Also by S. C. Gwynne

SELLING MONEY

THE OUTLAW BANK

RANDOM HOUSE   NEW YORK

THE
OUTLAW
BANK

A WILD RIDE INTO
THE SECRET HEART OF BCCI

JONATHAN BEATY

AND

S. C. GWYNNE

Copyright © 1993 by Ramjac, Inc.

Library of Congress Cataloging-in-Publication Data
Beaty, Jonathan.
The outlaw bank: a wild ride into the secret heart of BCCI/
Jonathan Beaty and S. C. Gwynne.
p. cm.
Includes index.
ISBN 0-679-41384-7
1. Bank of Credit and Commerce International—Corrupt practices.
2. International finance—Corrupt practices. 3. Money laundering.
4. Bank failures. 5. Criminal investigation—United States.
I. Gwynne, S. C. (Samuel C.), 1953– . II. Title.
HG1978.B4 1993
364.1′68—dc20   92-50153

Manufactured in the United States of America
98765432
First Edition

FOR LINDA AND KATIE

ACKNOWLEDGMENTS

Although our names appear on the front of this book, there were many colleagues and friends who helped to make it possible.

The Outlaw Bank grew out of an eighteen-month-long series of articles in *Time* magazine, whose managing editor, Henry Muller, and chief of correspondents, John Stacks, let us run with the story and placed considerable resources at our disposal. Their support was unwavering, despite threats of multimillion-dollar lawsuits from figures connected to BCCI and despite strong assertions, especially in the early days of the story, from law enforcement authorities who claimed that we had it all wrong and that the government wasn't trying to bury the real facts. Throughout the project, *Time*'s deputy chief of correspondents, Joelle Attinger, provided constant guidance, sympathy, and much-needed "reality" checks. Her assistant, Ann King, did so many things for us, often under deadline pressure, that we scarcely know where to begin to thank her. Steve Koepp, Geoff Colvin, and Barry Seaman, who edited our *Time* articles, showed extraordinary patience with our chronic lateness and helped make an abstruse subject understandable to our readers. The work of others in *Time*'s business section—John Greenwald, Bernie Baumohl, Sue Washburn, and Jane Van Tassel—was similarly invaluable. Although our names were on the several journalism awards that *Time* eventually won for the BCCI stories, staff writer John Greenwald wrote a number of the

articles based on our reporting and reports from other *Time* correspondents. We would also like to thank Bob Marshall and Nick Jol-
lymore, *Time*'s legal counsel, for their excellent and attentive reviews
that helped make our stories bulletproof: Despite the threats of lawsuits, none actually materialized.

We were also the beneficiaries of the extraordinary talents of our
book researcher, John Dickerson, who did everything from building
our state-of-the-art computer data base to tracking down leads to
baby-sitting some of our more intimidating sources. John was in every
sense a full partner in this enterprise.

Some of the reporting reflected in this book came from others within
Time's News Service. Adam Zagorin, *Time*'s Brussels bureau chief,
came through in the clutch several times with information and interviews we could not have gotten on our own. Correspondent Rich
Behar, Houston bureau chief Dick Woodbury, and former New Delhi
bureau chief Ned Desmond all contributed excellent and original material to our *Time* articles. Miami bureau chief Cathy Booth was an
unsung contributor: In the best tradition of journalism, she declined
a deserved byline on a story containing an important breakthrough
about the government's cover-up efforts in order to protect her source.
Rome-based *Time* photographer Rudi Frey ventured far beyond the
call of duty to help us out, as chronicled herein. We owe a great deal
to all of our colleagues at *Time* magazine, but perhaps our greatest
debt is to John Stacks, whose determination to unravel the mystery of
BCCI made it all possible.

Many sources on several continents helped make this story possible:
Some of them risked their lives, and many of them risked their reputations and jobs. We cannot name many of the honest and dedicated
people in law enforcement and government who provided information
simply because they believed the truth was more important than
political expediency, nor can we identify all of the former BCCI employees who came forward but still fear retaliation. The exception to
that latter category is Masihur Rahman, the former chief financial
officer of the bank, who first explained to us the financial legerdemain
that resulted in the disappearance of billions of dollars. Rahman later,
and bravely, made this information public in testimony before a Senate subcommittee.

But we can thank the following: Jack Blum, the former Senate
special counsel, who more than anyone else is responsible for exposing
the BCCI scandal; Senator John Kerry of Massachusetts and his aides
Jonathan Winer and David McKean, whose tireless efforts to uncover

the truth about BCCI provided us with much material; Joe Coyne, Virgil Mattingly, and the late William Taylor of the Federal Reserve, who were generous with their time; and James Dougherty, a Miami attorney who did much to advance the investigation of BCCI. We would also like to acknowledge the contribution of Shahid Javed Burki, the author of several scholarly works on Pakistan, who provided valuable insights about the country that gave birth to BCCI.

We appreciate the considerable efforts of our agent, Esther Newberg of ICM, in placing our manuscript and in staying close to it as it moved tortuously forward. The enthusiasm of Random House publisher Harry Evans launched this book, and our editors Ann Godoff and Ken Gellman at Random House were wonderful to work with and provided critical help in structuring it. Ms. Godoff's faith in the project never wavered and her constant support carried us past moments of doubt. The excellent eye of our copy editor, Patty Romanowski, also helped shore us up.

And lastly, we'd like to thank John and Jodell Downs in Truth or Consequences, New Mexico, who made our time there writing this book both exciting and memorable. Every day, for the best part of a year, Mr. Downs unfailingly poked his head into our office and asked why we weren't typing. It kept us from missing our *Time* editors in New York.

CONTENTS

Part Four: THE COVER-UP

CAST OF CHARACTERS

Agha Hasan Abedi: Pakistani financier who founded BCCI in 1972 with the intention of forming the Third World's first multinational bank.

Kamal Adham: The former head of Saudi Arabian intelligence and brother-in-law of the late King Faisal; shareholder in BCCI and First American Bank.

Sani Ahmed: Head of BCCI's protocol department in Pakistan until moving to Washington, D.C., to run BCCI's representative office.

Asaf Ali: Pakistani multimillionaire and arms dealer.

Robert Altman: Former president of First American Bank and Clark Clifford's law partner/protégé. Altman also served with Clifford as BCCI's chief American counsel from 1978 to 1990.

Amjad Awan: Former manager of BCCI Panama who handled Manuel Noriega's personal banking.

Munther Ismael Bilbeisi: Expatriate Jordanian involved in coffee smuggling, arms dealing, customs violations, money laundering, and paying bribes and kickbacks.

Jack Blum: Former investigator and chief counsel to Senator John Kerry's Subcommittee on Terrorism, Narcotics, and International Operations.

Lord Callaghan: A former British prime minister, Callaghan was a paid economic adviser to BCCI.

Roy P. M. Carlson: Bank of America executive who orchestrated BofA's original investment in BCCI, and who, at Ghaith Pharaon's request, became head of National Bank of Georgia.

Jimmy Carter: Thirty-ninth president of the United States who accepted millions from Abedi and BCCI for charitable organizations.

Clark Clifford: Former chairman of First American Bank and chief U.S. counsel to BCCI; advised Democratic presidents since Truman.

James Dougherty: Florida lawyer for Lloyd's of London who investigated Munther Bilbeisi and BCCI.

Arif Durrani: Pakistani arms dealer recently released from a U.S. federal prison for illegally providing HAWK antiaircraft missile parts to Iran.

Eddie George: Deputy governor of the Bank of England.

Gokal brothers: Pakistani brothers Abbas, Murtaza, and Mustafa, who ran the Gulf Group, a London-based shipping company. The Gulf Group is believed to be BCCI's largest debtor.

Fazle Haq: Pakistani general who smuggled U.S. supplies through Pakistan's North-West Frontier Province into Afghanistan.

Eugene Holley: Former Georgia state senator who introduced Bert Lance to Abedi.

Zafar Iqbal: Took over as head of BCCI in late 1990, after the firing of Abedi and Naqvi.

Richard J. Kerr: Acting CIA director who in 1991 confirmed that the agency had used BCCI to move money around the world.

John Kerry: Democratic senator from Massachusetts and chairman of the Subcommittee on Terrorism, Narcotics, and International Operations of the Senate Foreign Relations Committee.

A. R. (Abdul Raouf) Khalil: Current high-level officer in Saudi Arabian intelligence and key BCCI front man.

T. Bertram (Bert) Lance: President Carter's budget director and former chairman of National Bank of Georgia.

Robin Leigh-Pemberton: Governor of the Bank of England.

Gerald Lewis: Florida state comptroller who refused to renew BCCI's license to operate in the state after the 1990 Tampa money-laundering conviction.

Middleton "Sandy" Martin: Sheikh Zayed's American lawyer.

Sami Masri: A BCCI operative.

J. Virgil Mattingly, Jr.: The Federal Reserve Board's general counsel who spearheaded the agency's investigation into BCCI's secret ownership of First American.

Ghanim Faris al-Mazrui: Head of Sheikh Zayed's Private Department and BCCI board member.

Khalfan al-Mazrui: Head of the Karachi office of Sheikh Zayed's Private Department.

Robert Morgenthau: Manhattan district attorney.

John Moscow: Assistant district attorney who directed the BCCI investigation for Robert Morgenthau.

Robert Mueller: Head of the Justice Department's criminal division.

Swaleh Naqvi: BCCI's chief operating officer who took over after Abedi's 1988 heart attack.

David L. Paul: Real estate developer and owner of CenTrust Savings Bank of Miami.

Ghaith R. Pharaon: Flamboyant BCCI front man who acquired Georgia National Bank and Independence Bank of Encino. Also a shareholder in Attock Oil, BCCI, and CenTrust Savings Bank.

Masihur Rahman: Former chief financial officer of BCCI.

William Ryback: Deputy director of banking supervision at the Federal Reserve.

Charles Saphos: Chief of the Criminal Division Narcotics section of the Justice Department who wrote Florida regulators after BCCI's Tampa conviction asking that the bank be allowed to remain open.

William Taylor: Head of banking supervision at the Federal Reserve Board.

William von Raab: U.S. Customs commissioner who headed the agency during the Tampa money-laundering investigations.

Zayed bin Sultan al-Nahayan: Head of Abu Dhabi's ruling family and president of the United Arab Emirates. Reportedly one of the world's richest men, he now owns BCCI.

CHRONOLOGY

1972   Declaring his intention to form the Third World's first multinational bank, Agha Hasan Abedi organizes the Bank of Credit and Commerce International.

1975   Using Abbas Gokal as a front, BCCI attempts to acquire Chelsea National Bank in New York. Regulators reject the bid because of concern about BCCI's involvement.

1976   BCCI opens its Cayman Islands subsidiary ICIC, which becomes BCCI's repository for loans to privileged insiders.

1977   **October:** Eugene Holley introduces Bert Lance to Abedi.

1978   **January:** With Abedi's help, Ghaith Pharaon finalizes his acquisition of National Bank of Georgia from Bert Lance. On the same day Abedi pays off Lance's $3.5-million bank loan.

February: BCCI orchestrates a hostile bid for Financial General Bankshares of Washington with the help of Bert Lance. FGB, in turn, sues Lance, Abedi, BCCI, and the Arab investors for making an illegal attempt to take over the bank.

February: Joseph E. Vaez, an officer in the Office of the Comptroller of the Currency, submits a report on BCCI that characterizes it as a bank dangerously out of control.

March: The Securities and Exchange Commission files suit against BCCI, Abedi, Lance, and others in connection with the purchase of Financial General Bankshares stock. With Clark Clifford's help, the investors settle the suit and agree to make an offer for all outstanding stock.

1979   **December:** The Soviet Union invades Afghanistan. As a result, Pakistan becomes a key strategic priority for the United States.

1981   **August:** Based on Clifford's assurances that there will be no link between BCCI and Financial General Bankshares, regulators approve the sale of Financial General to Middle Eastern investors connected with BCCI.

1982   **August:** Lance introduces Abedi to Jimmy Carter.

1985   **January:** Douglas Mulholland delivers a CIA report on BCCI's ownership of First American to Treasury Secretary Donald Regan.

October: Using Ghaith Pharaon as a front man, BCCI illegally acquires Independence Bank of Encino for close to $23 million.

BCCI helps Adnan Khashoggi finance the sale of arms to Iran as a part of the Reagan administration's Iran-Contra effort.

BCCI suffers over $440 million in losses from options trading through its trading subsidiary Capcom.

1986   **September:** The CIA issues a report saying that BCCI has owned First American since 1982. The report is seen by the State, Treasury, and Commerce departments but is not forwarded to the Federal Reserve.

1987   **July:** Pharaon becomes a partner in David Paul's CenTrust Savings Bank of Miami.

First American Bank buys the National Bank of Georgia from Ghaith Pharaon for $227 million.

1988   **February:** Clifford and partner Robert Altman sell their stock in First American—bought less than two years earlier—to BCCI front man Mohammed Hammoud for more than $30 million in cash and stock profits.

February: Abedi's heart attack and later heart transplant end his direct control of BCCI. Swaleh Naqvi becomes the bank's chief executive.

September: Amjad Awan tells investigators that BCCI owns First American and National Bank of Georgia.

October: American Customs agents arrest five BCCI bankers in Tampa, Florida. Other bankers and narcotics traffickers in London and several U.S. cities are also arrested on money laundering and other charges. BCCI says in a statement: "The bank wishes to state categorically that at no time whatsoever has it knowingly been involved in drug traffic related money laundering."

1989   **April:** Stifled by federal inaction, Jack Blum visits Manhattan District Attorney Robert Morgenthau to persuade him to take on the BCCI case.

1990   **January:** BCCI pleads guilty to money laundering in Tampa, Florida, but receives no stiff sanctions. Bank remains open and forfeits only $14 million.

March: The first Price Waterhouse audit is completed. Report reveals a black hole of at least $1.7 billion in the bank's accounts.

April: A second Price Waterhouse audit is completed; it details thousands of irregular transactions and reveals that BCCI, not the Middle Eastern investors, holds controlling shares of First American.

April: Sheikh Zayed acquires 77 percent control of BCCI.

July: A Florida jury convicts five Tampa BCCI officers of conspiring to launder cocaine profits.

1991 **March:** The Fed orders BCCI to sell any shares that it acquired illegally in First American Bank of Washington.

May: Coffee importer Munther Bilbeisi is indicted on charges of tax evasion stemming from a coffee-smuggling scheme financed by BCCI.

July: Regulators worldwide seize BCCI offices and place more than 75 percent of the bank's $20 billion of assets in sixty-nine countries in government hands.

July: New York State grand jury indicts BCCI and its two principal officers, Agha Hasan Abedi and Swaleh Naqvi, for fraud, bribery, grand larceny, and money laundering.

July: The Federal Reserve Board fines BCCI $200 million for illegally acquiring control of three prominent U.S. banking institutions: Washington's First American Bank, National Bank of Georgia, and Miami's CenTrust Savings.

August: Clark Clifford and Robert Altman resign as chairman and president, respectively, of First American.

December: BCCI's liquidators plead guilty and agree to forfeit $550 million.

1992 **July:** Khalid bin-Mahfouz is indicted by a Manhattan grand jury.

July: Kamal Adham pleads guilty in New York and agrees to cooperate with Morgenthau and the Justice Department.

July: Clark Clifford and Robert Altman are simultaneously indicted by Manhattan District Attorney Robert Morgenthau and a federal grand jury. Kamal Adham plea-bargains and agrees to cooperate with prosecutors.

INTRODUCTION

THE DEVIL'S PAYMASTER

"Mr. Bond, power is sovereignty. Clausewitz's first principle
was to have a secure base. From there proceeds freedom of
action. Together, that is sovereignty. I have secured these
things and much besides. No one else in the world possesses
them to the same degree. They cannot have them. The world
is too public. These things can only be secured in privacy. You
talk of kings and presidents. How much power do they possess?
As much as their people will allow them . . . And how do I
possess that power, that sovereignty? Through privacy.
Through the fact that nobody knows. Through the fact that I
have to account to no one."

—IAN FLEMING, *DR. NO*

Dr. No, the island monarch with thin, cruel lips and immodest designs
on the fate of the Western world, would have been fascinated by the
scandal that blossomed around the Bank of Credit and Commerce
International (BCCI) in the summer of 1991. It was a conspiratorialist's conspiracy, a plot so byzantine, so thoroughly corrupt, so exquisitely private, reaching so deeply into the political and intelligence
establishments of so many countries, that it seemed to have its only
precedent in the more hallucinogenic fiction of Ian Fleming, Kurt
Vonnegut, or Thomas Pynchon. As tales of its global predations were
spattered across headlines all over the world, its apparent influence
reached almost absurd proportions. This was a bank that had taken
the popular notion of a "global electronic village" and made a mock-
ery of it, a bank that was at once everywhere and nowhere, whose
dirtiest secrets were hidden deep in the impossible tangles of its
offshore networks.

BCCI suddenly bloomed as a sort of supermetaphor for the 1980s, the decade that celebrated the likes of Robert Maxwell, Ivan Boesky, and Michael Milken and unleashed upon the United States a horde of freebooters in the banking and thrift business. But nothing in the history of financial scandals even approaches the $20-billion-plus heist at BCCI, which sixty-two countries shuttered forever in July 1991 in a paroxysm of regulatory vengeance. No single scandal had ever involved such vast amounts of money. Superlatives were quickly exhausted. BCCI was the largest criminal corporate enterprise ever, the biggest Ponzi scheme, the most pervasive money-laundering operation in history, the only bank—so far as anyone knows—that ran a brisk sideline business in both conventional and nuclear weapons, gold, drugs, turnkey mercenary armies, intelligence and counterintelligence, shipping, and commodities from cement in the Middle East to Honduran coffee to Vietnamese beans.

Though it was fundamentally a financial fraud, BCCI itself was not a bank in any conventional sense. Or, more precisely, banking was only a part of the global organism, the ingeniously constructed platform from which its other lines of business were launched. Taken collectively, it was more of an armed Renaissance city-state of Machiavelli's era than a modern corporation. This "bank" possessed its very own diplomatic corps, intelligence network, and private army, its own shipping and commodities trading companies. And BCCI itself was so thoroughly enmeshed in the official affairs of Pakistan that it was often impossible to separate the two.

BCCI was bigger even than that: It was the unsettling next-stage evolution of the multinational corporation, the one the theorists had been predicting for years but which never seemed to be able to shed its sovereign boundaries. (General Motors and Mitsubishi are both good examples of this—huge companies with holdings and operations all over the world that nonetheless persist in being fundamentally American and Japanese entities.) In taking that step, BCCI became truly stateless and very nearly invisible to the authorities in each country where it did business. The BCCI scandal shows what sort of frightening mischief can be made in a world where trillions of electronic dollars routinely wash in and out of international financial markets.

Nor was BCCI a conspiracy. In much of what it did, BCCI reflected the way the world works. The organization was designed to mimic the way the world's largest corporations and banks move and hide their money. It was no accident that BCCI was incorporated in Luxembourg, one of the least regulated nations on earth and a favorite haven of the money men at the Fortune 500. It was no accident that it ran its wildest manipulations through what amounted to a branch in the Cayman Islands—a place long favored by major banks to hold offshore money away from the ken of the IRS and banking authorities. BCCI had mastered these black arts so well that it became the bank of choice for the intelligence agencies of the Western hemisphere, who found its deeply secretive methods more and more useful. BCCI was necessary to them; it was part of the way they worked, too. It was those alliances, along with bribery on a grand scale, that allowed the criminal bank to flourish for two decades with effective immunity from the law.

This is the story of how the wealthy and corrupt in Latin America managed to steal virtually every dollar lent to their countries by Western banks, creating the debt crisis of the 1980s; how heads of state such as Ferdinand Marcos, Saddam Hussein, Manuel Noriega, and others skimmed billions from their national treasuries and hid them in Swiss and Caymanian accounts forever free from snooping regulators; how Pakistan and Iraq got materials for nuclear weaponry and how Libya built poison-gas plants. BCCI is also the story of how governments manage to put together arms deals with supposedly hostile governments, as in the case of Israel's clandestine trades with Arab states, or the United States' supplying weapons to both Iraq and Iran in violation of its own laws. BCCI is a paradigm of how our national borders have been rendered porous, despite the best attempts of law enforcement; it is about terrorism and how terrorism is financed; it is about how drugs enter the United States and Europe and how the drug lords disguise and conceal their ill-gotten gains. The BCCI scandal affords a rare and representative glimpse at the trillion-dollar-plus underground market of secret money that moves at will in and out of the world's most sophisticated and highly regulated economies. For all of these reasons, no authorities anywhere were in a hurry to shut down BCCI: The bank was as useful to governments as it was to crooks, and indeed, governments became active participants in the fraud. In the United States BCCI became the subject of a massive and decade-long cover-up. For the investigators and the reporters who finally cracked it, the most difficult task of all was breaking down the formidable walls erected by their own law enforcement agencies. Penetrating the cover-up became the key that finally unlocked the BCCI scandal.

The great-man theory of history holds that individuals propel events, that Robespierre created the last and most violent convulsion of the French Revolution, and not the other way around; that Lenin—not the larger dialectic of history—gave birth to the Communist state in Russia. The counter-theory argues that these people became great because they were in the right place at the right time and were products of historical events they did not control. It is difficult to say which of these fits Agha Hasan Abedi, the diminutive son of petty bureaucrats who founded BCCI in 1972 and handcrafted what by the early 1980s became one of the most powerful private organizations on earth. He is undoubtedly a great man, though in the West he will be remembered more for his bad deeds than for his good ones. Like the bank he built, Abedi himself was ahistorical, existing in the margins and footnotes of "official" history. Until BCCI self-destructed in 1991, due largely to Abedi's neglect, he was known to few outside the magic circle of powerful elites he had drawn about him. Now that will all change. He made his own luck in the passion with which he flung himself at his own destiny. He was also lucky, for that same destiny led him to the very axis of one of the great power shifts in history.

Before Abedi was anything else, he was the world's most energetic errand boy, a bright-eyed factotum and a salesman who believed that the customer was always right. He took the notion of "customer satisfaction" beyond even the most progressive of the West's new management theorists who began cropping up in the 1970s and 1980s. He would purvey anything, anywhere, to anyone who smelled remotely like a customer. That would include everything from exotic rugs to bags of cash and male prostitutes, though Abedi himself was ascetic. He was both a visionary and a romantic. He was a Muslim, but no ordinary one. Though born into the Shiite sect of Islam, he later drifted into the religion of the secretive Sufi sect, which claimed a direct and personal relationship with God based on love. By contrast, mainstream Islam was built around fear and submission. The business style he created—the management theory of the bank—was unlike any ever seen before in a large company. He incorporated his Islamic mysticism into the palpable driving force of the bank: Advancement was based on spiritual progress, and Abedi took Islam's emphasis on the good of the family and society ahead of individualism and trans-muted it to an intensely democratic theory of management. All would devolve into corruption, and Abedi's mysticism would eventually sound like a hodgepodge of California New Age gobbledygook and Dale Carnegie. Yet it was a powerful original vision, and it constituted the early strength of the bank.

Abedi was perhaps the most brilliant pure businessman the developing world has produced. He built the first Third World bank that could stand with the giant colonial European banks that had dominated the underdeveloped world for more than one hundred years. He was among the first to anticipate one of the most jarring economic shifts in history: the rise of the Islamic nations of OPEC (Organization of Petroleum Exporting Countries) in the 1970s. And he was perhaps the first—certainly the first in the banking world—to see the opportunity that lay in hundreds of billions of dollars of petrodeposits.

Writing about BCCI is a formidable task. Not only because its criminal operations took place in seventy-three countries over a span of nearly twenty years, but also because of the sheer volume of the documentation. To attempt to grasp the totality of BCCI is to be quickly overwhelmed by a tidal wave of facts, histories, anecdotes, and allegations. Any book seeking to detail all of the bank's activities everywhere would run easily to several thousand pages. Tracking BCCI is also something like playing three-dimensional chess. As BCCI evolved from a story about a corrupt bank to a story about intelligence agencies, weapons dealing, geopolitics, and government cover-ups, so did the cast of characters. The reader will note, with little surprise, that many of our sources originally gave us information in "not-for-direct-attribution" or "off-the-record" interviews. In the instances where we describe that information here in a manner that reveals the source, we have done so only after obtaining permission from the particular individual. That includes sources whose actual identities remain protected.

The protection of sources has been a particular problem in writing this book, since several expressed fear of being killed or harmed because they talked to us. Our continuing concern for their safety has led us to take measures to conceal some identities, although the quotes we have used are precise. Thus the names of two important sources who became characters in this book, the weapons dealers Heinrich and Ali Khan, are pseudonyms. The real identity of Condor, the senior United States official who confirmed some of our findings, is not revealed for obvious reasons. And finally, we have used the fictitious name Ali Mirza for the BCCI executive who was secretly tape-recorded by federal law enforcement figures as he described BCCI's criminal activities. Some state and federal investigators probing the BCCI case know the real identities of Heinrich, Ali Khan, and Ali Mirza, but we have tried to make it difficult for the bad guys. Although BCCI no longer (officially) exists, only a handful of its people have been arrested. The rest are still out there, and many of them remain potential threats to our sources.

The writer's dilemma, then, is how to take this mountain of abstruse data and make sense out of it, and how to capture on paper the real excitement and drama of one of the great scandals in history. We have tried to solve that problem in three ways. First, by abbreviating the long history of BCCI's financial transactions, which were designed to be so bewilderingly complex that even the bank's own auditors could not follow the internal trails of money. Second, by providing some description of the political settings in which the bank flourished. For example, it is not possible to understand BCCI and Agha Hasan Abedi without some understanding of Pakistan, the country in which the bank was born. Nor is it possible to fathom the cover-up in the United States without understanding the dynamics of America's foreign policies and how they influenced government figures to allow BCCI to remain in the shadows.

Third, and less conventionally, we have told a large part of the story from our own points of view. We have described in detail what it was like to report the BCCI story for *Time* magazine, and we have described the experience of watching the global mystery of BCCI unfold in front of us, in cities from Miami to San Francisco, London, Casablanca, and Abu Dhabi. We have used this technique because we felt it would be easier to communicate the meaning of BCCI through our personal experiences. We also felt that the story of our own odyssey reveals some of the tension that gripped governments and regulators as BCCI's empire began to unravel and threatened to expose the dirty secrets of those who used the bank. Many of those secrets are the kind that threaten the reputations of governments and august figures, and most of them remain buried, either in BCCI's hidden archives or in government office files protected by national security classifications. We have uncovered some of them.

This book is the fruit of two years of investigation and research, and in the process we have interviewed scores of sources and followed hundreds of paper trails. But just as we have chosen to provide samples of BCCI's financial manipulations rather than a numbing history of every event, our account of reporting the story focuses on several main sources rather than on detailing every confirming statement provided by secondary and tertiary sources.

Another reason to tell our own story is that we were part of a relatively small group of people who actively pursued BCCI prior to the bank's seizure in July 1991. In the vacuum created by the absence of federal law enforcement, and against the activist role played by BCCI and its agents to cover up the story, a handful of reporters and a handful of congressional and state-level investigators were left to uncover the scandal.

As we broke the news to the public through the pages of *Time*, we also became brokers for information that went far beyond the material that appeared in the magazine. Within the limits of confidentiality we shared some of this information with others in the hunt and long chase after the truth in the BCCI saga.

To accommodate all of these considerations, we have broken the book into four sections. The first is a narrative of our own journey as reporters into the scandal's heart. It is intended to provide a sense of what it was like to track BCCI in the days before its sweeping criminality was known. The second part is an attempt to telescope the history of BCCI into three chapters and to introduce the characters who became the driving forces behind the bank. The third part resumes the narrative from our point of view as reporters, after we discovered that BCCI was something far larger and more sinister than just a bank. The final section deals with the cover-up and the failure of governments all over the world to do anything about BCCI despite their clear knowledge of what it was and what it was doing. We hope this helps make a complicated subject more easily understandable.

TRUTH OR CONSEQUENCES, NEW MEXICO
JANUARY 1, 1993

PART ONE

THE CHASE

CHAPTER 1

BACK CHANNELS

It started the way an investigative story should start: in San Francisco's Chinatown on a fogbound winter night, in the candlelight and shadow of the Empress of China Restaurant. There was a meeting between two old allies.

It had been arranged a few days earlier in *Time*'s Los Angeles bureau, when Jonathan Beaty had received a phone call from Washington, D.C. It was Jack Blum, who was both a friend and a source, suggesting that they get together for a talk. When Beaty explained he was headed for San Francisco on an assignment, Blum said that, by coincidence, he too was going to be in San Francisco to meet with a client. They could meet for dinner Tuesday. This was early February 1991. Operation Desert Storm was in full cry and the world's attention was riveted on Baghdad and Kuwait City. Not much else was going on, and in the news business the war was the only game in town. Beaty was tracking weapons-related technology sales to Saddam Hussein, and he had momentarily forgotten that he didn't believe in coincidence.

Occasional meetings at well-appointed restaurants for dinner, or lunch for that matter, were a ritual for the two men, who had first met in Washington during the latter years of the Carter administration, when Beaty was a correspondent in *Time*'s Washington bureau. Blum, a lawyer who had been a Senate investigator for the Foreign

Relations Committee, had been a valuable source of information for Beaty's investigative and political stories. Their conversations, which Beaty called "interviews" for the sake of his expense account, were almost always conducted in restaurants favored by the Washington elite, where even the tips amounted to more than either would ordinarily pay for a meal out of his own pocket. Beaty insisted that the magazine was happy to subsidize these forays, which was perhaps an exaggeration.

It became an important connection: They traded information, and Blum had helped guide Beaty—and *Time*—through some of the darker thickets of Washington politics. He was an exceptional student of the genre: Like some Audubon of the Potomac, he could gaze across the power-broker restaurants where he and Beaty dined, name the denizen, and describe the feeding habits and mating rites of the species who held real power in the permanent federal bureaucracy.

Blum had arrived in Washington in 1965, fresh from Columbia Law School, and found a place with Senator Phil Hart as an investigator for Hart's antitrust subcommittee. His work caught the attention of Senator J. W. Fulbright, who moved him to the Senate Foreign Relations Committee, and by the mid-'70s Blum had made a permanent place for himself in Washington as a counsel to Senator Frank Church's subcommittee on multinational corporations. His investigations of the Lockheed payoff scandals had, among other things, helped topple a Japanese government, sent Japanese Prime Minister Kakuei Tanaka to jail, and brought about the abdication of the Queen of the Netherlands. The committee's investigations had exposed ITT's improper activities in Chile, fingered Robert Vesco and the $3-billion global Ponzi scheme called IOS (Investors' Overseas Services), and been a driving force behind the creation of the Foreign Corrupt Practices Act. Former CIA Director Richard Helms's answers to Blum's questions in a closed-door session of the subcommittee led to Helms's being indicted for perjury. Few congressional investigators have ever had that sort of run.

Blum did not look the part. He appeared as he must have as a schoolboy: studious, with a round, almost cherubic face, fine brown hair with a lifetime cowlick, and serious, intent eyes magnified slightly by thick glasses. He was now approaching fifty, a tall man with a large frame who usually looked permanently rumpled in gray slacks and a nondescript blue blazer the size of a small tent.

In 1976 Blum had gone into private practice, where he stayed for ten restive years. But in spite of his singular ability as an investigator, an encyclopedic memory, and a network of invaluable contacts, Blum had never gotten rich as a Washington lawyer. It wasn't just the old bromide—that he was too honest and candid for the delicately shaded ethics of Washington. He was by nature a crusader and a moralist, a supporter of causes lost before the battle was joined. He was smart enough to know that quixotic clients with a just cause seldom paid handsomely for legal help. But in a town where careers are built by passing through revolving doors, he was not inclined to change sides. Unlike, he sometimes thought, so many former hotshot assistant U.S. attorneys who built reputations as prosecutors and then made millions defending the drug dealers and swindlers they once had tried to put in jail. Although he kept these uncharitable views to himself, he was still controversial. He was an outsider who understood how things worked, he was intolerant of political horse-trading, and he talked to reporters. All of which meant that the old pols, the inside players, and potential big corporate clients viewed him with a degree of alarm. It would be fair to say that Jack Blum had as many enemies as he had friends in Washington. He had plenty of each.

Blum had reentered the public sector in 1986, as special counsel to Massachusetts Senator John Kerry's Foreign Relations Subcommittee on Terrorism, Narcotics, and International Operations, where he had spearheaded probes of drug trafficking. Kerry, the recently elected junior senator from Massachusetts, was making a name for himself. His subcommittee had produced a report—hotly protested along partisan lines—that accused the Reagan administration of selectively interfering with the criminal justice process and abusing the ethics of its own "war on drugs" to protect its clandestine support of the Contras.

In the years after his Washington tour, Beaty returned often to the capital and kept up the tradition, meeting Blum in restaurants to trade war stories and political gossip. But Beaty had not seen much of Blum since the lawyer left Kerry's subcommittee for private practice in 1988.

The Empress of China, where the menu featured flaming baby quail and thousand-year-old eggs, was an appropriate place to renew the old ritual, but Beaty wondered why Blum had insisted on a meeting yet been reluctant to tell him what he had wanted to talk about on the phone.

It didn't take long for Blum to come to his point. They were still waiting in the bar for a table when Blum asked him if he was ready to hear a story that might take a little time to tell.

much do you know about BCCI? The Bank of Credit and
ce International? You remember. José Blandón brought it

did remember, vaguely. BCCI floated up from a group of two
or three hundred corporate names that had, at one time or another,
come to his attention as being linked to criminal enterprises. In early
1988 Blandón, a Panamanian diplomat and a top aide to General
Noriega, had been a star witness for Senator Kerry during the hearings Blum had orchestrated, and Beaty had covered the sensational
proceedings for the magazine. The cultured former general counsel of
Panama was the first credible witness to publicly finger Noriega for
taking a generous cut of the Panamanian drug business and named
BCCI as one of Noriega's banks.

Beaty shrugged, unable to figure out where Blum was headed. He
recalled that Blum had taken a sudden interest in BCCI after learning
the bank was at the epicenter of Noriega's financial dominion, but he
had been little interested in what seemed to be just another offshore
foreign bank running drug money. Banks like that were a dime a
dozen in Panama.

"A BCCI branch in Miami was busted for money laundering a few
months after your hearings, but not a lot ever came out of it," Beaty
offered.

The reporter had been surprised to learn that BCCI even had a
branch in the United States. There had been a government-orchestrated media splash when the feds arrested a few of the bankers and
a lot of cocaine cartel people they had lured to a bachelor party in
Tampa, the final act in a two-year U.S. Customs sting operation code-
named C-Chase. William von Raab, head of the Customs Service
throughout the Reagan administration, had crowed that it was the
most important money-laundering case in history, but in the end the
bank had plea-bargained out for a relative slap on the wrist.

Blum nodded and took a deep breath. "There was something wrong
with that plea bargain," he said in a low voice. "It was part of a very
big fix. But that's only the beginning of what there is to know about
BCCI. It's a global criminal empire, and the bank is about to go down
in the largest financial scandal in world history."

Beaty stared and, without being conscious of it, started patting his
pockets for a pen and looking for a dry cocktail napkin. The lawyer
usually talked as if he expected to read his words back in a transcript
someday and wasn't given to hyperbole.

"How do you know this?" Beaty asked, leaning forward to hear

Blum, who looked around the room before continuing in an even quieter tone.

"Jonathan, you once asked me why I left my job with the Kerry subcommittee, and I never really answered you. Well, the answer is that I proposed a serious investigation of BCCI and was brushed aside. My contract was coming to an end, and suddenly there were no funds to renew it. A high-level cover-up of everything concerning BCCI was set into place after Customs stumbled across their money-laundering operation in Miami, and it's still in place.

"Are you sure you want to hear more?" Blum smiled slightly. "It's a long and complicated tale, and if you have any plans for the future, I guarantee hearing it will ruin your life." Beaty lifted an eyebrow, and the Washington lawyer began his story.

Blum's strange odyssey began in the spring of 1988, after Senator Kerry's hearings on drug trafficking and money laundering had veered into Manuel Antonio Noriega. Blum was curious about BCCI and had become more so when he drew a blank in checking with the usual official sources. The banking regulators told him that BCCI had agency branches in New York, San Francisco, Los Angeles, Houston, and in Florida, in Tampa, Miami, and Boca Raton, but they had little more to offer. Then he put out word of his interest through his old-boy network and waited. Somewhere among those retired intelligence types, the active spooks and semispooks, the friends in law enforcement and places like the General Accounting Office, someone should know something.

When the call came, it was from a top-level BCCI executive who was leaving the bank. He had heard that Mr. Blum was asking questions and he had a story to tell if Mr. Blum was interested, and if his name could be kept out of it.

Blum received the call in his office—the "rat hole," he called it—on the fourth floor of the Hart Senate Office Building. Senators' offices are wainscoted in fine wood and thickly carpeted, but those amenities are spared in the warrens of the permanent committee staff. So Blum was a large man behind a very small desk strewn with stacks of papers and crowded on three sides by gray metal bookcases and a massive, light-green combination safe that held transcripts of closed-door testimony and subpoenaed documents. Outside his minuscule domain, which was enclosed by panels that did not reach the ceiling, was an ante-room, usually a bedlam, housing in close proximity a secretary, two young aides, and an elderly copying machine. When he had finished the phone call with the banker, Blum asked the secretary to book him a seat on an evening flight to Miami. BCCI's Miami branch was a large and successful ninety-person operation that looked after the bank's interests in Latin America. To the office at large Blum announced he had just found a witness who promised to explain what happened to Noriega's money.

"I can't tell you his name," Blum said. "I've never revealed it. Think of him as Witness A. But he told me that I wasn't getting anywhere with my inquiries because I didn't understand what I was looking at. He said I wasn't going to find anything by looking at corporate reports, or trying to trace other businesses the bank owned, or even who owned the bank. The bank was set up to hide illicit financial transactions, and the real business of the bank was to handle the accounts of roughly three thousand high-net-worth criminal clients. He went on to say, for example, that they bought a bank in Colombia just to get access to the drug-cartel money, and he described the relationship between the bank and General Noriega in Panama. Noriega was looting his own country, and BCCI had given him his own personal banker in Miami, Amjad Awan, to handle the accounts."

With visions of a $20-billion full-service bank for criminals in his head—nobody had ever heard of such an entity before—Blum pushed the Senate Foreign Relations Committee for subpoenas. He wanted the bank's Miami records, and he wanted to talk to Amjad Awan. Blum learned from the U.S. Attorney's office in Tampa that Awan was a target of the C-Chase undercover team that was laundering drug proceeds through BCCI's Miami branch, but the banker was unaware of that, and he agreed to meet Blum at his home in Annapolis to talk about BCCI. The sharply dressed banker was careful not to say anything self-incriminating, but he talked about the bank's large network of criminal clients, talked about drug-money-laundering operations around the world, and then dropped a bombshell.

Awan, the former head of BCCI's Panama office and then the bank's marketing manager for Latin America and the Caribbean, told Blum that BCCI secretly owned and controlled First American Bank.

"First American is a $11-billion interstate bank holding company based in Washington, D.C.," Blum explained, "with offices from Florida to New York. BCCI secretly controls other United States banks too, but I'll get to that."

Flaming baby quail and elaborate menus ignored, Blum absentmindedly ordered chow mein and fried shrimp, while Beaty added to the distress of the hovering waiters by collecting enough candles from nearby tables to see his notes. He knew he hadn't a chance of remembering the details if he didn't write them down.

Days after Blum had taken a sworn deposition from Awan, in October 1988, the authorities pulled the plug on the elaborate Tampa sting operation, arresting Awan, several other BCCI bankers in Florida and Europe, and more than two dozen narcotics traffickers. The BCCI case was now completely in the hands of the Justice Department, which was preparing for the trials that would not take place for another fifteen months. But Blum was still dissatisfied. He had tried to talk the Florida prosecutors into expanding their view of the bank to incorporate the world criminal empire sketched by Awan and the cooperative anonymous banker from Miami, but there was no indication that the Justice Department or Customs was pursuing any of the leads that could have taken them deeper into BCCI.

"I wasn't getting anywhere either," Blum recounted. "By March I was winding up the subcommittee investigation because we had run out of time. I was unhappy because BCCI still hadn't turned over all the bank records I had subpoenaed. Their lawyers, Clark Clifford and Robert Altman, were stalling me at every turn."

Beaty's antennae twitched. He had never heard of Robert Altman, but Clark Clifford, a former secretary of defense, was one of the most famous and powerful lawyers in Washington.

Blum had been packing up subcommittee records to send to the Senate archives when he got another call, this one from a former client. The client, a former intelligence operative, had just talked to a man who had once been a BCCI officer. "I can't tell you his real name, but let's call him Ali Mirza.* The BCCI banker told him that the bank had fixed our Senate investigation and had gone all out to close the Justice Department investigation of the bank.

"I told him, 'Look, I'm out of this business, call Customs in Tampa.' He calls them and tells them about it, and then he calls me back and tells me the BCCI banker still wants to talk to me and will meet me in Miami. So then I call Customs and arrange to have a motel room near the airport wired."

Blum spent three days in the motel debriefing Mirza and working him around to testifying. The adjoining room was crammed with electronics gear manned by Customs agents and one IRS agent. Once, an assistant U.S. attorney listened in to see how things were going.

"Mirza described efforts to influence the Senate subcommittee, he

---

*Ali Mirza is a pseudonym for a former high-level BCCI officer. His real identity is known to law enforcement and a handful of reporters. Jack Blum never publicly revealed the names of the witnesses he took to the federal investigators, and their names were very closely held throughout the investigation.

talked about the bribery of the Georgia legislature, he named U.S. politicians whom BCCI had loaned or given money, and said BCCI secretly owned First American Bank, as well as the National Bank of Georgia and Independence Bank out in California."

Beaty was riveted. "And all this was taken down on tape? What happened to it?"

Blum shrugged. "I don't know. Mirza wasn't the only one taped. A week later I brought my original BCCI banker source, Witness A, to Miami for a similar taping. As far as I know, the feds didn't follow up with either witness.

"You've got to understand the situation here. The government had been following my investigation. Undercover agents from C-Chase were tape-recording Awan when he told them about BCCI's reactions to the Senate subpoena we issued. Awan told the undercovers that one of BCCI's lawyers, Robert Altman, advised him to flee the country. He said he didn't want to go because he liked Florida and he thought he didn't have anything to fear. He told the undercovers on tape that BCCI secretly owned First American Bank and that First American Bank's owners of record are just straw men for BCCI. That means Clifford and Altman have lied to U.S. banking regulators."

Beaty held up his hands, totally confused. This was coming too fast. "What do Clifford and Altman have to do with First American Bank? You said they were BCCI's lawyers."

"Clifford and Altman are BCCI's lawyers in the United States, but Clifford is also chairman of First American Bank, and Altman is the president."

The reporter shook his head, trying to clear his mind. It was beginning to sound like *Alice in Wonderland*. As Blum explained it, the shareholders who owned BCCI—wealthy and important men from the Middle East—had purchased First American Bank nine years ago over the objections of the Federal Reserve Board, which didn't want to let BCCI take over an American bank. Clifford got the banking regulators to approve the deal by swearing that even though the same group of investors would own both banks, there would be no other connection between the two. First American would be independently managed, and BCCI would have no control over its operations.

"What I'm telling you," Blum said, "is that the BCCI shareholders aren't the independent investors they were portrayed to be. In reality most of them are just front men for BCCI, a criminal bank deeply involved in the drug business, and therefore BCCI secretly owns and controls one of the most important banks in Washington, D.C.

The bottom line is that BCCI is using Clifford and Altman as ultra-respectable-looking front men to run their American operations."

Beaty grimaced. "This is getting a little dense, Jack. You're saying Clifford, one of the biggest powers in the Democratic party, and his partner, this Altman guy, are part of some criminal scheme, fronting for this giant criminal bank? And that the Justice Department has known all about it for years and isn't doing anything?"

Blum smiled, an impish twinkle in his eye. This was serious business, but he had always enjoyed blowing Beaty's mind.

"I told you, we're talking serious cover-up here. I haven't even mentioned that Bert Lance was in the middle of the First American takeover and that Jimmy Carter flew around in BCCI's corporate jet, have I? When Carter stepped out of the White House, he no longer had the use of *Air Force One*, so Abedi bought a retired White House jet, an *Air Force Two*, and made it available to him. And Abedi gave a lot of money, maybe millions, to Carter's charitable foundation and to build his presidential library."

"Oh shit, Jack." Beaty gave a theatrical groan as he dutifully wrote down: "Lance and President Carter involved with BCCI." He was torn between excitement and disbelief. He and Jack went back a long way, and he thought the lawyer was one of the most honest people he knew, but this was becoming surreal. He scrambled for firmer ground. "And who is Abedi?"

"Agha Hasan Abedi is the founder of BCCI. It's his bank." Blum spelled out the name. "He's a Pakistani, very mysterious, and he put BCCI together in 1972. The bank is one of the largest private banks in the world; it grew at a phenomenal rate and has offices in about every country in the world and claims to have $20 billion in assets. But Abedi had a heart attack just before the indictment and is back in Pakistan now. The bank has been unraveling ever since, but we'll get to that later."

The restaurant was nearly empty, and the waiters stood around making it obvious that they were anxious to clear the table and go home. Beaty looked through his notes, scrawled on napkins, notepaper, and the back of an American Express receipt. He felt like he had just been pummeled.

"But what happened to all this information?" Beaty asked.

"That's just it. Nothing. Nothing has happened. I heard later that while I was in Florida, Clifford had a meeting with his close friend Senator Claiborne Pell and got him to extend the deadline for my subpoenas for thirty days, which meant that whatever documents they decided to turn over came in after I left. Obviously I thought the U.S. attorneys in Florida were going to use the information we gave them, that they would use the witnesses we gave them, who told them how big a criminal bank this really was. But you were right: They gave BCCI a plea bargain and fined the bank $14 million, which was just the amount of drug money they took in from the undercovers. The federal government let the bank remain open for business as usual. Florida shut down BCCI in the state, but they're still operating in New York and on the West Coast. The undercovers did an incredible job, and at least some of them thought they were going back for another round at BCCI, but it never happened. My two witnesses kept calling me, saying, What's happening? When is anyone going to talk to us? Awan's sitting in jail—he was convicted of money laundering—but he never testified at his trial, and I hear that nobody has asked him any questions yet. It's all been buried."

Beaty signed his credit card receipt, and the two men stood up, stretched, and stepped into the night. They walked down Grant Street toward the arched entrance to Chinatown.

"There is an investigation, though. When Justice didn't do anything, I took all this to Robert Morgenthau, the D.A. in New York. He's moving."

Going to the legendary New York district attorney had been a shrewd move, the reporter thought as he waited to hear what was coming next. Morgenthau had been the U.S. attorney for the Southern District of New York in Nixon's day, and when the White House discovered his investigation of campaign money that flowed through Maurice Stans, finance chairman of President Nixon's reelection campaign, he had been fired. Undeterred, he had run for district attorney of Manhattan, and he had been there ever since, politically unassailable and independent as a hog on ice.

"You're going to have to get this from somebody else," Blum finally said. "But it's been a big investigation, and now there is a New York grand jury, and they are on the verge of indictments. I think they have enough to ask for an indictment of Altman, but they have yet to prove that Clifford knew what was going on."

Blum looked at the reporter, who was smiling. "There's more, but you're going to have find someone else to tell you this, too: I hear that the Federal Reserve Board is finally going to step into this. BCCI is hemorrhaging. Sheikh Zayed, the ruler of the United Arab Emirates in Abu Dhabi, who is a big shareholder in BCCI, stepped in a few weeks ago and bailed the bank out, and now he effectively owns the bank. But he ordered up audits, and billions of dollars are missing. The Fed is worried that if BCCI crashes, First American might be endangered and the FDIC would have to cover the loss. And that could be a political disaster for the Bush people."

Beaty nodded. That made sense. The savings and loan scandals had been bad enough, but most people didn't know how close to the edge the whole banking system was skating. The biggest banks were holding enough bad loans with junk bonds as collateral to make everyone nervous, and the Federal Deposit Insurance fund was stretched thin. He had been told that First American was an $11-billion-asset bank and if it had to be bailed out at the taxpayers' expense, it could get messy.

"Who can I talk to at Morgenthau's shop?"

"The guy running the investigation is John Moscow. He's the head of the white-collar fraud section and is the lead prosecutor on this. But he doesn't talk much."

"Will you call him and put in a word for me? Tell him I can keep my mouth shut." Blum nodded but didn't look encouraging.

The next day Beaty called John Stacks, *Time*'s chief of correspondents. Stacks was abrupt, irascible, and one of the best newsmen anywhere near the top of the magazine's increasingly corporate management structure.

"Hey, Beaty! What have you got? Have you found Saddam Hussein's suppliers yet?"

This was going to be tricky: Asking to be taken off an assignment always was. "Look, John, I've got the mother of all stories here and I've got to go to Washington." The correspondent had no idea what the story lead should be in the welter of allegations he had been given. Stories, or possible stories, ran off in every direction. He started rattling off the high points from his notes. When he finally ran down, there was silence.

"You say Clark Clifford might be indicted? You better check it out."

Bingo. Beaty grinned. "What about Sam Gwynne? I haven't talked to him yet, but he could be a big help on something like this. He really came through on that money-laundering cover last year." Gwynne had been an international banker before he became a *Time* correspondent, and if anybody could sort through this, he could.

"So talk to him. But he won't have much time. He's taking over as national economics correspondent and is going to be moving to Washington. I think he's there now on a story."

Beaty located Blum at his Powell Street hotel, and the two men agreed to meet a few days later in Washington at a restaurant near McPherson Square. "Don't forget," the reporter said, "You're going to have to go through this again for Sam Gwynne." He didn't bother to add that he needed to hear it again too. On this one you couldn't tell the players without a scorecard.

Beaty headed for the San Francisco airport and an indirect flight to Washington. He knew someone who might know something about all this, and if the man did, and if he was willing to talk, it would be worth the side trip. Standing at a pay phone just before boarding his flight, Beaty finally reached Gwynne at his hotel.

"Sam, I've got a story to tell you that's going to ruin your life."

CHAPTER 2

CURIOUSER AND CURIOUSER

Gwynne, a scotch and water in hand, sat on the edge of his bed and warily watched Beaty pace the hotel room. The older reporter gestured as he retold Blum's story, pausing from time to time to pluck a name from his jumble of notes. Gwynne closed his eyes for a moment. Maybe, he thought, this had made more sense when Beaty had first heard it.

This could be a hell of a story, but Gwynne wasn't sure he was entirely flattered that Beaty had asked for his help. Beaty's specialty was the journalistic equivalent of a high-wire act performed without a net: high-profile stories frequently drawn from unorthodox sources or sources he couldn't name in print. It was typical that the magazine had once dispatched him to Libya to ask Muammar el-Qaddafi if he had really sent a hit squad to assassinate President Reagan.

Beaty was one of a few highly independent correspondents *Time* saw fit to feed and clothe. For more than a decade he had been the magazine's resident investigative journalist, and that meant, among other things, following leads too bizarre for the sensibilities of more establishment correspondents. It meant spending time in the company of mercenaries, cops, crank and cocaine dealers, conspiratorialists, intelligence agents, Mafiosi, and disgruntled government staffers, many of whom became friends. Beaty's unusual modus operandi, his inclination to work from the outside in, and the life-styles of his sources had long ago passed into *Time* lore. He was the only *Time* correspondent who belonged to the National Rifle Association and owned a bulletproof vest. Beaty was not destined for a management role.

Time correspondents were most likely to be drawn from Yale, Harvard, or Princeton; Beaty was a U.C. Berkeley dropout who had graduated from the bohemian scenes of San Francisco's North Beach in the late 1950s and wandered into journalism a decade later. In four years he had worked his way through covering the police beat and city council meetings for a small Southern California daily to freelancing articles for *Time* magazine. His newspaper exposés had terminated the careers of a mayor, several city councilmen, and a crooked deputy district attorney. In the mid-'70s he was the chief investigator for Los Angeles County Supervisor Baxter Ward, the former television newscaster who made a name for himself by attacking political corruption. Beaty ran Ward's public hearings examining the fitness of the county sheriff, the district attorney, and the county assessor, investigations that forced the resignation of the assessor, who had been the political kingmaker of Southern California. And that had landed him in Washington as *Time*'s investigative reporter.

Gwynne was much more the sort with whom *Time* was comfortable, a presentable prep-school-and-Princeton type who had come to journalism from a career as a banker. During the international lending boom of the 1970s and early 1980s he had worked as a loan officer for a couple of multibillion-dollar banks, mostly pumping money out to the Third World in Asia and the Middle East and traveling to places like Tunis, Jedda, Kuwait City, Dubai, Bangkok, and Djakarta. He left banking, conveniently, a few months before the sovereign bankruptcies of Mexico, Brazil, the Philippines, and other countries triggered a $600-billion debt crisis. He quickly discovered that he was one of the few bankers in captivity willing to talk about what had gone wrong out there in the Third World and why American banks had so gleefully flushed so many billions down a rat hole. Gwynne had done that for a living.

He wrote a book about it, thereby pigeonholing himself for a long time as an "economics" writer. He banged around Southern California working as a reporter for *The Los Angeles Herald Examiner*, a freelance writer, and editor of a business magazine. After a stint as *Time*'s Detroit bureau chief, he was coming to Washington as national economics correspondent. Though he had worked with Beaty on a *Time* cover story about money laundering in 1989 and had done the odd investigative piece for other publications, Gwynne by background and temperament was not an "investigative" reporter.

Now Gwynne was worried about the credence Beaty was giving the word of Jack Blum.

"I know you've worked with him for years," Gwynne said when Beaty finally ran down. "But this guy is talking about a worldwide conspiracy nobody has ever heard about. Bankers who pay off presidents. A bank that just moves money and doesn't make real loans and doesn't have any real capital. And why did he wait for almost two years to tell you about the Kerry investigation getting derailed?"

"I don't know yet. Look, let's just talk to him, and you make your own judgments. But, one way or another, this is starting to break." He waved a copy of *The Washington Post* Blum had given him, now five days old. A small headline on the front page read: WHO CONTROLS FIRST AMERICAN BANKSHARES? AFTER 9 YEARS QUESTIONS LINGER ON FOREIGN TIES. Inside, a large picture of Clark Clifford dominated page 3. The story was by Jim McGee, a reporter neither of them knew.

Gwynne had already scanned the article. "All right, there seems to be a connection between First American and BCCI, but this doesn't even hint at the stuff that Blum told you about. Why would the feds ignore information he says these witnesses gave them?"

Beaty grinned broadly and fished in his briefcase for a large brown envelope. He had been saving the best for the last.

"So look at this."

Gwynne pulled a sheaf of typewritten pages out of the envelope and began to read, looking up at Beaty from time to time in growing amazement. It was a report of a debriefing of a BCCI officer. The older reporter was smiling like a Cheshire cat. "Don't look smug. How in the hell did you get this?"

Beaty explained that he had visited an old government source the night before. He described the source's job and why the source had decided to be helpful but didn't name him. "We can't use any of this in print yet, and if anyone discovers we have it, we've got to say that it just came in over the transom. But the guy being interviewed in that report has to be the same guy Blum calls Ali Mirza. Keep reading: Blum didn't even begin to tell me all the stuff this Mirza dumped out for the feds."

Beaty and Gwynne met with Blum the next day at the McPherson Grill, a Washington version of a trendy New York restaurant imitating a trendy ferns-and-blond-wood West Coast restaurant. The place had been chosen with care. It was loud, crowded with younger Washington technocrats, lawyers in starched white shirts, and secretaries from the Securities and Exchange Commission building next door. In the darker, more exclusive capital watering holes, power players closely eyed neighboring tables to see who was talking to whom.

The three men took a table in the back, and at Beaty's prodding, Blum summarized. For Gwynne's benefit he focused on what he called "the biggest Ponzi scheme ever pulled off by anyone, anywhere." The notion of a financial institution playing a Ponzi game was not a new concept. In the 1980s some of the renegade savings and loans that had done the most damage in the United States had operated this way, soliciting government-insured $100,000 brokered deposits by offering interest premiums and using the stream of new money to cover old losses. That was the way a financial Ponzi worked: As long as the deposits kept coming in, holes in the balance sheet could be patched up and the regulators kept at bay.

The first difference between BCCI and those savings and loans, Blum said, was scale. Agha Hasan Abedi had spun a global Ponzi, operating out of the unregulated havens of Luxembourg and the Cayman Islands. Nobody had ever done anything on this scale before, nor had anyone ever danced so artfully through the interstices of international regulation. For all practical purposes this was an unregulated bank. And the word was that a billion dollars, perhaps far more, had gone missing.

"But the far weirder difference," Blum continued, "is that this bank has no capital at all. As far as I can tell, it never did have any. And it's not in the business of making loans."

To Gwynne this sounded implausible. He had only Beaty's word that Blum knew what he was talking about, and Blum was already pushing the limits of credibility. A bank without capital—a bank that had never had any significant capital—was not imaginable, nor was a $20-billion international bank that was not in the lending business. How did it stay afloat?

"You can't run a bank in that many countries without capital," Gwynne said. "I can't see it."

"That's the magic of BCCI," Blum calmly pushed on. "The bank got its start-up money when the ruler of Abu Dhabi let Abedi handle the remittances from expatriate Pakistanis working in the Gulf. There were hundreds of thousands and eventually millions of these guys all sending money home every month. It was enough money that it shored up Pakistan's entire economy, and Abedi got the float—and the float meant that he always had a few million dollars sitting in his bank, on the way from a Pakistani worker in the Gulf to his family back home. The slower the remittance, the bigger the float. Abedi treated it like capital."

That was a good answer. "But what about the shareholders, the people who bought stock in BCCI? What happened to that money?"

"That's the brilliant part. Apparently, the bank put loans on the books to wealthy Arabs to buy stock in itself but never handed over the money. The bank would hold on to those shares as collateral for the loans, which were, of course, never repaid. At some point they liquidate the loan and seize the collateral. Nothing actually moves anywhere, but millions in assets have been created on paper. It's circular. And in the process BCCI appears to be underwritten by some of the most wealthy people in the world. See?"

The notion, Gwynne thought, was breathtaking. Banks were by nature highly fictitious entities: Most of their "funds" were imaginary units of value, and even financial idiots knew that they did not actually keep their deposits on hand. But what Blum was talking about sounded like an entirely fictitious bank—a work of pure imagination. Deposits became capital; deposits became profits; deposits were used to cover losses and patch holes. There was, in short, nothing but deposits, and many of the deposits were not in fact deposits at all; they had been whisked down this or that offshore sinkhole, never to be recovered. As for lending, Blum said loans were used primarily as a tool of control, or to buy influence. BCCI lent money to powerful politicians and their families. There were certainly loans, but they were not the bank's main purpose.

Blum embarked on a description of the bank's big depositors, share-holders, and front men. This was the glamorous part: Abedi had assembled a glittering group of the richest and most powerful people in the Middle East, the rulers of four countries, fabulously wealthy commoners, and princelings from Saudi Arabia. His deposits came rolling in from the petrodollar-rich treasuries all over the Middle East.

Blum was very definitely playing out in deep left field; yet the deeper he and Gwynne got into technicalities such as letters of credit, acceptances, loan accounting, and wire transfers, the more Blum held his own. He clearly understood what he was talking about, and he was clearly not crazy. Gwynne decided he was going to have to trust Beaty's instincts. Beaty, who had been nervously waiting for that moment to pass, finally broke in.

As far as he was concerned, the big story was the cover-up, and he had been thinking only about the tapes—the hours and hours of tapes that the government lawyers and investigators from C-Chase had collected—of Blum's BCCI bankers describing political influence, the secret ownership of First American Bank, plans to scuttle Kerry's subcommittee, and all the rest. Blum had said the tapes had disappeared.

"Let's talk about the tapes from the mysterious Ali Mirza," Beaty said. "Was he your Witness A or Witness B? Or should I mention that I've discovered someone else who was talking to the government? Maybe we should call him Witness C."

Blum's face froze into an expressionless mask.

"Is this a copy of the report your intelligence friend made about his meeting with the source you call Mirza?" Beaty asked.

"How the hell did you get this?" Blum was genuinely astounded.

"I can't tell you," Beaty replied. "All I can say is that it came from somewhere in the government."

Blum flipped quickly through the folder. Then he reached down, opened his briefcase, and fished out some papers. It was a memo identical to the one Beaty and Gwynne had. Blum laughed out loud, but he didn't sound too amused.

"A copy of this was delivered to the Customs team and federal prosecutors in Florida, but I don't know where else it went. So now you have it too. Do you have any idea of what you're sitting on?"

The report was composed of two unsigned memos, typed on plain bond in the numbingly flat bureaucratic style of official investigative reports everywhere. They gave detailed statements made by Ali Mirza during a meeting on March 17, 1989, and during a second meeting on March 20. All together, there were nine pages of closely spaced text. The report began with a statement that Ali Mirza, "hereinafter referred to as the source," had sought the meetings with some urgency.

Mirza, the writer said, began by inquiring in an odd way about the Kerry hearings. He seemed to know all about them and he was worried that he, too, had come under FBI surveillance because Amjad Awan, BCCI's head of Latin American operations, had called to tell him about receiving a subpoena from Senator Kerry's subcommittee. Awan told him that he contacted the bank's president, Swaleh Naqvi, in London to tell him about the subpoena. Naqvi told Awan to take a plane to Washington to see Robert Altman, and Altman told Awan to shred his documents and leave the United States immediately. Awan, the source said, was afraid that he would be fired for having disobeyed Naqvi and Altman, but he didn't want to leave Florida because his children were in school there.

Mirza then described BCCI's obsession with Blum, whose investigation clearly had frightened BCCI in a way that the Justice Department had not. He referred to a man named Syed Ziauddin Ali Akbar, another mysterious Pakistani with whom Blum had had an odd and inconclusive interview in the summer of 1988. Akbar had been sent to find out what Blum knew, and what he was planning to do.

> Source said that he had also been in contact with another BCCI person who had been implicated in the activities under investigation, a Mr. Akbar . . . Akbar had met with Mr. Blum and after meeting had told his colleagues in BCCI, including source, that "Blum knows everything about the bank, every detail," and words to the effect that "we are finished." At this point source said, "Blum really went right to the jugular."

The "source" then described the fixing of the troublesome Jack Blum.

> At this point, source expanded his earlier statement about Jack Blum leaving by saying that in fact there had been a concerted effort by Democratic senators to "kill" the hearings and that this effort along with pressure that had been brought to bear on the U.S. State Dept. by the Pakistani government had been successful in curtailing further hearings. According to source, this effort had been orchestrated by several people, including Clark Clifford and Robert Altman, who had gone to contacts they had in the Senate. Source said Senator Coelho [sic] from California had been contacted (to my recollection it was not stated what Coelho was allegedly supposed to have done, but source mentioned his name several times).

Mirza also talked about Ghaith Rashad Pharaon, the flamboyant Saudi financier who had purchased the National Bank of Georgia from President Carter's confidant Bert Lance and later sold it to First American Bank. He said that Pharaon had engaged a Mr. Charlie Jones of Hindsville, Georgia, to help suppress further hearings and that Jones had been "paid a considerable amount of money to accomplish this task." Mirza named two U.S. senators Jones had enlisted "to do what was necessary to suppress the hearings and eliminate Jack Blum."

Beaty and Gwynne had already pointed out those passages to each other. *Eliminate Jack Blum.* It was increasingly clear why Blum was angry, why he was pursuing his private crusade against this bank. The BCCI people were giving him credit for having broken through in his investigation, while at the same time bragging that they had closed him down. Even more astounding was that the Customs, IRS, and Justice people in Florida had heard all of this—three and a half days of it, in fine detail—and yet had not opened an investigation.

Mirza also described at length Pakistan's involvement in applying pressure to curtail the hearings: "The Pakistanis having used the argument that such further investigation would destabilize U.S.-Mideast relations at a sensitive time." What could a Senate investigation of BCCI in the United States have to do with the country's Middle Eastern relationships?

There was just too much they didn't know. Mirza wasn't a nobody: He came from one of the leading families in Pakistan and he was privy to top management decisions within BCCI's American operations.

"This is it, isn't it, Jack? This Mirza is one of the witnesses you set up for the feds?" Beaty asked.

Blum was solemn. "I'm not asking any questions, but you can't use this, and you definitely can't mention Mirza's name. He doesn't know he was recorded. And if anybody knew that he talked to us, he would probably be killed."

One of the strangest and most compelling parts of the memo dealt with Pharaon. He, at least, was a familiar name, the kind of larger-than-life character the press loves: a smooth Saudi billionaire who flew around in his own jumbo jet, making deals between visits to his palaces and mansions scattered around the world. He was the first and most visible of the new generation of oil-rich Arabs to wash up on American shores. But Mirza had a very different take on him.

> Source said everything that Pharaon had came from BCCI. In effect Pharaon was an invention of BCCI. He explained that after Pharaon had returned from college, he in fact was "recruited" by Abedi and for years had been used to "front" for BCCI. This had been very useful for BCCI as Pharaon came from a respected Saudi family and had all the necessary Middle East credentials. Whenever the BCCI group wanted to buy anything that they perceived was difficult for them to acquire directly, Pharaon would be used. This included, according to source, the National Bank of Georgia, the Independence Bank, among others.

"That's fairly interesting," Gwynne said dryly, pointing to the passage. "If I remember correctly, the National Bank of Georgia held the paper on some large commercial loans to President Carter's peanut business in Georgia. If Abedi just used Pharaon to front his purchase of the National Bank of Georgia in 1978, that means the president of the United States owed money to BCCI."

"Yeah, but we've got nothing that shows Carter knew that," Beaty said. "But it is thought provoking: Abedi moved in right at the top."

The three men continued scanning the documents. They read Mirza's descriptions of payments and favors to Andrew Young, Jesse Jackson, and President Carter. He talked about BCCI's hidden investment in CenTrust Savings and described how lawyer Charlie Jones and Ghaith Pharaon met with banking regulators in Washington and somehow persuaded them not to shut down the fraud-riddled Florida savings and loan bank. Their efforts kept the bank open for more than an additional year, and when the regulators finally did get around to closing CenTrust, it cost the Resolution Trust Fund—or the American taxpayer—an estimated $2 billion. He said Abedi had needed a change in Georgia's banking regulations in order to take over the National Bank of Georgia and that he had handed out $1 million to influence the Georgia State Legislature to modify the law. And most important, he described Abedi's use of nominees—straw men—to control First American Bank.

Mirza was taking on some very powerful people. Why had he decided to come forward? Blum's friend, the ex-agent, said in the report that he believed Mirza had made his statements as an oblique approach to Blum. "The source," he wrote, "is still affiliated with the group and at the same time is preparing the way for a bid for immunity if things continue to deteriorate."

The report concluded on a chilling note:

> It is not for me to assess the value of the information that source has provided. However, if it is considered that the information is credible and would be of utility, I would recommend that he be brought in without too much delay. In this recommendation I would include the idea of furnishing the source and his family the necessary security safeguards. The group is well aware of the level of detail that source has, and somewhere in this process if they become aware that source is in contact with U.S. authorities he would be considered a threat to their security and survival. Given the nature of the people in the group it is certainly possible that they might attempt to physically eliminate the source or his family.

Whatever else it might be, the Mirza memo was the stuff reporters dream about. Between it and Blum's account, Beaty and Gwynne had been delivered, virtually in toto, a road map to much of the BCCI story. Other large investigative stories—such as Watergate—came out in tiny increments over a period of time. Much of this story had been laid out already; the problem was going to be proving it in the face of government denials, using witnesses in fear of their lives. Beaty and Gwynne shook hands with Blum, promised to let him know what they found as they began digging.

"What about John Moscow in Morgenthau's office, Jack? Have you talked to him about seeing me?"

"I told him about you. He wants to talk on the phone first, to sound you out. He'll call, probably tomorrow, but convincing him to meet is up to you."

"Has he seen this memo?"

"I don't think so, but he knows about it. I wouldn't doubt that Mirza is one of his witnesses."

Beaty and Gwynne looked at each other. There were wheels spinning within wheels here, and the two reporters retreated to try to sort out everything they had just heard.

To one accustomed to newspaper city rooms, *Time*'s Washington bureau has the look of a law office and the ambience of a decorator-designed rabbit warren. It is unnervingly quiet for a place that generates most of *Time*'s political stories, and is curiously civilized, even on a busy night. A visitor wandering through its labyrinthine pastel corridors, festooned with huge color photographs from *Time* and *Life,* hears little but the occasional whir of a laser printer, the soft babble of telephone conversations, or the *tip-tip-tap*ping of fingers on a computer keyboard that has become the trademark sound of modern journalism. Nothing could be further from the *Front Page* newsroom than the eighth-floor suite of offices at Connecticut Avenue and L Street.

Camped in two of the bureau's empty offices, Beaty and Gwynne found the three stories that had been written so far on BCCI and read them closely. After BCCI's money-laundering conviction in early 1990, a handful of reporters had taken another look at the relationship between Abedi's BCCI and Clifford's First American Bank. In May 1990 Larry Gurwin, a freelancer writing in the Washington business monthly *Regardie's,* had described at length the intimate ties between BCCI and First American's shareholders. Most of them, the article said, were shareholders in both banks, and all seemed to have the same "investment adviser"—Agha Hasan Abedi.

The same month, Peter Truell and John Fialka raised many of the same questions in *The Wall Street Journal*. They also caught the fact that some of Noriega's money laundered through BCCI had passed through accounts at First American Bank in Washington. Truell and Fialka also had discovered that the C-Chase undercover agents had taped Amjad Awan telling them that BCCI really owned First American, but they didn't question why those tapes had never been played for the jury. Both articles suggested that if BCCI did not control First American, there was at least something all too coincidental about the many links between the two banks.

The stories, now nine months old, apparently failed to catch the attention of the federal law enforcement agencies presumably interested in foreign banks sneaking into the United States under false colors. But they had alerted *The Washington Post*, and the *Post* wielded enormous power in Clifford's backyard. In the summer of 1990 the *Post* assigned Jim McGee, the reporter who had exposed Gary Hart's alleged sexual infidelities on the front pages of *The Miami Herald*, to investigate First American's ties to BCCI. The result, published some seven months later, was the most thorough piece yet on the subject, and one that stopped just a hair's breadth shy of accusing Clifford and Altman of felonies.

It had been an arduous, nervy affair for the *Post*, in part because of Clifford's good name in Washington, and in part, insiders said, because of Clifford's close and long-standing relationship with *Post* publisher Katharine Graham. And First American just happened to be *The Washington Post*'s bank; every reporter and editor received paychecks bearing its name. By the *Post*'s own account, McGee interviewed Clifford for fifteen hours over several months, exploring every alleged connection between the two banks. That is an extraordinary amount of time, both for the newspaper and for Clifford. It was a measure of Clifford's stature in the capital that McGee was forced to proceed so cautiously. Though the *Post*'s editors pulled the punch— neither the headline nor the article's conclusions reflected the substance of what McGee was saying—the piece nonetheless rocketed the Clifford–First American–BCCI story to prominence in Washington. It was not yet national news.

McGee reported that Abedi personally screened the appointments of some of the most senior executives in First American. BCCI officers had arranged for the purchase of First American branches in New York. BCCI had arranged, financed, and acted as midwife in First American's 1987 purchase of the National Bank of Georgia. And BCCI had made loans to some of those same shareholders in order to purchase First American. While all this was going on, Clifford and Altman were not merely chairman and president of First American, respectively. They were also First American's chief legal counsel, an odd arrangement that caused *The Washington Post* to wonder, carefully, whether there might be a conflict of interest.

Clifford and Altman were also BCCI's lead counsel in the United States. The firm had dished out an incredible $20 million to orchestrate that bank's defense against money-laundering charges in Tampa. With such a wide and deep purview, it seemed impossible that both men could be ignorant of what was going on. Clark Clifford later put it better than anyone: "I have a choice of either seeming stupid or venal." This was his biggest problem. By pleading ignorance, the man reputed to be the smartest lawyer in Washington would seem to be lying.

To their credit, *Regardie's*, *The Wall Street Journal*, and *The Washington Post* had ventured out to suggest that the emperor was wearing no clothes. Yet after the *Post*'s revelations in its February 3, 1991, article, there had been no follow-ups in other newspapers.

The *Post* had not mentioned, and presumably hadn't known about, a New York grand jury on the move. That fact, if they could confirm it, was now Beaty and Gwynne's precious news lead. More important, the Mirza memo potentially spun the story into both a domestic and international scandal of much wider scope and suggested that the real reportorial game had just begun.

Beaty and Gwynne were drawing up lists of people to interview when the phone call that triggered their next move came in. It was John Moscow, calling from New York. Beaty talked to him for a few minutes and then rushed into Gwynne's office.

"We're in! I'm leaving for New York right now to meet Moscow this evening."

"Great work. What did he say?"

"Not a lot. He was pretty guarded on the phone. Mostly I was telling him what great reporters we are. I didn't ask him whether a grand jury was hearing evidence, but he did acknowledge that Blum had come to them last year and that as a result they had begun an investigation. So far everything Blum has told us has checked out. That must have been an interesting meeting."

It had indeed been a dramatic affair when Jack Blum walked into Robert Morgenthau's office in late March 1989.

Blum was received cordially. The Washington lawyer and the district attorney knew each other slightly, but Blum was well aware of Morgenthau's reputation. There are only a relative handful of people in the United States in positions of influence who have devoted their careers to exposing government and business corruption, and fewer still who have managed to retain those positions for very long while doing so. Morgenthau knew Blum had been running Senator Kerry's hearings into drug-money laundering, so Morgenthau was prepared to listen attentively when the former Senate special counsel declared he had a very important story to tell him. The district attorney offered Blum a cigar, and when he declined, lit his own and leaned back in his blue leather office chair and nodded. "This is about the biggest bank fraud in the history of the world," Blum began.

The investigator had not come to Morgenthau by impulse; he had debated with himself for weeks about what to do with his knowledge. If you thought you had stumbled into a vast criminal enterprise that had unlimited money and the sophistication to buy influence on such a magnificent scale that even the U.S. Justice Department covered its eyes, there aren't too many people to turn to. It had not escaped Blum that the Justice Department takes its orders from the White House. In a very real sense, Morgenthau may have been the only law enforcement game in town.

Morgenthau was then seventy years old, a lean figure with silver hair, a high domed forehead, and a patrician manner. He was soft-spoken, courtly, and one of the most important men in New York. There were several reasons for this, and perhaps the least of them was that he was the most renowned district attorney in the nation. It is an old-fashioned term, but Robert Morgenthau was esteemed because he was an influential man of high principle raised in a tradition of public service. As Blum later told a reporter, he came to Morgenthau because he was a man with "a reputation for absolute integrity and propriety and the willingness to do whatever has to be done." Morgenthau was extraordinarily well connected in the social, liberal, and judicial circles of power in New York and Washington, and he used those connections without hesitation.

The office that Blum sat in for the fateful discussion that day is a reflection of the man who has occupied it for fourteen years. It is large, cluttered with books, papers, and the memorabilia of a lifetime of public service. The walls are covered with photographs and awards, dominated by an Oliphant cartoon blown up to epic proportions. The cartoon depicts a younger Morgenthau, wearing a Sherlock Holmes hat and holding the leashes of a pack of bloodhounds, following the footsteps of Maurice Stans, President Nixon's campaign finance chairman, to the locked door of a cash-stuffed Swiss bank. The paintings are not masterpieces: They are counterfeit Dufy paintings confiscated in an art fraud case. The framed letters from Franklin Delano Roosevelt and Lord Lothian to Henry Morgenthau, Jr., Robert Morgenthau's father, are real, as are the fondly inscribed photographs of virtually all the Kennedy clan. On his desk there is a picture of his forty-five-year-old second wife, Lucinda Franks, a novelist and former Pulitzer Prize–winning *New York Times* reporter, and their two young children.

The Morgenthaus have been part of the political establishment of the city, and the country, since 1886, when Robert Morgenthau's German-Jewish great-grandfather immigrated from Bavaria. Robert's grandfather made a fortune in real estate and became ambassador to Turkey under Woodrow Wilson; his father was Franklin Roosevelt's secretary of the Treasury. Bob Morgenthau had been a friend of the Kennedy family and as a result had been named U.S. attorney for the Southern District of New York—long the most important U.S. attorney's bailiwick in the nation—when Kennedy reached the White House in 1960. Morgenthau's Washington connections, and his reputation as a crusader, were built in that office, and the Oliphant cartoon on his wall is a pointed reminder of his independence.

The D.A.'s straight shooting had kept him in public office for thirty years as the top federal and local prosecutor in a city that long ago institutionalized patronage politics, kickbacks, municipal corruption, and electoral manipulation. Morgenthau was remarkably free of political insecurity: Unlike most elected officials, he couldn't cite to the nearest decimal point the plurality that kept him in office, because it had been years since he faced a serious challenge.

The office also provided a different kind of clue to the reason why Morgenthau might be predisposed to pick up the torch that Blum sought to pass. The tall windows that line the room are covered with New York grime, and the view outside the next-to-the-top floor of Hogan Plaza, the run-down building named after New York's first crusading district attorney, is equally grimy. Below, on the streets of Lower Manhattan, within a traffic-jammed quadrangle bounded by courthouses and government buildings, there is always a milling crowd, a depressingly visible manifestation of the endless flow of the lost and desperate entering and leaving the creaking, overburdened Manhattan criminal justice system. Most of them, victims and perpetrators alike, have been damaged, directly or indirectly, by the drug trade.

On the floors immediately below Morgenthau's worn office are the far dingier, peeling-paint offices of 570 assistant district attorneys, who carry the highest caseloads in the country, buried in an avalanche of local crime. These men and women prosecute 110,000 cases a year that range from murder to domestic violence to racketeering charges against Mafia dons. Thirty thousand of those cases are drug cases, and drugs figure somewhere in the majority of the remainder, whether the charge is murder or theft or child abandonment.

Morgenthau had realized for years that arresting small-time drug dealers in an effort to stanch the tide was futile, and that to do something effective one had to attack the financial conduits that made it all possible. The banks. The untouchable, respectable banks. The Bank Secrecy Act of 1968, the first law that forced reluctant banks to open at least some of their records to law enforcement, was drafted in Morgenthau's offices. Now Jack Blum was telling him about an international bank that was born in the drug trade, a bank that laundered drug money as part of corporate policy, and a bank that apparently remained open because its enormous cash flow bought influence in the corridors of power in Washington. And in Karachi, London, Paris, Lagos, Panama City, Buenos Aires, Bahrain, La Paz, Brasília, and Beijing, to name just a few other places. A bank with imposing offices on Park Avenue and hidden control of an American bank with offices from Florida to New York that gave it access to the trillion-dollar-a-day New York–based international electronic transfer system.

After Blum had laid out his story, nearly two hours in the telling, and concluded that, in his opinion, no one was going to prosecute BCCI, Morgenthau had only one question: "Is there evidence of money laundering through New York?" Yes, Blum told him, and there was evidence that BCCI also owned First American Bank, which had major offices in New York.

Michael Cherkasky, Morgenthau's chief of investigations, who had been called into the office to listen to Blum, was appalled that his chief seemed ready to step into the case. As Cherkasky later told Marie Brenner, a writer for *Vanity Fair* magazine, Blum's story sounded ridiculous. "He said the entire Third World was involved and that they had bought and sold entire governments and maybe some United States officials. It was a fascinating tale—this guy was telling us the world was corrupt!" But Cherkasky's real worry was pragmatic: Where would he find the resources to pursue a complicated international case, which could take years, when the office was already so overburdened?

And what about the critics who were sure to surface and demand to know why the D.A. was spending city taxpayers' dollars on a foreign adventure while New Yorkers were being mugged and shot? Morgenthau was a pillar of the Democratic party, but so was Clark Clifford, and Clifford had powerful friends. Morgenthau, however, was seemingly untroubled by questions of jurisdiction or resources.

"If New York is the banking center of the world and the money is laundered through here, there is our jurisdiction," Morgenthau declared. "If the United States attorney is not doing it, I'm doing it."

Cherkasky picked up the telephone and asked John Moscow, his top investigator, to come upstairs. He had a new case.

CHAPTER 3

INTO THE LOOKING GLASS

As the other passengers from the Metroliner flowed past him, Beaty paused by the arrival gate to gaze around Penn Station. A small overnight bag dangled from a shoulder strap, and his right hand gripped a bronze-colored metal briefcase. The travel-dented but still gleaming Halliburton was conspicuous. It was an easy identification signal that the reporter often used when he arranged meetings with strangers in public places.

Beaty leaned against the wall, still looking for a middle-aged man wearing a loden-green coat. The day's crush of commuters leaving New York for the suburbs had peaked; still, there were hundreds of people in the cavernous station. It would have been less complicated for Beaty to have taken a taxi downtown to the district attorney's offices, but John Moscow had shied away from that suggestion and insisted he would be pleased to meet the train. A courteous gesture, but Beaty understood that Robert Morgenthau's man wouldn't want to be seen talking to him, even by his colleagues. That was thought provoking, and Beaty had decided it was a good omen. He had been warned that Moscow gave away very little. Still, people who didn't want to be seen talking to a reporter usually had something to say.

The loden-green coat, wrapped around a powerfully built man in his forties, materialized in front of Beaty. It was John Moscow, the head of white-collar fraud. The two men introduced themselves, shook hands, and headed for the Thirty-third Street exit. Beaty was a little surprised at Moscow's appearance, although he wasn't sure what he had been expecting. Maybe somebody more academic. Blum had mentioned that Moscow was a Harvard Law School graduate and commented on his intelligence, but this man looked more like a button man for the mob than an intellectual. He was big, around six feet tall and a couple hundred pounds or more, with hooded eyes and a nose that appeared to have been broken at least once. He looked street smart and tough and talked out of the side of his mouth, like a wiseguy who never said anything that wasn't confidential or incriminating.

Outside in the cold night air Moscow turned away from the line of waiting cabs and suggested a walk: They could flag down a cab later or perhaps stop somewhere for a drink. It turned out to be a very long walk, since the D.A.'s man was wary of walking into a place where either of them might be recognized. At first the reporter, who was cold and ready to duck into any Seventh Avenue dive, thought Moscow was a bit paranoid. But as they talked, it began to dawn on him that this whole thing might be bigger and more complicated than even Blum had envisioned. Beaty had expected the prosecutor to be cautious about a meeting with him simply because he had a case before a grand jury, but that hardly justified this much concern about security.

"You didn't want to talk on the telephone, but you can't be worried about taps—?"

Moscow slowed down. "My investigators have been placed under surveillance . . . by unknown parties." He thought for a minute, framing his words. "And bugs have been found in certain offices that were not placed there by regular law enforcement."

Beaty waited for Moscow to elaborate, but apparently the subject was closed. It was, Beaty would learn, a typical Moscow answer: precise, exact, frustratingly limited, and a little awesome in its implications. Engrossed in conversation, the two men circled the same four blocks a couple of times and then headed north toward Central Park and Beaty's hotel some two dozen blocks away. They took turns carrying Beaty's overnight bag, but the reporter held tightly to his briefcase, which contained the Mirza memo.

"Look, John, I've got this report by some spook talking to a BCCI guy named Mirza. Do you know about it?" Beaty wasn't prepared for the answer he got.

"I've seen it, and I've talked to Mirza about it. He confirms most of it, and he's worried that someone is going to put a contract out on him." They stood on a corner waiting for the light to change. "But I've never heard the tapes—those debriefing tapes Blum told you about, where Mirza and some other people talked for several days. We've tried to get them. At Mr. Morgenthau's request, the Federal Reserve sent two examiners to Florida to ask the Tampa prosecutors whether they had any evidence that BCCI controlled First American, and they denied knowing anything. Then I asked Justice, and I asked Customs in Tampa specifically about the Mirza tapes and requested copies, but they denied any knowledge of them. They told me they didn't exist. They lied. They don't know I had already found Mirza and talked to him, and that he had told me about the session with Blum in the hotel room."

The light had changed and changed again, but neither man noticed. Beaty groped for a follow-up question. There was no use asking why. Why was becoming a little overwhelming.

"Uh, yeah. Jack said this person that wrote the report was a former CIA guy. Is that true?"

"I really can't tell you anything more about that."

This time the answer reduced the reporter to silence. Talking with Moscow, he was learning, was like consulting the Delphi oracle: You received a pronouncement, a veiled revelation of truth, and went away trying to figure out what it meant. Beaty realized he had just been told that Blum was not exaggerating: There was a cover-up going on, for reasons unknown, and the CIA or somebody still close to it was acutely interested in what was being done about BCCI.

The Mirza memo was a treasure for more reasons than one. Because he had it, Beaty could ask Moscow to confirm or deny information he already held. That was the way the game was usually played, and it made Moscow a little more comfortable, since he clearly wasn't going to volunteer much. With a flash of insight Beaty realized that Morgenthau and his people were anxious about having hooked a leviathan they might not be able to boat. There was more to this than Clark Clifford's involvement.

By the time Beaty and Moscow had hiked as far as the Time & Life Building on Fifty-first Street, the reporter was insisting that they stop somewhere—anywhere—so he could write down some of this. By then he understood why Moscow was so wary about being seen and agreed that his hotel, the Parker Meridien on Fifty-sixth, would be out of the question. Too many lawyers, particularly too many lawyers and high-level officials from Washington, stayed there. They chose the faded splendor of the Dorset Hotel after peering through a window:

The piano bar was nearly empty. Inside they peeled off their topcoats, and Moscow unwound his wool scarf. Beaty saw that the green car coat had been hiding a reassuringly conservative gray suit and pin-striped shirt. The Californian was still having trouble with Moscow's New York accent, and his statements were often enigmatic to the point of obscurity, but Beaty had decided that Moscow was a very smart man. If he whispered out of the side of his mouth it was because, indeed, everything he said was either confidential or incriminating.

The picture Moscow presented was clear enough, although the financial details were mind-bending and there were many loose ends. Morgenthau's people had learned enough from a handful of BCCI officers to advise the Federal Reserve that there was evidence BCCI owned and controlled First American Bank. The proof, however, was contained in internal audits and audits conducted by Price Water-house, BCCI's outside accountants in London—audits that neither the accounting firm nor the Bank of England would turn over to Morgen-thau or the U.S. Federal Reserve.

BCCI had been posting multimillion-dollar losses since its indict-ment in 1988 and Abedi's heart attack the same year. When Sheikh Zayed bin Sultan al-Nahayan of Abu Dhabi had come to the rescue, he had injected almost $1 billion and now held 77.4 percent of BCCI. He had demanded audits, which apparently showed further billions missing. Moscow suspected the black hole on the ledgers might be as large as $4 billion. The Bank of England had frozen up when it learned that one of London's biggest foreign banks was insolvent. Instead of shutting down BCCI, it had been sitting on the bad news while trying to talk Zayed into putting up more money. Scotland Yard, which at first had cooperated in Morgenthau's inquiries, now also was stiffing the American investigators.

Moscow was a very frustrated man. Instead of receiving help from the agencies that should have been concerned, the Manhattan D.A. was being blocked by high officials around the world. Luxembourg, where BCCI was incorporated, cited banking privacy laws that pro-hibited its giving anyone the time of day; the Bank of England, where BCCI was headquartered before Zayed stepped in, was silent. The U.S. Justice Department was thwarting Morgenthau at every turn. Justice was shocked to learn of Morgenthau's probe and refused to let his investigators interview Amjad Awan.

An hour later the Dorset Hotel bar was still forlornly quiet. Beaty signaled the waiter to bring the bill, but when it came, Moscow refused to let him pay and they split the tab. Outside on the street they shook hands again, and Moscow gave his final piece of counsel: "Look at the Tampa plea bargain."

It was one in the morning when Beaty called Gwynne in Washington to pass on what he had learned. "Here's the important part: Jack wasn't ranting and this is all for real. I'm pretty sure there is a grand jury, although Moscow wouldn't come right out and say so, and Clifford and Altman are under investigation—although he wouldn't say that directly, either."

Beaty sounded excited. "The Mirza memo is real, and I think Mirza has probably already testified before the grand jury. And the feds are blocking this big time. Get this: Morgenthau made an official request for the Mirza tapes and was told they didn't exist."

"But what do we do next? I take it that all this was off the record?"

"Way off the record, and even then I'm getting this by hints and implications. These guys think their own telephones may be bugged, and somebody's been tailing the D.A.'s men. Moscow's trying to give us a road map to get us started, but he's allergic to direct statements. You can't give this guy lessons on how to deal with the press: His father was the chief political correspondent for *The New York Times*.

"What to do is I'll talk to the office in the morning and get us both cleared for a while. You've got to get on the phone to the Fed, first thing. Everything is about to come unraveled. It's a good guess that the Federal Reserve is going to have to make a move, so do your banker's thing."

"I'm already doing it, but you haven't given me a chance to get a word in edgewise. I talked to a state banking regulator late this afternoon, and there's a rumor that the Federal Reserve has issued a cease-and-desist order barring First American Bank from transferring any money to BCCI and has forwarded a criminal complaint to the Justice Department. The Fed has determined that BCCI secretly controls First American, and they want to make sure BCCI doesn't loot First American now that things are coming apart. And they're going to make the order public in a few days."

"Make it public?" Beaty marveled. "A criminal complaint? They never do that. It could cause a run on the bank.

"Maybe your guy is right: Moscow says the Fed is really pissed off. Those are the words he used. The Fed and Morgenthau have been working together on this for quite a while. If the Fed is going to make it public, it's going to do it to force the Justice Department to take some action; apparently there have been criminal referrals to Justice about BCCI before and nothing happened. Justice has been stiffing them too. The Fed doesn't care about a run on BCCI; that's Abu Dhabi's problem. But the Fed is plenty worried about First American going down with them and taking the FDIC fund with it."

"I guess it was worth a trip to New York," Gwynne deadpanned, "but did you learn anything important?" Beaty made a choking sound. "All right, okay, I'll start phoning around in the morning and try to confirm this. You better get some sleep. It sounds like you've got a fevered brain. Let me know what Stacks says."

Beaty, who had treated himself to a suite with a large bedroom in minor defiance of expense account rules, fell asleep on the sofa with his clothes on. His last thought was that he was going to have to call his wife and tell her that it might be a few days before he could get home.

Wednesday morning John Stacks listened quietly and without expression as Beaty, seated on the blue couch in his boss's large corner office, ran through the story. The chief of correspondents wore a crisp white shirt and tortoiseshell eyeglasses that only slightly softened a disconcertingly direct gaze. He was known as a tough-minded man. Behind him a wall of windows overlooked the Hudson River twenty-four floors below, and the opposite wall was covered, floor to ceiling, with a map of the world. Colored pins marked the locations of *Time*'s twenty-five bureaus. Joelle Attinger, deputy chief of domestic correspondents, sat next to the reporter and took notes on a yellow legal pad.

Beaty quickly ran through his conversations with Blum and Moscow and explained the mysterious circumstances surrounding the Mirza tapes.

"Just the fact that the government had evidence about the illegal ownership of First American and sat on it tells you there's something very wrong happening here. And Gwynne's got word that the Federal Reserve is about to make all this public."

Stacks didn't respond directly. "Why are we being told all of this?"

Beaty shrugged. "We know where Blum is coming from. He's outraged. As far as Morgenthau's office is concerned, I think maybe we've been adroitly steered there. They're frustrated and maybe getting a little desperate. Morgenthau can't keep an investigation going forever, and they're still getting blocked at every turn. He got the Fed moving, but the FBI won't assign any agents to the case. And I got the impression that Morgenthau is taking a lot of personal heat for picking on Clark Clifford."

Attinger looked up. "So what should we be doing?"

"Everything. This thing is huge. It's going to be a worldwide scandal, and the D.A. probably has a half-dozen people assigned to it, maybe not even that many full-time. Morgenthau isn't looking for publicity. He's looking for investigative help and some way to lever the Justice Department into cooperating instead of sitting on evidence. There are leads going off everywhere that go beyond his prosecutorial sights, and his man Moscow is willing to talk about things that aren't directly related to the grand jury. He says that whatever role Clifford and Altman played, that's just a minor part of the whole BCCI story." Beaty shot a quick look at Stacks. "I kind of told him that *Time* would be prepared to devote major resources to a story like this."

Stacks maintained his deadpan. "Well, what about a first story first? By Friday can we say a New York grand jury has targeted Clark Clifford and that the Fed has linked the two banks? Do you have to talk to Morgenthau?" Friday night was the magazine's deadline.

"Maybe. Everything was off the record, so we need confirmation elsewhere. Gwynne's trying to pry something more out of the banking regulators on the Fed action. Morgenthau's out of pocket, but I trust Moscow. He's a real straight-arrow type. And I may have the grand jury thing by the back door; there are subpoenas out, so a criminal investigation will be fairly easy to confirm in court records now that I know where to look. Moscow told me a kind of funny story, about Clifford and Altman's lawyer coming in to say they were innocent, but that Altman wanted immunity if he was going to come in to talk."

Stacks looked at him blankly.

"Well, maybe you had to be there to think it was funny," Beaty continued. "Anyway, the lawyer is Bob Fisk, the former U.S. attorney and the biggest criminal lawyer in town. If Clifford and Altman have a criminal lawyer and Altman's been invited in to talk, we can probably say they're among the subjects of the probe even if we can't say they're the targets. And if the Fed has made a criminal referral to the Justice Department, the FBI will be forced to investigate them, too. But Morgenthau's real target is BCCI itself, and he's convinced the Bush administration is trying to bury the whole subject. I don't think they have any idea why."

"All right. Do it. The two of you can work out of the Washington bureau. It's already Wednesday, so just give me a one-column story for the Business section. If you can confirm it. You don't know enough yet to write any more, and that much will get us into the game. I'm top-editing this week, so make sure I see it."

Time magazine had just lurched into the BCCI saga.

.   .   .

By Thursday morning Beaty had joined Gwynne in the Washington bureau, where they camped in the two partially furnished spare offices. Gwynne already had begun a telephone marathon, with calls out to banking regulators at the Comptroller of the Currency, the Federal Reserve, and Treasury, and to state regulators in New York, Washington, Virginia, and Florida. He was working his way up through their secretaries, public affairs pooh-bahs, and assistants.

The lights on his desk phone blinked steadily as return calls came in. He couldn't say, wouldn't say, exactly what he wanted, which was confirmation that the Fed was going to issue an order prohibiting BCCI from transferring funds out of First American. It sounded routine and technical, but in the banking world it would be a sensation. Such an order would be the first public disclosure that the Federal Reserve had determined the two banks were a single entity. And it would signal that one of the biggest private banks in the world was in dire financial condition and the Fed suspected criminal activity. A direct question from Gwynne would cause the doors to slam shut. Banking regulators work behind a wall of secrecy fortified by the convenient convention that the public should be last to learn of a bank's failing health.

So Gwynne was chatting amiably, asking for background information as if he had all the time in the world while anxiously watching the clock as he fished for anything that might help him finesse an oblique confirmation from the Federal Reserve. In this button-down arena it was going to be oblique or nothing. Beaty, running between interviews of his own, poked his head into Gwynne's office and grinned at the sight.

Gwynne's khaki wash pants, boating shoes, and small, round horn-rims were the fatigue uniform of East Coast Establishment Man. Beaty might have held it against him on principle, but he had to give Gwynne credit for keeping the tension out of his smiling voice as he talked away, even though his forehead was beaded with sweat. This new partner might be a preppie—there was no denying the New England ancestry, Princeton and all of that—but he was surely a good reporter. Beaty decided on the spot that it must have been yuppies he hadn't liked all along: Preppies could be all right as long as they were the real thing.

Gwynne punched off the phone with a flourish and looked up, triumphant. "That's it! We've got it! One of the state regulators who fought the Fed decision to let the BCCI shareholders buy First American in the first place told me exactly what is happening. The Fed isn't talking, but they just got back to me and said I shouldn't leave town, because there is going to be a major announcement Tuesday." Gwynne wrote the first draft of the six-hundred-word short. Beaty, who had confirmed that grand jury subpoenas were out, rewrote the part about New York investigating Clifford and Altman. Both reporters fiddled with the final phrasing and then blipped it to New York by computer. The first BCCI story was in the bag.

Beaty volunteered to stick around for the closing of the story and waved Gwynne out the door. Their main work was finished, but there would be fact-checking queries from the researchers in New York, and on this one *Time*'s libel lawyers would probably have questions, too.

It was eleven o'clock when the news desk in New York called and Beaty learned that their scoop had disappeared from the radar screen. One of the lawyers had grave doubts about the wisdom of making serious charges without authoritative attribution, and the story had been killed.

By the time Beaty found the lawyer in question, he had slipped sadly from the understated and professionally detached demeanor so valued at *Time* Edit. The attorney, a young woman from the general counsel's office who was making her debut in the Friday-evening libel slot, was not sympathetic to the argument that his record for accuracy made up for the lack of attribution in a potentially libelous story. How did they know that Clifford, a very important man who would surely sue if they were wrong, was a suspect? A grand jury was a secret proceeding, was it not? How did they know the Federal Reserve was going to take an action not yet taken? Did they have this in writing?

Beaty was reduced to sputtering. The woman obviously knew little about the news-gathering business, but in fact they had no sources they could name, and their proofs were a matter of reporting expertise and experience. Both Beaty and Gwynne had been told what they were told by people who spoke so carefully they could later swear they had violated no confidence. Confirming information already in hand was often a matter of hints between professionals. Beaty knew prosecutors, and Gwynne knew bankers, but he couldn't explain that the Federal Reserve person knew exactly what Gwynne was looking for, and the revelation that an announcement was forthcoming was, in context, a calculated answer. Or that he had been told a funny story about an innocent man asking for immunity.

Beaty hung up abruptly. He could think of no other avenue of appeal. John Stacks had left for the night and couldn't be located. The senior business editor, Geoffrey Colvin, a highly talented editor on loan from *Fortune* magazine, was sympathetic but not about to overrule a libel lawyer on a story he knew nothing about.

Time magazine is an intricate piece of machinery that somehow produces six million copies of its product every seven days, and by Friday night, the hundreds of parts in that machine are all spinning at maximum r.p.m. to achieve the weekly miracle. Early pages, converted by electronic alchemy to binary code, have already been beamed by satellite to printing centers around the world, and the presses are rolling in Djakarta, Chicago, and London as the correspondents, writers, researchers, and editors in the dowdy Time & Life Building in New York are still struggling to compose and arrange the right words and pictures for the "front of the book," the hard-news sections that are printed last. By Friday night the giant machine is a juggernaut that can be steered with increasing difficulty but not slowed down. As the speed of interrelated events increases to orbital escape velocity, fewer and fewer people are allowed near the helm: Course corrections at this point are prohibitively expensive. At midnight there was no one left on the bridge except flag-rank types, but Beaty decided to try anyway.

The top editor, who had spiked the story after hearing from the young lawyer, was busy and curt. No, John Stacks had not briefed him on the background, and it was too late to argue with the lawyers. If the story was so damned important, why had Beaty waited until the last minute to turn it in? It was two in the morning when Beaty reached Henry Muller, *Time*'s managing editor, with an unprecedented request. Muller, who was known for his unfailing courtesy, strained that reputation as he made it clear he was busy editing an overhaul of the Desert Storm cover story. He had already heard Beaty was making loud protests, he said, but he ran the magazine by delegating authority and he wasn't about to overrule a top editor. And why had Beaty brought the story in so late, anyway?

The correspondent muttered something impolitic about bringing in breaking news when he got it because he thought he worked for a newsmagazine. It was his last dumb statement of the day. Absorbed in the banking story, he had all but forgotten there was a war going on and was only vaguely aware that some pundit had said *Newsweek*'s war coverage was better than *Time*'s and there was considerable tension on the thirty-fourth floor as a result. Beaty stared at the hotel room wall until 7:30 in the morning, then called Stacks at home to announce his resignation.

In the normal course of events, weeks might have passed before *Time* magazine looked seriously at BCCI. It appeared to be just another business story. Only the unlikely involvement of Clark Clifford distinguished it from any other bank fraud case. That was minor titillation for *Time* editors, who ordinarily would have scheduled a page-long piece at some point and thought no more of it. But the insignificant brushup over Gwynne and Beaty's spiked story, known to only a handful of people, tilted the table. That particular handful of people ran *Time* magazine, and their attention had been drawn to BCCI and to Beaty and Gwynne's strange collection of allegations.

"I thought you quit," Gwynne said, teasing, as Beaty walked into the bureau Tuesday morning. Both had come in early to read the BCCI stories they expected to see in the *Post* and *The Wall Street Journal*. If the Fed was going to make the announcement, at least one of the morning papers probably would have been tipped off the night before. In Washington, the town of leaks and counterleaks, every bureaucrat knew the working deadlines of the major dailies and newsweeklies.

"I only quit for Saturday," Beaty replied, trying not to sound sheepish. "Stacks called back Sunday to see if I was serious, but I was over it by then. He promised that that novice lawyer would be kept away from our stories. . . . Hey, it's in the *Journal*!"

The paper had it all laid out. The Federal Reserve had announced it was investigating whether BCCI had acquired shares in First American Bank without prior approval and had ordered a halt to practically all transactions between the two banks. A criminal referral had been made to the Justice Department.

The reporters whooped and grinned at each other. They had missed breaking the story, but they had been vindicated. Their sources had been certified reliable and they hadn't embarrassed John Stacks, who had taken a couple of pokes at the Edit side on their behalf when the episode was rehashed on Monday.

It became a real news item as the other papers followed *The Wall Street Journal*'s lead: FED PROBES FOREIGN LINKS TO FIRST AMERICAN: OVERSEAS ASSET TRANSFERS BARRED AS SAFEGUARD headlined *The Washington Post*. *The New York Times* speculated about a divestiture order forcing the sale of First American. The Associated Press and Reuters carried stories, and the networks put it on the evening news. Beaty and Gwynne quickly got marching orders from New York. The magazine had scheduled a major piece, due the following week, to give Beaty and Gwynne time to pass up the competition. That gave them ten days. They were to write the story themselves, as well as report it, and they could tap bureau resources around the world. No one mentioned the killed story, or ever would. On the other hand, no one mentioned Beaty's intemperate reaction. The two reporters were being given the chance to put up or shut up.

They racheted up to wide-open throttle, but as the twelve- and fourteen-hour days clicked by they wondered if they were going to produce much more than the sound and fury of a high-speed run.

There was no shortage of leads. The problem was what to make of them. There was, for example, the puzzle of how Senator Kerry's BCCI hearings had fizzled out. Beaty and Gwynne, in fact, had the oddest of first encounters with the Massachusetts senator and his staff, with whom they would work closely for the next two years.

John Kerry was one of the most interesting new faces to come into the Senate during the Reagan years. He had been a war hero in Vietnam, and later one of the founders of Vietnam Veterans Against the War. In 1971 he gained national attention by throwing away his medals at an antiwar rally, an act that seemed doubly remarkable because it had been done by a graduate of Yale whose mother also happened to be part of the vastly wealthy Forbes family, Boston Brahmins for more than one hundred years. Though he was barely into his second term, Kerry already had made a splash with his investigation into the drug trade in Latin America and into the affairs of Panamanian dictator Manuel Noriega. He had encouraged Jack Blum to pursue the BCCI connections suggested by José Blandón. Yet Kerry had also been in the middle of what Blum said was a deliberate and successful effort to squelch his probe. That was why Blum had gone to Morgenthau, and ultimately to the press: He believed deeply that he had been fixed.

Had Kerry been somehow involved in that? Beaty had run a check of Kerry's campaign funds through the Campaign Research Center in Washington and found, to his astonishment, that $4,000 had been donated to Kerry by Clark Clifford, Robert Altman, and two other members of their law firm the same month that Blum was terminated. Gwynne's call to Kerry's office inquiring about this triggered a panicky half-hour-long session with Kerry's aides Jonathan Winer, David McKean, and Larry Carpman. Kerry himself called later to try to straighten it out. The last thing he wanted was a story saying that he had received money to kill off Jack Blum. A number of phone calls later, Beaty and Gwynne decided to drop the seemingly damning contributions from their story. The money had definitely moved, but there was no apparent quid pro quo, and the amount was comparatively insignificant. It was also clear from Beaty's financial background check of the senator that Kerry wasn't rolling in sudden money.

But that still left the mystery of precisely how Blum had been torpedoed. If not by Kerry, then by whom? The most likely candidate seemed to be Claiborne Pell, the Rhode Island senator who chaired the Senate Foreign Relations Committee, under which Kerry's Subcommittee on Terrorism, Narcotics, and International Operations operated. When Blum had talked to Beaty he had been chary about pointing the finger at Pell, even though Beaty was aware that Pell had little love for Blum and had not been happy with Kerry's investigations.

But apparently Blum had been franker when talking to another reporter in Boston. *Time*'s Boston bureau chief, Bob Ajemian, had looked into this at Beaty and Gwynne's request and had wired back: "In describing the numerous efforts to block the BCCI probe, Blum holds special blame for Foreign Relations Chairman Claiborne Pell. 'Pell was utterly hostile,' Blum told a Boston newspaperman this week. Blum says Pell refused to grant the subcommittee more time and had little interest in the investigation. Blum was dropped from the payroll in May 1989, even though he had informed Pell that he had only recently come across damaging evidence linking BCCI to First American."

Still, nothing definitive could be hung on Pell, who had made no secret of the fact that he thought Kerry's headline-grabbing hearings inappropriate to the dignity of the Foreign Relations Committee. The same vagueness that swirled around the affair also permeated other aspects of the case: the allegations of undue political influence in the Mirza memo; the Justice Department's unnecessary plea bargain in the Tampa money-laundering case and its denial of the existence of the Mirza debriefing tapes. It became quickly apparent that Beaty and Gwynne's inside knowledge did them little good.

At every approach they were stonewalled with bland denials, and there was only eerie silence from regulators and enforcement agents usually willing to explain their version of events to the press as long as their names weren't mentioned. Sources within the Justice Department and the intelligence community who for years had cooperated with *Time* magazine acted as if they had never heard of BCCI before they read about it in the papers.

The front door to the Justice Department was barricaded. The designated spokesman said he could not talk about BCCI matters, past or present, because of the criminal complaint just forwarded from the Federal Reserve. "We can't comment on ongoing criminal investigations," he said.

Gwynne pounced on that: "Does that mean we can say that the Justice Department has already initiated a criminal investigation of BCCI? What about First American and Clark Clifford?"

"I didn't say that. These matters are under review. There's nothing else I can say."

The two reporters could only fume, their frustration compounded by the knowledge that the Fed had made the criminal referral public only because the Justice Department was dragging its feet.

They knew the U.S. attorneys in Tampa and Miami would give them nothing that wasn't politically acceptable, so they drew up and divided a list of assistant U.S. attorneys who had worked on the BCCI money-laundering case and began calling them. They learned nothing. No, they were told, there was nothing unusual about the plea bargain with the bank. No, it was not unusual that the five defendants had been allowed to live in luxury apartments provided by the bank, guarded by off-duty Florida police paid by BCCI, for months before the trial instead of waiting out the time in jail. No, it was not unusual that millions were spent in their defense. They knew nothing about any tape recordings of former BCCI bankers describing the bank's criminal activities while government agents listened in.

The only chink in the armor came from one of the assistant prosecutors who had left Justice for private practice. He said the decision to allow the bank to trade a guilty plea for a modest sentence, while the government dropped its charge that money laundering was BCCI corporate policy, had come as a surprise. In fact, he said, he had expected an aggressively wider case against the bank. He believed the plea bargain decision came from Washington but had no firsthand knowledge. He didn't want his name used. The interview was encouraging but by itself would hardly support an accusation of misfeasance.

Gwynne and Beaty enlisted Elaine Shannon, who covered the Drug Enforcement Administration, Customs, and Justice for *Time*, to make end runs around the public affairs office. Shannon, author of a book about the cocaine trade that lionized the DEA, had remarkable access to the higher levels of the justice system. She knew a lot of agents in the field.

The next night Shannon appeared at Gwynne's office, where he and Beaty sat amid piles of papers in the pall of cigarette smoke. "I think you're getting bad information," she said, "especially if it's coming from Jack Blum. I've talked to all the top people, and they think he's a loose cannon."

Beaty and Gwynne looked at each other. They had carefully avoided mentioning Blum to anyone except John Stacks in New York.

"And there doesn't seem to be anything wrong with the plea bargain," she continued. "They explained it to me in detail. The part that says the government won't prosecute for any other criminal activities they know about is standard. It's in every plea bargain, and besides, it bound only the U.S. attorney in Tampa."

Shannon did have one piece of concrete information. No one she had contacted at Customs or the FBI had heard of Ali Mirza, but if anyone knew anything it would be Bonni Tischler, the Customs officer in charge of the Tampa office who had supervised the long-running C-Chase sting.

Beaty called the Tampa Customs office the next day. What he heard sent him pounding down the hall to Gwynne's office. "We've got something, Sam. It was unbelievable—Tischler was actually screaming at me. Apparently we're not the only ones tracking the Mirza tapes: Some other reporter—she didn't say who—had already asked her about it this morning and she was still livid. Whoever that was, I think she blew him off. She was going on and on about the irresponsible press and protecting confidential informants and what a shit Jack Blum was. And then she admitted it! She said there were tapes. She claimed she didn't remember what was on them and she didn't know what had happened to them. I asked her whether they had made transcripts and if they had been forwarded to Washington, and she really came unglued. I think she said no, but it was all pretty confusing."

"No wonder. You put her in the position of either having to blame Washington for deep-sixing them or saying Customs had failed to pass on crucial information. Just look at it: The Federal Reserve people had already been there asking questions, and they've got Morgenthau pounding on the door of Justice, saying he knows about the tapes and where are they, and then they denied they had them . . ." Gwynne smiled at the thought. It was easy enough to picture the situation in Tampa. "This is the woman who thought she was going to be named director of Customs because of the C-Chase operation, and now it's all gone to hell. They know they've been sitting on a time bomb and all of a sudden the press calls and says, 'Hey, fellows, the jig is up.'"

Beaty was still on an adrenaline high. "She started off by denying it, but I told her that we had this cold and that we were going with it this week whether she denied it or not. I said we understood that her task force sent copies of the tapes to the FBI special-agent-in-charge in Miami, and that's when she started shouting."

Gwynne smiled again. If Beaty used go-for-broke interview techniques like that very often, it was little wonder that some of his colleagues in Washington muttered about him. He wasn't winning any friends for the bureau.

Deadline was approaching rapidly, and although the correspondents had learned a good deal about the history of BCCI and the public persona of Agha Hasan Abedi, they made no more progress toward confirming the tantalizing snapshots of BCCI's criminal empire presented in the Mirza memo. They would go with what they had.

Three weeks after Blum and Beaty met in San Francisco, *Time*'s first BCCI story, headlined A CAPITAL SCANDAL, reached the newsstands the last week of February. "The biggest bank in Washington and a legendary American political adviser are ensnared in a probe involving a shadowy money-laundering enterprise," explained the subtitle. If their story had no answers, Beaty and Gwynne at least managed to put the right question into print: "The question that won't go away: How could an outfit like BCCI control a large U.S. bank without regulators knowing or doing anything about it?"

The magazine allocated four pages to the article—a lot of space in *Time*'s format—and they used some of that space to introduce the major characters and explain the complex affair.

> The link that investigators are now talking about is . . . comprehensible enough to anyone who has ever had a mortgage. They say BCCI lent the investors the money they used to buy stock in First American, with the shares pledged as collateral, just as a mortgage holder pledges his home as collateral. Investigators say those loans are "nonperforming"—the bankers' term that means they aren't being repaid. Everyone knows what happens in that case: The bank gets the collateral, in this case the controlling shares in First American. And presto, an unregulated foreign organization takes over an American bank without U.S. regulators knowing about it.

They had to tiptoe through some of the links:

> Investigations in Washington, New York City, and Florida are probing deeper into the bizarre affair and uncovering evidence of

startling regulatory inaction, if not political chicanery. Clifford, 85, says he and his law partner Robert Altman, president of the bank, "have run First American for long years at the highest ethical level, and we are proud of our stewardship." But he acknowledged to *Time* that he has retained a criminal-defense attorney to represent him in connection with the matter.

But the key stroke in the story was a piece of inside baseball: By smoking out the missing Mirza tapes, the reporters intended to send a message—to the few who would know what it was about—that they were aware of the tapes' contents. Panic, they knew, drove sources and witnesses into the arms of reporters and prosecutors. Without naming Mirza, they told Blum's story of taking the BCCI witness to the feds.

> Federal agents in an adjoining room listened to this key BCCI player for three days as he continued to explain BCCI's machinations. He described plans to use political influence to derail the Kerry inquiry. Supervising Customs agents said the tapes of this executive's remarks had been in their possession and that official reports had been completed, but they declined to say where the tapes and reports had been forwarded.

The gambit did flush out one key source, but the reporters had underestimated the Justice Department's commitment to limiting the scope of any BCCI investigation. After Beaty and Gwynne wrote about the tapes, Morgenthau's office again demanded copies from Justice and Customs. Even though Justice had to acknowledge that the evidence existed, it again refused to provide copies to the New York D.A. on the flimsy excuse of protecting a confidential informant. When Morgenthau offered to send a notarized release from Mirza granting permission for the transfer of the tapes, the answer again was no—this time on the grounds that Mirza had mentioned the name of another confidential informant who had to be protected. In the end, realizing that Morgenthau could produce limited confidentiality waivers from the witnesses, the Justice Department relented and turned over the information. The dodging maneuvers after the *Time* story quoted Customs saying the tapes existed consumed more than another month of critical investigating time.

CHAPTER 4

PIERCING THE SCAM'S HEART

That the dumb act in Washington extended even to the State Department was something Beaty and Gwynne discovered as soon as they began looking into BCCI's origins in Pakistan. Although BCCI described itself to American regulators as an international bank owned by rich, successful Arabs, its founder, the mysterious Agha Hasan Abedi, was a Pakistani, and it was run largely by Pakistanis. The reporters, gearing up for the next story, were intrigued with Mirza's contention that the government of Pakistan had pressured the United States to limit prosecution of BCCI. Mirza's version of the bank's creation, if true, indicated that the bank had criminal leanings from the start. He had told investigators that while Abedi was indeed a clever banker, he also benefited from the backing of a Pakistani named Fazle Haq, who was—Mirza said—heavily engaged in narcotics trafficking and moving the heroin money through the bank. The reporters reasoned that Mirza should have known what he was talking about there, having come from an aristocratic and highly placed Pakistani family.

"Haq had become more powerful," Mirza had said, "after the arrival of the Khomeini regime in Iran. Although the shah had beheaded drug smugglers, Khomeini bested him in this regard and went after drug traffickers with a vengeance. The result of this increased pressure was that drugs which had been smuggled from Afghanistan through Iran were now coming through Pakistan, which only resulted in further enriching Haq's power." Haq was connected with several "elite" Pakistani families and had many allies in the Pakistan government and military supporting his activities, Mirza had said, and "the funds that were generated by the narcotics trafficking were put into the bank."

Time's library turned up a reference to a Lieutenant General Fazle Haq, appointed governor of Pakistan's North-West Frontier Province in 1978. If it was the same Haq, then there was a certain logic to Mirza's assertions. The North-West Frontier bordered Afghanistan, and the Khyber Pass connecting the two nations had been controlled by smugglers for generations. Neither Gwynne nor Beaty was an expert on Pakistan, but both knew the semicovert U.S. supply line to the Afghan freedom fighters—organized after the 1979 Soviet invasion—passed through the North-West Frontier Province.

Even more intriguing were implications that the U.S. government was well aware of BCCI's connections to the heroin trade. In a second meeting with the unidentified intelligence man, on March 20, 1989, Mirza told the agent he had just met in New York with Mr. "Happy" Minwallah, one of former Prime Minister Benazir Bhutto's closest advisers.

"Minwallah had told source at their meeting that on January 5, 1989, Ambassador Oakley [U.S. Ambassador to Pakistan Robert Oakley] requested a secret meeting with Bhutto. The only other person at the meeting was Minwallah. Oakley told Bhutto that he was aware that BCCI was heavily engaged in various kinds of criminal activity and was the subject of investigation. Oakley, on behalf of the United States government, asked Bhutto to cancel the investment banking license that had been issued to BCCI. This license had been given to BCCI during the last days of the Zia regime."

The memo went on to say Bhutto agreed to cancel the license, and did so, but

> . . . there was considerable opposition to her action, not only from the generals who support BCCI but also from persons in the government, in the bureaucracy, who are also paid by BCCI, e.g., the current foreign minister. On this point source says most of the government senior people are being paid by BCCI and have been for a long time. Oakley informed Bhutto that this information had been brought to Pakistan from Washington by the number-two man of either the CIA or FBI—not the station chief or legate but

someone actually from Washington. The CIA/FBI representative did not meet with Bhutto. The meeting was arranged purposely [sic] to exclude officials of the Foreign Ministry and others in the government, as it was felt that too many of them were involved with BCCI.

There was not a breath of this sort of thing in any story yet published about BCCI. It was a tantalizing angle, but the reporters quickly learned they would get no help confirming it from the State Department. Beaty made the usual round of calls seeking background information from the appropriate regional and country desk officers over at Foggy Bottom, but each time he broached the subject he was referred to Public Affairs, the front door at State. At Public Affairs, no one could find an official who had ever heard anything about someone named Haq being involved in the heroin trade, or anything about BCCI, or a U.S. government meeting with the Pakistani prime minister about BCCI. Nor had anybody ever heard anything about Pakistan laying on heavy diplomatic pressure for leniency after BCCI was indicted in Florida.

"There's a war on, you know," one high-level State spokesman told Beaty after he got through on his seventh call. "It's hard to reach anybody, but I never heard of BCCI before the newspaper stories this week."

Beaty pretended to be irate, which wasn't difficult. "Well, *Time* magazine is about to print that Ambassador Oakley had a secret meeting with Benazir Bhutto to complain about BCCI's involvement with the drug trade. Why don't you see if that ratchets up enough attention to get an answer from someone?" He hung up and went to Gwynne's office.

"I'm getting stiffed at every turn on Pakistan. Has Shannon found anything about Haq yet?"

Unaccountably, Shannon's sources at DEA's Washington headquarters claimed they knew nothing about Haq. She had then begun directly calling agents in Islamabad and Karachi.

"She says there's nothing there," Gwynne said with a shrug. "They don't have anything firm on Haq, and they've never heard of BCCI being involved in the Pakistan heroin trade."

"Bullshit!" Beaty exclaimed. "The DEA out there is into political intrigue up to its eyebrows. I knew a State Department narcotics suppression officer who told me that when he was doing a duty tour in Islamabad, the American ambassador refused to forward any DEA reports to Washington about Pakistani officials' involvement in the drug trade. I'm leaving for the weekend: I'm going to go talk to Condor. He's only going to be in the States for a couple of days."

Gwynne nodded. Beaty had already told him a couple of stories about Condor, code name for his most highly placed American intelligence source. Only John Stacks knew who Condor really was. Gwynne had noticed that Beaty was reluctant to go to Condor for anything more than verification on really important stories. And when Condor confirmed something, it appeared in the magazine as a flat statement of fact, without attribution.

Over nearly fifteen years Beaty had built a relationship of mutual trust with Condor. Even so, it remained a delicate association and one he rarely exploited. It survived because the reporter had never come close to burning his source and Condor had never given bad information. The latter was an important consideration: Beaty was wary of sub-rosa contacts with covert agents. He believed that the CIA sometimes cultivated a reporter by feeding him small leaks so the journalist would later accept a major piece of disinformation when the spooks needed to put a certain spin on the news. "Carrying water for the agency" was how Beaty described it.

Condor, however, was something else. In the years Beaty had known him he had advised some of the top policymakers of several administrations and filled a variety of important government posts. Although Condor never quite said so, Beaty knew he had been an active intelligence agent at one time. Condor had ascended to such a high level that Beaty had no idea to whom he reported.

He didn't give away state secrets, but sometimes—for reasons never explained—he was willing to give *Time*, through Beaty, geopolitical background briefings that were breathtakingly candid. It wasn't a one-way street: Both men were in the information-trading business, and Beaty realized he was one of the government man's sources. An investigative reporter with an international *Time* beat picked up a good deal of knowledge. Beaty never called on Condor without bringing something worthwhile to exchange. They rarely met face to face, and never in Washington.

This time they were getting together at the country estate of a friend, within a couple hundred miles of the capital. The reporter packed a bag, took a cab to the train station, and climbed aboard an Amtrak local. He stepped off the train several stops short of his destination, grinning to himself at his junior-league trade craft. He rented a car and drove the rest of the way, intermittently getting lost on country roads that passed Colonial homes and white-fenced pastures dotted with thoroughbreds. Condor was waiting when he arrived a little after nightfall. Their hosts mixed drinks and chatted with them for a few minutes, then left them alone in the paneled study.

Beaty spent half an hour sketching what he knew about BCCI and the Justice Department's curious lack of interest in it. Then he drew the Mirza memo from his briefcase and dropped it on the desk with a flourish.

"You'll be interested in this, I think. You might even know the man who wrote it."

Condor read the report quickly without commenting. He looked up at Beaty for a long moment, then read it through again, still without speaking.

Beaty prompted him: "We're just starting to chase down the stuff about political influence in this country, but I'm over my head with this Pakistan information. State says they don't know anything at all about any of this. Justice won't talk to us. The DEA says they don't have anything on a Pakistani general named Haq, who is discussed here, but I found an old *Time* story saying he was arrested in a big drug-mafia crackdown. What do you think?"

"They're all lying to you. When Zia was president of Pakistan the U.S. deep-sixed everything they knew about Haq, because he was our man. The arms supplies for the Afghan rebels were being smuggled through his district, but everybody knew that Haq was also running the drug trade. BCCI was completely involved. This was more than a State Department problem; this was a White House concern. There were national security issues here that transcended worries about drugs and money laundering."

Beaty sat transfixed as Condor went on.

"We were working with the Pakistanis, trying to slow it down, but we couldn't afford to expose it. After Zia was killed we wanted the heroin labs in Pakistan shut down, but these were tough guys and they weren't afraid of Bhutto. I don't know about a specific meeting between Oakley and Bhutto over BCCI, but you have to be careful about what 'Happy' Minwallah says. He hates Haq. When Bhutto ordered Haq's arrest, she was trying to demonstrate to us that she was doing something about the drug problem. But near the end of her tenure she was canceling trips abroad because she feared that the drug mafia and her political opposition would get the army to declare martial law again. The opposition included Abedi. And, as you know, the generals did get rid of her. The charges against Haq disappeared."

Beaty was stunned. For a moment he couldn't think of a sensible next question. "Why do they call him 'Happy' Minwallah?"

"Minwallah was Benazir Bhutto's bagman. People like Airbus and Boeing used him as an agent, and the word in the U.S. business community was that if you wanted to get a deal done with Benazir, you had to keep Minwallah happy. After a while the name stuck."

Condor talked for another hour about BCCI's doings in the Middle East in general and Pakistan in particular. "BCCI's brightest days came when Zia was firmly in power, and throughout the '80s they knew they had the war as cover. Whatever they wanted to do, they knew the U.S. was going to remain silent. The bank started during the petrodollar boom, but when the oil dollars began to dry up they moved into the drug trade and the weapons business."

Beaty looked up a passage in the report. "Mirza says here Haq was deeply involved in arms sales and did business with 'first name unknown Ibrahim, the brother-in-law of Saudi King Fahd.' Is there something there I should be looking at?"

Condor smiled. "That would be Khalid Ibrahim. King Fahd took a new wife, from the southern province of Baha, the daughter of Sheikh Ibrahim, the governor. They had a son, Abdul-Aziz. The king loves him greatly and he wants to make sure the kid is fixed for life, so he arranged for Khalid Ibrahim, the boy's uncle, to be his business manager. So in recent years, if you want to do an arms deal or an oil deal, you have to go through the al-Ibrahim clan. During the mid-'80s all the Saudis were bitching that Khalid was taking too big a cut. They'd sit around and eat pistachio nuts and drink coffee and complain. 'Someone's got to tell the king,' they'd say, 'it's not fair that on every major deal you have to bring in the al-Ibrahim family.' None of them wanted to confront the king alone, so in 1987 a group of senior princes went to the king with their complaints, and Fahd told them to fuck off. Now Khalid is uniformly despised, but you still have to do business through him."

Beaty could listen for hours to Condor's stories about how things worked in the Middle East, but he stuck to his point. "So this is important?"

"BCCI's role in the Middle Eastern arms business is far more extensive than a connection to General Zia ul-Haq's dealings. BCCI is the bank that makes things happen when the principals in a transaction can't be seen doing business together, and that includes governments. BCCI brokers most of Israel's arms trades with Arab states, for example. And the bank provides another very valuable service that it probably should thank your friend Jack Blum for."

Beaty looked surprised.

"Wasn't Jack one of the Church subcommittee's investigators? Well, the Foreign Corrupt Practices Act turned business upside down in the Middle East—you understand that paying commissions is part of the way you do business there and it isn't precisely considered bribery? When OPEC raised the price of oil, the United States went along with it. It was an incredibly civilized thing to do, but privately we threatened them with the use of military force and a food embargo if the oil producers didn't invest their oil dollars in Western banks and spend most of them on Western goods. The biggest purchases have always been in arms sales, and prior to the Corrupt Practices Act you couldn't make a sale without giving a healthy slice to an agent. The big commissions come from arms sales, although telecommunications could rival those on a particular day. The Saudis considered the use of agents one way of redistributing the wealth: The princes are always going to get their cut, but the use of go-betweens provided a way to give loyal commoners, such as Pharaon, a piece of the action.

"So when the Saudis and the Emirates outlawed the use of agents and prohibited commissions in arms sales—the royal families were horrified at the thought of being embarrassed by accusations that they condoned bribes—BCCI solved the problem. Abedi's bank simply structures the kickbacks and agent commissions into the financing of the deal, so they can't be seen, and the bank pays everyone off."

Beaty was beginning to feel overwhelmed. There was too much to grasp all at once. "You mentioned Ghaith Pharaon. Mirza says he's just a front man for Abedi. And my partner on this story, Sam Gwynne, is talking to one of Pharaon's former business associates who says the same thing. When did Pharaon fall in with Abedi? We thought he was a billionaire in his own right."

"His first name is pronounced 'raith.' He had money, but like many Arabs, when the price of oil went into the toilet his cash machine came to an end and his operations fell apart. He had assets, mostly long-term investments in U.S. real estate, but he stiffed a lot of creditors and went bankrupt in Saudi Arabia.

"The Saudis liked his father, a Syrian doctor who treated King Abdul-Aziz, but they didn't like him. He was too arrogant. You're supposed to perfect this Bedouin thing: Others may give you the title of sheikh, but you take it reluctantly, you don't assume it yourself. It's very Victorian.

"His visibility was too high for the Saudi taste. He had bought a bank with a U.S. senator or somebody in Chicago; he was in Georgia with Abedi—but seeking influence in America was *not* his job. The 'special relationship' with America was not so firm then, and senior Saudis worried that Ghaith appeared to be speaking for Saudi Arabia and that he was giving the wrong image. The conventional wisdom in the Middle East has it that around 1984 or so Ghaith was summoned to see Crown Prince Abdullah, who was vacationing in Spain. It is said that the prince slapped him in the face and said, 'You have become insolent and pompous, and you think mistakenly that you have joined our family.' It would be my hunch that after that he became solely Abedi's man."

It was very late when Beaty drove back to Washington so preoccupied in his thoughts that he got lost twice.

At the bureau in the morning Gwynne handed him a message from the State Department. It said Ambassador Oakley had been contacted and he had cabled back denying any knowledge of any such meeting with Bhutto in 1989 or any directive from Washington concerning BCCI. Unfortunately, the message said, the cable from Oakley was classified. Beaty could not see a copy of it, but he should feel free to call if he had further questions.

Beaty crumpled up the message and threw it in the waste basket. "Wait till you hear what Condor had to say!" he told Gwynne. "We're not talking about some agency in the government knowing about BCCI's criminal track record and failing to pass the information on to the bank regulators. We're talking about White House knowledge. No wonder nobody wants to talk to us."

Gwynne grabbed at the stack of notes Beaty was waving at him. "Oh swell. This has all been so simple I was getting bored. What are we going to do next?"

What came next was a TWA flight to London for Beaty. It had nothing to do with Condor's revelations. This was three-dimensional chess, and while they'd been concentrating on one board, the players on the other boards kept moving. Adam Zagorin, *Time*'s Brussels bureau chief, had been tracking down leads in Europe. He was having little luck pressing Ghaith Pharaon's lawyers in Paris for an interview with the Saudi, who was reportedly lying low on his yacht in the Mediterranean. But Zagorin's search for former BCCI banking officers was looking up. He was in the midst of telephone negotiations with one of his targets in London, and he advised Beaty in a message sent through the New York news desk. The man, Mr. M., might not show, he said, but on the off chance, did Beaty want to join him for the interview? Beaty immediately made a reservation to depart from JFK and caught the Metroliner to New York.

It was John Moscow who had called his attention to the fact that BCCI had just laid off nearly one thousand employees in London. The dischargees had been raising a public fuss over being tossed without notice and apparently without benefits. Moscow had theorized that among all those unhappy former employees there must be a senior officer who might want to talk. It was too bad, he said, that there was no one there to listen. Beaty took the hint. He knew that Morgenthau had neither the manpower nor the resources to send someone to London on a cold search. Beaty did—at least for the moment.

Moscow muttered the names of three potential candidates. At least Beaty thought he had. The names were just mentioned in an out-of-context comment that drifted off, as so many of Moscow's sentences did. Beaty added a name of his own and sent the list off to Adam Zagorin with a plea for help. Zagorin had tracked down the jackpot of them all. Until last year, Mr. M.—Masihur Rahman—had been BCCI's chief financial officer.

On the way to the airport in New York, Beaty took a cab to meet Moscow for lunch at an inexpensive Italian restaurant in Lower Manhattan. The reporter was in a good mood, as he always was when setting off on a hunt. "What do you want me to bring you back from London, John?"

Moscow rocked rapidly in his chair—an unconscious habit that signaled his mind was running at high speed—before answering with a smile: "The Price Waterhouse audits."

Beaty laughed. Why not ask for the Holy Grail? "Sure, John, if I see any copies lying around, I'll pick them up."

The audits, revealing a multibillion-dollar hole in the bank's ledgers, had started the unraveling of BCCI. The Bank of England was guarding them as if they were a national secret, refusing to provide copies to Morgenthau or the U.S. Federal Reserve. Moscow had an idea of what was in them: Two Federal Reserve officers had been permitted a brief look at the audits but were not allowed to make copies. That peek, along with Morgenthau's prodding, had propelled the Federal Reserve into issuing the restraining orders against BCCI and First American Bank and requesting a criminal investigation by the Justice Department.

After landing in London, Beaty checked into the historic Brown's Hotel and was still unpacking when Zagorin arrived. The slim, cerebral American was an old friend from their days in the New York bureau. He was a perfect choice for the task of tracking BCCI players: As a scholar he had learned Arabic and as a journalist he studied the extremely rich. Zagorin had friends in all the right circles.

"Rahman is very nervous about this," Zagorin said, "but he's agreed to meet us here at the hotel tomorrow at 4:00 P.M. I've had to promise him that we won't reveal that he's talked to us and that we won't publish anything without his permission. He's afraid the bank will harm his family. He wasn't going to come but he was intrigued that you would come so far to see him: I've told him a lot of lies about what a great reporter you are and how you'll be able to help him."

Brown's fills up in late afternoon for tea, so the reporters reserved the Alexander Graham Bell Room for the meeting. Bell's first telephone was on display in one corner of the Nineteenth Century drawing chamber. Beaty and Zagorin were having tea and sampling a tray of breads and marmalade when Rahman slipped into the room. He was dignified, exquisitely courteous, and very nervous. "I am sorry," he announced, "but I have changed my mind about the wisdom of talking with you. I will stay only for tea; I have come only so you would not think I stood you up after your journeys."

The courtship with Rahman was delicate and lasted over five hours. Rahman excused himself from time to time to call his wife. "It is a signal, you see. If I do not call her, she will know something has happened to me. She is very distraught and worried about the children. We have had many threats."

It was an extraordinary tale: Rahman, born in Calcutta, the son of a chief justice of the supreme court, had been brought into United Bank by Abedi and Swaleh Naqvi in 1966, and moved with them when Abedi created BCCI. He had brought with him the original handwritten ledgers of the bank's first year of operation in Abu Dhabi, and described the first bank building—a simple structure on a vast ocean of sand next to Abu Dhabi's one paved road. He told the entire history of the bank.

It took hours to get to any hard facts. Rahman was defensive about the bank's reputation. BCCI's problems came, he suggested, only because Abedi—a man driven by his own vision and a "passionate belief in himself"—began taking "shortcuts" because he "was trying to capsulate the time remaining to him . . . his only thing was a shortage of time" in which to realize his vision. "There is a great deal of good in BCCI; you don't get to be a $28-billion bank by drug money."

Beaty looked up from his note taking: The figure just mentioned by the former chief financial officer could be arrived at only by adding the assets of First American Bank to BCCI's stated worth. Beaty said nothing.

Gradually, a story emerged that no one—beyond the inner circle of BCCI management—had heard before. After BCCI pleaded guilty to money laundering in January 1990, Price Waterhouse, whose audits had given the bank a clean bill of health for years, suddenly took another look. It "discovered problems everywhere" in a worldwide audit in March of that year. This was such a disaster that Rahman was placed in charge of an internal audit committee that was to verify the Price Waterhouse figures. Although the management team put the best possible face on it, its findings showed matters were even worse than the outside auditors had portrayed. The books were in a shambles. Hundreds of millions of dollars had been loaned or transferred from one account to another without paperwork; hundreds of millions more had simply disappeared. Knowing the report could not be withheld from the Bank of England, which loosely monitored BCCI's operations in Britain, management quickly concocted a plan: Sheikh Zayed would contribute $700 million to cover the first gaping hole in the books, and they would present to the English bank a plan to "restructure" BCCI under Zayed's nominal control and move its headquarters back to Abu Dhabi.

"The Bank of England was told on April twentieth," Rahman explained, "and the same day, the plan for a takeover by the Abu Dhabi government was presented. First, the temperature went up, and then the temperature went down."

Beaty could easily picture the scene: The Rolls-Royces and Bentleys pulled up in front of BCCI's opulent London office for the emergency board meeting that signaled the darkest day in the high-flying bank's history. The undoubted horror of the Bank of England representatives as they learned that one of the largest foreign banks in England, a bank they had allowed to expand to nearly forty offices in London alone, a bank that employed former Prime Minister James Callaghan as an economic adviser, was about to come crashing down taking thousands of British depositors with it. And then the intense relief as the smooth-talking BCCI managers assured them that the ruler of Abu Dhabi, one of the richest men in the world, was stepping in to make good the shortfall, and that they had a plan to restructure the bank. All the regulators need do was to keep silent while BCCI quietly repaired the damage.

Rahman, however, doubted the sheikh had any idea of what he was buying into or how big a hole he was being asked to fill. "There is no way to discuss commercial matters with them," he said dismissively. "You talk camels or get them girls." He portrayed Zayed's court as smothered in "young turks from the bank who would do absolutely anything" to accommodate their Arab clients. He described a cabal of BCCI bankers around Crown Prince Khalifa, Sheikh Zayed's heir apparent and nominally BCCI's major shareholder, who believed they could keep real control of the imploding bank. Khalifa's reputation as a playboy, whispered about in Abu Dhabi, was no secret in Europe; he had purchased Ringo Starr's house in London, where the police would cordon off the streets whenever he threw parties.

The more Rahman talked, the more Beaty and Zagorin realized the awesome scope of the fraud within BCCI. The soft-spoken Pakistani described what he called a secret bank within the bank—International Credit and Investment Company Holdings (ICIC) in the Cayman Islands—into which perhaps billions of dollars in deposits were improperly diverted before they disappeared altogether. He said that even though he was the chief financial officer, knowledge of that secret conduit was kept from him and he did not discover it until the internal audit. He was incensed that BCCI's employee benefit fund, designed by Abedi to provide retirement income and profits to the fourteen thousand people who worked for the bank—especially the senior officers—had also disappeared down that black hole in the Cayman Islands to cover hundreds of millions in unexplained losses. He drew organizational charts of BCCI's incredibly complex holdings to show the two correspondents how the money flowed.

It was nearly midnight when Beaty told Rahman that, as much as the magazine would like to help, this was all too incredible to be put into print. "Who would believe the auditors would certify the bank's accounts if it was this bad?"

"I can show you," Rahman insisted. "I have copies of all the audits in the trunk of my car outside!"

Zagorin stared; Beaty felt suddenly light-headed. He had only been bluffing.

The three of them stepped outside and, nervously looking over their shoulders, slipped down the dark street like thieves to Rahman's gray Mercedes parked at the curb. Rahman's stories of his life being threatened, of shots fired through his windows, and of Scotland Yard posting guards at his house were too detailed not to be believed. During one of Rahman's calls home, Beaty spoke with his wife to assure her that he was truly with *Time* magazine. She was a frightened woman.

Rahman opened the trunk and removed an armload of folders and papers, and the three men climbed into the car. Beaty began flipping rapidly through pages, holding them under the dashboard light and taking notes here and there. Gwynne would never believe this, he thought. He would never believe these audit reports. There were scores, hundreds, thousands of loans in staggering sums for which there had been no repayment for years. The Gokal Brothers shipping company held $404 million in loans against $62 million in collateral, and, in the dry language of accountancy, the examiners cast doubt on the value of that collateral. Ghaith Pharaon and his brother, Wabel, had outstanding loans totaling $288 million, yet, the auditors noted, "There are no loan agreements, promissory notes, or correspondence with the customers."

And Rahman was right about the auditors. One Price Waterhouse review of the bank's Cayman Island holdings—the black hole—dated October 18, 1985, certified BCCI's books without qualification even though it included the following statement in its certification:

"Customer deposits consist of confidential accounts which are not conducted as open accounts requiring periodic dispatch of statements. Furthermore, because of company policy we have not been able to confirm any deposit balances directly with customers, and therefore it is not possible for our examination of such accounts to extend beyond the amounts recorded."

Beaty thought he was beyond surprise. "Good grief, they certified the books without confirmation or checking of any kind! That's not possible."

He turned to the banker. "Mr. Rahman, you need more than *Time* magazine's help. You were the financial officer, and the dishonest people you say are now running the bank are going to blame you for much of this when it comes out."

Rahman nodded sadly.

"The only person I can think of who can give you the kind of protection you need is Robert Morgenthau, the district attorney of New York. He's an honest man, and you simply must talk to him. Take the audits to him. You need a powerful protector."

Beaty and Zagorin spent another half hour in earnest conversation with Rahman, and he tentatively agreed to take the audit reports to New York. He had nowhere else to turn; by his own account, the Bank of England was working to bury the BCCI scandal before more of it became public. His own lawyers, he believed, had sold him out. They were urging him not to go public with information about the bank.

Back in New York Gwynne and Beaty worked feverishly to put the story together, the days and nights running together as the Friday deadline grew closer. This time they knew they were far out ahead of anyone else in the press. Gwynne, doggedly following the skein of allegations outlined by Mirza while Beaty was in England, had made a major strike. Mirza had described Ghaith Pharaon's efforts to persuade U.S. banking regulators not to close down CenTrust Savings Bank of Miami, a giant S&L riddled with fraud and bad loans. Pharaon, Georgia lawyer Charlie Jones, and David L. Paul, the owner of CenTrust and a major Democratic financial backer, had flown to Atlanta to talk the Federal Home Loan Bank Board (FHLBB) into helping. A senior regulator remembered in scathing detail the visit from "the Arab, the Cracker, and the Jew." Pharaon had been sweating as he told them how rich he was and how much money he was prepared to put in to shore up the ailing S&L. The trio, the regulator had said, had been turned down cold and told they would have to go to Washington if they wanted to appeal.

Gwynne had reached the chairman of the the FHLBB at the time, M. Danny Wall, and wrested from him the grudging admission that he too had met with the trio and approved a scheme to keep the Miami S&L afloat.

The confirmations did much more than shore up the correspondents' faith in Mirza's accuracy. They had finally found an example that demonstrated that BCCI machinations had cost the U.S. taxpayer heavily. Pharaon had parked $25 million of BCCI's money in CenTrust long enough to allow the S&L to pass a curiously unstringent regulatory review and had then withdrawn it. The illegal maneuver allowed CenTrust to remain open for another year before the regulators finally shut it down. The cost to the taxpayer for that added burst of life: nearly $1 billion.

Beaty jetted to Georgia to ask Bert Lance about Lance's role as adviser to Abedi and to request Lance's help in obtaining an interview with President Carter, who had refused to speak to Beaty about the $10 million Abedi had given the former president for his charitable work. Carter still refused, but Lance acknowledged he knew about the reported $1 million that BCCI had given Charlie Jones to facilitate the relaxation of Georgia's banking laws and permit the sale of Lance's old bank—the National Bank of Georgia—to First American. Lance scoffed at the thought that bribery was involved, since, he said, the legislature was going to modify the law anyway. He considered the alleged million-dollar payment a tremendous joke, since it was far more money than would have been needed if payments had been required. (Lawyer Charlie Jones refused to answer numerous telephone calls from *Time* requesting his side of the story.)

On deadline day Beaty and Gwynne, who had been awake for the previous two nights, struggled to get the words down on paper through a fog of fatigue and a series of harassing phone calls. Clifford called Beaty, insisting in his sonorous voice that it was all a mistake. When the reporter told him that he was planning to write that Clifford had taken in more than $10 million in legal fees from BCCI, the lawyer solemnly told him that it was not more than $1 million. Beaty made the change with misgivings and discovered later that Clifford had lied. The reporter did, however, manage to ignore a particularly strange threat from the dean of power brokers.

"I don't know how your magazine could allow this kind of treatment after all I've done for *Time*," the old man said smoothly. "After all, I handled your problems with the postal commission for years: I think you should ask somebody about that."

Beaty professed ignorance and agreed to talk to someone about it, but he was too old a hand at the magazine not to know what Clifford was talking about. Since *Time* and *Life* magazines mailed millions of copies a week to subscribers, postal rates were a critical issue. Beaty didn't even want to think about what Clifford might have done for the magazines, but he figured that was all ancient history. He would bring up the subject of Clifford's oblique threat after deadline.

A far more troublesome call came from John Moscow. Beaty had gone over some of what he had learned from Rahman with Morgenthau's man, and told him with some glee that he should expect a package wrapped in plain brown paper to be dropped over his transom any day. But now Moscow was worried. *Time* had learned so much from Rahman, whose name they could not use, that the forthcoming *Time* article would appear crammed with inside information leaked from the grand jury. Clifford's powerhouse lawyers would crucify Morgenthau.

It was almost comically ironic: Moscow still didn't have the audits, and Beaty had never once asked him a question about anything directly connected to the grand jury probe. Moscow, sometimes to Beaty's great frustration, had been scrupulously professional about not leaking legally confidential information, but nobody was going to believe it.

Gwynne and Beaty talked it over but couldn't think of a solution: They were caught in the middle by having to protect their sources. Then, through the mental fog that was slowing them down, Beaty had a brainstorm. All they had to do was demonstrate that *Time* held the

Price Waterhouse audits before Moscow got his copies. Then, if pressed, Moscow could honestly say he hadn't leaked the information, since the magazine had managed to get the incriminating audit papers independently before he did.

Gwynne looked at Beaty strangely. "Swell. Good idea. But we don't have the audits; all we have is your notes."

Beaty waved two pieces of fax paper in triumph. "But Sam, we do." Zagorin had talked Rahman into faxing them two pages of the audit so they could prove to *Time*'s lawyers that Beaty had actually seen the material. One of the pages detailed Pharaon's dubious loans. "It's not too late: All we have to do is photograph these and put them in the magazine. We don't have to say in the story that we have the Price Waterhouse audit, but it will sure look as if we do!" They rushed off to the photo department.

The four-page *Time* story entitled "Masters of Deceit" received national attention. The layout included photographs of Agha Hasan Abedi, Abu Dhabi's Prince Khalifa, and Saudi tycoon Pharaon under the heading "Money Men." Photos of President Carter, Indian Prime Minister Indira Gandhi, Pakistani President Zia, and British Prime Minister Callaghan fell under the heading "Charity As a Front." David Paul (big perks, big yachts, big bonuses, and a money pipeline to BCCI that helped persuade regulators to keep his business afloat) was shown along with a picture of his world-class yacht. Behind them all was a large page from the audit showing Pharaon's bank loans and the auditors' remarks that millions were passing through his account with "drawdowns not supported by requests from the customers," which the magazine explained was accounting jargon for money moved out of accounts without documentation of any kind.

The article was a series of hammer blows: Pharaon was described for the first time as a front man for Abedi; Clifford and Altman were described as now under scrutiny by a New York grand jury seeking to determine whether the pair were knowing front men; and President Carter was zinged for taking millions from Abedi—including $1.5 million long after BCCI was indicted and convicted for laundering drug money.

Beaty and Gwynne returned again to their favorite theme: ". . . the Justice Department's apparent reluctance to expand its investigation of BCCI after the bank was convicted of money laundering last year."

They quoted a former U.S. prosecutor involved in the case: "I thought we were going to continue . . . we were aware of the BCCI connection to First American, but nothing ever happened."

And they quoted a letter from Charles Saphos, then chief of the

Justice Department Criminal Division Narcotics section, written to the Florida comptroller after the bank had been convicted, requesting that the State of Florida allow BCCI "to be permitted to operate in your jurisdiction . . . at the request of the Department of Justice." (In spite of the request, which was oddly worded to indicate that Justice might wish to monitor certain accounts at the bank, the Florida comptroller ordered BCCI's doors closed in his state.)

Beaty and Gwynne were on a roll, and the magazine was backing them to the hilt. The bank, said *Time,* was one of the most complex and secretive banking networks ever developed, and it served tax evaders, intelligence agencies, political bribers, arms dealers, narcotics traffickers, and national leaders bent on looting their countries.

Beaty fell asleep at his computer terminal while making the final corrections to the story, and Gwynne finished the job for him.

CHAPTER 5

TO ABU DHABI AND BEYOND

SENATOR KERRY: "One thing that has attracted a lot of attention in this is the whole so-called Black Network, which we have not heard a significant amount of evidence on. We've read about it, but always through indirect sources, et cetera.

"Individual bank officers have testified to incidents of threats and to efforts to intimidate them or keep them quiet, or so forth.

"My question to you is, that was a pretty extensive network that was outlined and some fairly dark activities. To what degree does your intelligence data correspond or document that kind of activity with respect to the BCCI bank?"

MR. KERR: "We probably can expand on that in closed session. But it seems to me that the most obvious answer and the accurate answer in this session would be that the things that we have described to you earlier as illegal activities obviously constituted a fairly sizable activity on the part of the bank.

"There also, presumably, you know, was a legitimate side of the banking operations—loans, et cetera. So I think part of it is seeing this kind of two-sided organization as seen by the nature of the intelligence that we collected over that extensive period of time to show that there was, in fact, a group, a side of that which participated in, if not illegal—well, it certainly was illegal—but also kind of shady activities. My assumption is that there is also a more formal legal side of it. Whether there was, quite simply, a neat line between the two, I personally don't know. My instincts would tell me that's probably not the case."

—SENATOR JOHN KERRY AND ACTING CIA DIRECTOR RICHARD KERR, HEARING BEFORE THE SUBCOMMITTEE ON TERRORISM, NARCOTICS, AND INTERNATIONAL OPERATIONS OF THE SENATE FOREIGN RELATIONS COMMITTEE,   OCTOBER 25, 1992

The pilot had turned out the cabin lights, and most of the passengers slept as the British Airways 747 bored through the moonlit June night at 34,000 feet, bound for Casablanca. Near the middle of the airliner, Beaty and another man sat in the dark with their heads close together. One of them spoke steadily in a low voice that sometimes dropped to a whisper. Beaty wrote rapidly on a yellow tablet while holding a miniature flashlight in the other hand to avoid using the overhead reading lamp, which would have bathed them in light. When a stewardess brushed past in the narrow aisle, the speaker, an olive-skinned Arab wearing dark slacks and a stylish brown leather jacket, fell silent. His eyes were opened wide in the darkness, and perspiration beaded his forehead despite the air-conditioned chill.

Beaty looked up from his notes and stared at his companion. The reporter had been traveling with the Palestinian—a defector from BCCI's Karachi branch—for more than a month, waiting impatiently to hear the full details of his story, and this was payoff time. It was difficult to credit what he was hearing. What would you call it, he thought, corporate terrorism?

"Don't stop now. We're landing in another hour, and I swear if you haven't lived up to your promise by then, I'm abandoning you at the airport. I'm not going to talk to Khalfan until I've heard the whole thing." Sheikh Khalfan al-Mazrui was the director of Sheikh Zayed's Private Department in Karachi, the entity that administers the fabled wealth of Abu Dhabi, and as such he was ultimately responsible for the operations of BCCI in Pakistan. He was going to meet them in Casablanca. Neutral territory.

Sami Masri began talking again, the hushed words tumbling out painting a detailed, vivid picture of the Bank of Credit and Commerce International's global involvement with drug shipments, smuggled gold, stolen military secrets, assassinations, bribery, extortion, covert intelligence operations, and weapons deals. These were the province of a Karachi-based cadre of bank operatives, paramilitary units, spies, and enforcers who handled BCCI's darkest operations around the globe and trafficked in bribery and corruption.

As the plane began its long descent, both men sat silently, lost in their thoughts.

Beaty's strange odyssey with Sami Masri had begun forty-three days earlier on May 9, 1991, when the news desk in New York called the reporter at home in Hermosa Beach, California. Beaty and Gwynne had been traveling constantly since the end of February, and a weary

Beaty had arrived in Hermosa Beach the night before, carrying a bouquet of roses for his wife and the promise of a few days off. The house had been crowded with friends for a welcome-home party, and when the call came the next morning the jet-lagged reporter was still trying to clear the cobwebs out of his brain. It was Barry Seaman, the deputy chief of international correspondents.

"Sorry to bother you at home," Seaman said politely and insincerely, "but I'm duty editor this weekend and we have a very nervous-sounding caller that you might want to talk to. He's at Kennedy Airport and says he just got in from Karachi. He wanted to talk to the publisher. I had a difficult time understanding him, but he claims he has some hot BCCI documents and a story he wants to tell us. He's at a phone booth now waiting for you to call him. His name is Steve Winters, and he says he can bring the bank down."

Beaty groaned and dialed the number. Ten minutes later he called the news desk back.

"There might be something here, Barry. At least he knows who all the players are, people I've heard about whose names have never been in the papers. But with that accent his name can't be Steve Winters."

"So what do you think?"

"He sounds pretty scared, which means he might actually have something, and he claims to be broke, which means he's going to try and put the bite on us. But I think you're right: We better check it out. Linda will divorce me if I leave tonight, so I arranged a room for him at the Hilton at JFK and got the manager to charge it to my credit card. Winters, or whoever he is, agreed to wait there until I show up on Sunday. You sure you want to pay for all this?"

Seaman laughed. "Since when did you start worrying about what things cost? Let me know if it turns out to be anything."

Beaty, carrying his identifying metal Halliburton briefcase, was signing in at the registration desk when his man appeared. As the reporter had guessed, Steve Winters was an Arab. He was young, late twenties or early thirties, muscular, and had wavy black hair, large brown eyes, and a dark full mustache. He wore a brown leather jacket, travel-wrinkled slacks, and expensive Italian loafers with no socks. They introduced themselves and shook hands. Winters's palm was wet with perspiration, and his brief smile didn't connect to his eyes. He had a bad case of nerves.

"It would make things easier if you told me your real name," Beaty said as they sat in Winters's room. "Steve doesn't seem to fit."

"Not yet. Perhaps never. We have to have an understanding. This is very dangerous for me. I read *Time*'s story in Karachi and decided to come to New York, perhaps to talk to *Time*. You somehow have the audit report on BCCI, and they are worried about how much you know. But there are many things that you don't know. There are things you can't imagine. Very important people have been paid off. Or they are blackmailed. People have been assassinated."

The reporter looked at the magazine the Arab was holding. It was their second story—the one headlined "Masters of Deceit" that had pushed them ahead of the press pack—now a month old.

"You work for BCCI?" Beaty asked.

"Not exactly. I can give you information, documents, that will expose the bank and Clark Clifford. But if I do, how much will it be worth?"

Beaty hid his exasperation. "Until I know what you have, I can't offer anything. Let's just talk for a little bit." The magazine wouldn't pay for information, but Beaty wasn't about to give the standard lecture on the impropriety of checkbook journalism at this early stage.

It took hours of talk to pry out the essentials. Winters's real name was Sami Masri, and he was the brother-in-law of Khalfan al-Mazrui, of Sheikh Zayed's Private Department in Karachi. Beaty found it equally interesting that Khalfan was the brother—if he understood the complicated lineage being described—of Ghanim al-Mazrui. Ghanim, the reporter knew, was the director general of His Highness's Private Department, as well as the director of the Abu Dhabi Investment Authority and a longtime director of BCCI. Ghanim effectively ran Abu Dhabi, and next to Sheikh Zayed himself was probably the most influential person in the United Arab Emirates. Masri had a pipeline to the top.

Masri also wanted $25,000 in return for his information on the bank. Masri was working in some capacity for the bank's criminal cadres, although he wouldn't say so directly. He thought Sheikh Zayed, whom he seemed to revere, didn't realize the bad guys were really running the bank's worldwide operations. He wasn't sure whether his brother-in-law, Khalfan, realized the extent of the bank's black operations.

Masri didn't view his demands as unreasonable. "It isn't much money. I've spent that much on holiday. If I talk to you, turn over documents to you, I could be killed. I will have to begin a new life, perhaps take a new identity, and I will need something to live on until I can find a job and then regain my inheritance."

Beaty temporized. "Speaking of new identities, how did you happen to come up with the name Steve Winters?"

This time Masri's smile was reflected in his eyes. "He's a CIA agent in Karachi we work with."

"We?"

"The people I was telling you about that do the black work. The . . . the—how would you say it in English—the Black Network. They do a lot of intelligence operations with the CIA. Some bad things. That's part of the reason I want out of this life, I want to change. I'm a married man now."

"The Black Network, that's what you call it?"

Masri nodded. "There is a word in Urdu, in the Pakistani language, but that's as close as I can come in English."

Masri didn't realize it, but he had just hooked the reporter. Beaty suggested they check out of the slightly seedy airport hotel and take a cab to the Parker Meridien, his usual hotel in midtown Manhattan. He rented two suites and continued negotiations.

"Look, Sami," the reporter said at last, "I can't pay you twenty-five thousand dollars. I can't pay you anything. That just taints the information, and my editors wouldn't trust it. But I think we can help each other out."

Beaty wondered if Henry Luce had just turned over in his grave, but he had sorted out a couple of central facts from Masri's disjointed and fragmentary account of his life, and he had an idea.

Masri had shown him papers that indicated he was at least telling the truth about his family. He was a Palestinian with a Jordanian passport, but he had been raised in Abu Dhabi in favored circumstances. His mother was a companion to Sheikh Zayed's favorite wife, and his sister had married into one of the most powerful families in the Emirates. Sami had spent some time at an American university on a scholarship provided by Zayed.

Perhaps he had, as he claimed, decided to pull the plug on BCCI after he read *Time*'s story and concluded things were unraveling. Certainly others were beginning to jump ship. But no matter how he dissembled, the facts also seemed to be that Sami had outraged his family by marrying an airline stewardess just a month before and had been disinherited. He had shown Beaty a picture of his wife, Pamela, a pretty blonde with pale blue eyes from Australia, who worked for one of the Emirates' airlines. The reporter knew that good-looking women from around the world sought jobs with the Arabian airlines so they could meet enormously wealthy sheikhs, but respectable Arabs simply did not marry Christian women. Beaty had also noted the size of Sami's bar tab at the Hilton, which he had just paid, and concluded that all in all, the young, temperamental Mr. Masri had become a general disgrace to his family.

"Look, Sami. You're in a bind whether you talk to me about BCCI or not. You've had to sign your inheritance over to your brother-in-law, Khalfan, to administer. You don't know what to do about Pamela. You say that the tension of your work with the Black Network is pulling you apart. You know all these things about BCCI's criminal activity, and you think the bank is going to crash. And you say Khalfan and Sheikh Zayed don't know the extent of the bank's problems or its illegal networks.

"Here's what," Beaty continued. "There's a better use for this information than trying to sell it to *Time* magazine. Help me find some proof of what you're telling me, and let's both go tell Khalfan and Zayed about it. You would be a hero: the only subject of Sheikh Zayed who dared to tell him the truth about the sinking bank he's pouring billions of dollars into. You would redeem yourself, and BCCI would not dare incur Zayed's wrath by trying to retaliate."

Masri poked at the idea suspiciously. "What would you get out of all this? If this happened, the sheikh would never want to make it public."

Beaty knew altruism was a suspect motive. "Zayed would reward me too. I would be giving you the umbrella of *Time*'s protection so you could privately bring this to his attention. I'd ask that Zayed direct his people to answer questions about Clark Clifford and Robert Altman. My magazine is really only interested in Clifford's role in all of this."

Beaty wondered if his nose was growing longer.

In the end Masri reluctantly agreed. They would go to Abu Dhabi and Beaty would pay the expenses. In return Masri would act as the reporter's translator. Perhaps, as the reporter suggested, he would be enriched by Zayed's favor. "But I will need a place to stay while we organize this. You do not understand the Arab way of doing things, and it will take time. And I cannot turn the documents over to you until Pam is safely out of the Emirates. She is working in Dubai."

Beaty grinned. "No, you said Khalfan and Prince What's-his-name Sultan are meeting with all the BCCI heads in London this Thursday and Friday. Let's leave tomorrow and see if we can get anybody to talk to us."

At the Time & Life Building the next morning, Joelle Attinger had only one question: "Where's the story?"

"Who knows? It's a long shot, but my young friend just might lead us to someone in Abu Dhabi who will talk. The *Post* and the *Times* haven't even been able to get anyone into the country. And if I actually see His Highness Sheikh Zayed bin Sultan al-Nahayan, it will be a coup no matter what he says." Beaty, who was no linguist, had been practicing pronouncing Zayed's name.

"I spoke to John Moscow this morning and he thinks the question of whether Sheikh Zayed, or Ghanim al-Mazrui, his number-one man, knows about the bank's criminal activity is one of the keys to unraveling this. Besides, the first stop is London, and there are people there we want to talk to anyhow. Gwynne will keep working things from this end." Beaty didn't have to explain that he didn't have a game plan beyond a decision to shake the pillars of the temple.

He also didn't mention that John Moscow had tried to argue him out of going to Abu Dhabi. "You're underestimating how much they don't like you," the prosecutor had said. "You don't know who this guy is. He all but says he's a terrorist working for BCCI and he wants to take you to the Middle East? I don't think you're being very smart."

Beaty was far too busy to see the quixotic nature of his quest. However, before the day—spent in the British consulate on Third Avenue near Fifty-third Street trying to obtain an instant visa for Masri—was over he had his first taste of what traveling with his new source was going to be like. In a world rattled by terrorist acts, a Palestinian traveling on a Jordanian passport was viewed with automatic suspicion. Nor did Masri have a look about him that inspired confidence. There were a lot of places, Beaty would learn, where Sami Masri would not be allowed out of the airport. There were other countries where, for reasons of his own, he would not step off the plane.

They caught the last flight out of New York and twelve hours later checked into the London Inter-Continental Hotel near Hyde Park. Beaty preferred Brown's Hotel, but he had a life-size picture of the sockless and arrogant Masri amid the staid Londoners taking afternoon tea in Brown's historic but dowdy lobby. There were plenty of robed sheikhs wandering about the ornate lobby of the Inter-Continental.

Beaty had never thought it was going to be easy, but the first days in London left him feeling as if he were pushing through a room filled with feather pillows. The London meeting Sami had heard about between the heads of the bank and Abu Dhabi's representatives failed to materialize. It took Sami two days to locate Khalfan on the telephone. Beaty talked to him briefly and learned that a London meeting had indeed been scheduled, which restored Sami's sinking stock. But the sheikh, who had little English, didn't want to talk about anything important on Pakistani telephones. Beaty thought he understood. His Highness's Private Department in Karachi had a staff of hundreds, but nearly 80 percent of them were BCCI employees seconded to Zayed's personal staff. Beaty promised to fax a letter to a secure number, but Sami warned him earnestly that nothing was secure within BCCI's domain in Karachi.

Beaty took a cab to the London bureau to get *Time* letterhead stationery and composed a careful letter. He introduced himself as one of the *Time* reporters covering BCCI:

> While preparing a new article on the subject I met Mr. Masri, who has convinced me that I have inadequate information about Abu Dhabi and its role in restructuring BCCI. I have been given to understand by Mr. Masri that His Highness is an exceptionally honest man of goodwill. I would be glad to reflect that in my story, and I appreciate your assistance in obtaining a visit to Abu Dhabi and an interview with His Highness so I may see for myself the truth of his reputation. I will talk to you Saturday about arrangements and place myself in your hands. I am sure this will reflect credit to yourself, *Time* magazine and His Highness.

The reporter thought this was a particularly Arabic approach. He had made a veiled threat—yet a threat unconnected to his real intentions—and then offered an idea of intangible rewards. Sami had given Khalfan enough oblique hints to enable him to read between the lines. *Time*, Sami had indicated, was preparing a bombshell article that could expose BCCI's attempt to persuade the Bank of England to allow BCCI to bail itself out with the sheikh's money and restructure itself largely by changing its name. Beaty knew there was furious activity going on behind the scenes in England, Abu Dhabi, Karachi, and—as far as Beaty was concerned—in the United States, to contain the BCCI problem before more people got burned. Condor had told Beaty that Saudi Arabia had joined with the United Arab Emirates to put tremendous pressure on the Bank of England and the British government to let the investigation fade away. The withdrawal of Arab oil money from London's investment houses was a serious threat, and at this point only Morgenthau was keeping an old-boys'-club settlement at bay. The district attorney had made it known that he wouldn't be party to a settlement that left BCCI's management largely intact throughout the world to continue business under a different name.

Beaty wasn't going to be allowed to discuss his real agenda—the criminal nature of BCCI—on the phone, so the trick was to convince a wary Khalfan that they had to meet face to face. Then the game would be to convince Khalfan that he, and Sami, should talk directly to Ghanim al-Mazrui. No one saw Zayed without Ghanim's approval.

The reporter was more candid with Middleton "Sandy" Martin, Zayed's attorney in Washington, D.C., whom Beaty had met in the lawyer's office two weeks earlier. He now phoned Middleton at home to ask if he could expedite permission for a visit to Abu Dhabi.

"Mr. Beaty, only Ghanim al-Mazrui can approve that. I'm in communication with him almost daily, and I'll ask, but I think it's doubtful. If you will fax me a copy of the letter that you sent to Khalfan al-Mazrui, I will send that to Abu Dhabi, along with my recommendation that he see you. I've tried to tell them in Abu Dhabi that they have a public-relations problem they must deal with."

A splendid understatement, Beaty thought. The magazine had learned that the two editions carrying the BCCI stories had been censored in Saudi Arabia and the U.A.E., the stories cut out of the magazines.

"Mr. Martin, you've told me Sheikh Zayed is an honest man. I want to see him because I have evidence that BCCI is more involved in criminal activity than anyone suspects, and I believe people around Zayed are keeping this information from him. I'm willing to tell Ghanim everything we've learned, and in return perhaps he would be willing to answer some questions about Mr. Clifford."

There was a long silence. "You can't have heard worse than I have. BCCI employees have come to me, too, with accounts that are extremely disturbing. I'll let you know."

Sandy Martin was an enigma, and Beaty had no idea whose side he was on. He was a partner in Patton Boggs & Blow, one of the most powerful firms in the capital, and it had been Martin who disclosed to the Federal Reserve that the Price Waterhouse audits, the audits ordered by Sheikh Zayed when he took control of the bank in April 1990, had revealed that millions, perhaps billions, of dollars were missing. Martin was wary of the press and closemouthed, but he had told Beaty a couple of extraordinary things in the off-the-record session in his office. He told the reporter that BCCI might be one of the largest criminal enterprises in the world. That was stunning to hear from a lawyer whose firm was involved in BCCI's defense, but then

Martin had made it clear that he, personally, was retained by His Highness. The lawyer handled Zayed's real estate investments in the United States and had done so for the past eight years. A government source had told Beaty that Zayed's investments in the United States amounted to a staggering $50 billion, or more, but Martin refused to either confirm or deny that estimate.

Martin's other mind-bending statement slipped out when Beaty casually commented on photographs of the Himalayas on his office wall. A world-class mountain climber, Martin then complained that after months of planning and preparation he wasn't going to be able to scale K9, the peak next in height to Mount Everest, on his coming vacation. Beaty politely wondered aloud why not.

Martin looked at him strangely. "Because they say that if I go to Pakistan, I'll be killed." He refused to say who "they" were, but it was obvious from his wording that it was BCCI in Pakistan he feared. That comment was the major reason Beaty had been prepared to give temporary credence to Sami Masri's claims of a Black Network operating within BCCI.

Martin was more than just a lawyer, however; he was another piece in the jigsaw puzzle. A recent *Village Voice* article had declared that Martin was a former Defense Intelligence agent, but he was far more than that. When Beaty asked him about his former government role, Martin said he had never been a DIA officer but a national security adviser to the Joint Chiefs of Staff at the Pentagon before leaving government for a private law practice.

"Damn, Sam, just think about it," Beaty later told his partner. "This guy wasn't just some DIA agent—he was one of the people running defense intelligence—and then he leaves a job like that to go directly to work for the president of the United Arab Emirates, investing his petrodollars in the U.S. And Zayed was the main money behind BCCI even then: What kind of coincidence is that? No wonder nobody in the government wants to touch BCCI."

Three more frustrating days in London passed before word came back from Abu Dhabi. Martin called to say that Ghanim was not prepared to talk to *Time* magazine at this time. Perhaps in another week or two.

Beaty, ready to commit mayhem, made reservations to fly back to Los Angeles and got into a shouting argument with Masri. The Palestinian was a difficult companion. He spent his days in his room drinking room service whiskey, raging about Pamela's refusal to leave Abu Dhabi, and speculating endlessly about whether she was unfaithful.

At night he wanted to visit the nightclubs, where he almost instantly spent his per diem—which Beaty parceled out daily—as well as the reporter's. At dinner the night before, at the Hard Rock Cafe, the reporter had handed him his last hundred dollars and the Arab promptly tipped the waitress fifty.

Beaty was caught in the middle of a lovers' quarrel he had to resolve: Masri stubbornly refused to talk further about the Black Network—or to retrieve the documents incriminating Clark Clifford he claimed to have in safekeeping—until his wife was safely out of the Gulf. Pamela told Beaty on the phone, sweetly enough, that she would meet them in the States when she got time off from work in two or three weeks and asked if Sami was being faithful to her.

"They don't teach this in Journalism 101," Beaty snarled at Masri, but Masri only looked at him blankly.

"Do you think she loves me?" he asked.

Back in Hermosa Beach, Beaty stashed Masri at a surfers' motel near his home and called Sam Gwynne to explain that everything was going to hell in a hand basket. Gwynne, however, was making some progress. He had been talking to James Dougherty, a Lloyd's of London lawyer in Miami who was locked in a civil legal battle with BCCI. Dougherty, Gwynne said, had a ton of documents he was prepared to share.

"I'll leave Sami here and meet you in Miami tomorrow," Beaty said. "Maybe I'll never see Sami Masri again." They decided to stay at the Grand Bay Hotel in Coconut Grove. The Grand Bay was famous as an elegant hotel favored by drug dealers: Many *Miami Vice* episodes had been filmed there, and the undercover Customs agents from Operation C-Chase had used the hotel for meetings with BCCI's Amjad Awan.

Gwynne and Beaty spent three days with Dougherty, reading his records and interviewing the witnesses he had accumulated, and then took off to pursue their own witnesses and leads. The lawyer was warring with an expatriate Jordanian weapons dealer and coffee smuggler named Munther Ismael Bilbeisi, who lived a gaudy Florida millionaire's life in Boca Raton, Florida. Over the years Bilbeisi sold millions of pounds of coffee smuggled from Central America to United States buyers. His vast operation was supported by the payment of bribes and kickbacks from Honduras to New York and the phony paperwork and money-laundering services provided by BCCI. He told friends that BCCI had set up a special branch office in Boca Raton just to handle his accounts and those of a few other high rollers. Dougherty uncovered the scheme after Bilbeisi sued Lloyd's of London when the insurance underwriters refused to pay Bilbeisi's 1986 $6-million claim for commercial losses on a coffee shipment and the alleged theft of a Sung Dynasty vase from his Boca Raton mansion.

The reporters decided that the Bilbeisi affair was a good case study of BCCI's support of illicit activities, especially since Dougherty complained that the Justice Department had refused to investigate the case even though he had offered documented evidence and witnesses. They were rushing the story to completion when Beaty received a phone call from Sandy Martin and a message from Sheikh Khalfan al-Mazrui. Khalfan would meet Beaty and Sami Masri in Casablanca and Beaty should apply to the United Arab Emirates ambassador in Washington for visas to Abu Dhabi.

Beaty flew back to Hermosa Beach to bail Masri out of the Sunrise Motel. He had refused to leave Masri enough money to pay for his accommodations, assuming that his translator would blow the rent in the nearby beachfront discos. As Beaty had predicted to Gwynne, Masri was in shaky shape, despite daily phone calls from Beaty. Without the reporter's steady encouragement, Masri spiraled into wild depressions, worried about his coming ordeal in Abu Dhabi. Declaring that he would tell Khalfan and Sheikh Zayed about BCCI's Black Network—which would also be a confession—was one thing; facing the reality of that move was another.

Beaty and Masri joined Gwynne in Washington on June 12, and Beaty began a shuttle between the Moroccan and U.A.E. embassies to wheedle visas from the reluctant ambassadors. Just getting Masri into Casablanca proved a problem, and in the end Beaty declared that the Jordanian was a *Time* employee traveling with him on assignment. Beaty and Gwynne typed up an impressive letter on *Time* stationery, and Gwynne talked the Washington bureau office manager into signing it.

"This is just to get a visa for one of Beaty's sources," Gwynne told her, indicating vaguely that New York knew all about it. The gossip in the Washington bureau was proving correct: The straitlaced Gwynne was becoming corrupted by his association with Beaty.

Before departing, Beaty had two long telephone conversations with Condor, who gave him a detailed briefing on the political situation in the Emirates in general and in Abu Dhabi in particular. As the BCCI story unfolded, Condor had developed a keen interest in Beaty's progress. Abu Dhabi was considered a vital American ally in the Middle East, especially since Operation Desert Storm, and the BCCI affair was now affecting national security interests.

"Zayed is a shrewd old Bedouin and is well respected," Condor told the reporter, "but he's not getting any younger, and the BCCI scandal may affect the succession." In addition to being the ruler of Abu Dhabi, Zayed was the president of the United Arab Emirates, and it had long been assumed that his heir, probably Prince Khalifa, would automatically assume the presidency of the U.A.E. "Zayed's rivals for ruling the Emirates, such as Sultan al-Quassami in Sharjah, would like to see the succession to presidency of the U.A.E. restructured, but they don't dare tell Zayed that, and they wouldn't move against him. But Khalifa is a different story: He's not excessively clever and he's not often sober. If the U.A.E. is going to be embarrassed by the BCCI scandal, then Zayed's enemies may make a move. It's a question of how these smaller sheikhdoms are going to hang together."

Condor believed that Zayed's advisers were keeping the truth about BCCI's desperate financial straits and pending criminal charges in the United States from the old sheikh. "Zayed is surrounded by people who have benefited from BCCI's activities, and they talked Zayed into recapitalizing the bank. He took the money out of public funds, the Abu Dhabi Investment Fund, and the central bank. I don't think he knows how bad things are."

Condor also warned Beaty that people around Zayed would try to prevent him from seeing the sheikh. "Just assume that your hotel room and telephone may be bugged and your luggage and papers will be closely examined. If you run into trouble go see Ned Walker, the American ambassador in Abu Dhabi. It wouldn't be a bad idea to check in with him when you arrive." The government man concluded with a quick rundown of BCCI's vital role in the Middle East as a middleman in weapons deals and as a broker of intelligence. Beaty was startled: This was far more than Condor had revealed in earlier conversations and went beyond anything Sami Masri had yet told him, although Masri's snippets of information about the Black Network fit into the pattern.

John Moscow was also full of advice and warnings. He provided a couple of names of BCCI officers in Abu Dhabi who might or might not talk and suggested a list of questions to ask if Beaty actually got to Ghanim al-Mazrui. "Call me every now and again and let me know how things are going," Moscow said.

Beaty and Gwynne finished a first draft of the Bilbeisi story and Beaty and his now-subdued Arab companion caught a cab for the airport.

.   .   .

Sami had postponed talking in detail as long as he could. Now, on the plane from Paris to Casablanca, he began describing the Black Network.

"They recruited me in 1984 when I was going to college in Pittsburgh," Masri began. "They called me on the phone, they knew me from home, they knew a lot about me, and it was easy to relate to them. When they showed up, they were just normal people, very humble, down to earth."

"What nationality were they?"

"They were young white people, Persians, Armenians out of Jordan, Pakistanis living in the Emirates. They all spoke Arabic, most of them with a Palestinian accent.

"It was all very friendly at the beginning. They gave me money, there were parties and women, and then they began to explain the power and connections they had and suggested that I join their organization. They told me I would learn later what the organization was really about. They were always there for you and they just sort of took control of everything. They taught me about leadership, gave me books to read—books on how to deal with people, on psychology. They talked about not showing your emotions. They were always saying, 'That's what a leader does, and you should behave like a leader.'

"In 1985 I got my first operation: There were six people, and I was in charge; I had instructions, support, cash. We went out of Karachi to Bangladesh and then to India. We had documents, passports, and we flew to England. People were waiting for us there. They picked up the stuff and gave us new passports and travel documents. I got paid $50,000 and the others got $10,000 each. I found out later that this first operation was an easy one; it was meant to go like clockwork to give us confidence. We got into the really heavy things later."

Beaty didn't look up from his legal pad and, deliberately sounding bored, asked, "And what was this 'stuff' you delivered in England?"

Sami ignored the question. "All of a sudden they started talking to us differently; it was almost like boot camp. It wasn't friendly anymore. We trained with arms, and there was other special training: breaking and entering, setting up bugs and eavesdrop devices."

"What were you doing with all this?" Beaty asked.

"We were acting as couriers, delivering documents and gathering military and industrial information . . . government secrets. I was sent to interrogate people—people that were targeted. We would learn everything about them; we would do that ourselves or hire detective agencies. At times when there were people we wanted to recruit, or people who had information that we wanted, we would put hundreds of thousands of dollars in their bank accounts before we talked to them."

Beaty looked up and forgot to sound bored. "You just put money in someone's account?"

"It is a very good technique if you can afford it, and we had unlimited money. If you look at your bank account and see that you have a million dollars that you didn't think you had . . . it is much harder to return that money than it is to turn it down in the first place. And in some circumstances, you are already compromised just because the money is in your account and you can't explain it."

"Who would you give the money to? I mean, what kind of people were targeted?"

"People we wanted to work with us. Generals, politicians, government officials, bank officers, it was in all countries."

"And this was BCCI doing this?"

Sami toyed with the glass of cognac on his tray. Beaty had noticed that Masri had drunk little alcohol for the past day or two and had correctly deduced that he was concerned about the coming meeting with his puritanical brother-in-law.

"The organization was bankrolled by BCCI. They wanted complete domination of key countries. For example, they talked about complete control of Panama. You know about Noriega, they were his bank. But also BCCI was paying for the Mossad's operations in Panama, and they were taking care of the Colombian drug transactions. They—the bank—were funding both sides in Nicaragua. We were handling the money that the Saudis were giving the Contras as a favor to the United States, but on the other hand, the Kuwaitis were paying the Sandinistas just to spite the Saudis. There were some arms deals for them out of Libya and Cuba, and BCCI financed those.

"BCCI was getting a lot out of Nicaragua. The organization paid personal money to Ortega, and he gave us facilities: We could fly planes in and out for money transfers without worrying about customs, and we had access from the sea. Ortega became one of BCCI's favorites: They dumped Noriega for Ortega. BCCI delivered Noriega to the U.S. Justice Department, you know, but there were a lot of BCCI documents in Panama that disappeared because they would have implicated too many people."

Masri stopped talking, and the reporter let the silence grow as he thought. This was far more than he had bargained for, and he couldn't decide whether he believed any of it or not. How would you check this out? He had already learned that what seemed implausible on the face of it could be true when it came to BCCI. He knew from his own reporting experience that Israel would work with anyone who furthered Israeli goals, and it was true the Mossad had an influential presence in Panama, which was a key transshipment point in clandestine weapons deals. He also knew there had been something of a quiet scandal within U.S. law enforcement circles over BCCI documents related to Noriega that had apparently disappeared. How would Sami have known that?

"Sami, tell me more about the Mossad."

"What do you want to know? We trained together in Karachi for covert operations. We gathered information for the Mossad, spying on the Gulf States because we were so close to the ruling families there that we were familiar with foreign policies. The Israelis sold U.S. arms, technology, expertise to Pakistan, India, Sri Lanka, and BCCI brokered the deals. BCCI would loan money to the countries for the purchases, but some of it that came to Pakistan was a gift. Ghaith Pharaon was involved in fifty Scud B adjusted missiles that North Korea sold to Syria. BCCI didn't finance that deal; they paid for it upon instruction.

"They gave the Mossad, Israel, the use of their agents in the Emirates. BCCI was friends to everybody."

"You said before that you worked with the CIA."

"We did joint operations; BCCI was financing Israeli arms going into Afghanistan. There were Israeli arms, Israeli planes, and CIA pilots. Arms were coming into Afghanistan and we were . . ." Masri searched for a word, "facilitating.

"BCCI's motive was to strengthen its ties to the agencies. We were looking to the future. But it wasn't all tied to arms. Once there was a shipment from Colombia, via Fiji and Manila, to Karachi by ship. The network unloaded it in Karachi, a CIA agent from Indiana named Steve was in charge, and we had to get it out of the port using trucks to the airport, where we loaded it on an unmarked 707. I was there, I carried the money to give to Karachi customs. The payoff to customs was a half-million rupees, which is about $25,000. I knew that supervisor: He had asked to take the night shift that night because something was coming in. I don't know what the shipment was: It was in huge wooden crates, we had to use a crane instead of the forklifts."

"When was this?"

"The load left Karachi in April 1989. It was the nineteenth, I think. The plane left Karachi going out over Turkey and Iran, and they got

Air Pakistan to abort a scheduled flight at the last minute so this plane would appear to be Air Pakistan, but then it diverted to Czechoslovakia. I heard its final destination was the East Coast of the United States somewhere between Virginia and Vermont."

"What do you think was in the crates?"

"I don't know. We moved gold, we moved guns, we moved drugs. This shipment started in Colombia."

Beaty was reluctantly impressed. He had spent so much time with Masri that he had developed a keen ear for his exaggerations and deceptions. But this was almost a different Sami, speaking in detail and with assurance. He had other detailed stories about "intelligence ops" with the agency, including deliveries of crates into the war zone across the Pakistan border. This was surely a view of the bank that went beyond anything Beaty had heard from anybody. If even a fraction of what Masri said was true, they were all going to have to drastically revise their thinking about BCCI as simply a financial scandal. But this was all difficult to accept even as a working hypothesis. The CIA?

"Sami, did Abedi direct the organization, the Black Network?" It was a test question. Beaty knew enough to know that if a network within the bank was controlling, or coordinating, the illegal activities, Agha Hasan Abedi would be careful to keep layers of insulation between himself and the operatives. Abedi was a shadow, the man always behind the scenes providing prompts from offstage left.

Masri didn't answer for a moment. "I don't know, I only saw him a few times, but I never talked to him. In Karachi he would talk to Zafar Iqbal and Sani Ahmed. But it was BCCI's organization. They paid the money. There is very tight security; nobody knows who works in other cells. Sometimes strangers would come up to me and give me an envelope and it would be money, a bonus for a job that was just done, or it would be instructions for me to go somewhere, to some country and meet with someone. I was told that Refaat Assad, the former commander of the defense battalions in Syria, the brother to the president, was behind the setup of BCCI's intelligence operations. You should ask him. He's now living in Spain or Portugal in exile after a disagreement with his brother."

Beaty smiled to himself. Now there would be an interview. "But you say the CIA was using BCCI, using your organization?"

"The CIA was doing things for us, delivering information, and we did things for the agency. We picked up people for them, we found people for them, we assassinated people for the agency. There is nothing that the organization would not do. We were big in drugs, drug smuggling, drug financing. Our planes flew from Karachi to Singapore, to South America, planes packed with money. In a couple of countries our planes would even have a military escort: In Pakistan we had F-15 escorts. There was a shipment of Bolivian coke one time to Karachi; a lot of the time the money came in from South America or Miami to Karachi."

"Sami, that doesn't make sense. Heroin and hash come *out* of Pakistan . . . why would anybody send cocaine into Karachi?"

Masri looked puzzled at the question. Cocaine was a commodity. "I told you I would tell you what I know. I don't know where it went. The BCCI people around the sheikhs, they would provide cocaine for their young people, the Westernized sons. They provided cocaine, cocaine and young boys, for the royal families. But this shipment from Bolivia, that was a bulk shipment."

The reporter hadn't missed the reference to Prince Khalifa, Sheikh Zayed's heir apparent. Masihur Rahman, the former BCCI chief financial officer he had interviewed in London, had made the same accusation about BCCI's efforts to corrupt, or influence, Khalifa. He decided to let that one pass for the moment: There was too much to ask about. "You say there were assassinations?"

"I told you we used intimidation. That was mostly in Pakistan. The Pakistanis are easy to intimidate. You might send a man his brother's finger with his ring still on it. They discovered that one BCCI man, a protocol officer, had sold his home and was liquidating his assets. He was going to flee without telling anyone. They got brigands from the North-West and they came in and raped his wife and killed his brother. That is the only man I know myself for sure they killed."

"But the CIA? You don't really know about any assassinations linked to them?"

"Only things I heard. We helped them in Southeast Asia—Burma, Hong Kong—where we had more effective agents."

The plane was beginning to descend. They would be landing soon.

"And what about the United States? What did the Network do in America?"

"We only sent the crème de la crème to the United States. There were more than a hundred Network people there, but none of them were BCCI people. I mean BCCI bankers. But BCCI was the brains, the paymaster, the front, and really the major operator."

"But you don't know if they bribed anyone?"

"There were lots of Americans who were put on the payroll: These

were the people we had gotten to through blackmail, extortion, bribery. I don't know who all: There were judges, state policemen, the
FBI, the Justice Department, whoever we needed help from. When
they had an operation, they wanted it to go smoothly. They had a
saying: 'A dog barking with you is better than a dog barking against
you, and if it is your dog, you have to throw him a piece of meat.' It
was easy in the United States because we knew the weaknesses in the
United States. It was always money. You give a guy a loan and then
he didn't have to pay it back."

"So who did you get to? Do you know anyone for a fact?"

"Senator John Tower, they knew his weaknesses. They sent him
women, young beauties from Lahore, and then they got videos and
films."

"Did you see any of these videotapes?"

"No, but I heard them talk about this in meetings. They talked
about President Carter. It was a big thing about the money to Carter."

Beaty kept taking word-for-word notes, but on this subject Masri
seemed only to be repeating BCCI gossip about events before Masri
went to work for the Network. He talked of Senator Howard Baker
meeting with the organization's men in Europe, and how then–Secretary of State Cyrus Vance had made a secret trip to Pakistan in
advance of Carter's later public visit. Vance, and later Carter, had
been hosted by BCCI's protocol department rather than Pakistani
officials, which Masri thought a good joke. The "contributions" to
politicians Sami had heard about all took place in the Carter era.

How strange, Beaty thought. Ali Mirza, who was a great deal more
specific on how the bank bought influence in the United States, had
also talked only about Carter-era politicians. Mirza had talked about
loans to Andrew Young, cash to Jesse Jackson, contributions to Carter,
and of course about loans and money to Bert Lance. And the million
dollars provided to influence the Georgia legislature to pass that banking bill. It was as if Abedi had given up trying to buy influence after
Ronald Reagan was elected, but that hardly made sense. The Reagan
administration was awash in officials who cut corners, and many of
them had gotten nailed for it.

"So these were just things you heard? Who was in charge of this?"

"Sani Ahmed, the head of the protocol department. He set these
things up. When I was there a great deal of cash, millions, was being
sent to the Washington office. It came from Switzerland to Karachi,
and Ahmed would take it to the United States to the Washington
office, but I don't know where it went from there. Sani did money

laundering big time, and the arms deals in Guatemala, Nicaragua, Iran. BCCI, the organization really, was supplying arms to the Contras. I do know for a fact that they picked up surplus and stolen arms all around the world to give to the Contras. And arms from the Israelis. Hasenfus, he was paid by BCCI: We all knew that." Eugene Hasenfus had survived when his plane, carrying supplies for the Contras, was shot down over Nicaragua. Identification he was carrying linked him to the CIA, and the incident ignited the Iran-Contra scandal.

"Sami, do you have any proof at all of any of this?" Beaty was beginning to feel beleaguered. This was a shotgun blast of allegations.

"The BCCI vault in Karachi. They keep records. I've been in the vault, it is twenty meters by twenty meters of reinforced concrete and I was told it was one of the biggest vaults in the world. It was built by the same people who built Saddam Hussein's bunkers. There were separate companies from Belgium, Austria, Germany who all had a part of building the security system." The lights in the plane had come on, and Masri had dropped his voice to a whisper.

"One more thing, Sami," Beaty said. "You haven't said anything about Clark Clifford."

Sami Masri was still whispering in his ear when the seat belt sign came on. They were landing in Casablanca.

It was nearly dawn when Beaty finally got into his room at the Casablanca Hilton. He made a time zone calculation and called Sam Gwynne.

"You're never going to believe all this, Sam. I don't want to go into details on the telephone, but our boy says Mr. A., the fellow who founded the bank, was working directly with William Casey. He says they knew each other." He gave Gwynne a tight synopsis of Masri's disclosures, couched in slang with oblique references only Gwynne would catch. If the National Security Agency telephone surveillance computers catch this conversation, he thought, it's going to sound like two big dope dealers making a deal.

"How much of it do you believe?"

"Christ, I don't know. The stuff about the people from Langley sounds pretty far out, but our boy has lots of details. I think he's exaggerating how important he is in all of this, but he talked for a couple of hours, and his story is internally consistent. Khalfan is supposed to show up here in a day or two, and if he repeats this for him I think we're going to have to take it seriously. Our boy is scared shitless by Khalfan. He's putting his head in a noose by making these allegations. Abu Dhabi's not going to take this as a joke."

"Well, maybe you're onto something. I just got to Dale Murray. Remember he was Ghaith Pharaon's partner in Chris-Craft, the boat-building company? He testified before a grand jury in Florida and told them how Pharaon and BCCI paid off everyone in the Argentine government from the president down and pulled off a big debt-equity swap scam."

"Equity swap?"

"Yeah, they bought bad Argentine loans from U.S. banks for pennies on the dollar, and then the Argentine government bought them back from Pharaon and Murray for full value. Then Pharaon kicked back half the profit under the table to government officials."

Beaty closed his eyes. "Has it occurred to you that we're in over our heads? Call Joelle for me and tell her I got here okay and that the canary finally started singing. I'll stay in touch."

Khalfan al-Mazrui arrived at the Inter-Continental two days later, traveling with his family, a large entourage of servants, and enough luggage to fill half the cargo hold of an airliner. His wife, Sami's sister, had been shopping in Paris.

"*Salaam*, Mr. Jonathan, it is so much a pleasure to meet you." His English was halting and careful. They touched palms.

"*Wa alaykum as salaam,*" Beaty managed to stumble in reply. The reporter was impressed. Khalfan was tall, younger than Beaty had anticipated, perhaps in his mid-forties, and dressed in snowy white linen robes as finespun as silk. The hotel staff, who wore formal Western evening dress and had been merely polite to the reporter when he checked in, were suddenly fawningly attentive.

The sheikh spoke rapidly to an uncharacteristically diffident Sami, who then turned to the reporter. "Khalfan requests that you join him for lunch this afternoon."

At four o'clock Beaty found himself sitting cross-legged in a circle of robed and turbaned men from Abu Dhabi in a very large tent on the outskirts of Casablanca. With much laughter the reporter was shown how to take a handful of saffron rice from one of the large communal platters and knead it into a ball. A white-bearded elder cut pieces of fish from the platter and placed choice morsels in the reporter's mouth. This was not going to be a power business lunch.

Nor was there going to be one soon: One day, and then another, passed, and Khalfan gave no indication that anything important was waiting on the agenda. On Wednesday Khalfan invited him to take coffee in the hotel's ornate main lobby, where brightly colored birds flew freely above the trees growing in the marbled expanse. He was

invited to discuss philosophy, and Khalfan delicately inquired about
the reporter's knowledge of the Zionist conspiracy. Beaty dodged as
adroitly as he could. "Perhaps," Khalfan said at last, "you and Sami
would like to join me in my suite."

As far as Beaty could tell, Khalfan's suite took most of an entire floor
of the hotel. They settled themselves in couches, and Khalfan opened
his hands in a gesture for them to speak.

Beaty talked for a long time, pausing only for Sami's translation,
outlining his knowledge of the bank's history, of Abedi's assumption
of increased authority within Sheikh Zayed's Private Department, and
then moved into what he knew about the bank's criminal activities.
Beaty watched Sami closely: He was pale and frequently wiped his
palms on his pants leg but appeared to be translating accurately,
judging by Khalfan's questions and responses. All expression had disappeared from the sheikh's face, and he was soon taking copious
notes. Beaty, reading from his own notes, told Masri's entire story,
weaving it into his own wider perspective of the bank's activities. He
didn't directly finger Masri as a member of the Black Network but
from time to time he pushed him into explanations so that Khalfan
could not mistake where some of this information was coming from.

At the end Beaty made his pitch: Masri, as well as his sources
within the U.S. State Department, had convinced him that Zayed was
unaware of the bank's true nature. Perhaps Zafar Iqbal was keeping
this critical knowledge from the sheikh, since Zayed's own lawyer in
the United States was convinced the ruler did not realize the fate that
was to befall the bank he now owned.

Coached by Sami, Beaty knew that Zafar Iqbal, who had recently
been named by Abu Dhabi to head BCCI and the effort to restructure
the empire before the international regulators moved, was Khalfan's
arch-rival for power within the Emirates. It was left delicately unmen-
tioned that if Zayed was being kept in ignorance, it was just as likely
that it was Ghanim al-Mazrui who was withholding information.

Khalfan was silent for more than a minute. "And you, Mr. Jonathan, what is it you wish?"

"To be given access so that I may write a fair story which explains
Sheikh Zayed's honorable intentions."

Khalfan looked unimpressed. Beaty realized that sounded too good
to be true.

"And to be given access to any BCCI documents relating to Clark
Clifford and his knowledge of BCCI's hidden ownership of First
American Bank in Washington," he added hastily. "*Inshallah* [God
willing]."

Khalfan nodded approvingly. "Perhaps you should go to Abu Dhabi. I will make a telephone call. You have your visa: His Excellency the ambassador spoke well of you. I must return to Paris, but I will join you at the Inter-Continental in Abu Dhabi in three days, *Inshallah,* as God wills, and we will see if Ghanim al-Mazrui has the time to see you. Matters are very hectic now."

Beaty and Masri stood up to leave. "Sami, why don't you stay and visit with me for a few minutes. Your sister wishes to know how you have been and what you have been doing since you so suddenly left Karachi."

Outside the large double doors to the suite Beaty let out a long breath. At last glimpse, Sami Masri looked like a man standing on very thin ice. It couldn't happen to a nicer fellow, Beaty thought.

When they flew into Abu Dhabi the next evening, Masri was so apprehensive he could hardly talk. There were subcurrents that Beaty didn't understand, and as the reporter was waved through immigration, armed guards appeared and led Masri away. Beaty waited for nearly two hours before Masri returned, but Masri refused to talk about what had transpired.

Days passed without word from Khalfan, and Beaty discovered that the Inter-Continental, a new glass-and-bronze tower set on the beach, was a gilded cage. It was the *hajj,* the Muslim religious holiday when pilgrims travel to Mecca, and because of the important visitors who had come to Abu Dhabi for the holiday, security at the hotel was extraordinary. White-robed guards cradling machine guns followed their sheikhs. Abu Dhabi was a gleaming new city, but if one parted the lush green curtain of trees and shrubs surrounding the city like an emerald wall, one peered out into the endless waste of the desert.

Beaty stuck near the hotel, waiting for the telephone call from Ghanim. It took three days to arrange a courtesy visit with the American ambassador, Ned Walker, as Condor had advised. Walker was a busy man. He was pleasant, but Beaty learned little more than the fact that Sheikh Zayed had an income of $30 billion a year and that the ambassador had no inclination at all to discuss BCCI. At night he ate his meals in solitary splendor. Masri had all but disappeared, and that was quickly becoming a problem.

If Beaty was restive, Masri was becoming less and less manageable. His arrogance, which had dwindled to apprehension as it became clearer to him that he might indeed have to confess to Sheikh Zayed, returned full-blown. He reappeared the third night in the company of several robed men, one of whom he introduced as an officer in Abu Dhabi intelligence. "Secret police," Masri hissed in Beaty's ear. The reporter thought the men looked sinister but then dismissed the thought. Masri was getting to him.

The next morning Masri, who had been raging over his still unresolved problems with Pamela, announced he was going to visit her in Dubai, a two-hour drive up the Gulf Coast. He had decided to divorce her immediately, he said, and disappeared once again.

Beaty wondered if Masri's new friends had a hand in that decision. To kill time he took a drive into Abu Dhabi, but he had the distinct impression that he was being followed wherever he went and returned to the hotel. He again dismissed the thought. Until Condor unexpectedly called him from London.

"Jonathan, I don't want to alarm you, but I think you may be in danger. I'd stay close to the hotel. If you have trouble, call Ned Walker: I advise you to do this as soon as possible."

Beaty was still thinking that over the next morning when Masri called from the lobby downstairs. He was back and he had brought Pamela with him. The reporter met them in the elegant ice cream bar and took Pamela's measure. She was attractive and more wholesome-looking than he expected. Somehow he had thought she would be harder-edged. Masri did most of the talking. They had to find an Imam to certify the divorce, and the formalities should be completed by the end of the day. Beaty soon excused himself.

"I'm sorry to have to meet you under these conditions, Pamela," he said. He looked at Masri. "I would have thought she was worth reforming for."

Masri sneered.

When Beaty returned to his room he found a note from Sami under his door.

> Jhon [sic]:
> I will call you this evening and I would like P. to talk to you. Explain to her not to make it easy for me to obliterate her and her family. I don't want to hurt her but I might because she knows too much. It is not my choice. Thanks.

Beaty didn't know what to make of it. Perhaps it was more bravado, but during the past month Masri had told him several times that he told Pamela everything about his work with the Black Network. Pamela had been holding some of the documents Masri claimed he had taken from BCCI's Karachi headquarters before he fled. And Pamela had acknowledged to Beaty that she was indeed holding documents that Sami wanted kept safe. She was to have delivered them to Sami in the United States.

Beaty swore. Seven days without word from either Khalfan or Ghanim. It was beginning to unravel.

When the telephone rang again it was Bob Marshall, *Time*'s lawyer in New York who handled the magazine's libel problems. Marshall, usually unflappable, was over the edge, his voice tight with tension. "Beaty, you've gotten us sued for a hundred million dollars!"

The reporter's stomach felt like he was in a rapidly dropping elevator. "What?"

"Munther Bilbeisi. The story you and Gwynne said was airtight."

"It was. It is. I've never had that much documented backup before."

"He's outraged that *Time* called him a weapons dealer, a smuggler, a bribe payer, and part of BCCI's corrupt empire."

The elevator dropped another ten floors. "Bob, we had him cold: There's a warrant out for his arrest, he's about to be indicted on more charges, and he had fled to Jordan."

"Well, he's a friend of King Hussein, and he is filing suit for one hundred million dollars because he says our story is 90 percent wrong. I know your facts are correct, but he can probably get a judgment against us in Jordan. We want you to catch the next available plane to Amman and go talk to him."

Suddenly there was a loud knocking on Beaty's hotel door. The reporter promised the lawyer he would call him back right away. It was Pamela, her mascara smeared with tears. It looked as if the side of her face was bruised. Masri had thrown her out of their room, she said, and locked the door. She had no money with her and it was too late to call anyone who might drive her back to Dubai. Could he rent a room for her tonight?

Beaty took her down to the reception desk and signed for the room. He left her standing in the lobby and took the elevator back to his own room. Half an hour later there was another pounding on his door. When he opened it, Masri, shirtless and looking wild, threw Pamela to the floor and slammed the door behind him.

"You've given me the excuse I've needed now, Beaty!" he screamed. Pamela curled up in a fetal position, and Beaty looked on openmouthed at the Arab. Masri was hyperventilating and his abdominal muscles were corded.

"This is a Muslim country and you've interfered in my marriage!" Masri yelled. "I can do whatever I want to you and nobody will say a word. You've interfered once too often: It's all over for you! Nobody wants you in this country: You're a dead man!"

Beaty caught his breath, which had suddenly left him. "Knock it off, Masri. We're here to see Sheikh Zayed, not to play games."

"I'm not playing games. I've been stringing you along all this time to see how much *Time* magazine really knew. Now it's over. Who do you think those men I was with the other night were?"

"Masri, I don't have time for this. I'm going to have to leave for Jordan to talk to Bilbeisi. He's sued the magazine. But I'll be back. You want to be on the right side when I talk to Ghanim."

Beaty had told Masri about the Bilbeisi story: Masri was quite familiar with the Bilbeisi clan in Jordan.

The Arab began laughing. "That's right. You go to Jordan. That will make things easier. That's my country. Those are my people! You will never be heard from again."

Beaty got Pamela out of the room first, and then talked Masri into leaving by threatening to call hotel security. He bolted the door and lay back on the bed. He was hyperventilating himself.

The phone rang: It was Bob Marshall again.

"Beaty, you never called me back. Have you made arrangements to go to Jordan yet?"

"Uh, Bob, I've got a few problems here. I don't think it would be a good idea for me to go to Amman now. I'll call Bilbeisi and let you know." The lawyer had given him Bilbeisi's telephone number. Beaty dialed, and Bilbeisi's wife answered.

When the coffee merchant came on the line the reporter introduced himself and said that his New York office had relayed a message that Mr. Bilbeisi was upset. Bilbeisi was sputtering.

"You have told lies about me, Mr. Beaty! You have ruined my reputation! Your editors said that you will come and talk to me about this. I have given them twenty-four hours before I file suit."

Beaty tried to explain that he was quite prepared to talk to him but that he didn't want to come directly to Amman from Abu Dhabi. "There are some people here, not connected to you at all, who have threatened to harm me if I go to Jordan."

"You will be safe here, Mr. Beaty," Bilbeisi said in a suddenly smooth tone of voice. "This is my country and I am quite influential. I will have you met at the airport by the military, and they will escort you to my home. You will be safe within my hospitality. You have been listening to lies spread by that Lloyd's of London man in Florida."

Great, Beaty thought. "I'll call you back," he promised.

Marshall refused to budge, insisting Beaty had to leave in the morning to try and pacify Bilbeisi before he made good his threat. Beaty, who would have gone to almost any lengths to avoid his courage being questioned, stubbornly refused to say exactly what his problem was. "Bob," he pleaded, "I'll go to Jordan, but I just don't want to leave from here to get there. There are some people I'm trying to shake, and things are complicated. I'll fly back to the States and then fly right back."

That wasn't satisfactory. The round trip would take longer than the twenty-four-hour deadline. Beaty talked to Attinger and then waited for a return call. There were high-level conferences going on at the Time & Life Building. It was noon in Abu Dhabi when Attinger called back.

"Okay, Jonathan, it's all been arranged. Stacks is going to fly out to talk to Bilbeisi, and you can finish your business in Abu Dhabi. Bilbeisi was impressed enough that the chief of correspondents was going to come personally that he agreed to hold off until he got there."

Damn. Now Stacks was going to have to pull his bacon out of the fire. "What did Stacks say?" Beaty asked, a little apprehensively.

"You know him. All he said was that he could use the frequent-flier miles."

"Uh, Joelle, this might be a little more dicey than John thinks. Masri has turned coat on us, and things are a little uncertain."

Attinger explained that the magazine had the bases covered. They had arranged for Stacks to interview either King Hussein or the crown prince immediately after he met with Bilbeisi. "I know Bilbeisi is a shady character, but he won't dare make a move. You let us know what's happening with you."

Beaty called Ambassador Walker and was told to come immediately to the embassy. Beaty hadn't seen Masri, but on the way out of the hotel he stopped to talk to the hotel manager and explained that he had been forced to fire Mr. Masri, his employee, and that he was a bit worried that Mr. Masri might do something violent. The manager promised to station security men in the room next to Beaty's until the matter was resolved. Beaty had the distinct impression that none of this was coming as a surprise to the manager.

At the embassy he gave Walker a quick rundown on Masri and sketched out what the magazine had learned about BCCI and its activities. Then he handed the ambassador a photocopied transcript of his interview with Masri on the flight to Casablanca.

"You might find this interesting," he said dryly. "I have a friend in government that believes the BCCI affair is now touching on national security matters. I'd appreciate it greatly if you would run a check on Masri and let me know what you find. Maybe he's all bluff."

Leaving the embassy, Beaty began laughing to himself. He had broken one of his own rules by handing over the interview to the ambassador, but Masri had obviously aborted his agreement to protect him. His laughter was at the thought of the consternation that was going to hit the CIA when they read the report, probably within a few hours. Masri's allegations spelled out in detail the agency's dealings with BCCI as well as the names of politicians who might or might not be involved.

He had been back in his room for only a few minutes when Ambassador Walker called.

"Mr. Beaty, we've run a check on the individual we discussed. We believe he is a very bad customer, and we suggest that you leave Abu Dhabi immediately. We've booked a seat for you on tonight's plane to London, and we'll keep an eye out until you're safely out of the country."

Well, maybe Sami wasn't bluffing after all. "What if I left for Jordan? My magazine has an assignment for me there."

Walker was firm: It was better that he leave the Middle East entirely for a while.

Beaty couldn't sort out all the security people who loitered in his hallway and in a room next door until the time came for his evening flight. Most of them were hotel security, he presumed—which also meant they were connected to Abu Dhabi intelligence, according to Condor's briefing. And he assumed that Condor had sent in a "friend" as he promised, and no doubt Walker had someone about.

When he walked down to the lobby to leave for the midnight flight, there was a crowd scene. He spotted Sami Masri standing expressionless within a circle of hard-faced security men. Masri didn't look at him. Beaty left for the airport in a small convoy, and boarded the plane without going through any formalities.

Beaty looked out the window at the lights of Abu Dhabi far below as the plane climbed to cruising altitude. Masri was right about one thing, he thought: He certainly wasn't wanted in this country.

CHAPTER 6

END OF EMPIRE

"Wherever you turn, whatever you are looking at, all is unreal.
You are living in a world of unreality."

—BCCI AUDITOR IAN BRINDLE,
PRICE WATERHOUSE SENIOR PARTNER[1]

Sami Masri was not what people in the news business call a reliable
source. He drank. He was subject to sudden, wild mood swings. He
was broke, without a country, in disgrace with his own family. He
feared he might be killed if he returned to Pakistan, arrested if he
stayed in the United States. Now he had apparently gone renegade
again. And he had threatened Beaty's life.

But as Beaty and Gwynne tore into the transcript of Beaty's air-
borne debriefing—the same transcript that was no doubt being studied with equal intensity ten miles to the west at CIA headquarters at
Langley, Virginia—they were struck by the precise and consistent
detail of Sami's account. Now, in the quiet of *Time*'s Washington
bureau, he and Gwynne could study it for truth and continuity. They
went over it again and again, checking it against what they knew of
the recent history of Pakistan and the Middle East, looking for obvious
errors or invention.

"This is pretty wild stuff," Beaty said. "What's even wilder is that
I don't think he's inventing it. But he's hard to figure. I think there are
times when he's exaggerating his own importance. And there are
other times when he's being evasive because he's afraid of being
indicted in the U.S. It's as though he's got his foot on the brake and
on the gas at the same time."

"Like he can't quite make his mind up," Gwynne mused, leafing again through the transcript, crammed margin-to-margin with Beaty's neat handwriting. "But he isn't nearly clever enough to make details like this up. They're too odd and too precise." Gwynne had met Masri on two occasions, more or less to baby-sit him while Beaty was off looking after his own business. He had used the time to interrogate Masri about his motives for talking to *Time*. Gwynne had concluded that he had at least three different motives, any combination of which might be in play at a given moment: Masri's desire to do something good in order to reinstate himself in the graces of his family and Abu Dhabi's ruling establishment; Masri's desire to see the bank taken down, and with it any number of his enemies; and Masri's intermittent, irrational belief that *Time* might pay him real money for his services. Withal, Masri did not seem to Gwynne to be a very complicated person. He had seemed callow, and very scared.

The question now was what to do. Masri had drawn a picture of BCCI sharply at variance with all previous accounts of the bank. Blum had never whispered about any of this, nor had Moscow or Fed officials or the investigators at Senator John Kerry's office. Condor had perhaps hinted at it in his descriptions of the Pakistani drug trade, and BCCI's weapons business, but had provided no details. Masihur Rahman had talked about threats on his life, and on the lives of others, but had never specified who these people were or who they worked for. If Masri was right, then BCCI was not really a bank at all, but something far more complex.

Beaty and Gwynne ordered in some Chinese food and spent the evening discussing Sami Masri's eye-opening tale. By midnight they finally agreed that though they could not be certain of the truth of some of the particulars, they believed the substance of what Masri had said, which meant that they believed that BCCI was less a bank than an armed state. But to move forward with a story for the magazine, they needed to confirm Masri's tale from other sources, and they would have to triple-source the larger points, such as the existence of ties between the CIA and BCCI. No one had ever heard of such things before. The two reporters would have to work extremely quickly, and there was little margin for error. John Stacks had approved a cover story that would tie together everything they knew about the bank, and he wanted it soon.

To complicate matters, both reporters felt that something momentous was about to happen, some very big piece of news. Many of the usual information networks had gone strangely silent; it was like the unsettling silence in nature that precedes an earthquake. BCCI simply could not be allowed to continue to operate much longer. Although the scandal had received wide press coverage, the bank that Beaty and Gwynne had portrayed as a global criminal was still open for business around the world. They had now been writing about the bank for four months, as had reporters at *The Wall Street Journal*, *The Washington Post*, *The New York Times*, and other publications. It was now the end of June 1991, and none of this reporting seemed to have had the slightest effect on the U.S. Justice Department, which had done nothing about the bank since the 1990 Tampa plea bargain. No regulators had taken any action against the bank anywhere in the world. In Djakarta and Bogotá and Lagos and New York and Los Angeles, BCCI's branches and agencies still opened their doors each day, sent millions of dollars in wire transfers ricocheting around the world. In seventy-odd countries, ten thousand BCCI employees still collected paychecks. More than a million depositors still kept their money in its vaults, and an assortment of sovereign central banks still naively trusted BCCI with large reserves. Something, somewhere, had to give.

Confirming Masri's story was not as hard as Beaty and Gwynne had first thought it would be. Though there was a lot of frantic phone work, the nature of it changed and became easier once they knew which questions to ask: Before Masri, it had not occurred to them to inquire about intelligence operations, drug and weapons sales, or other unusual activities.

The first outside confirmation of Sami Masri's story came from a source Gwynne had approached several weeks before on a tip. Over several decades in the weapons business, the man had worked for two of America's largest defense contractors and participated in deals all over Europe and the Middle East. Unlike so many of the sources Gwynne and Beaty gathered while stalking BCCI, this one was entirely legitimate. The sort of stuff he specialized in was aboveboard—government-to-government sales of weaponry and materiel approved by the U.S. Congress. At the time Gwynne found him, he had a good job with a reputable defense contractor.

Still, when Gwynne asked if he knew anything about BCCI, there was a long silence followed by a request for total anonymity. Gwynne reluctantly granted it. As usual, it was difficult finding anyone at all to go on the record about the bank.

The man's story was remarkable. He had worked in Europe for many years, he said, and he had run into BCCI dozens of times. Everybody in the weapons business knew about BCCI, he said, and almost everybody feared them. They appeared to work all ends of the business, from straight financing to brokering and even to dealing for their own account. They also employed some very formidable street-level muscle.

"We were representing a joint venture chasing a sale of military equipment to the Belgian government," said the man. "We had gone pretty far down the line when suddenly BCCI showed up, representing the Italians. I was staying at the Hilton in Brussels, and I got a phone call from a BCCI guy asking me to come down to the lobby. When I go down, there's a BCCI guy, a Pakistani, and next to him is this 220-pound French guy named André, the kind of guy who stuffs people in car trunks. They have business cards with a BCCI logo. So André says: 'You're getting out of this thing. This is our deal.' Then the other BCCI guy says: 'You're out, and go and tell your client you're out.' They scared the hell out of me. BCCI had two functions, as bagmen, and as thugs. They pushed the competition out."

The man returned to his room and called his boss, who told him he had already been contacted in Southern California by the same people bearing the same message. The source told other stories about this cadre of BCCI employees who, like the French thug André, were not in any sort of financial business. They were either weapons dealers or street-level enforcers. The story he told stretched across a decade, from Europe to the Middle East. Though he did not assign any special name to these people, their jobs sounded very much like Sami Masri's.

Meanwhile, Beaty had also gotten back in touch with a Pakistani weapons dealer named Ali Khan, whom he had interviewed months before. When they had first met, Khan had rattled on about BCCI's involvement in weapons dealings and with Western intelligence services. To Beaty, it had all sounded too fantastic; he had heard none of it before, and it linked with nothing he knew about the bank. Besides, Khan had been nervous, unwilling to document any of it. But now Beaty returned to his notes and found extraordinary similarities between Masri's story and the Pakistani's account, which had detailed both weapons deals and what amounted to mercenary armies. Khan had spoken of the extensive intelligence connections BCCI had, including the American CIA. From Khan he now heard a detailed account that corroborated a significant portion of Sami's tale. "Look," he told Beaty. "These people work hand in hand with the drug cartels; they can have anybody killed. I personally know one fellow who got crossed up with BCCI, and he is a cripple now. A bunch of thugs beat him nearly to death, and he knows who ordered it and why. He's not about to talk."

The puzzle was slowly coming together. Next came a piece of genuine good luck. Beaty and Gwynne had put it out that they were looking for CIA connections to BCCI. One day Beaty received a call from a source who, like most others, insisted on anonymity. But unlike most of the others, this man was influential in the American corridors of power, and immensely credible as a source. Even John Stacks had been impressed. The source said he had called as a personal favor to his old friend Bob Morgenthau. It became so important to keep his identity secret that he was referred to among the five people at *Time* who actually knew who he was as "Famous Name."

Famous Name delivered in detail the confirmation that the CIA had used BCCI extensively, especially in connection with covert U.S. operations in Central America. He said that, even before Oliver North had set up his network for making illegal payments to the Contras, the National Security Council—an arm of the White House—was using BCCI to channel money to them through Saudi Arabia. He also confirmed what Beaty and Gwynne had thought to be one of the more fantastic aspects of Sami's story, that the Defense Intelligence Agency (DIA) had been involved with BCCI's covert operations. He told Beaty flatly that the DIA maintained a slush fund (i.e., completely off the official books) with BCCI to finance secret operations. Famous Name was a special case, and the first and only time Beaty and Gwynne had broken the standard "double-sourcing" rule of investigative journalism. Since they were certain that no one else could or would confirm this account, Beaty had gone to *Time*'s managing editor, Henry Muller, to request special dispensation. Muller had approved the use of Famous Name for that single yet critical piece of information.

Sami Masri's tale was proving true with alarming speed. However Masri might have altered some of the circumstances of his own role in Black Network activities, he was clearly right about the real nature of the bank and its connections to the intelligence community. Now, through Blum, Beaty and Gwynne heard yet another version of a covert-ops network linked closely to BCCI. When Blum had arranged to interview BCCI banker Amjad Awan, he had gotten strong warnings from his back channels. An old law enforcement friend had warned him about BCCI, saying that the Customs agents had encountered what seemed to be a mafia in the employment of the bank. They killed people. They kidnapped people. The undercover agents had stumbled into this when the BCCI people had offered these services to the undercovers, Blum had said. "And it scared the shit out of them.

They eventually wanted to set up a special unit to go after it, but somebody in Washington pulled the plug," Blum said. According to the details Blum's source had provided, the network that the Customs agents uncovered was apparently running independent contracting jobs in and out of Central America and Florida. Precisely as Sami had said they were. It figured: If BCCI was dealing with the Colombian cocaine cartels and moving arms about the world, it would need a cadre of hard types.

Meanwhile, Beaty and Gwynne's premonition—fueled by subtle hints from the Fed—proved to be right. At 1:00 P.M. on July 5, in an unprecedented sweep, the regulators finally moved against BCCI. In Britain, the United States, Canada, the Cayman Islands, Spain, France, and Switzerland, they swooped into BCCI's offices and informed startled bank officers that their bank was being shut down. The seizure covered more than 75 percent of the bank's putative $20 billion in assets. The news exploded in the Third World, where BCCI held large deposits, often from central banks. Within days Hong Kong's financial markets erupted in a full panic, as $1.4 billion of depositors' funds were frozen, including an estimated $200 million from the government of China. In Pakistan the government was able to keep the bank open only with armed guards at the gates to prevent a wholesale run. In neighboring Bangladesh authorities would soon claim that BCCI had "looted" the country, leaving it with huge losses. All over Africa, nervous central bankers put on optimistic faces and privately wondered if they or their countrymen would get their deposits back. In Cameroon, Congo, Ivory Coast, Gabon, Senegal, Sierra Leone, and Ghana, depositors were frozen out. At least one third of Cameroon's national reserves was frozen and would eventually be lost. Nigeria lost $200 million. The final reckoning would not come until much later. For BCCI's 1.4 million depositors who had placed an estimated $20 billion with the bank, there would be less than $2 billion of real assets to pay them off.

There was no precedent in history for what had happened. Never had any bank as large as BCCI been shut down, nor had anyone ever done such a thing on a global scale. The seizure was excruciatingly painful for the Bank of England, under whose august nose Abedi and Naqvi had spun their global deceit. Among the hardest hit were the depositors in the U.K., where the Bank of England froze $400 million in 120,000 accounts held largely by Indian and Pakistani families, Ugandans, and other immigrants. There were in addition some sixty British municipalities that had placed $160 million in funds with

BCCI. Twelve hundred BCCI employees lost their jobs. Ironically, many of the depositors had been pulled in by a characteristic BCCI scheme: The bank offered a program whereby deposits were placed in the names of relatives living overseas, thereby avoiding British tax. The Bank of England moved quickly to stall a panic by offering depositors partial compensation.

But the most visibly angry of all of the victims of the seizure were Sheikh Zayed and his chief lieutenant, the secretary general of the Abu Dhabi Investment Authority, Ghanim al-Mazrui. They were infuriated. This was partly because, after months of congenial dickering about the restructuring of BCCI, the Bank of England had abandoned them and left them twisting in the wind on July 5. The shutdown had coincided with a meeting of BCCI's board in Luxembourg to discuss the bank's reorganization and new capital infusions from Zayed. The deal was to have been signed a mere ten days later.

Behind Zayed's visceral reaction to the takeover was the stark reality that he himself had been the principal mark in Abedi's con game. He had been coddled into pumping $1.5 billion in new capital and another $1.5 billion in deposits since mid-1990. That money was gone, never to be recovered. And that was not all. When oil prices dropped off a cliff in the early 1980s, Zayed had sought Abedi's advice. More than ever before, he needed counsel on how to manage his money. This led to a watershed in BCCI's history: the de facto merger between the sheikh's so-called Private Department and BCCI, which led to the creation of a special Karachi section of the Private Department, which employed several hundred people, most of them seconded from BCCI. The result was the financial rape of both Zayed and the Abu Dhabi Investment Authority by BCCI and its allies in the sheikh's Private Department. By the mid-1980s several hundred million dollars were discovered missing, drained off by employees in Karachi. Though this was hushed up, and a new manager—Khalfan al-Mazrui—sent in to clean it up, this was yet another reason why Abu Dhabi had been so frantic to cut a deal: BCCI had favored the higher-ups in the Private Department with large loans and stock deals, and one of the recipients of that largesse was whispered to be Ghanim al-Mazrui. Zayed and his various state agencies together lost as much as $8 billion in the shutdown of BCCI.

The global seizure of BCCI meant that there would be no easy solutions for Zayed. It was more than a bit ironic that this leader of a former British protectorate would be solicited within a week of the seizure by the Bank of England. No less a figure than Bank of England

Governor Robin Leigh-Pemberton went to Abu Dhabi, hat in hand, to request that Zayed now formally indemnify the bank's depositors.

While the West speculated on why it had taken so long for authorities to shut down BCCI, the reaction in Pakistan was one of angry disbelief. Though Abedi had been sick since his first heart attack in February 1988 and was living quietly in the affluent Defense Officers' Society in Karachi, he remained a towering figure to many Pakistanis, revered as a courageous Third World entrepreneur whose bank had been hounded by racist Western financial interests. The circumstances of that heart attack, in fact, had contributed nearly as much to his personal stature as had his charitable giving. He had been stricken while dressing for a state dinner with Pakistan President Zia and Sheikh Zayed. Both rushed to his bedside to comfort him. Aghast at his apparently critical condition, Zayed put his own jet, equipped with life-support systems and medical equipment, on standby. The next day Jimmy Carter arranged for a leading heart transplant specialist to fly to London, where Zayed's plane quickly took Abedi, flanked by BCCI's own corporate jet.[2]

Now most of the Pakistani press came quickly to the enfeebled former chairman's defense. The English-language *Daily News* told its readers that "Jewish pressure" led U.S. authorities to crack down on BCCI.[3] In the newspaper *Dawn* the president of one of Pakistan's largest chambers of commerce described the action as a "Zionist-triggered conspiracy against the Muslim world as part of a new world economic order."[4] The chief minister of the province of Sind said in no uncertain terms that "the West and Israel were responsible for the closing of the bank. BCCI was the Third World bank, and it took to the challenge of breaking the hegemonistic control of the Jewish lobby and the world's financial institutions."[5] A Karachi businessman named Rubab Khan observed, "This is part of the Western plot to seize all the money and assets of the Arabs and drive out the Pakistani bankers from international banking."[6]

As the bank he built went down, and with it the life savings of hundreds of thousands of ordinary people from the developing world who had trusted him, Abedi held court in his spartan, pure-white drawing room with members of the Pakistani press. Dressed in "an immaculate, beige kurta-pajama suit of raw silk" he told them: "I am not responsible for the current crisis in the BCCI. I have not had anything to do with the bank since I was sidelined after my heart attack in Lahore in February 1988. . . . I don't blame anyone, neither in the West nor Sheikh Zayed. These things happen."[7] He insisted that the bank was strong when he left it, and that its failure was the result of "mismanagement."

Though reporters present uniformly described Abedi's speech as slurred and his words often incomprehensible, he made the announcement that, even as he spoke, he was in the process of starting yet another bank. It would be called "Progressive Bank" and would start within the month, he said. When asked about the allegations of fraud, Abedi mumbled and pointed his finger upward, repeating "God knows better." Did he agree that his grand design was fatally flawed? "I wanted a bank which would be honest and good for humanity," he replied. Would he appear in England to answer charges? "My health won't permit it. In any case, what's the point of talking about it anymore?" What would become of all the businessmen who lost their savings? "They will recover, get loans from other banks, *Inshallah*."[8]

The greatest mystery in all this was the size and location of Abedi's personal bank account. He had secretly controlled a large portion of the shares of BCCI, but those were now worthless. So his wealth, whatever form it was in, lay somewhere else. He is almost certainly worth billions, but the very secrecy that allowed him to set up his untraceable international banking network also allowed him, in the end, to hide whatever fortune he had amassed. After the bank's seizure a group of depositors in London held a seance using a Ouija board in a resourceful but unsuccessful attempt to find the number of Agha Hasan Abedi's secret account at the Union Bank of Switzerland.[9]

Though the Bank of England had pulled the trigger on BCCI on July 5, 1991, and had thereby started a global chain reaction that had smashed Agha Hasan Abedi's brainchild into tiny pieces, it had done so only reluctantly and only after waiting an extraordinary amount of time. It had been cowardly rather than heroic; it had moved only when forced to do so by a formidable U.S. alliance between the Federal Reserve Bank and the Manhattan district attorney. Though the Fed does not have the power of subpoena, nor can it bring indictments under U.S. law, it is in many ways the most formidable of U.S. government agencies, both in its political independence and in its ability to move swiftly, unilaterally, and with decisive force in its own domain. That summer Morgenthau did something that no one had ever done before, something that required special legal dispensation, and something that probably only Bob Morgenthau could have pulled off: He put the Fed on his own grand jury, thus tightly binding together the two investigations.[10]

It was Moscow who got the first big break for the new alliance. In October 1990 he heard from a still-unidentified source that the bank's longtime accountants, Price Waterhouse, had conducted an audit of BCCI and presented a report to BCCI's board on October 3. The source said that the audit contained records of immense loans to nominees, or front men, which proved that BCCI owned First American. The report also allegedly contained evidence of huge previously undocumented losses. Moscow immediately called Tom Baxter of the New York Fed, and within days the New York offices of Price Waterhouse were besieged with calls from both the district attorney's office and the Federal Reserve, asking to see a copy of the audit. A SWAT team from the legal and enforcement divisions of the Fed showed up at the accounting firm's door, demanding the audit. Citing client confidentiality, Price Waterhouse repeatedly refused to cooperate with either Morgenthau's office or the Fed in any way.[11]

At the same time, Morgenthau and Moscow were pestering the Bank of England for audit information, with the same empty results. Because of the secret agreement among the bank, Price Waterhouse, and Abu Dhabi, the Bank of England could not afford to let the information out—least of all to Morgenthau. "The secrecy had become critical now that they all knew about the ongoing criminal investigation in New York City by the District Attorney," said the Kerry subcommittee in its final report. "Each made a strenuous effort to prevent the District Attorney from obtaining Price Waterhouse audit reports which contained the information that if known would destroy the bank."[12] Bank of England officials maintained a close silence—a posture totally at odds with their sworn duties.

That proof was being withheld deliberately from the official who had long been the Fed's spearhead on the BCCI–First American case: William Ryback, head of the bank's international supervision division. Over the years Ryback had returned again and again to the supposed connections between the two banks, only to find a cold trail. He had heard the charges made by Amjad Awan, stating that BCCI owned First American. That was provocative, but he considered it hearsay, and he had never been able to lay hands on the documents that would confirm it. After having been reassured many times by Clifford and Altman that there were no proprietary connections between the two banks, Ryback was now mad.

In December Ryback made a momentous journey to London, one

that quickly paid off Morgenthau's efforts to link the two investigations. Armed only with what he had heard about the audit from Moscow, he had called BCCI President Zafar Iqbal, the man who had recently taken over BCCI when Zayed had summarily fired Abedi and Naqvi after seeing that same October report, and had asked to see the audit. Evoking the awesome power of the U.S. Fed, he stopped just short of a full-scale threat.

"Ryback just said, We demand to see this," recalls the Fed's general counsel, J. Virgil Mattingly, Jr. "He said the Fed finds it completely unacceptable that you are withholding it. He was able to forcefully demand to see the report."[13]

Given the fact that BCCI still operated two large agencies and a representative office in the United States and held hundreds of millions of dollars in assets in U.S. banks, one thing BCCI did not need was an irate and intractable Fed.

Ryback was thus the first American official to glimpse the particulars of the fraud. What jumped at him while he sat in BCCI's plush emerald-carpeted London offices on 101 Leadenhall Street reading the October 1991 audit were more than $1 billion in loans to an entity coded "XYZ Corp." The loans were all secured by stock in XYZ; not a dollar of the loans had ever been repaid. Ryback hastened to Iqbal and, guessing, asked: Was XYZ really First American? Were those loans made to front men? Iqbal told him he was right.

Ryback's feelings about what he saw are revealed in the understated style of a confidential Fed memo dated December 18, 1990, by his associate Thomas McQueeney. "Bill feels that BCCI has been lying to us for years," wrote McQueeney, "and he would like to have Clark Clifford and Robert Altman investigated for their role in withholding this vital information from us. Bill said he . . . would like to go to the board for a divestiture order."[14]

Though Ryback had seen the evidence, he was forced by Iqbal to agree that he would not bring it back home. Nor would the Bank of England, which possessed the audit, let him take a copy back home. Thus began a bitter squabble that would go on for months. Robin Leigh-Pemberton would not let Ryback have it because he knew that Ryback would give it to Morgenthau. And the Bank of England, continuing its delicate negotiations with Zayed, absolutely could not afford to let that happen.

But the Fed would have its own documentation soon enough. In December the Fed's general counsel, the trim, determined, soft-spoken Virgil Mattingly, received a very strange visit in his imposing office at Twenty-first and C streets in Washington, D.C. The caller was Sandy Martin, Sheikh Zayed's American attorney.

Martin had neither been summoned nor prompted in any way, yet on December 21 he walked into Mattingly's office and told Mattingly and Ryback in detail about the shareholder loans through which BCCI exercised hidden control over First American Bank. Recalled Mattingly: "He gave me a list of the shareholders that had been filed in the most recent report. He went through the list name by name and identified people who had loans from BCCI secured by stock in First American. He said 60 percent of the stock of CCAH [Credit and Commerce American Holdings, the holding company that owned First American] was pledged, and that the loans were nonperforming." Mattingly could not believe what he was hearing. "My reaction was shocked, surprised," he said. "This was highly unusual that someone would come in and admit something like this. I mean, a lawyer walks into the general counsel's office at the Federal Reserve Bank and admits this stuff? I told him that BCCI was in violation of the Bank Holding Company Act."[15] For some reason, Martin had voluntarily admitted to his client's felony.

Mattingly met again with Martin in the second week of January 1991. Martin had returned from Abu Dhabi, where he had gotten a privileged look at the most damning set of documents known to exist: the six thousand or so files that Swaleh Naqvi had personally maintained, containing records of the worst and most complex of BCCI's manipulations. He brought back some of these and gave them to Mattingly. For the first time, the Fed had hard evidence of nominee loans.

That same month Mattingly summoned Robert Altman to his office. Altman and his partner Clifford had also just returned from a trip to the increasingly popular oasis of Abu Dhabi. They had gone there to plead with the new owners of the bank for more capital. During all the furor over BCCI, First American's own deepening woes had been overlooked. A disastrous real estate portfolio had driven the Washington bank deeply into the red, and their repeated appeals to BCCI for more money had been ignored or put off. Within a few weeks First American would announce a $180-million loss for the previous year. Now there was more bad news for Altman. Mattingly explained that he had seen evidence that BCCI had acquired the stock of First American. Altman said he had no idea of what Mattingly was talking about. Altman said then, as he had said before in letters to Bill Ryback, that he knew nothing about any shareholder loans to anybody.

That assertion would quickly be proven false. Altman, who was both clever and cool under fire, had made a serious mistake. He had neglected to mention that he and Clark Clifford had received $18 million in BCCI loans to purchase shares of stock in CCAH. He had said nothing about the $10 million in profits the two men had made from the subsequent sale of that stock to another shady BCCI front, Mohammed Hammoud. The contradictory evidence came to Mattingly a few days later, again from the mysterious Sandy Martin, whom he had asked for a complete list of loans to shareholders. When Mattingly received it, in the third week of January, it included some new names. "I remember opening the envelope and looking at it," said Mattingly. "It showed money lent to Clifford and Altman—a lot of money—to buy shares in First American."

Though it was far from the most important evidence they had received, that single piece of news angered Mattingly and the others more than anything else. It triggered an immediate criminal referral to the Justice Department and orders to BCCI and First American to "cease and desist" from any interaction or funds transfers. Once Altman had stepped on the tripwire, the Fed geared up for a full investigation. In March 1991 the Fed dispatched a team of three officials to Abu Dhabi to secure documents.

For years the Bank of England had watched the wild growth of the Pakistani-run bank with rising apprehension. Since the middle 1970s the supervisors at Britain's principal regulator of banks had been frightened by BCCI's staggering rate of growth. In 1978 the Bank of England refused to give BCCI a full banking license—a formality, more or less, but an important one. Despite that, however, BCCI was permitted to grow virtually unsupervised throughout the 1980s in a country famous for its tight enforcement of prudent banking practices. In 1987 the bank had begun to probe BCCI, using the criminal bank's own auditors, but nothing came of its investigation. In their palatial offices in the heart of London's financial district, Bank of England Governor Robin Leigh-Pemberton and Deputy Governor Eddie George had seen the disastrous 1990 Price Waterhouse audit. They had been told point blank that many of BCCI's transactions were "fraudulent and deceitful," and that Price Waterhouse could not determine how far the fraud reached. Yet in the spring of 1990 the Bank of England agreed to a plan to let BCCI move its headquarters from London to Abu Dhabi, and to arrange for Sheikh Zayed to take over the bank. By so doing, the Bank of England had conspired to conceal

BCCI's horrific problems from its depositors and creditors. According to the final report of the Kerry subcommittee:

> By agreement, the Bank of England had in effect entered into a plan with BCCI, Abu Dhabi and Price Waterhouse in which they would keep the true state of affairs at BCCI secret in return for cooperation with one another in trying to avoid a catastrophic multibillion-dollar collapse. From April 1990 forward, the Bank of England had now inadvertently become partner to a cover-up of BCCI's criminality.[16]

Driving all of this was His Highness Sheikh Zayed bin Sultan al-Nahayan, who was adeptly playing carrot-and-stick with the English authorities. The carrot was money, tankerfuls of it, enough money to plug the gaping holes in BCCI's balance sheet and pay off the hapless British depositors. The prospect that this political land mine could be neatly defused with a check from Zayed kept George and Leigh-Pemberton, already deeply embarrassed about the bank's failure to act earlier, timidly hoping it would all go away. It was not difficult to imagine the headlines: DEPOSITORS LOSE EVERYTHING, BANK OF ENGLAND TO BLAME. (Those *were* the headlines later that summer.) So it was in a sort of quiet panic that Bank of England officials had been politely discussing this matter with Zayed's Private Department for some nine months. They even had a plan, something like a $5-billion quid pro quo. Zayed, who had stepped in as the new majority owner in October 1991 and had pumped in $1 billion to shore up losses, would be pumped for more. The pivot of the negotiations, as far as anyone could tell, was the relative embarrassment of both sides: Zayed's loss of face as the owner of the bank and abettor of Abedi, and the Bank of England's genteel, Anglo-Saxon shame at having let BCCI fleece its depositors for so long.

Though it seemed during that late spring of 1991 that nothing was being done about BCCI, there had been a subtle yet critical shift in the thinking down on Threadneedle Street at the Bank of England. Since John Moscow had first learned of the secret October audit, both he and the Fed's Ryback had doggedly pursued both a hard copy of that audit and other documents held by the Bank of England. The speed and resolution with which both were moving suggested that action would soon follow: indictments from Morgenthau and some sort of sweeping action from the Fed. The Bank of England—the only legitimate regulator with immediate leverage over BCCI—stood alone with the terrible evidence (i.e., the Price Waterhouse audit) of how much money had disappeared and how irretrievably bad the situation had become. The political stakes were considerable. BCCI had a formidable presence in the United Kingdom: 25 branches, 120,000 depositors, and $3.2 billion in assets. The central bank had the power to take away BCCI's license and thereby shut it down in the United Kingdom. But that didn't solve the problem of the depositors losing their money, and that did not salvage the Bank of England's reputation. By the very zealousness of their investigations, the Fed and the New York district attorney's office had shaken the Bank of England from its torpor. Now Robin Leigh-Pemberton and Eddie George had to do something.

What they had to do became sharply apparent on June 27. Three months earlier, the British central bank had commissioned yet another, more detailed audit of BCCI by Price Waterhouse. This was supposed to have assisted in the restructuring plan, back in better days when it seemed that Zayed alone could solve the BCCI problem. But the receipt of that audit, which presented in brilliant detail the scale of the fraud, set in motion the events that would quickly and bitterly end the empire of Agha Hasan Abedi.

The document that brought down everything had a curious lineage indeed, coming as it did from the very same prestigious company that had whitewashed BCCI's accounts for years. One of the cornerstones of the fraud was Price Waterhouse. As one of the world's largest accounting firms, it wielded enormous influence, and a clean, or "unqualified," audit from the company meant easy access to credit and capital; it meant the regulators kept their long noses out of your files; it gave depositors confidence. In short, an unqualified Price Waterhouse audit neatly purveyed all a bank needed to survive and prosper. Until the October audit that Bill Ryback traveled to London to see, all audits of BCCI had presented a bank that, while growing very quickly, was otherwise unblemished.

That was, of course, patently false. Anyone who looked critically at the bank's accounts would have known immediately that something was wrong. Just how far BCCI had veered from prudent banking practices was glaringly obvious as far back as 1978. That year the Office of the Comptroller of the Currency (OCC), the largest U.S. regulator of banks, had run its own audit on BCCI, part of a larger audit of Bank of America, which then held 30 percent of BCCI's shares. The conclusions of the audit—which, along with all the other early warning signs of BCCI's condition, was made to disappear by the U.S. government—were stark enough: The bank's explosive growth had created strains on management; the bank had no lending limits, often had no documentation at all supporting its loans, and was whizzing money around the world from affiliate to affiliate and leaving no paper trail. Money was disappearing in "unsecured borrowings" into the International Credit and Investment Company Holdings (ICIC) in the Cayman Islands. Worse than that, the bank's portfolio of bad loans was expanding at an unsettling rate: Bad or questionable loans constituted three and one half times BCCI's capital. One client alone—the Gokal shipping family from Pakistan—had $185 million in loans, or 290 percent of the bank's capital funds. Either of those would have been enough to shut down most banks in America and in Europe, no questions asked. Though this was BCCI in its infancy, its sins were readily apparent to a subordinate bank examiner at the OCC.

That year the bank got a nice, clean bill of health from its two auditors: Ernst & Young, which handled the main European books, and Price Waterhouse, which looked after the Cayman Islands. This use of two firms to account for one company was highly unusual, but this was Abedi's way of ensuring that no one save himself and Swaleh Naqvi would ever view the sprawling entity in its entirety. This arrangement, however, did not last, and in 1986 Ernst & Young resigned the account, believing correctly that it could not conduct a true audit without access to the growing number of accounts in the Cayman Islands.

That left Price Waterhouse as BCCI's sole auditor, and it was Price Waterhouse in the critical years 1987, 1988, and 1989 that delivered unqualified audits of a bank with no capital, a bank whose accounts had become so devious, so grossly manipulated, that even the auditors themselves would later admit that the bank's financial history could never be reconstructed. Yet Price Waterhouse did know that things were amiss, and they knew certainly as early as 1985, if not earlier. That was the year they gave BCCI an "unqualified opinion" while noting that the bank had inadequate loan loss reserves, had no lending limits to individuals, kept little or no current financial information on any of its clients, and made loans without collateral. Even BCCI's own staff did not know the names behind thousands of numbered accounts.[17] Those are the accounting firm's own observations. Though the reason for Price Waterhouse's behavior is still the subject of violent controversy, documentary evidence would later suggest one possible answer: Among its many attempts to curry favor, BCCI made $597,000 in loans to Price Waterhouse from its Barbados office.[18]

In spite of this egregious track record, in early 1991 the Bank of England hired Price Waterhouse to run an "independent" audit of BCCI. As though to expiate for past sins, PW actually *did* an independent audit, one that revealed what the accounting firm itself called "one of the most complex deceptions in banking history."[19] That audit, delivered in June 1991, contains the best analysis to date of how BCCI devised and executed the multibillion-dollar fraud. After what insiders estimate was eight full years of rendering bogus accounts, Price Waterhouse had finally delivered something akin to a real version of the bank, as surreal as it may have looked to the outside world.[20] Still missing were "accountings" of BCCI's other businesses, including weapons, drugs, mercenary armies, and a variety of commodities. Though immensely profitable and funded directly with depositors' money, these would never turn up on any audit.

The June 1991 audit revealed with brutal clarity what had become of Abedi's sweeping vision of the transnational Third World bank. BCCI had been built from oil, from the enormous wealth that flowed into the Middle East after the huge OPEC oil price increases of the 1970s. But this fantastic engine of growth, one that led Abedi and many others to believe that BCCI could become the largest and most powerful bank in the world, soon began to sputter. In 1979, during the days of BCCI's glorious ascendancy, OPEC produced 31 million barrels of oil a day. By 1983 a collapse in demand dropped that production rate to a mere 18 million barrels a day—a 43-percent decrease.[21]

The great windfall was over. But it was worse than that, because the OPEC countries, upon which BCCI depended for most of its deposits, had been spending as though it would never end. Saudi Arabia is a prime example. From a high of $119 billion in earnings in 1981, the kingdom's revenues had gone into free-fall: By 1984 they had fallen to $36 billion, by 1985 to $26 billion. The country's development program was cut back sharply, and the world's richest oil barony even started to run large budget deficits.[22] The same held true for Abu Dhabi and the United Arab Emirates, the once-golden and ever-renewable source of Agha Hasan Abedi's working capital.

This was the first shattering blow against the empire. Deposits were the lifeblood of the bank, and for its grand deception to function properly BCCI needed an ever-fresh stream of new money. A Ponzi scheme, in which new money is used to cover old losses, crashes the minute the funds stop flowing. The second was the bank's massive exposure to Gulf Shipping and Trading and its affiliates, the global shipping giant run by Abedi's close cronies the Gokal brothers, Mustafa, Abbas, and Murtaza, who had used BCCI money to build one of the world's great shipping empires. In their late-1970s heyday, the Gokals chartered more ships in one year than did the countries of China and India combined. By the late 1970s a recession in the shipping industry, nearly as bad as the later recession in the oil business, plus a series of bad investments in other businesses, had made it impossible for the Gokals to repay their loans, which topped out at $831 million in 1990. The third blow was an estimated $1 billion in losses incurred between 1977 and 1985 in the bank's treasury operations—the result of wildly imprudent commodities trading and outright theft.

What the auditors found in early 1991 was the wreckage left by the extensive and duplicitous efforts to cover up those losses, to make BCCI appear to be something that it was not. At the core of the deception were some six thousand secret accounts kept personally by former Chief Executive Officer Swaleh Naqvi. So far as anyone knows, the only real reconciliation of BCCI's unreconstructible accounts took place in Naqvi's head. (Abedi, it is said, wasn't particularly good with numbers.) Unless Western law enforcement is able to pull him in—he now languishes in Abu Dhabi under house arrest, at the mercy of Zayed—it is unlikely that the full story will ever be known.

But the audit provides at least a road map. As the auditors themselves said, all is unreal. The bank's capital, for example. Though BCCI started out with a very little bit of real capital from Zayed and Bank of America, much of the later capital on which the bank was built (the capital base, which includes monies from sale of stock plus the accumulated earnings of the company, had risen from $2.5 million in 1972 to $845 million at the end of 1990) was, concluded Price Waterhouse, illusory. The logic, and the method, relied on an ingenious circularity. When Abedi needed new capital funds, he would create and sell stock, usually to one of his prominent Middle Eastern nominees like Kamal Adham or A. R. Khalil, top-ranking men in Saudi intelligence, or Ghaith Pharaon, who among them had more than half a billion dollars in such loans. (Pharaon by himself had $288 million, down from a high of nearly $500 million in the mid-1980s.) The money to buy that stock would be given to the nominees in the form of a loan from one of BCCI's secretive Caymanian affiliates. BCCI would then hold its own stock as collateral for the loan, which never had to be repaid.

The result was a bank made larger by the amount of the loans, and new capital out of thin air. The audit estimated that at least 55 percent of BCCI's stock had been sold in this way, and investigators have suggested a far higher amount.[23] This was also one of the mechanisms by which Abedi, who nominally did not own any shares in the company, actually controlled BCCI and owned it outright. The shares of stock never left his vaults. And when Abedi needed additional capital to absorb losses from fraud or from operations, he simply pumped up BCCI's own stock price by making more loans to the fronts to buy stock. The same basic set of front men were used by BCCI to secretly purchase First American Bank, and the movement of shares was similarly circular. The audit revealed that the fronts had been paid $47 million for their roles as nominee stockholders. Add to all this the probability, according to the audit, that the bank itself had never been profitable, and it would seem as though Jack Blum's seemingly incredible assertion back in February that BCCI was "a bank without capital" was true after all. The effect of the loss of $1 billion in securities trading was, oddly, to wipe out the bank's false capital, a very strange turn of events that led to manipulation of accounts whose very goal was to restore money that had not existed in the first place, layering one fiction on top of another.

From fake capital we move organically to fake deposits and fake loans. Buried in Naqvi's esoterica were $600 million in "unrecorded deposits." That is, depositors had actually put real money into the bank, but the bank had not accounted for it. It could therefore be used as ready capital to plug holes or as instant cash, disguised as a transfer from a BCCI affiliate, run in through ICIC and out the other side again. These unbooked deposits helped fill the enormous hole created by BCCI's treasury losses. The important thing was that they could be anything Naqvi and Abedi wanted them to be.

There was also the curious case of BCCI's "Islamic banking unit." Islamic banking, as purveyed by BCCI, was nothing more than a sham accounting trick that sidestepped the Koran's interdiction of usury. A strict Muslim was allowed neither to pay nor to charge interest. Instead, Islam enjoined its followers to make equity, or ownership investments, on which they could earn a fair return as the enterprise prospered. So instead of taking a "deposit" and paying interest on it—though that is precisely what it was doing—BCCI's Islamic banking unit invented a fiction called a *"murabaha"* transaction that would allow depositors to convince themselves that the money they earned came not from "interest" but from the profits of an enterprise. The fiction was created by buying commodities—real, tangible goods as opposed to the abstractions of banking—and then selling them for a profit. In fact, it was nothing more than a trick, a simultaneous, offsetting purchase of commodities, creating artificial "proceeds" of that sale that were remitted to depositors. To all appearances the client was not "depositing" money, he was investing it. And the "interest" he received masqueraded as profit on his investment. This was enormously popular with the stricter Islamic banks in the Middle East. But it turns out that these funds, too, vanished off the balance sheets and into Naqvi's secret books as unrecorded deposits. In the case of the Faisal Islamic Bank of Egypt, $358 million disappeared this way.

There were also billions of dollars in false loans, which were the most common method BCCI used to cover losses. Two good examples were $168 million to A. R. Khalil, and $121 million to Sheikh Mohammed bin Rashid al-Maktoum of the ruling family of Dubai in the United Arab Emirates. The way these were used illustrates perhaps the most common mechanism of fraud. To take just one example, the Gokals were unable to pay even the interest on their $831 million in outstanding loans. This created a problem for BCCI, because to write off those loans would have wiped out both its real and illusory capital. So the illusion had to be created that the loans were performing, a sleight of hand Abedi had begun practicing as early as 1978. BCCI would book a loan to Maktoum or Khalil without their knowledge or consent. The loan would then travel out of BCCI's main office to a branch or affiliate somewhere in the bank's global system. There the ingenious "routing" system took over. Routing was the bank's internal money laundry, a method of concealing the true origin and nature of funds washing through its accounts. Favored routing vehicles were Banque de Commerce et de Placements, a BCCI subsidiary in Switzerland, the Kuwait International Finance Company (KIFCO), owned by the same fronts that owned First American, and the National Bank of Oman, in which BCCI held a large stake. Naqvi's office was the source of all routing instructions, which would typically involve transferring the fake loan proceeds to one of the routing vehicles, which would then remit funds through the system, disguising them to look like interest payments on the nonperforming loans to the Gokals or any one of hundreds of others. The "special duties account" through which these funds ran held an average daily balance of $1.6 billion of such money at its peak in 1986.[24]

The worst of the account manipulation surrounded the bank's worst loans, according to the audit, and almost all of that manipulation was booked through ICIC, in its impenetrable haven of the Cayman Islands.

Agha Hasan Abedi and Swaleh Naqvi had discovered the Caymans back in the middle 1970s. By 1976 they had set up an offshore system that cloaked them in a virtually impenetrable veil of secrecy, both in their movements of money inside the bank and in the ownership of BCCI and its subsidiaries. That was the year they incorporated ICIC (Overseas), which consisted of three Caymanian entities—the BCC Foundation, the ICIC Staff Benefit Trust, and ICIC Business Promotions—and which owned some 41 percent of BCCI itself. It was here, within the untraceable labyrinth of shares and accounts, that the dirtiest of BCCI's financial dealings took place.

The sunny, paradisaical Cayman Islands are at once a shining example of what is wrong with the world of finance and the reason no one wants to do anything about it. Beneath the veneer of respectability carefully polished by the big banks with offices there, the islands thrive on three principal commodities: money evading taxes, money from drug sales and other criminal activities, and illegal capital-flight money zooming out of the Third World. The tax games played so aggressively by the world's largest corporations needed a playing field, and if places like the Caymans, Monaco, Liechtenstein, the isles of Jersey and Man, Panama, and Andorra did not exist, one could argue that they would have to be invented to accommodate a very certain need. The criminal element simply slid in comfortably behind the reputable corporations and used the same mechanisms for their own ends. In turning to the Caymans for secrecy, Abedi and Naqvi were merely mimicking what their larger and more respectable First World brethren had been doing for more than a decade. By 1991 the tiny island of Grand Cayman contained 550 banks and trusts and $400 billion in "offshore" deposits, making it the number-one offshore financial center in the world. Forty-six of the world's fifty largest banks had Caymanian licenses. In all, 22,000 companies are registered in the islands, engaged in everything from shipping and trading to insurance, finance, and real estate.[25]

The Cayman Islands are a tax haven of the first order. There is no personal or corporate income tax, no inheritance or estate tax, and no tax disclosure treaty with the United States. And the Caymans' severe secrecy laws effectively prevent any tax or law enforcement authorities from prying into accounts. "When the IRS comes around, all you have to do is show them the wire transfer of your funds from the United States to the Caymans," sniffed a Florida tax attorney. "That's pretty much the end of the line for taxes, because the money can't be touched by the IRS."[26] The elaborate system of secrecy is maintained and enforced by something called the Caymans Protection Board, which controls citizenship, visas, and work permits. This is critical, since most of the accountants, lawyers, judges, and police are not Caymanians and need work permits to continue making money in paradise. Planes regularly come and go carrying cash from Latin America, and boats, over which there is no control at all, can come and go as they please.

To understand how the Caymans work, you have to understand the miraculously artificial banking concept called "booking." Booking is a spatial concept, having to do with the actual "location" of money. Let us say a bank in the United States makes a credit card loan in the state of New York. For tax or other reasons, the bank decides to "book"—or locate—the loan in North Dakota. This is done by a stroke of the pen. The bank simply decides that that is where the loan will be. The same can be done with deposits, and the concept can be just as easily transferred offshore. It was, and is, that simple. Most large banks have similar arrangements. Of the 548 registered banks in the Cayman Islands, only 68 have actual offices and staff there. Booking is a fiction, as were Eurodollars and most offshore branches.

To bring this spatial-monetary conundrum closer to home, imagine that you are on the road, several thousand miles from home. You need cash, so you venture down to the local bank, which happens to be linked into the computerized Cirrus system, and withdraw your cash from an automated teller machine (ATM). Consider for a moment the location of your money. Normally, you might think of it as "sitting" in an account at your hometown bank in, say, Portland, Oregon. Yet you just pulled $200 out of a machine in Waquoit, Massachusetts, so that is where your money must be too. Your money is everywhere and nowhere; or, more precisely, your money—really nothing more than a metaphysical beep on the general ledger of the banking system—is exactly where the system says it is. Which could just as easily be Grand Cayman Island as Waquoit.

Though the Caymans were merely a bookkeeping device used by men who sat at desks in London, the accounts booked there remained invisible to European authorities. ICIC constituted a bank within the larger bank and was by far the largest of the rabbit holes down which funds vanished.

All of which raises a persistent question: Who actually performed the manipulations? The Price Waterhouse audit suggests part of the answer. First, they were almost all Pakistani employees in a bank in which Pakistanis were a small minority. Second, though Price Waterhouse blacked out the names of the individuals in the audits it finally released to investigators, their job descriptions remain, and they reveal much about what the core London executive staff did for a living. Twenty-one people were charged, variously, with the following duties: setting up nominee shareholdings; false confirmation of audit requests; false loan accounting; secret side agreements with shareholders; routing of funds to avoid detection of source and origin; creating fictitious loans to cover up misappropriated funds; rerouting deposits through ICIC; misappropriation of depositors' funds without depositors' knowledge; creation of loans with "no commercial substance" in the names of people without their knowledge.[27] Together with what former BCCI employees have called a network of "one hundred entrepreneurs" who worked smaller frauds at BCCI branches around the world and assisted in "routing" actions, and Abedi and Naqvi themselves, an approximate estimate of how many were involved in significant criminal activity comes to something like 140 people.

What is perhaps most striking about the fraud is the utter chaos of it all. BCCI had no central computer system to keep track of its $20 billion–plus in assets. Its accounting system was ancient, and most of the ledgers investigators have seen are handwritten. In the more corrupt branches, managers literally kept little black books in which they would record, as Naqvi did with the larger accounts, account manipulations, falsified routings of funds, and off-books deposits and loans. Many of the books were kept in the Urdu language. Indeed, one way that so much money disappeared was that it simply was not recorded.

One BCCI officer who worked in the bank's Paris branch recalled how money would routinely disappear out of BCCI's African offices, in this case, in Gabon. "A lot of it is in how they kept the books," he says. "The Libreville office borrows from BCCI's Paris office twenty-five million dollars. They then make a loan to their borrower. Libreville books the profits from the interest on their loans but does not book the expense of paying interest to Paris." Thus, Paris books profits, and Gabon books profits, and the expense, or loss, never shows up anywhere. This was multiplied exponentially on a global scale, and explains why much of the bank's profits were fictitious.[28] What is frightening about BCCI, despite its vast global manipulations, is the probability that it could have continued its fraudulent ways for many years if petrodollars had continued to flow into its vaults.

On June 28 Robin Leigh-Pemberton and Eddie George decided to act. The baleful revelations in the Price Waterhouse audit and the certainty that Morgenthau and the Fed would take action had left them no choice. That day the Bank of England officially informed the Federal Reserve Bank of the impending seizure of BCCI in the United Kingdom. The next day William Taylor and other Fed officials flew to London, where they met with the Bank of England and regulators from Luxembourg and the Cayman Islands, and put in place the plans that would destroy Abedi's bank.

The global regulatory action they took on July 5 finally unleashed the Furies against BCCI. With BCCI bursting into headlines all over the world, *Time* was even more anxious to get the cover story that Beaty and Gwynne were trying desperately and under enormous pressure to pull together. They finally delivered it in mid-July, and *Time* magazine was soon on the newsstands with a cover story entitled "The World's Sleaziest Bank." The subtitle spelled out just how far Beaty and Gwynne—and *Time*'s editors—had traveled in their understanding of BCCI: "Exclusive: How BCCI became a one-stop shopping center for criminals and spies—and how the U.S. is trying to cover up its involvement." Until then, no one had suggested that BCCI was more than a financial scandal, albeit one spiced with allegations of drug-money laundering and the famous names of some of the bank's clients. And *Time* had not accused the government of a cover-up in any major story since Watergate.

The story began with what Beaty and Gwynne believed was a necessary redefinition of the bank:

> BCCI is more than just a criminal bank. From interviews with sources close to BCCI, *Time* has pieced together a portrait of a clandestine division of the bank called the Black Network, which functions as a global intelligence operation and a mafia-like enforcement squad. Operating primarily out of the bank's offices in Karachi, Pakistan, the 1,500-employee Black Network has used sophisticated spy equipment and techniques, along with bribery, extortion, kidnapping and even, by some accounts, murder. The Black Network—so named by its members—stops at almost nothing to further the bank's aims the world over. . . . The strange and still murky ties between BCCI and the intelligence agencies of several countries are so pervasive that even the White House has become entangled. As *Time* reported earlier this month, the National Security Council has used BCCI to funnel money for the Iran-Contra deals, and the CIA maintained accounts in BCCI for

covert operations. Moreover, investigators have told *Time* that the Defense Intelligence Agency has maintained a slush-fund account with BCCI, apparently to pay for clandestine activities. . . .

The story also blamed the federal government for hindering the investigation:

> In the U.S. investigators now say openly that the Justice Department has not only reined in its own probe of the bank but is also part of a concerted campaign to derail any full investigation. Says Robert Morgenthau: "We have had no cooperation from the Justice Department since we first asked for records in March 1990. In fact, they are impeding our investigation, and Justice Department representatives are asking witnesses not to cooperate with us."

Beaty and Gwynne offered for the first time the notion that the failure of the Justice Department to act might have been a result of BCCI's links to U.S. intelligence:

> The bribes and intelligence connections may offer an explanation for the startling regulatory inaction. The Justice Department has hindered an investigation by Massachusetts Senator John Kerry, whose Subcommittee on Terrorism, Narcotics and International Operations was the first to probe BCCI's illegal operations. According to Kerry, the Justice Department has refused to provide documents and has blocked a deposition by a key witness, citing interference with its own investigation of BCCI. To date, however, the Justice Department investigation in Washington has issued only one subpoena. "We have had a lot of difficulty getting any answers at all out of Justice," said Kerry. "We've been shuffled back and forth so many times between bureaus, trying to find somebody who was accountable. These things are very serious."

In the face of vigorous government denials, Beaty and Gwynne also quoted Blum for the first time in the magazine:

> According to Jack Blum, Kerry's chief investigator in 1988–89, the lack of cooperation was so pervasive and so successful in frustrating his efforts to investigate BCCI that he now says he believes it was part of a deliberate strategy. Says Blum: "There's

no question in my mind that it's a calculated effort inside the
federal government to limit the investigation. The only issue is
whether it's a result of high-level corruption or if it's designed to
hide illegal government activities."

Beaty's and Gwynne's sources had clearly moved the BCCI story
forward in July. They had indeed redefined the bank for the rest of the
world. But the implications of that redefinition were almost frightening. BCCI had been seized and shut almost everywhere. But what
these sources had told the *Time* reporters suggested massive corruption that had taken place well outside the scope of ordinary banking.
It all suggested that, far from ending, the real BCCI story—the story
of the bank that could get you anything—had just begun.

That same week the rest of the global media finally cranked up. The
Time story helped create a firestorm in the press that boosted the
BCCI story out of the business sections of newspapers and magazines
and onto the front page. The revelations about the Black Network
were picked up by the media around the world. So too were the
allegations that the CIA was linked to BCCI and that BCCI had
played a role in the Iran-Contra machinations.

The same day *Time*'s story broke, *The Guardian*, a respected British newspaper, carried a detailed story describing a link between
BCCI and the notorious terrorist Abu Nidal. According to *The Guardian*'s sources, the Nidal group had long used a London branch of BCCI
to move the money it used to mount attacks on Western targets, and
MI5—the English equivalent of the CIA—had known about the accounts. There seemed to be no doubt that the BCCI bankers knew
exactly who they were dealing with: One of the bankers at the London
branch described how anxious they had been to provide every service
to the terrorists in order to keep their multimillion-dollar accounts.

The CIA, which rarely responds to any allegation, immediately
issued a flat denial of *Time* magazine's description of the ties between
the agency and BCCI. The denial was a strategic mistake. Within days
British newspapers reported that the CIA had maintained accounts in
BCCI's London offices to pay scores of English citizens who were
providing information to the American intelligence agency. And the
London *Financial Times* supported *Time*'s contention that the CIA
had used BCCI in Pakistan by reporting that Pakistan's finance minister had confirmed that the CIA used BCCI branches in Pakistan to
channel money for covert operations involving the support of the
Afghan rebels.

The *Financial Times* story also raised the stakes: The finance minister, the paper reported, had also said that the CIA, and other American intelligence agencies, had maintained slush funds at BCCI branches and that these funds were used for payoffs of Pakistani military officers and Afghan rebel leaders.

The CIA issued a curtly worded statement saying they would investigate the allegations. Meanwhile, Acting CIA Director Richard Kerr appeared before a group of high-school students and admitted for the first time that BCCI did in fact hold CIA accounts. With no one to ask hostile questions, Kerr asserted that these were normal accounts, the sort of accounts the CIA maintained for its global operations. After denying it for months, the agency had found what it thought was a graceful, quiet way of letting the cat out of the bag.

But the real free-for-all came with the Justice Department. Beaty and Gwynne's previous stories had tagged Justice for foot-dragging, but there are no words to spare in a *Time* magazine article, and only a few sentences delivered that message. Now the charge was blazoned across the cover of the magazine. The day after it appeared, Attorney General Richard Thornburgh dispatched the head of his criminal division, Assistant Attorney General Robert Mueller, to ABC's *Nightline* show, hosted by Ted Koppel, to refute *Time*'s charges. It would prove a tactical mistake.

Koppel invited Beaty, Gwynne, Jack Blum, and Senator John Kerry to appear on the same show. Television, which had previously provided little more than sound-bite coverage of Clark Clifford's involvement, was now about to play a major role.

Koppel opened with a detailed background report, then shifted to live coverage in Washington, where Mueller, Kerry, and Beaty sat in the ABC studio. Beaty remained mute as Kerry and Mueller dueled politely over whether the plea bargain with BCCI in the Tampa money-laundering case was a giveaway. Mueller insisted that the Justice Department had won a major victory. He also disputed any charges that his department had not proceeded vigorously with further investigations, and he ignored Senator Kerry's attempt to bring up the subject of the missing tapes of Blum's interviews with the former BCCI bankers who talked about political payoffs and BCCI's secret ownership of First American. When Koppel tried to point out that the assistant attorney general had not answered the senator's question about the missing tapes, Mueller ignored him too and bragged that BCCI's offices in Florida had been shut down as a result of information the Justice Department provided the Florida banking regulators.

Kerry was beginning to sputter, and Beaty, outraged enough at

Mueller's deceptive tactics to forget that he was on national television, jumped in. "But Mr. Mueller—I'm sorry, but the senator is quite accurate. You may have provided the reason for shutting down the bank by convicting it of money laundering, but then a very high-level person in your own department turned around and asked the State of Florida to keep this bank open, despite the fact that your own prosecutors had testified that drug-money laundering was a policy of the bank and that it wasn't a matter of employees taking some kind of independent action. When you plea-bargained out, you let the bank go and took the low-level employees, which is kind of in reverse."

Mueller came back strongly. "I disagree—I adamantly disagree with that . . . and secondly, there was an exchange of letters between Justice Department personnel and personnel in the Florida regulatory agency. And what was told the agency was that if they made a determination that BCCI was to stay open, we wished them to monitor certain accounts of narco-traffickers so that we could review those records and seize those—"

"I'm sorry, sir," Beaty said, "but that letter did not mention narco-traffickers at all."

"Have you read—"

"In fact," Beaty added, "it was one of the most bizarre letters that many of us have seen."

Koppel, realizing the television audience had no idea what they were talking about, broke it up and turned to *Time*'s charges that U.S. intelligence agencies employed BCCI as a means of funding covert operations and asked if that might have had something to do with the Justice Department's limited response to evidence.

"That is absolutely incorrect . . . there is just no truth to the allegation and unsupported allegation that the intelligence community is in any way trying to shape or stop this investigation," Mueller stated.

"Well, let me—" Koppel began.

"Mr. Mueller," Beaty cut back in, "we haven't made the accusation that this has been shaped by the intelligence community. All we have tried to do is point out the rather stunning lack of curiosity and aggression on the part of the Justice Department."

"I take—well—" Mueller began.

"And I can cite you, sir, numerous occasions when witnesses have come forward and been ignored by you. The very tapes that Senator Kerry has referred to, of witnesses talking about the link between First American Bank and BCCI and of payments to American officials, disappeared. Those tapes had been listened to by U.S. attorneys from your own office."

"Mr. Beaty, no tapes have disappeared," Mueller replied.

"Two months ago you denied to Mr. Morgenthau and his department that those tapes even existed!" Beaty shot back.

"Mr. Beaty, no tapes have disappeared," Mueller repeated. "Any allegations or evidence that have been provided to us either by you— and you have provided information and sources to us—or by Senator Kerry or any other source has been looked at and is being pursued, has been pursued, or will be pursued in the future."

The show ended as Koppel tried, unsuccessfully, to pin down Mueller on just what tapes were being referred to. Beaty's mind was racing too fast for him to want back into the now confusing exchange. Mueller's last statement to him was awesome in its implications: Beaty had not brought either information or sources to the Justice Department. To Morgenthau, yes. To Justice, no. It could only mean, it seemed, that the CIA had passed on his notes of his interview with Sami Masri to Mueller at Justice. The Casablanca transcript, it seemed, was now taking its place with the "missing" Mirza memo.

The global seizure of BCCI was merely the opening salvo in what was quickly becoming a concerted regulatory campaign against the bank. The Justice Department, as usual, was nowhere to be found, but on July 29 Morgenthau announced indictments against BCCI and its former top officers, Abedi and Naqvi, describing the case as "the largest bank fraud in world financial history." In doing so, he sent the first clear message that he was going to finish what the seizure had started. He was going after the individuals who had perpetrated the fraud, and no amount of foot-dragging, lack of cooperation, or outright hindrance of the investigation by the Justice Department or any other U.S. government agency was going to forestall it. In the truest sense, Morgenthau stood alone on that day among world law enforcement as the only one who had dared take on BCCI.

That same day the Federal Reserve initiated a massive civil action against the bank. It fined BCCI an unprecedented $200 million and moved to ban its key front men from banking in the United States. Those fronts, said the Fed, had been involved in secret deals that included phony loans to purchase shares in three U.S. banks: First American, National Bank of Georgia, and CenTrust Savings Bank of Miami. They included Ghaith Pharaon, Kamal Adham, A. R. Khalil, and Faisal Saud al-Fulaij, the former chairman of Kuwait Airways. The Fed had thus severely chastised some of the most powerful men in the Middle East. Their action merely hinted at the scope of the scandal that was to unfold in the following months.

PART TWO

THE RISE OF
THE OUTLAW BANK

CHAPTER 7

OUT OF THE BLUE

"You have seen how their greatness dawned by the Call, their Call spread by religion, their religion became mighty by prophecy, their prophecy conquered by Holy Law, their Holy Law was buttressed by the Caliphate, their Caliphate prospered by religious and worldly policy."

—ABU HAYYAN AT-TAWHIDI, "KITAB AL-IMTA WA'L-MU'ANSA"

The tiny Cessna two-seater came out of the eastern skies and made landfall near the desert town of Abu Dhabi. It was a small aircraft to have come from the east, which meant that it had come from across the Persian Gulf, from out of the Iranian desert. Other than the pilot, who had been reluctantly recruited for the mission, its cargo consisted of one neatly dressed Pakistani banker with immaculate black hair swept up and back from his prominent forehead. His name was Agha Hasan Abedi. He carried several ornate Pathan rugs. It was 1965 and this was Abedi's first trip to the British-controlled Trucial Coast, a hodgepodge of tribal baronies on the northern border of Saudi Arabia best known to history for their exploits as pirates and slave traders. He had come with the implausible notion of paying an impromptu call on the emir, and of presenting the rugs as gifts of goodwill. Abedi was president of a Pakistani bank, one that he had started eight years before and had built into the country's third largest. Now, like a traveling salesman rolling into a Kansas prairie town, he was hunting new business. Though no one could have known it then, the *chug-chug-chug* of Abedi's plane was the sound of the future arriving in Abu Dhabi.

He had chosen one of the oddest places on earth—East or West—to go looking for a new client. Abu Dhabi in those days boasted barely two dozen buildings of any substance. Most of the streets were unpaved, most of its dwellings barely more than shanties. Surmounting the town was the ancient stone palace of the emir, a Bedouin prince named Shakhbut bin Sultan al-Nahayan. What made this feudal kingdom such an odd place in 1965 was that it stood poised on the brink of unimaginable wealth. Oil had been discovered in the Gulf waters just off the coast of Abu Dhabi in 1959. It had been a major strike, reminiscent of the first finds in Kuwait and Saudi Arabia twenty years before. A second strike on land followed in 1960, and the money had just started to flow in the mid-1960s. In spite of the town's flyblown appearance, it was already clear that Abu Dhabi was going to be immensely rich; just how rich no one could have guessed then.

Odder still were Shakhbut's ideas about money. He knew that banks existed, but he could not have described how one worked nor why anyone would want to give a bank his money. He had no personal experience that would help him to understand the financial concepts of interest, deposit taking, or check writing. Wealth, as he understood it, was measured in camels, weapons, tents, and rugs. So Shakhbut kept his sack of money, which had begun to grow exponentially fatter with new oil revenues, under his bed where he could see it, feel it, and comfort himself that he was becoming a rich man. He was broken of this habit only when the rats and mice of the royal household began to eat his horde of cash.[1] Though this convinced him to have the cash hauled over to the vault of the newly established British Bank of the Middle East, he was in the habit of summoning the startled and bleary-eyed bank manager in the middle of the night and requesting to see it.[2] Though the banking system in Abedi's Pakistan was archaic by modern standards, it was still several hundred years ahead of the Bedouin notions of finance in Abu Dhabi.

Abedi presented himself at court and was given an audience with the emir, who promptly and coldly rejected the Pakistani's offer of banking services. Abedi returned empty-handed to Karachi. But he had no intention of giving up this splendid idea of opening up the oil-rich Gulf. Within a year the roughhouse politics of Abu Dhabi would open that door again. Though the al-Nahayans were ignorant of the complexities of Western finance, they were smart enough to see that Shakhbut was not the man to grapple with the stunning changes that were already rumbling through the tiny sheikhdom. In 1966 the ruling family, led by Shakhbut's younger brother Zayed bin Sultan al-Nahayan, deposed and exiled the emir, and Zayed ascended the throne.

Though his ideas were considerably less medieval than Shakhbut's, Zayed's background as a tribal chieftain still had more in common with the Arabia of the Middle Ages than with the Western world of the Twentieth Century. He was the product of a primitive and violent life. Eight of Abu Dhabi's prior fifteen rulers had been murdered, and five had been driven out. Only two had died without violence while still in power.[3] By any historical measure, Shakhbut was lucky.

Perhaps the best account of Zayed's early life was written by the explorer Wilfred Thesiger, who spent several months with him in the late 1940s. Thesiger writes that Zayed was "a powerfully built man of about thirty with a brown beard" and describes him sitting on the bare sand next to his rifle, wearing a Bedouin smock, a dagger, and a cartridge belt. He lived in a mud fort with walls ten feet high and on behalf of his brother supervised six small villages in the oasis of Buraimi, near what is today the border of Abu Dhabi and Saudi Arabia. Zayed's chief preoccupation throughout most of his life was the *ghazzu*, or Bedouin raid, the object of which was to secure either territory or camels, usually the latter. According to Thesiger, Zayed could ride, shoot, and fight and "had a great reputation with the Bedouin."

Zayed's passion, which he shared with many other Gulf princelings, was falconing. The sport consisted of setting trained peregrine falcons upon the relatively helpless houbara (known to the West as MacQueen's bustard), a bird the size of a hen turkey that half flies and half runs from the winter wastes of Iran and Iraq to the warmer and more pleasant wastes of the Persian Gulf. Zayed was happiest when he was falconing, camped with a small band of armed retainers in the primitive desert with slaughtered goats and cauldrons of rice cooking on the wood fires, boys fighting over a raw camel's liver, salted and dripping with blood, and the brass coffee mortar ringing the call to supper.

Before oil was struck, the tribes of the Trucial Coast scratched out a meager living from fishing, some primitive farming, and pastoralism. It was a hardscrabble existence to begin with, and life had become progressively harder as traditional businesses dried up. Piracy and slave trading had died out before the turn of the century, and even the once-thriving pearl trade evaporated in the 1930s. Zayed had spent his life as a prince of a tiny corner of a small oasis in a destitute country. He was not modern in any sense of the word. He knew nothing about money, banking, business, or trading. He had never traveled outside of his country.

While little else had changed, there was no ignoring the prodigious oil strikes on land controlled by the emir. And it was both the smell of oil and the prospect that Zayed would be more open-minded than his brother that brought Abedi to make a second dangerous pilgrimage across the Persian Gulf from his comfortable home in Karachi. He landed on a runway in view of the palace, and made his way through the buzzing crowd of fortune seekers, sycophants, and opportunists that in the middle 1960s had already begun to gather outside the palace walls. He presented the Pathan rugs and introduced himself as a banker and a Muslim from the Third World who understood the ways of Western money. He introduced himself as a man the sheikh would find useful. The sheikh would soon find him very, very useful.

This nattily dressed man with flashing black eyes and big ideas about the future of oil was more than just an aggressive Pakistani banker or an innovative financier. Abedi was always larger than that, in part because he saw his life and destiny in sweeping historical and religious terms. When in later years he delivered his mesmerizing speeches promising the empowerment of the Third World and the return of Islam to the glorious days of Muhammad and the caliphs of the Seventh Century, he was speaking from his own experience of the world. Abedi was the product of the cataclysmic forces that played upon the Indian subcontinent for more than one hundred years before he arrived, rugs in hand, to buttonhole a Stone Age sheikh in Abu Dhabi. What he did then and later was deeply rooted in the history and origins of Islam and Pakistan, and cannot be fully explained without a backward look at his own twisted cultural lineage.

The story of Agha Hasan Abedi begins sixty-five years before his birth in the town of Mahmudabad, in the glittering Muslim kingdom of Oudh in north-central India. Oudh was one of the most powerful kingdoms in the Moghul Empire, which had ruled large sections of India since the Seventeenth Century. The Moghuls were Muslims, a small but powerful minority group in an otherwise Hindu and Parsee India. In the early part of the Nineteenth Century, the British conquest of India had encroached most violently against this group, and in 1857 the Muslims of north-central India—including those under the rule of the rajah of Mahmudabad—made one last bloody attempt to reclaim the power and influence they had lost. The insurrection, which became known to every British schoolchild as the Great Mutiny (though its Islamic participants still call it the War of Independence),[4] was brutally suppressed by the British, thus shattering completely the political power of the kingdoms of the old Moghul raj. More than a million died in religious riots.

One of the victims of this vast paroxysm of Muslim violence was Agha Hasan Abedi's great-grandfather. He had been a courtier to the rajah of Mahmudabad, part of a class of well-educated, Urdu-speaking senior and petty bureaucrats who managed the rulers' estates and took care of the details of official business. For his participation in the mutiny and disloyalty to the British raj, Abedi's forebear was hanged in a cage in the streets of Lucknow to serve as an example to the rest of the insurgents.[5]

By the time of Abedi's birth in that same city in 1922, the remnants of the powerful Islamic kingdoms had fallen into a long and gentle decline. Stripped of most of their political power by the British, and isolated in a sea of Hindi culture, the rajahs were nonetheless tolerated to manage their lands, collect their taxes, and operate as satraps in the British Empire. And Abedi's family continued to do what it had done for generations: serve the rajahs of Mahmudabad as administrators, revenue officers, and private secretaries. In 1922 the decadent princely state of Mahmudabad was still one of the largest and richest in northern India, and despite the ravages of the mutiny, its rulers could still trace their lineage back to the grand and powerful Moghuls of the Seventeenth Century. From a golden throne in a vaulted palace, the rajahs collected more than a million dollars a year from 530 villages and uncounted thousands of hamlets.[6]

Though Abedi's father and grandfather had never risen to the rank of senior advisers to the rajahs, they were considered to be among the inner circle of confidants.[7] As such, they had both solid, respectable middle-class status and a view into the shimmering luxury of the rajahs' lives. Though accounts of Abedi's father's profession vary— from chef to the rajahs to tax collector to farm manager—perhaps due to Abedi's own revisionist accounts of his birth, he was clearly a well-established courtier at the palace in Mahmudabad.

It was in this culture that Agha Hasan Abedi lived until he was in his early twenties. As a child he had listened to tales of baroque luxuries, of the glory days of the Moghul raj, and of the bloody struggle against the British conquest. He also grew up intensely aware of his status as a double minority. Not only was Abedi a Muslim (Muslims made up only 20 percent of the population of north-central India), but he was also a Shiite Muslim, and in all of British-ruled India, Shiites accounted for only 15 percent of Muslims. The Shia are to Islam what puritanical fundamentalists are to mainstream Christianity—a minority sect known for its "obsessive attention to work, politics, and religion."[8] In contrast to the more dispassionate and detached Sunni Muslims, the Shiites are passionately demonstrative and are fond of putting on elaborate shows of penance and mourning. Shiites have a mystical bent as well, reflected in their devotion to martyrdom, belief in saints, and worship at the tombs of holy men. Shia Islam is more political as well, as in Khomeini's revolutionary Iran. Abedi's family were intensely religious, teetotaling Shiites, who dutifully observed all Islamic rites. Islam pervaded, and would continue to pervade, every corner of Abedi's life.[9]

None of this early life was lost on him. Abedi's experiences as the son of a courtier would provide the model he would use later to transmute the institutional structure of the benevolent and patriarchal Moghul raj into his own version of a modern multinational corporation. Abedi learned patronage and power at the feet of the rajahs, and he learned charity. Despite their lavishly appointed palaces, the rajahs obeyed Islam's insistence on almsgiving as one of the Muslim's principal moral duties. In times of economic trouble they and their retainers would ride out to the villages and distribute donations to the needy. They were proud of their patronage of culture as well, giving grants to Muslim poets and religious scholars. Abedi would later become famous in the Third World for his charity and philanthropy. The rajahs were, as Abedi would soon become, generous, impulsive, and romantic. "Abedi grew up moored to a rich Muslim tradition," wrote Najam Sethi, "including the sense that patronage and power are the essence of empire. Abedi's philanthropy and his fondness for perfume, gourmet cuisine, fine clothing, art, and the color white for its purity can all be attributed to his Lucknavi Muslim heritage."[10]

Abedi's first lesson in patronage led him at the age of twenty-five into the big city of Bombay, India's financial capital, and into the world of banking. After graduating with a degree in law and English from Lucknow University, he had sought work but immediately found what it meant to be a Muslim looking for work in a society where Hindus, with warm British encouragement, held most of the jobs. A phone call from his father's boss, the rajah himself, landed him a job at a new Islamic institution called the Habib Bank. He worked as a petty clerk, sitting behind a dirty counter, shuffling wads of rupee notes, and filling out ledgers. He settled into an arranged marriage.

He would not be in Bombay long. That same year, 1947, witnessed one of the most violent demographic upheavals in modern history: the migration of fourteen million Muslims from India to the newly created nation of East and West Pakistan, and the deaths of three million people in the violent civil war that accompanied the birth of the state. "This movement of . . . people had no precedent in history," wrote Pakistani historian Shahid Javed Burki. "Even the better-recorded movements of later times—Bengalis to India in 1971, in the late 1970s, Afghans to Pakistan in the early 1980s—did not involve so many people or occur over such a short period of time."[11] The end of the British raj meant that Muslims of north-central India, including Abedi and his family, would now feel the full fury of Hindu prejudice.

That year Abedi joined the mass migration, along with virtually all of the urban Muslims from north-central India and the old heart of the Moghul Empire, traveling west to the newly created state of Pakistan. The arrival of this group had a profound effect on the new country. Into a predominantly rural society still flush with feudal traditions of clan, family, and religion came a bright, educated, and highly motivated group of urbanites. They were called *mohajirs* (refugees), and they were utterly unlike either the Muslims of present-day Pakistan (provinces of Sind, Punjab, Kashmir, and the North-West Frontier), or those from the provinces of Bengal and Assam that became East Pakistan.

The effect of the Great Mutiny of 1857 had been to leave the provincial governors and the landlords without much wealth or power. The culture that emerged was both industrious and egalitarian, and it was the *mohajirs*, most of whom quickly settled in the larger cities of Lahore, Karachi, and Islamabad, arriving full of fervor and dynamism, who pioneered the new country's economic development and effectively staffed the national administration in its early days. As a whole, they constituted something like a ready-made middle class in a backward agrarian nation. Though they had been hurt more deeply than any other group by the rise of British authority, the educated Muslim elites of north-central India were in fact itching to expand outward and upward and were eager for power and influence. Wrenching though it was, their mass flight into Pakistan gave them just the opportunity they had been waiting for. Though Abedi was still a double minority—only now he was a Shiite *mohajir* in a land of mostly indigenous Sunnis—he was luckier than most. His job in the Habib Bank moved with him to the city of Lahore, the scene of some of the most violent fighting of the civil war in 1946 and 1947. He would start his career as a banker in a semifeudal country that had virtually no banking industry at all. Abedi came into a financial vacuum in 1947. He and his fellow *mohajirs* would quickly change that.

Over the next decade Abedi settled into what looked like a solid career at Pakistan's fastest-growing and most innovative bank, a circumstance due largely to the fact that it was staffed by men from the progressive provinces of north-central India. Abedi rose quickly to branch manager and then into the corporate hierarchy of the Habib Bank. By the late 1950s he was restless and ready to strike out on his own. Showing a talent for recruitment and persuasion he would later use to astonishing effect on a global scale, he found just the man to help him do it: Mian Yusif Saigol. Saigol was a leading textile manufacturer, and his clan one of the "twenty-two families" whose fortunes would dominate Pakistani commerce in the decades to come. According to Mian Yusif's son Naseem Saigol, Abedi simply "convinced my father that he should have a bank. Dad gave him a check for 10 million rupees [$2 million] and appointed my elder brother Shafiq as director with Abedi under him."[12] Thus did Abedi in 1959, with no capital of his own, launch a rival to his old employer and the first new bank in Pakistan since independence. He called it United Bank Limited. Though it never attained international stature during Abedi's tenure, United proved to him that his dreams of a multibillion-dollar transnational bank were possible. Though its beginnings were humble enough, United Bank became the blueprint for empire.

United quickly grew fat with deposits, and Abedi quickly showed the style, flamboyance, and innovation that marked his ascent in the world of finance. United became the first bank in Pakistan to computerize its records and the first to introduce the notion of "customer service." Another policy that set Abedi apart—and would be a hallmark of his banking style throughout his career—was lending to poor farmers and small-business people. He would set up branches in remote farming areas that had never seen banks. "These were hardly profitable," said Mian Saigol's son Azam. "But Abedi had always been keen on serving poor farmers."[13] Even more reminiscent of the paternalism of the rajahs of Mahmudabad, Abedi set up charities at the bank for widows, orphans, and students from poor families.

By the time he made his journey to Abu Dhabi in a single-engine plane, Abedi was a man to be reckoned with in Pakistan. He counted among his friends many of the leading business people in the country, and he maintained a close acquaintance with Field Marshal Muhammad Ayub Khan, the military dictator who had seized power in a 1958 coup. But modest wealth and social status fell far short of his ambitions. However successful Abedi might be, United was still a local bank in an underdeveloped country, and that meant that there was a natural limit on how much capital—how many new deposits—the bank could absorb. Before anything else, Abedi believed in deposits; he dreamt of deposits. Deposits were the building blocks of empire, and he believed that if he had enough of them he could buy anything. His solution to the problem was to seek a type of deposit that had not yet acquired the name that would become a household word in the English-speaking world by the mid-1970s. Abedi made two critical decisions. First, his ambitions could not be satisfied within Pakistan; he would have to cross borders. Second, he decided to hunt petrodollars. He was the first banker in the Third World, and among the first anywhere, to see that dollar deposits from Middle Eastern oil exports would turn the banking world on its head and make many enterprising people rich along the way.

Agha Hasan Abedi and Zayed bin Sultan al-Nahayan are the beginning and the end of BCCI. Abedi thought it up, and built it up; Zayed got the smoking wreckage dropped into his lap twenty years later. Zayed was the golden and ever-renewable source of Abedi's precious deposits. Abedi was Zayed's eyes on the world. Their relationship started that day in 1967. Zayed was impressed, and Zayed had been wondering anyway what he was going to do with all that money. He had received a few timid overtures from the West, but he distrusted the West. Here was someone from a poor country, a Muslim who knew about banking, a man Zayed could trust.

The courting of Zayed in those early years was classic Abedi and typical of his later approaches to ruling elites around the world. He was single-minded, persuasive, and would do anything to please a client. At the beginning that meant frequent visits and gifts. After a few visits Zayed took Abedi falconing, and falconing gave Abedi the idea that would cement the relationship for good.

Though the houbara had been plentiful in Arabia for most of Zayed's life, an odd sort of ecological disaster—from Zayed's point of view anyway—had taken place in the 1960s. The houbara had been hunted out in much of the Gulf, thanks mainly to the advent of oil money and the opportunity afforded any sheikh or wealthy businessman with a Land Rover to venture off into the desert and become a *bedu* for a day.[14] Four-wheel-drive sport utility vehicles had arrived en masse in the Arabian Peninsula. Abedi's solution—he always seemed to have one—was to invite Zayed to Pakistan, where Abedi would handle all the details of accommodations and would take Zayed to the province of Baluchistan, where the houbara was still plentiful. Through the sheer zealousness of Abedi's lieutenants, these visits were triumphs of logistics. Zayed no longer squatted in the desert with his rifle and cartridge belt and a small band of retainers. Abu Dhabi's new money—which, for all practical purposes, was Zayed's money—meant that falconing trips were now attended by a large entourage, driving modern Jeeps and Land Rovers and carrying huge white air-conditioned tents and scores of exotic birds. Abedi's zeal in attending to Zayed's needs impressed the emir, who also found Pakistan to his liking.

By the early 1970s Zayed had begun to pump petrodeposits into Abedi's bank. It was Abedi's bank that handled the purchase of a number of large homes for the sheikh's use while in Pakistan. United Bank managed these properties and others, handled all details of all of Zayed's trips, which meant food, lodging, and entertainment ranging from camel races to trips to Lahore's red-light district for more than one hundred people in the entourage. And Abedi quickly capitalized on his connection to Zayed to set up meetings with the ruling elites in Kuwait, Bahrain, Saudi Arabia, and the other emirates, whom he took on similar hunting trips in Pakistan. Abedi, now the head of the third-largest and still the fastest-growing bank in Pakistan, became Zayed's closest financial adviser.

We will never know what Abedi might have done with United Bank Limited or how far he might have taken it. In 1971 Agha Hasan Abedi and his miraculous little bank ran headlong into the buzzsaw of nationalization and the formidable personality of a unique Third World statesman named Zulfikar Ali Bhutto. Bhutto was swept into power in Pakistan on a wave of populist rhetoric following yet another tectonic shift in the subcontinent's history. What had been West Pakistan had lost both a war with India and East Pakistan's battle to secede from its western partner. West Pakistan surrendered, and the new country of Bangladesh was created. The loss discredited the military regime of General Yahya Khan, and in December 1971 Bhutto was sworn in as Pakistan's new president.

Bhutto's brand of populism was aimed directly at the twenty-two families, who in the preceding two decades had gathered a disproportionate amount of the country's wealth. Many of these families—which included Abedi's close friends and partners the Saigols and other powers such as the Gokal family—were of course deeply involved with United Bank. In January 1972 Bhutto announced his decision to nationalize Pakistan's banking industry. Abedi's bank was taken from him, and because Bhutto feared his power to influence events, he placed Abedi under house arrest.

Abedi reacted curiously to this violent and abrupt change. As far as anyone can tell, he neither sulked nor considered the loss of his bank to be a serious setback. While confined to his house, he summoned several of his old colleagues and held small dinners where he would talk excitedly about his new idea. One account of these days comes from Masihur Rahman, later to become BCCI's chief financial officer. "At that time I was getting feedback from friends that Abedi wanted to see me," said Rahman. "I was cautious at first, because I myself had been detained, and it was a difficult political climate. But I finally went to see him. He had a nice house and a nice garden, and for a few minutes we talked about our families. Then he explained to me his vision of a Third World bank. I said, 'You are amazing. You're under arrest and you're talking about a new bank.' He said flatly that in ten years we would be millionaires, and this would be the biggest bank in the world." Later, after Abedi had been released from detention, he came to Rahman's sister's house one night for dinner, talking ever more excitedly about his idea. When Rahman later asked his sister, who had been a bit overwhelmed by Abedi, what she thought of the man, she replied, "I looked into his eyes and saw God and the Devil sitting in perfect harmony." Few others saw anything more than a rabidly ambitious banker.

Abedi's vision was precise. He would build what no one had ever built before: a globe-straddling, multinational Third World bank that would break the hammerlock the giant European colonial banks held on the developing world. "Nothing had changed much since the colonial days, as far as banking was concerned," said Rahman. "Invariably the gunboats arrived, then the missionaries arrived, then came the banks." Western capital moved only very selectively into the developing world, and often with long strings attached. Abedi believed that, by treating the Third World as a full partner, he could beat the big colonial banks at their own game. His would be a large corporate bank but would also bank the small-business people whom the Western banks would not touch. The capital and deposits to fuel the bank's growth would come from the one part of the developing world that had resources—the countries of the oil-producing consortium OPEC.

Abedi's problem was that he had no capital and little legitimacy outside of Pakistan. He had, however, been in and out of the Arabian Peninsula enough to know that a number of big Western banks were already hungrily eyeing that part of the world. Their problem was access, and access was what Abedi, after five years of traipsing through royal corridors, had in abundance. At that precise moment in time Abedi had the best Rolodex in the Middle East. His relationship with Abu Dhabi was unique, and though it would always remain his strongest calling card, he had also assiduously courted the ruling families and leading merchants in Saudi Arabia, Dubai, Kuwait, Oman, and Qatar. He clearly had something to trade, and he had an idea who might be interested.

During his years at United Bank Abedi had cultivated the friendship of a Dutchman named Dick Van Oenen, the local representative of Bank of America in Karachi, who had an office in Abedi's United Bank building. In the early 1970s Bank of America was the largest bank in the world, and its ambitious chairman, A. W. "Tom" Clausen, was fairly drooling at the prospect of opening up the Arabian Gulf. Though Van Oenen was a mere rep—in those days that meant looking after a handful of government and banking relationships, and serving as tour guide and travel agent when the grandees from San Francisco came to town—he too had big ideas. Van Oenen decided to take Abedi to the United States to pitch his idea back at the home office.

At what Abedi would later refer to as the "historic lunch" in San Francisco in early 1972, he was at his persuasive best. He effectively promised BofA management the keys to the kingdom—superb access to the coffers of OPEC. In exchange, BofA would take a 30-percent share in the new bank for some $625,000 and a seat on the board of directors. Complete control of the day-to-day affairs of the bank was ceded to Abedi. This last was the key point. Abedi had made earlier approaches to other banks, including American Express International Bank. They had been interested, but were unwilling to pay Abedi's price. BofA agreed. In subsequent weeks Abedi convinced his friend Zayed to put up another $1.875 million. Abedi had the capital base for his new bank.

In a ballroom at the five-star Phoenicia Hotel in pre–civil war Beirut, Abedi and a group numbering about one hundred that included many *mohajirs* from Mahmudabad and nearby cities in north-central India who would form the core of the bank's management launched a company Abedi called the Bank of Credit and Commerce International. It was not a Pakistani bank in any sense of the word, and in fact would be shortly banned from Pakistan by an irritated Ali Bhutto. Two years later, BCCI was formally incorporated in Luxembourg—a place where Van Oenen had told Abedi he would be free of First

World regulatory interference. Its first six offices were located in the Gulf emirates of Abu Dhabi, Sharjah, and Dubai, and in London, Luxembourg, and Beirut.

Though Abedi could not claim full credit for it, the timing of BCCI's launch was nothing short of miraculous. The institution he had created in order to absorb and manipulate oil deposits stood just thirteen months away from an event that would initiate the greatest transfer of wealth from haves to have-nots in history. The Yom Kippur War in October 1973 led to an Arab oil embargo against the West, which resulted in a fourfold increase in the price of oil. Countries such as Saudi Arabia, Kuwait, and Abu Dhabi were no longer just rich; they were shamelessly rich and politically powerful. Yet another fortuitous event had been the departure in 1971 of the British from the Trucial Coast. Abu Dhabi and the other kingdoms were now independent and federated into a group called the United Arab Emirates. Both the U.A.E.'s president, Zayed bin Sultan al-Nahayan, and its vice president, Sheikh Mohammed bin Rashid al-Maktoum, considered Abedi a close adviser. Both had built—with Abedi's help and guidance—second homes in Pakistan.

Nineteen seventy-two was a propitious year in other ways for Abedi's new bank. It marked the beginning of an unprecedented international banking boom, driven by a magical and relatively new commodity called the Eurodollar, that would last for twenty years and would move some $600 billion from the First World to the Third World. Banks would soon be falling all over themselves to get a piece of the business Abedi had been nurturing quietly for years. Then there was the stunning rise of Islam itself, centuries dormant, in the wake of OPEC's good fortunes. Though Gamal Abdel Nasser's attempts to advance secular Arabism had failed, Saudi Arabia's King Faisal's push for Islamic solidarity in the years after the 1967 Six-Day War with Israel had not. Abedi's bank was an Islamic bank, too, he told his willing listeners in Arabia, peppering his speeches with religious jargon and talk of social values, and advancing the wildly attractive notion that a bank based on the principles of the Koran could go toe to toe with the bullies of Western banking. The same year Abedi launched his bank, Pakistan's new prime minister made what he called a "journey of discovery," loudly touting Islamic values in the very same countries Abedi had been cultivating. "Bhutto's emergence as the ruler of Pakistan coincided with both a renaissance in the world of Islam and the strengthened reputation of the Persian Gulf–dominated OPEC," wrote S. M. Burke in *Pakistan's Foreign Policy.* "Muslim nations were alive with activity, and the oil producers among them enjoyed unprecedented leverage in international economic and financial circles. The Islamic states could neither be taken for granted nor forced into submissiveness."[15] It was considered the mark of Bhutto's rise as a powerful Third World statesman when in 1974 he convened the Second Islamic Conference in Islamabad, playing host to the newly powerful elite of the Arab world. Though Abedi would always have a stormy relationship with Bhutto, Pakistan's sudden prominence helped him, and he could not have picked a better time to launch his Islamic bank.

Nor could he, in retrospect, have picked a better place to mine his early petrodeposits. Though he cleverly incorporated the bank in Luxembourg, where bank regulation was done with a nod and a wink, BCCI's power base was always the United Arab Emirates. By the middle 1970s the two entities had virtually merged. By 1990, however reluctantly on his part, BCCI became Zayed's bank. But there was nothing quite like the Wild West atmosphere in Abu Dhabi in the 1970s. Zayed may not have been the "Jed Clampett of the Middle East," as Americans staying at some of his new four-star hotels used to joke. But he was a financial ingenue with a newly minted horde of money, a horde that got much, much bigger after the Arab oil embargo. He was like Jed Clampett in that he went immediately for the big house in Beverly Hills and the swimming pool, and that he was simply not aware that most of the people who showed up on his doorstep were fortune seekers, and quite often dishonest fortune seekers.

Historian J. B. Kelly offers this wonderful snapshot of Abu Dhabi in those days. "Zayed's court is packed with a host of imposters, intriguers, sycophants and flaneurs (most of them northern Arabs) who ceaselessly jostle with one another for his attention and favor," writes Kelly. "Flattering, wheedling, shamelessly soliciting for personal ends, they swarm about the person of the ruler like so many flies. . . . Of the hundreds or even thousands of émigré Egyptians, Palestinians, Syrians and Iraqis who reside in Abu Dhabi only a minority are men of ability and integrity whose presence confers a positive benefit. The rest are mostly self-seekers who conspire and compete among themselves for position, money, preferment or advantage, ceaselessly intriguing to supplant rivals with nominees or placements of their own."[16]

This was Zayed's Abu Dhabi. It was also Abedi's Abu Dhabi, and it was precisely because of the arrival of all of these flimflam artists that Zayed needed Abedi. The sheikh did not trust the West, and he was being preyed upon by ethnic Arabs. As early as 1978, *Forbes* magazine was writing about three major financial scandals in the United Arab Emirates leading to the collapse of two offshore banks and the hasty retreat of a Bangladeshi bank. What made Abu Dhabi such a wonderful hunting ground for these types was the sheer speed with which Zayed was taking the tiny kingdom into the Twentieth Century. The building boom was prodigious: a sparkling international airport, dozens of new glass-and-steel high-rise buildings, parks everywhere. In the early morning the first things that greeted a visitor's eyes were the ubiquitous water trucks manned by Pakistanis from the poorer areas like Baluchistan and the North-West Frontier. They were watering Abu Dhabi into existence.

They were also part of a massive migration of laborers, especially Pakistanis, to the Middle East. Almost all the real "work" in those days was hired out to a motley collection of Palestinians, Egyptians, Koreans, and Pakistanis. This was part of the new order in the Gulf: The newly rich residents of the United Arab Emirates, growing ever more complacent with their large government allowances, pension plans, and health benefits, became less and less inclined to work, relying instead on the energetic hustlers from poorer countries. Of these, the Pakistanis were regarded as the most energetic and productive. They did all sorts of jobs, ranging from menial to clerical. Pakistan also provided special contingents of soldiers to the United Arab Emirates, Iraq, Kuwait, Oman, and Saudi Arabia. Though their purpose was ostensibly "training and technical assistance," many were de facto insurance policies for the ruling elite. There were more than ten thousand of these Pakistani soldiers in Saudi Arabia alone.[17]

More than anywhere else, the countries of the Middle East had turned to Pakistan for help in undertaking their breathless modernization. Beginning in the middle 1970s hundreds of thousands of Pakistanis began to pour into the oil-exporting states. By the 1980s the resident Pakistani labor force numbered three million, and its remittances to Pakistan would eventually peak at $2.9 billion. This was yet another piece of good fortune for Abedi's new bank. BCCI found itself the beneficiary of the "float" on most of these remittances. As earnings passed from the Pakistani laborer in the Gulf through BCCI on its way back home, the money would sit idle for a period of time. Because the remittances were constantly increasing, there was at any given moment a huge pool of these funds in the bank. Abedi could invest that money and earn interest. And it was this that accounted for the bank's first prodigious wave of growth. Not only that, but just as the impoverished Baluchis had been entrusted to plant Zayed's trees and water his gardens, so would another group of Pakistanis—the highly intelligent and highly motivated *mohajirs* from BCCI—soon be entrusted to keep track of much of the national wealth.

Abedi had told his associate Rahman during his house arrest that he intended to build the biggest bank in the world. If Rahman doubted him then, he had become a true believer by the late 1970s. Rapid growth of financial institutions was a feature of the 1970s, as big global banks intermediated between the huge excesses of dollars in the oil-producing world and the development needs of nearly everyone else. Bank assets were multiplying exponentially, and formerly conservative banks were pushing for the first time into unknown regions of the developing world. Yet even in that go-go climate, there was nothing like BCCI, a bank that, incidentally, was not playing the same international debt game that everyone else was. No large bank could even approach its rate of expansion. The bank that had started in 1972 with $2.5 million in capital and "deposits" that were really nothing more than the float on Pakistani remittances had by 1978 grown to be a $3-billion bank, something on the order of 1200-fold growth. By 1978 the bank that started with 6 tiny branches could boast 146 branches in 32 countries. Forty-five of those branches were in Britain alone, making BCCI the largest foreign bank presence there. Abedi's grand scheme was paying off with preternatural accuracy. His contacts in the oil countries were pumping up BCCI with petrodollars, even as his unique status as a Third World bank for the "little guy" had drawn in hundreds of millions from expatriate Indians, Pakistanis, and large expatriate groups such as the Ugandan refugees, who had been poorly treated by the British banks.

By the late 1970s Abedi was riding the whirlwind. No longer were he and his top lieutenants sharing a shabby storefront in Abu Dhabi. They had long since migrated to the mecca of the international banking business, the home of the Eurodollar, and the white-hot center of the debt boom: London. When he was not traveling—a rare circumstance in those days—visitors to BCCI's luxurious open-space offices could see Abedi at his desk, surrounded by the recruited elite of the Pakistani financial establishment and one or more of the bank's clientele, which already included some of the richest men in the world. As always, Abedi dressed nattily, showing a fondness for pink shirts, pinstriped suits, and lizard- or crocodile-skin shoes.

His life had changed. He now lived in a cozy rented house in Dulwich, a London suburb. He had married again in the mid-1970s after his first wife ran off with his best friend, a Pakistani stockbroker. His new wife, Rabia, a stunning former airline stewardess, had given him a child. As he would do all his life, Abedi downplayed his own wealth. Despite the often ostentatious life-styles of his associates, who had grown accustomed to cruising London in Rolls-Royces with clients, Abedi worked sixteen hours a day, lived in a modest home, kept a single Pakistani cook, and drove a dated Mercedes. He was an aficionado of Indian classical music and preferred reading management textbooks to hobnobbing with the social elite. While working in Karachi, he was never "a member of the city's smart watering spot that was frequented by Bhutto and his entourage, the Sind Club, while most senior BCCI officers were members."[18] His entertainment at home consisted of reading the paper in front of the television.[19] He would continue to cultivate this image of the modest man with modest means who had chosen not to profiteer from his extraordinary position. According to those who knew him then, he was an odd admixture of personalities: He could be alarmingly humble one moment and coldly arrogant the next. Everyone who knew him said he was most emphatically a man in a hurry.

Abedi's bank was by almost any measure the fastest-growing financial institution in the world. But the sheer pace of the growth obscured a more fundamental achievement. As he had reached out and captured petrodollars and deposits from ordinary people, he had built an organization the likes of which modern management theorists had never seen. "Abedi saw BCCI less as a 20th century multinational than as a 17th century feudal kingdom with international horizons," wrote Steve Coll in a splendid article in *The Washington Post* about Abedi's background in India.[20] Abedi had, in effect, grafted the structure, sociology, and cultural traits of the court of the rajah of Mahmudabad onto a modern London-based international bank. The result both scared and fascinated the phlegmatic bank aristocracy of the City.

We travel with the ever-changing procession of change.
We travel on the eternal bridge of change.
Above all, the instinct of the BCCI moves with the instinct of change.

In case you don't recognize the form, the preceding is a management poem, one of many written over the years by Agha Hasan Abedi, who had grown up entranced by the soaring, metaphorical language of the Koran. This one was published in the Bank of Credit and Commerce International's 1984 annual report. Before anything else, Abedi is a Muslim, a mystic, and a poet. What sounded to many, including his own employees, like fortune-cookie punditry was in fact Abedi's attempt to bridge the gulf between his own Islamic heritage and the exigencies of modern management. He was certainly eclectic but always within the traditions of Islam or its mystical Sufi offshoot, in which he was particularly interested. Even when the language lost its moorings, there is evidence that Abedi was perfectly serious about it because he believed that only a tightly conceived and universally accepted corporate ethic could bring him what he wanted. He also believed—according to many who knew him—that he was on a mission from God.

His sense of mission suffused the culture of BCCI. The first question on the many personnel circulars sent down to be completed by all employees was: "Do I serve a particular master, and, if so, who is my master?" The correct answer was: "God the Almighty."[21] Internal memos from upper management spoke incessantly of the divine nature of the bank's destiny. God had ordered up a bank that would be a mighty force for good in the Third World. And He had chosen BCCI to carry out His will. The bank's corporate purpose had nothing to do with profits for shareholders; it had to do only with serving God and humanity. Profits were merely a secondary effect, a sign from God that the bank was fulfilling its destiny.

The company that emerged at the front of the go-go pack in the late 1990s was a strange blend of Islam, Moghul raj, and Abedian synthesis. From the religion came "Islam's rejection of the personal, its insistence on sharing, its doctrine that society is always more important than the individual."[22] There was the fanatical insistence on humility, prayer, obedience to God's will, and the non-Western tenet that religion must be integrated into all aspects of daily life. From Mahmudabad came the egalitarianism that had evolved in the days of the raj's decline, and that the *mohajirs* had imported with them to Pakistan, a profound sense that power is drawn from patronage, and a great deal of sycophantic behavior by the lower-downs in the presence of the man they called Agha-saheb.

There was reason to kowtow; Abedi had changed their lives. Suddenly young men from the subcontinent were making the sort of money they had never dreamed of. One officer who had migrated from a $500-a-year job with the Indian central bank, for example, was now hosting lavish parties at London's most expensive hotels and earning a salary of $100,000. By the late 1970s such perks had drawn to BCCI the elite of the Third World banking world, including eleven senior executives who had been presidents of other banks, two former governors of central banks, and even the former heir apparent at Abedi's old employer and competitor, the Habib Bank.[23]

Yet the spiritual goads had an eminently practical effect, which was to unleash hundreds of "humble" bank officers who pursued the concept of customer service with a vengeance no other bank could match. At Heathrow Airport BCCI Rolls-Royces waited to whisk Middle Eastern clients away to shopping trips in the West End or dinner in the City. With the Rolls-Royces usually came bags of cash, dutifully carried by young Pakistanis who could be seen following this or that sheikh (or sheikh's wife) through the aisles at Harrods or one of the fabulously expensive jewelry shops of London. BCCI would handle all hotel accommodations and all entertainment. "We are attuned to the Arab way of working," said Ameer Siddiki, one of Abedi's closest lieutenants. "Arabs want personal service, Asian courtesy at its zenith. So you visit them at home on occasion, send them little gifts. The theory here is, 'Why should the customer come to us? We should go to the customer.' "[24] So complete was the service that BCCI officials were not infrequently awakened in the middle of the night to make good on a sheikh's gambling losses. It was difficult to argue with the results. BCCI not only drew in huge deposits but also began systematically to steal clients from British banks unwilling to be so solicitous of their needs.

From this fanatical drive to please its customers a darker side began to emerge. As BCCI rose in prominence, its officers continued to put on entertainments for clients in Pakistan. This had always meant such things as bustard hunts and camel races, but now the entourages of Middle Eastern potentates—in particular that of Zayed—were increasingly being entertained in less wholesome ways. Much of this sort of amusement took place in Lahore's legendary Diamond Market, the home of the famous "dancing girls." There, girls as young as twelve (and later, even younger) were dressed in silk harem pants and procured by BCCI officers for their clients. In the middle 1970s the man in charge of inspecting the girls was Zafar Iqbal, who would later become the chief executive officer of BCCI.

Though the bank's putative egalitarianism swam upstream against Abedi's domineering presence, BCCI was nonetheless highly progressive in its structure. In the bank's Leadenhall headquarters there were no private offices, not even for Abedi. There were no titles within BCCI. Even the higher-ups were designated only by the word *executive*. When the executives met, they sat around a perfectly round table meant to represent Abedi's idea of a "joint personality." This collective personality was supposedly what ran the bank. It had no geographic location, and it administered the bank by means of a system known as "The Concept"—a hazy amalgam of religious, mystical, and management concepts.

It was no accident that Abedi chose to stress the notion that the "bank" was merely a "concept" with no fixed spatial location. Having plunged into the maelstrom of international banking in London in the 1970s, Abedi's learning curve was astonishingly steep. He learned quickly that geography, or lack of it, was the name of the game. The currency that measured who was winning that game was the stateless Eurodollar, really nothing more than an imaginary construct that allowed banks to "place" certain portions of their assets "offshore." Eurodollars were a bookkeeping trick that everyone, including the regulators, agreed to play along with. The beauty of the system was that banks could park deposits and loans at will in odd little places like Nassau and the Cayman Islands, and by so doing could conceal them from any meaningful regulatory supervision.

Abedi and his lieutenants—particularly his numbers whiz Swaleh Naqvi, who like Abedi had grown up in north-central India—quickly recognized the already odd posture of BCCI. The bank had been incorporated in Luxembourg, the virtually unregulated financial haven that lacked even a central bank (like the U.S. Fed or the Bank of England), yet its shareholders (there were forty in those years) all came from the Persian Gulf, its headquarters were in London, and its principal· branches concentrated in the United Kingdom and the United Arab Emirates. No other bank presented such a spatially dislocated profile. Meanwhile, this band of hyperenergetic Pakistanis had sufficiently unsettled the august Bank of England that by the late 1970s BCCI was prevented from further branching and was refused "authorized status" as a British bank. Abedi's solution was to take yet a further step outside the boundaries of international regulation—a move that would effectively make BCCI a bank that was "offshore at all points." The bank had been formerly owned and controlled through a Luxembourg company called BCCI Holdings. In 1976 Abedi incorporated the ICIC in the Cayman Islands, through which much of BCCI's growing business would pass.

It seemed a small step at the time. After all, most major American and European banks had some sort of operations in Nassau or the

Caymans. Yet by doing so, Abedi effectively created the world's first truly stateless multinational corporation, a bank with offices all over the world, incorporated in Luxembourg and the Cayman Islands, run by a "joint personality" executive that had "no geographic location." By the late 1970s BCCI was both everywhere and nowhere, a Third World bank operating out of a First World city. As one of Abedi's chief lieutenants in the United States, Abdur Sakhia, would later testify: "We were an international bank with a worldwide network, and since we were not carrying any specific flag, we were not a British or a German or a Swiss bank, but we were purely an international bank. So if we were in Florida, we were Florida's bank. If we were in Jamaica, we were Jamaica's bank, and if we were in Barbados, we were a Barbados bank."[25]

As BCCI swept into the 1980s the bank was arguably the most successful in the world. Every two weeks a new BCCI branch opened somewhere, and more than $1 billion in new assets were being added each year. Though Western banking authorities resolutely refused to let Abedi into the club, and an increasingly nervous Bank of America had sold its equity, Abedi had built the world's first Third World consortium bank, one that had extraordinary access to the huge dollar surpluses being generated in the Middle East. His shareholders—Abedi claimed not to own a single share in his creation—were a glittering who's who in the Gulf: among them Saudi princes, the rulers of several of the United Arab Emirates, the richest commoner in Saudi Arabia, and the former head of Saudi intelligence. By the late 1970s BCCI had effectively merged with Zayed's Private Department, which handled and invested the Emirates' astonishing new wealth.

Abedi had made good on his promise to serve the Third World. Lavish green-and-gold-decorated BCCI branches with thick carpets and smoked-glass windows had sprung up in places like Kenya, Cameroon, Egypt, Zambia, Thailand, Turkey, and Brazil, and they were making loans and handling deposits for small-business men that the large colonial banks would not touch. With this loudly touted idea of the Third World consortium came a carefully cultivated image of radicalism. Abedi set up a Third World Foundation, which lavished millions of philanthropic dollars on the developing world. He funded a magazine called *South*, which from its London base trumpeted the empowerment of the nonwhite, non-Western world. The unease that Abedi inspired in Western banking authorities could be "neatly ascribed to imperialist resentment and greed."[26]

By the turn of the decade Abedi and BCCI were in an extraordinary position. The fall and subsequent execution of Zulfikar Ali Bhutto had given way to the military dictatorship of Zia ul-Haq, with whom Abedi had a close and cooperative relationship. As the oil surpluses rocketed upward—Saudi Arabia alone had already passed the $100-billion mark in 1980—it looked to many observers as though BCCI, as principal banker to the oil sheikhs of the Gulf, was ready to reap the windfall. This clip from *Business Week* in 1980 captures the conventional wisdom of the times and the way the world looked then to Agha Hasan Abedi:

> The Arab nations of OPEC are building a new international banking system that threatens to capture control of the world's financial resources in the 1980s in the same way they took control of the world's energy resources in the 1970s. While the different pieces of the Arab banking system are only now being put in place, it is already clear that the OPEC money weapon will join with the OPEC oil weapon in giving the Arabs unprecedented sway over the economies and policies of the West.
>
> On one level, the Arab banks will be the richest financial institutions in the world, with the ability to tap into the OPEC oil nations' fantastic wealth, which is expected to reach $1 trillion by 1985.[27]

Abedi's divinely ordained destiny was at hand: He would soon be able simply to write a check for Chase Manhattan, Citicorp, or any bank he chose. That would certainly come to pass. It was only a question of when.

CHAPTER 8

GILT BY ASSOCIATION

"Never wrestle a pig. You both get dirty, and the pig likes it."

—APHORISM ON JACK BLUM'S OFFICE WALL

"Clark Clifford could sell hams in a synagogue."

—REPRESENTATIVE CHALMERS WYLIE (R-OHIO)

In his London office Abedi dreamed of America. He spoke of it constantly with his colleagues. He believed he was building the biggest bank in the world, and from its posh London headquarters BCCI had taken on the look of a real player on the international scene. Yet any bank that fancied itself a global power had to have the ability to take dollar deposits and clear dollar accounts in the United States. Abedi had known from the start that he would need America: Dollars were the world's currency, oil was paid for in dollars, and national treasuries all measured their wealth in dollars. With the exception of a few stray Euro–Swiss francs and Euro–deutsche marks, most of the world's riches were measured in dollars, and all dollars eventually came home to roost in the United States.

Abedi did not have an easy time of it, as he had had in almost every other country in the world. To his great disappointment, the United States did not welcome the radical, Third World Islamic bank with open arms. Though Abedi did not recognize this or understand it at first, U.S. regulators saw BCCI as jerry-rigged according to Abedi's own wild spiritual logic, held together with baling wire and spit and glue, and operated well outside the conventions of banking in the

West. The warning signs were, from a Western point of view, unmistakable: BCCI was growing by quantum leaps. No bank in history had ever managed to sustain and control growth on the scale of BCCI in the 1970s—and it was operating without a net. "You had a $20-billion bank with no central bank regulator or lender of last resort," said one U.S. banker. "That gave most bankers a very nervous feeling about BCCI. Who's watching these guys?" No one knew how much its mysterious shareholders might be good for. Word on the street was that this was a marginal bank at best.

Abedi's first attempts to buy an American bank were almost comically transparent, showing just how little he knew about the market he so coveted. In 1975 the first of BCCI's front men emerged: Abbas Gokal of the immensely rich Pakistani shipping family, the single largest client of BCCI. Through him Abedi made an attempt to acquire Chelsea National Bank, but New York bank regulators soon enough discovered the puppeteer behind the curtain and blocked the acquisition. Nobody in the United States wanted, or would ever want, BCCI to acquire an American bank. Undaunted, another Abedi minion named Abdus Sami attempted to gain regulatory approval to buy a bank in 1977, this time for Bank of Commerce. So hostile were the New York State authorities that no bid was ever made. By mid-1977 it looked as though Abedi's unchecked ambitions had driven him permanently onto the rocks.

And here the American story might have ended, were it not for the intercession of a man once described as the "incarnation of the Southern novelist's most complex high-rolling salesman"[1]: T. Bertram Lance. He had gained quick fame as Jimmy Carter's budget director, then even quicker infamy when he was forced to resign his post ten months later under the harsh light of a congressional investigation. Lance had been the most interesting and intriguing of the Georgians who moved north with Carter after his election as president. Everything about him was outsized. He stood six feet five, and his weight fluctuated up and down through the middle 200s. He seemed prototypically Southern: an affable, shambling, slightly rumpled giant whose easy wit, deep Georgia drawl, and endless stock of barnyard metaphors were more suggestive of a Carson McCullers story than establishmentarian Washington. Lance was a poor boy who took a job as a bank teller in a small rural town, married the chairman's daughter, became president of the bank, then aligned himself with an ambitious state senator named Jimmy Carter, who named him to a cabinet post when he was elected governor.

When Carter announced he was leaving the Georgia governor's office in 1974, he supported Lance as his successor. Lance lost that election, and therein began his problems, for he had financed much of that campaign through overdrafts at his bank. In 1975 he became chief executive of the National Bank of Georgia—which coincidentally was the largest lender to Jimmy Carter's peanut warehouse—and borrowed another $2.6 million to finance his purchase of stock in the bank. The charges of financial improprieties later brought against him held, among other things, that Lance had improperly pledged certain of his bank's assets in exchange for that loan, and that he had once pledged the same stock as collateral for two loans. (After a lengthy investigation and subsequent trial, Lance was found innocent of these charges.)

Like Clark Clifford, Lance says that he had no inkling that he was being recruited by Abedi for nefarious ends. Yet in the critical years between 1977 and 1979, he became the lynchpin of Abedi's American strategy. He was replaced by others soon enough, but not before he had given BCCI the means to enter the U.S. market. He was in most ways typical of Abedi's marks: a well-connected politico with identifiable strengths and weaknesses. Bert Lance was not only $5 million in debt and watching the value of his stock plummet; he was also the best friend of the president of the United States.

Abedi had found Lance through an appropriately shady connection: former Georgia State Senator Eugene Holley, a man with the distinction of being the first person prosecuted under the Foreign Corrupt Practices Act for paying bribes in the Persian Gulf state of Qatar, and who in 1980 was convicted of bank fraud and sentenced to ten years in jail. Holley, a good friend of Bert Lance, was an old Georgia boy who had set up a Cayman oil company and promptly run up a debt of $17 million he could not repay. He had made a deal with Abedi on his Qatari oil concessions. Abedi had bailed him out.

Holley, who was both grateful and anxious to curry favor with Abedi and who knew of Abedi's intense interest in an American acquisition, came upon a way of returning the favor. In October 1977 Holley arranged a meeting between his friend Bert Lance and BCCI chieftains Abedi and Naqvi at New York's Waldorf-Astoria Hotel. This was less than a month after an embattled and deeply indebted Lance had resigned as Jimmy Carter's budget chief. Abedi was looking for someone with influence and connections in the banking business. Lance was looking for work and a way out of his financial predicament. It was to be a fortuitous meeting. Abedi was at his persuasive best, and Lance, sensing an opportunity, was a rapt listener. Abedi ticked off his credentials, then described his grand vision, couched in his idiosyncratic jargon. As Lance recalls the meeting, Abedi said, "I am building a bank headquartered in London that has a deep and abiding interest in problems of health, hunger, economic development, things primarily in the Third World, problems that we are all familiar with and problems that we all want to see resolved in one form or another."[2]

Lance, for his part, stuck to Abedi's high moral road. "I shared that concern," he said, "especially about economic development, because I had come from a poor section of Georgia, where I saw what the utilization of the resources of a bank could really mean to the people in that community through job creation."[3]

Once the altruistic foreplay was over, Abedi told Lance that he was interested in gaining a foothold in the United States. "My rejoinder to him," recalled Lance, "was that obviously you cannot be a global bank, an international bank, without some sort of presence in the United States. This is the most powerful, richest nation in the world, and this is certainly something you ought to look at."[4]

Indeed. Lance, who did not know that Abedi had twice made unsuccessful tries at American banks, was preaching to the choir. That was all Abedi needed. In spite of Lance's many protestations to the contrary, his selection to be point man in Abedi's drive into the U.S. market was the result both of who his friends were—Abedi recruited his confederates around the world according to the same criteria—and of the fact that the charges against him suggested a man who perhaps would not be as fastidious as some of the New York State regulators Abedi had encountered. For the next two years Bert Lance's business career accelerated with breathtaking speed, all thanks to Abedi.

The two men met again at BCCI's opulent London headquarters a few weeks later, and now they talked about specific deals. Lance suggested that Abedi look closely at a Washington-based bank holding company called Financial General Bankshares, Inc. Lance explained that Financial General had a unique franchise: While most banks could operate within only a single state, Financial General owned banks in several states. Lance said that Financial General's shareholders had split into armed camps. The time might be ripe for a takeover.

Abedi would scrupulously follow Lance's advice. But before the meeting was over, Lance made another suggestion more in keeping with his worries about his own financial problems. His own National Bank of Georgia (in which he held a 12-percent stake) was looking for a buyer, he said. Might any of Abedi's many clients be interested in a modest Southern bank? Abedi replied that he knew a Saudi Arabian investor named Ghaith Pharaon who had already acquired banks in the United States and was looking for another one. From the London meeting, Abedi moved speedily in lining up investors. By the time Lance and Abedi met again in Atlanta over Thanksgiving weekend, both the Financial General deal and the National Bank of Georgia acquisition were moving forward. Lance was to be the beneficiary of the latter, and he would soon lead the American effort in the acquisition of Financial General. Abedi's intervention meant that Lance's personal financial woes were about to end.

At the time that Abedi made his measured approach to Bert Lance, it is unlikely that he had ever heard of Clark Clifford. There is little reason he would have. The Republicans had been in the White House for most of a decade, which meant that the arch-Democrat had been plying his lawyerly trade more quietly than usual. But Lance turned out to be even more valuable than Abedi had thought. When Lance's troubles with the U.S. Congress and the media began to spiral out of control in the late summer of 1977, his boss and friend Jimmy Carter, frightened of losing his closest confidant, moved decisively to protect him. On Labor Day weekend he called another friend and adviser, a man with a history of being able to fix, smooth out, or otherwise make political problems disappear: Clark Clifford. Carter asked if Clifford would help Lance in his coming showdown with Congress. Although in a losing cause, Clifford and his young partner Robert Altman drafted the impassioned defense Lance delivered in a Senate committee hearing and sat beside him as he delivered it.

After his resignation, Lance continued to retain Clifford and Altman to help him sort out the rest of his problems. And so, when Abedi's investor Ghaith Pharaon agreed in late 1977 to purchase Lance's bank, it was Altman who handled the negotiations. At thirty-six, Pharaon represented the urbane, sophisticated side of the Arabian oil boom and within a few years would be one of the most visible of the thousands of rich Arabs who descended on America looking for a place to park their new wealth. He spoke elegant, lightly accented English, sported a trademark Vandyke beard, and dressed in $1,000 Savile Row suits. He was the first Arab to acquire control of a billion-dollar U.S. bank.

Lance had desperately wanted to sell his shares in National Bank of Georgia but had been unable to find a buyer. Less than three months after Holley introduced Abedi to Lance, the Pakistani had orchestrated the deal, even though Lance did not actually meet Pharaon until they closed the transaction. Abedi had arranged everything. Pharaon acquired Lance's stake for $2.4 million on January 4, 1978 (at $20 a share—$4 over the going rate—a handsome price, considering that no one else wanted it). That same day Abedi paid off Lance's troublesome $3.4-million loan from the First National Bank of Chicago. He did so by creating a loan in the same amount to Lance from the Cayman Islands—a loan for which there was no paperwork at all. That wasn't all Lance got. Around the same time another of BCCI's Cayman enterprises hired Lance as a consultant, at a salary of $100,000.

While he was bailing out Bert Lance, Abedi was also pursuing the acquisition of Financial General. Since he had been twice rebuffed by regulators, the approach would be made by nominees, front men who would acquire stock in their own names, mostly with money from BCCI. The way BCCI transferred ownership to itself was simple and elegant; it also happened to be a felony under U.S. banking laws. From December 1977 through February 1978, four such front men bought up nearly 20 percent of Financial General's stock, violating the law by failing to declare that they were acting as a group. These were no ordinary stooges; they were some of the richest and most powerful people in the Middle East: Sheikh Zayed of Abu Dhabi and the man who ran his money, Abdullah Darwaish; Kamal Adham, who had gathered up an estimated nine-figure net worth plying his connections on behalf of multinational corporations; and Faisal Saud al-Fulaij, formerly of Kuwait Airways.

The move was so naively transparent that the nominees were summarily sued, first by Financial General's owners, then a month later by the Securities and Exchange Commission. A new set of sheep's clothing had not succeeded in persuading anyone that this was not the wolf trying yet again to crash the U.S. market. The group immediately signed a consent order with the SEC agreeing to play by the rules and to make a public offer for Financial General.

On his end, Bert Lance was moving apace, earning his $100,000 consulting fee, acting as Abedi's eyes and ears in the Financial General deal. For a man with such thorny political and financial problems, Lance was seemingly uninhibited that spring. In March, still flying on his diplomatic passport, Lance went on an Abedi-financed junket to Pakistan, where he hunted bustard with Zayed and made the acquaintance of two of the four fronts: Kamal Adham and Abdullah

Darwaish. In April Lance was feted by oil tycoon Clint Murchison with a stag bash in the Maryland countryside, where senators, Jimmy Carter's closest aides, blue-chip corporate lobbyists, and a "sprinkling of Arabs" gathered for Murchison's annual wild-game feed and a chance to shake Lance's hand.[5] Meanwhile Lance was also busy recruiting his friend and attorney Clark Clifford. In February, just a few days before Financial General brought suit, Lance saw to it that Abedi, BCCI, and the front men had retained the firm of Clifford & Warnke as counsel. It was the beginning of a long and profitable relationship. Abedi's aide Abdus Sami sent a jubilant telex to his boss: "I met with Clark Clifford and explained to him our strategy and goal. He was happy to know the details and blessed the acquisition." In the same telex, he cautioned: "To keep individual ownership to below 5 percent we have to distribute the ownership to four persons of substance. . . . We have to be careful that our name does not appear as financier for most of them for this acquisition."[6]

Clark Clifford had passed into legend long before he hired on as BCCI's lawyer and adviser. He had been Washington's preeminent attorney for the better part of five decades. He had been a driving force behind many of the seminal changes in postwar America. He was without a doubt one of the most remarkable personalities ever to navigate the treacherous currents of national politics. Even at the age of eighty-four he was a striking presence, a man whose measured and mellifluous speaking voice and gently theatrical gestures seemed drawn from another era. A Washington lawyer once said that "listening to Clifford was like listening to God."[7]

The first thing to understand about this legendary public servant is that he was not really a public servant. Not in the sense that he spent much or even a reasonable percentage of his career in public service. That may seem an unlikely statement about the man-who-advised-four-presidents, but Clifford in fact spent a mere five of his forty-six years in Washington collecting a government paycheck. Clark Clifford's domain was the private sector, and it may be said fairly that for most of his career he took great pains to stay clear of the meager salaries, public accountability, and bureaucratic pirouetting that accompanied public office. He spent most of his time in the shadows of public life, slipping with considerable grace from the president's elbow to the corporate boardroom, always quiet and discreet, and almost always unseen. This was his special magic, and no practitioner of Washington's black arts ever did it better. Though Clifford's image of integrity in Washington was, as Reuters wrote in 1991, "as rock solid as the Washington Monument," he was perhaps described more accurately by the *Financial Times* as "the ultimate insider," a term that is conspicuously value-neutral.

That is not to say that Clark Clifford did not exert a prodigious influence on public policy, or that his reputation as a dominant force in Washington is somehow unmerited. Indeed, the fine hand of Clark McAdams Clifford can be seen in much of the political structure of contemporary Washington, and few people outside the Oval Office were ever closer to the engine room of history. Taken together, the accomplishments are breathtaking: As a top aide to Harry S Truman, he both masterminded Truman's come-from-behind victory over Thomas E. Dewey in 1948 and was the principal architect of "Fair Deal" politics; he was a co-author of the National Security Act of 1947, which set up both the Central Intelligence Agency and the National Security Council; he was a prime mover in the creation of the Department of Defense; he participated in the formulation of the Truman Doctrine, the policy of Soviet containment that lasted into the Bush administration. Though his one great political "mistake" was supposed to have been supporting his friend Stuart Symington (later vice chairman of First American) for the Democratic party nomination in 1956, he was nonetheless directing the transition from the Eisenhower administration to John F. Kennedy's New Frontier four years later. He was Kennedy's personal lawyer and among other duties advised JFK in the dark days after the Bay of Pigs invasion. After JFK was assassinated, Clifford became one of Lyndon Johnson's most senior advisers, eventually serving as secretary of defense, a job he took four days before the disastrous 1968 Tet Offensive in the Vietnam War.[8] Before he left the Johnson administration, he led the effort within the government to begin to extricate the United States from Vietnam. As a much older man, he counseled President Jimmy Carter on the Panama Canal Treaty and acted as Carter's special envoy to Greece, Turkey, and India. His advice and counsel has been solicited by virtually every major Democratic politician since Truman.

One could keep going at some length here, into such colorful details as the card games Clifford arranged for Truman, including one with Truman and Winston Churchill on a train ride to Fulton, Missouri, where Churchill delivered his famous "Iron Curtain" speech. But this is the public Clark Clifford, the one documented in reams of personal memoirs, histories, and policy papers. It is the private, ahistorical Clark Clifford who found himself stuck to the tar baby of the biggest banking scandal in history, the man whose stock in trade was his considerable talent for dancing effortlessly along the fine line between public and private America.

Clifford had come to Washington in 1945 as a naval aide at the White House and quickly worked his way to the top of the Truman staff totem pole. Yet at what was arguably the moment of his ascension, and the peak of his influence in the administration, he chose to return to private practice as a lawyer. In late 1949 Clifford left, according to his memoirs, both because he was psychologically exhausted and because, with a daughter entering college, he felt he had financial responsibilities to his family. After briefly consulting an old friend on the propriety of practicing law in Washington (as opposed to St. Louis, where he had been a trial lawyer before the war) and turning down an offer from Dean Acheson to join his law firm, Clifford went out on his own.

He quickly learned the market value of his contacts in government. The first phone call he received in his new offices was from Kenneth Stanley "Boots" Adams, chairman of Phillips Petroleum Company, who would later put Clifford on his board. His second was from Howard Hughes, requesting that Clifford represent Hughes Tool Company, RKO Pictures, and Trans World Airlines in Washington.[9] His law practice quickly flourished. In time he came to represent a who's-who clientele of the biggest and most powerful corporations in America: Firestone Tire & Rubber Company, Time Incorporated, General Electric, Schering-Plough (Maybelline Cosmetics and others), and many more. By the 1970s *Time* magazine reported that Clark Clifford earned more than $1 million a year, making him one of the highest-paid lawyers in the country at that time.[10]

With one important difference, of course. Though he held only one official government position after he left the Truman administration—as Johnson's secretary of defense—Clifford remained closer to the centers of power than many so-called public servants. It was in these years that he came into his reputation as a consummate troubleshooter—or "fixer," in the language of the capital. While still a senator, John F. Kennedy became the target of an allegation by investigative journalist Drew Pearson that Ted Sorensen, not Kennedy, had written Kennedy's Pulitzer Prize–winning book, *Profiles in Courage*. Kennedy turned to his lawyer Clifford, who orchestrated Kennedy's rebuttal so smoothly that he had a retraction from ABC News within the week. Later on, when President Kennedy and his brother Bobby were orchestrating their younger brother Teddy's run for the Senate, they learned that *Newsweek* had found out that Teddy had been forced to withdraw from Harvard for cheating. They called Clark Clifford to ask his advice. Clifford counseled them that Teddy should handle it forthrightly, then slyly planted the story with a "friendly journalist" for *The Boston Globe* that would allow Teddy a gentle out.[11]

When Lyndon Johnson's top aide, Walter Jenkins, was arrested in a YMCA for "homosexual conduct" in 1964, it was Clifford who was summoned and sent round to the newspapers to try to smooth it over. Later he wrote Bert Lance's spirited defense in the Congress against allegations of banking improprieties, and counseled former Speaker of the House Jim Wright before his 1989 resignation. He even did helpful little errands like helping Jackie Kennedy close a difficult real estate deal.

Fixes were not the only service sought from Clark Clifford. He was summoned to the White House not only to help JFK figure out what to do about the Bay of Pigs fiasco, but to advise Johnson on the Six-Day War in the Middle East in 1967. He did all this as a private citizen, nominally nothing more than a corporate lawyer with offices near the White House who, in between jaunts over to the Oval Office or to the offices of a cabinet secretary, received as clients some of the most powerful private business people in the United States.

What he had done in all this, perhaps by instinct, was to make that sort of behavior "a perfectly respectable career for young lawyers to emulate," in the words of Charlie Peters, longtime editor of the *Washington Monthly*.[12] Clifford had in fact set the postwar pattern of public servants moving on to sell influence that reached its apogee during the Reagan era. Marjorie Williams, writing in *The Washington Post*, observed:

> If Clark Clifford could be what he was—"advisor to presidents"—at the same time he was making millions of dollars, year in and year out, working for the biggest corporations in America; if he could nip across Lafayette Square from his office to help Lyndon Johnson sort out the Six-Day War in between helping General Electric and McDonnell Douglas and Knight Ridder and scores more to palliate the wearisome meddling of the federal government; if Clark Clifford could do all this, then surely the friendly relationship of political power and corporate wealth in Washington is just the natural order of things.[13]

Clark Clifford was all about access and connections. From that first phone call from Boots Adams he had played the game with quiet discretion. He was rarely mentioned in the media, and when he was, it was generally with awe and reverence. Still, little anecdotes leaked out over the years about this legendary public servant's fondness for private trade. His friend and client Jack Kennedy once joked that Clifford was not like so many others who sought to profit from their government service. "All he asks in return," Kennedy said, "is merely for us to advertise his law firm on the backs of one-dollar bills."[14]

Another tale was recounted by David Halberstam in *The Best and the Brightest*:

> The story is told of Clifford being called by a company president who explained a complicated problem and asked for Clark Clifford's advice. Clifford told him not to say or do anything. Then he sent a bill for $10,000. A few days later the president called back to protest the large size of the bill and also asked why he should keep quiet. "Because I told you to," Clifford answered and sent him another bill for an additional $5,000.[15]

Yet another tale had Clifford charging a client $10,000 for a single telephone call to the White House. Some or all of these tales may be apocryphal—it is impossible to check them out—and yet their tone and substance reflect the view long taken of Clifford by Washington insiders. Beneath the courtly exterior and melodious voice there was a razor-sharp businessman who sold his "access" more adroitly and more subtly than anyone before or since.

As rich as he made himself from his law practice, however, there is no evidence that Clifford had any real use for money other than as a yardstick to measure his stature in Washington. He worked most of the time, did not drink, smoked precisely three cigarettes a day, took his twenty-minute lunches at a humble cafeteria at a downtown YWCA, and was quickly bored whenever he tried to take a vacation. He had lived in the same Nineteenth Century clapboard farmhouse in suburban Washington since the 1950s. In the garage were a Jaguar— the most conspicuous luxury—and an aged Cadillac Fleetwood. The interior of his home was anything but lavish. Rugs were slightly frayed, and paint was chipping here and there. On the whole, a comfortable, cozy place that "displays the confident negligence of the upper class."[16] "Clark is a very simple soul, he really is," his wife, Marny, told *The Washington Post*. "I can't remember him ever, in all the years I've been married to him, wanting something."[17]

The same could not be said for his partner Robert Altman. Altman was the whiz kid at Clifford & Warnke whose ambitions and indefatigable appetite for work had endeared him to Clifford. By 1977, when Altman was only thirty, Clifford already thought enough of him to bring him in to help Bert Lance defend himself against a hostile Congress and to assign him to one of the firm's most important new clients, the Bank of Credit and Commerce International. Three years later, Altman would become president of the multistate bank holding company called First American.

As their relationship developed, the two became a formidable legal team, with Clifford playing the good cop—weighing in with his elder-statesman demeanor and impeccable credentials—and Altman the bad, calling later to threaten fierce reprisals. As Clifford entered his late seventies and early eighties, Altman's energy made him ever more valuable. What had evolved, in the words of Marny Clifford, was "almost a father-son relationship." Altman often dressed like Clifford in expensive double-breasted suits, mimicked some of Clifford's gestures, such as the famous "Clifford steeple"—a meditative gesture made by bringing his hands together at the fingertips to form a delta. Clifford was the best man at Altman's wedding and is the godfather and namesake of one of Altman's two children.

There, however, the similarities ended. If Clifford was a man whose wife could characterize him as never wanting anything in the way of material possessions, a man who was content to live in slightly tattered gentility, Altman was someone who wanted, and got, a great deal. First, there was the Wife. In 1984 Altman married actress and former Miss USA Lynda Carter, whose statuesque physique had made her famous as Wonder Woman on the mid-seventies television series of the same name. The wedding, which took place in Pacific Palisades, commingled Hollywood glamour and Washington elites. Clark Clifford and law partner Paul Warnke (the former Defense Department official and U.S. arms negotiator) chatted with such show-business luminaries as Loni Anderson, Barbara Mandrell, and Ed McMahon. Also in attendance was a well-dressed Pakistani named Agha Hasan Abedi, who offered Bob Altman's new wife her choice of cars as a wedding present. She chose a black Jaguar.

Then there was the House, a $2.6-million, 20,000-square-foot seraglio fitted out with sixteen bathrooms, a library, a fully equipped exercise studio, a music room, separate living quarters for servants, a tennis court and tennis pavilion, and a swimming pool. In the backyard an architect-designed waterfall spilled picturesquely into its own pond.

Altman clearly relished his new place among Washington's superlawyers, and his agenda reflected it. On certain days one might find him on Capitol Hill, defending the interests of clients like IBM, General Foods, and the drug industry before congressional committees. At other times he would act as president of First American, or he would look after his personal investments, which included the *USA Today* headquarters tower in suburban Virginia. He was known to fly to California on weekends to spend time with Lynda.

With the Wife, the House, the Partner, and his job as president of the largest bank in Washington, Altman in the 1980s climbed aboard a social rocketship. Though Lynda Carter was hardly a star of the first magnitude, she played brilliantly in a town surfeited with bureaucrats, lawyers, and policy wonks, and the bright, young, attractive Altmans were suddenly on everyone's A-list. They threw some of the best parties in town, including a birthday fete in early 1991 for White House economist Michael Boskin, attended by White House Chief of Staff John Sununu, among others. They gave spectacular Christmas parties, decking out the house with large-scale toy soldiers, enormous Christmas trees, and sleds, while white-gloved servants circulated with trays of artistic hors d'oeuvres. On football Sundays, less formal gatherings might include the powerful congressman John D. Dingell (D-Michigan) and his wife, Debbie, Transportation Secretary Sam Skinner (Sununu's successor as White House chief of staff), Commerce Secretary Bob Mosbacher, former House Speaker Jim Wright, George Bush's daughter, Dorothy, Chris Evert, and Martina Navratilova. In his early forties, Bob Altman was among the capital's most prominent and well-connected citizens.

Together Clifford and Altman had managed the rise of one of the fastest-growing banks in the United States. From $2.2 billion in assets in 1981, the bank had exploded over a decade to $11 billion, acquiring a number of smaller banks along the way. The number of employees had risen from 3,800 to 6,300. First American's shareholders had pumped in more than $600 million in new capital. Somehow Clifford had managed, after a thirty-five-year Washington career, to pull off yet another stunning achievement. That was the way it looked, anyway.

Clifford's presence in the 1978 Financial General takeover quickly tipped the scales in Abedi's favor. Clifford brought in the hotshot securities law firm of Wachtell Lipton Rosen & Katz and persuaded Abedi that he no longer needed Bert Lance, who had been promised the presidency of the bank. Clifford felt that Lance, whose trial for banking improprieties was about to begin, had become a liability. Meanwhile, Clifford and his young law partner were not only shepherding Adham, Fulaij, Darwaish, Zayed, Abedi, and BCCI through the thickets of the Financial General suit and serving as principal liaison with the shareholders of the bank. They were also riding point on the regulators, which meant the Fed and the banking authorities in the places where Financial General operated: New York, Maryland, Virginia, the District of Columbia, and Tennessee. Because Abedi could not let himself be seen pulling any strings at all, the entire affair quickly became a two-man show, and Clifford, assisted by Altman, put on a dazzling display of his talents.

By early 1980 the takeover had seemed to stall. After more than three years of infighting, Financial General had succeeded in what many observers believed was its goal all along: to use the legal fight to force up the bid. From an opening offer of $15 a share, the bid rose to $20, then $25, and now to $28.50.[18] Still, there seemed to be no end in sight to the litigation. And even if the two parties successfully settled their suit, there was the problem of regulatory approval: In 1979 the Fed had dismissed the group's first application.

Clifford solved both of those problems as perhaps only he could have. In early 1981 he received a call from an old acquaintance from the Johnson administration and one of the principal stockholders in Financial General: Armand Hammer, the legendary chairman of Occidental Petroleum.

"Why don't we declare an armistice?" Hammer said. "This war goes on interminably, and I'll come along and we'll sit down and talk this matter out." Clifford agreed; this was the sort of Olympian solution he preferred. Hammer brought several Financial General directors over to Clifford's Washington office. A day and a half later the dispute was settled in classic Cliffordian fashion.[19] The Arab investors would purchase Financial General from its current shareholders for a tidy premium: Many of them doubled their money.

The Fed and state banking officials weren't so easily put off. They were so openly skeptical, in fact, that they demanded a public hearing. If they were being told a well-coordinated lie, they wanted it on the public record. The meeting, which took place on April 23, 1981, was Clifford's masterstroke, and it was beautifully stage-managed. Present were Clifford, Altman, and four of the key "investors" in Financial General. They were led by Kamal Adham, whom Clifford and Altman insisted on calling "His Excellency," even though Adham was a commoner and bore no royal title of any kind. Adham told the regulators that he and his partners would be passive investors, and that BCCI would exercise no control over Financial General.

But it was Clifford's magisterial presence that carried the day. After all, this was not just a bunch of rich Arabs pledging their honor, though their prodigious wealth was clearly impressive—this was Clark Clifford, the man with the irreproachable reputation for integrity and public service. "There is no function of any kind on the part of BCCI," he assured them in that sonorous voice. "I know of no present relationship. I know of no planned future relationship that exists . . ."[20] Altman, addressing the question of the dummy companies that would be used as vehicles for Financial General's acquisition, said calmly, "There is no connection between those entities and BCCI."

And so the meeting went; each hostile question was parried in a calm and dignified way, as though there were not the slightest thing to fear. What Adham and the other shareholders told the Fed were lies and constituted felonies under U.S. banking law. Yet even more curious than what was said was what was left out. The Fed had no idea who those men flanking Clifford and Altman really were, though it had run routine checks of them through State, the CIA, and Commerce, and had found out nothing new. That Kamal Adham and A. R. Khalil were principals in the Saudi intelligence apparat and key liaisons with the CIA went unremarked upon. Not mentioned was Fulaij's $5-million loan from the BCCI subsidiary KIFCO; nor that KIFCO's, BCCI's, and Financial General's new shareholders all overlapped; nor that KIFCO had been used by Abedi to wrench control of the Pakistan national oil industry from Prime Minister Ali Bhutto. Nor that Fulaij was alleged to have taken bribes from Boeing Company as chairman of Kuwait Airways. The Federal Trade Commission alleged that he accepted at least $300,000 in payoffs from Boeing, though no penalties were ever imposed.[21] Nor, for that matter, that another investor who was present, Ali Mohammed Shorafa, listed as "director-general of the presidential court of Abu Dhabi," was also a weapons dealer.[22]

The meeting at the Fed was the last hurdle. Clifford had done what he was best at—he had persuaded others to accept his point of view. Which was, in the end, exactly why Abedi had hired him. Within a few months Clifford assembled a dream board of directors—a sort of preemptive strike against any further regulatory meddling in his bank—so laden with integrity and dignity and so suffused with government service that few would be able to question its motives or methods. The board included former Missouri Senator and Secretary of the Air Force Stuart Symington (vice chairman); former U.S. Ambassador to France and then-current president of the accounting firm of Arthur D. Little, General James M. Gavin; and retired General Elwood Quesada, who, along with David Rockefeller, had developed Washington's L'Enfant Plaza.

When Financial General tendered its shares and officially renamed itself First American in 1982, the number of shareholders had grown from the original four to fourteen. They included a veritable galaxy of the Middle East's wealthy and powerful, including Sheikh Zayed bin Sultan al-Nahayan; his son Khalifa; the members of the Abu Dhabi Investment Authority; Kamal Adham; Adham's personal assistant Sayed Jawhary; A. R. Khalil; Mohammed bin Rashid al-Maktoum; Humaid bin Rashid al-Naomi, the crown prince of the small emirate of Ajman; and Sheikh Hamad bin Mohammed al-Sharqi, ruler of the emirate of Fujairah.

Although all had been recruited by Abedi—who called on fifteen years' worth of networking in the Middle East to put the group together—not all were "fronts" in the sense that they were given BCCI loans to buy the stock in Credit and Commerce American Holdings (CCAH)/First American. Yet the seven straw men named in the Federal Reserve Bank's angry complaint nine years later—Adham (16.32 percent), Fulaij (8.58 percent), Khalil (8.49 percent), Jawhary (.51 percent), Sharqi (6.56 percent), Shorafa (6.51 percent), and Naomi (6.06 percent)—had conveniently been allotted a total of 53.03 percent of CCAH stock, giving Abedi majority control from the first moment. The real money and therefore genuine shareholdings, according to the Fed, belonged to the investors from Abu Dhabi and Dubai.[23] They would both argue later, convincingly, that they had been taken for a royal ride. This was merely the beginning.

In spite of Clifford's and Altman's repeated assurances to regulators that BCCI would have nothing to do with the management of First American, they were deeply involved with the rogue bank from the start. The very premise of the relationship—that the two would act simultaneously as lead U.S. counsel for BCCI, chief counsel for First American Bank, and chairman and president of First American— represented a staggering conflict of interest. Though they had said at the Fed hearing that BCCI would have "no function of any kind," and though they knew better than anyone of the deep suspicions that Abedi was using his Middle Eastern front men as stalking horses for his entry into the U.S. market, in 1982 they began traveling as often as once a month and at least four times a year to London, mostly to meet alone with Abedi on the subject of the management of First American Bank. Although Adham, as nominal lead shareholder, was occasionally present at these meetings, Abedi dispensed their marching orders. Clifford and Altman rarely spoke with the other shareholders, never spoke at all to many of them, and communicated with them by mail or through BCCI. As always, the capital that flowed into First American from the shareholders flowed through BCCI.

The justification for such an arrangement was that communications with those shareholders, who lived far away in the Middle East, were "difficult," and that Abedi was only facilitating the exchange of information between the investors he "advised" and their American management. This is the argument Clifford and Altman put forth. Yet this was patently absurd. Later, when asked by Senator Kerry what he thought about this arrangement, former globe-trotting BCCI executive Abdur Sakhia replied:

> Sir, I fail to understand, because I have heard both in the testimony and in the press how it was difficult to communicate with the Middle Eastern investors. I fail to understand that because the . . . list . . . involves people who did business in the United States, who came to the United States. They were not Bedouins in the desert who were being communicated to. They were intelligent people who owned banks and businesses. The Abu Dhabi Investment Authority has several billion dollars of investments in this country, and if they can manage those businesses, they do not need a channel via Mr. Abedi to First American. They could have done it directly.[24]

Even a member of Clifford's handpicked board of directors admitted that the directives came from Abedi. General Quesada told Jim McGee of *The Washington Post* that "he always understood that BCCI 'had a controlling interest in First American Bank in Washington' and had authority to give consent to FAB's plans. 'Or withhold it. They had that option.' " He also said: "They [Clifford and Altman] would go to BCCI with the capitalization amount and make sure they wanted to invest. See, they were the owners of the bank, so naturally we would have to go to them for consent on matters of major magnitude. Just like an American company." Quesada maintained all of this consistently during three interviews with McGee.[25]

What exactly were Abedi's instructions to the two men? At a July 28, 1983, meeting at the Inn on the Park in London, at which Altman made a comprehensive presentation to Abedi and Naqvi on First American's financial performance, Abedi lectured him on the concept of "joint personality"—the tight links he wanted forged between First American and BCCI. They discussed in detail the recruitment of key staff for First American Bank of New York (FABNY).[26]

It was at FABNY that Abedi exercised his greatest control, and the bank soon became a de facto arm of BCCI. When FABNY wanted to hire a chief executive officer, for example, leading candidate Bruno Richter traveled twice to London to meet and be interviewed by Abedi and then was screened a third time by Abedi in New York before being sent to Washington, D.C., to be hired by Clifford. The same thing happened when Richter began hiring his own staff. At the request of Robert Altman, Richter sent one of his top candidates, David Palmer, to London to meet Abedi. The meeting apparently went well, for Palmer was offered the job when he returned to New York.[27] Similarly, Abedi recommended two senior BCCI officials for senior positions at the New York bank; they were hired immediately. Abedi was even present in Washington when Clark Clifford interviewed Robert G. Stevens, the man who would hold the top job under Clifford and Altman at First American for seven years.

First American Bank of New York—Abedi's coveted presence in the vortex of the world's financial markets, for which he had big plans—saw yet another example of BCCI intrusion into the domain Clifford says he controlled. When FABNY wanted to acquire two branches from Bankers Trust in 1982, it was an employee of BCCI's representative office in New York who identified them and negotiated the purchase price, leading his counterparts at Bankers Trust to believe that BCCI was acting on behalf of a subsidiary. The same executive, Khusro Elley, soon afterward became a senior vice president at First American Bank of New York, for which he was recommended by Agha Hasan Abedi, who also kept him on BCCI's payroll.

Elley, an important conduit between Abedi and Altman, was responsible for looking after Abedi's interests in New York. While still with BCCI, for example, Elley met with Altman to discuss a broad range of management decisions: sublet of space, selection of FABNY's board, recruitment and hiring of staff, auditors, and lawyers, and even compensation packages. Through Elley and others, Abedi passed along orders to Altman. Abedi and Naqvi had personally visited New York and had chosen a Park Avenue location for the FABNY main office, even though Clifford and Altman objected to its cost. Altman was told pointedly by Abedi aide Shahid Jamil which auditors he was going to use.

Soon FABNY began marketing actively for BCCI, passing many of its international clients on. According to Gwynne's source in the weapons community, who had approached First American Bank of New York for financing on one of his deals, "As soon as I mentioned that this was an international deal," he said, "the Pakistanis showed up. From that moment on, it was always BCCI's deal, and this same thing happened on a number of occasions." Many of BCCI's international operations were integrated into the First American system, in terms of both deposits and a large volume of wire transfers. BCCI branches or affiliates kept a total of forty-seven different accounts with First American; between 1986 and 1990, 71 percent of incoming wire transfers to First American were from BCCI Panama, which happened to be among the most corrupt BCCI branches. In 1986 and 1987 First American deposited $74 million of its depositors' funds into accounts at BCCI Cayman Islands—a highly imprudent move for any American bank considering the losses then being suffered by BCCI and the lack of any central bank to shore up its balance sheet.

While all this was going on, Clifford and Altman were raking in large legal fees from both BCCI and First American. Though Clifford loudly proclaimed that he had taken only a nominal salary of $50,000 (Altman took none) from First American, he and Altman collected more than $15 million in legal fees for their work for both institutions.

Though Clifford and Altman spoke most often to Abedi during their London visits, the man they nominally reported to—the apparent lead shareholder of First American—was Kamal Adham. Of all the front men, none was more active, or more useful, than Adham; none was more suggestive of the extraordinary geopolitical reach of Agha Hasan Abedi. Abedi had met him in the early 1970s through an introduction from his friend Zayed. Adham was from the start the key man in the investor group that purchased Financial General. He referred to himself as the "informal chairman of the investors." In that role he came to know Clifford and Altman well; flanked by Abedi at BCCI's London offices, it was Adham who hired Clifford and Altman as chairman and president of First American Bank.

Kamal Adham was one of the true inside power players of the Middle East, a shrewd, jovial man who had for decades straddled the worlds of Middle Eastern business and politics. He was the half brother of Iffat, the favorite wife of King Faisal, who ruled Saudi Arabia from 1964 until his death in 1975. Adham had so impressed his royal brother-in-law that by the time he was in his early thirties, he was one of the king's closest confidants.

Like so many other enterprising Arabs in the 1960s and 1970s, when oil revenues were booming and foreign companies were lining up to sell their products, Adham had used his royal connection to commercial advantage. The way most commoners in the Middle East got rich off the oil boom was through a simple system known as "agency" arrangements. In order to sell a product or service in Saudi Arabia, you had to know someone in the royal family, which authorized all expenditures. If you did not know a princeling or a royal cousin, then you hired an "agent" who provided you access for a "commission." Though this commission often looks very much like a "bribe"—the U.S. Congress spent much time in the 1970s trying to distinguish between the two—it was nonetheless the way business was done, and few were better at it than Kamal Adham.

The list of his agency deals was long and illustrious. In the early 1960s Adham had used the royal influence to end-run Saudi Arabia's own oil minister and set up a deal with a Japanese oil consortium. (Kamal got 2 percent of the deal.[28]) He had many other such arrangements, all of which sprang from his access to the singular entity that was the Kingdom of Saudi Arabia. Since 1951, when he was only twenty-two, he controlled the franchise for Carrier Corp. air conditioners; he owned and operated a 7UP bottling plant; other companies he owned built roads, airports, and office buildings and imported elevators and computers.[29] By the mid-1960s Adham's influence was such that he simultaneously came to represent three defense firms and was being ardently courted by a fourth. Said Northrop representative Kermit Roosevelt, "Adham already has a piece of the Lightning deal, the Mirage deal, and the Lockheed deal and is trying to complete the square by an arrangement with Northrop." He also came to be the principal broker for weapons purchased by Saudi Arabia on behalf of Egypt.[30]

But perhaps his richest contract was with Boeing Company, which paid him millions of dollars in commissions to help it sell passenger jetliners to the fledgling Saudi airlines. One 1975 transaction shows just how helpful he was. That year McDonnell Douglas Corporation was closing in on a contract with the state of Egypt for six airliners. At the last minute, for no apparent reason, Egypt decided to buy Boeing jets instead. The way it worked was classic Middle Eastern business. Concerned that it would lose the sale, Boeing tapped another agent, Mahdi Tajir, a close friend of Zayed and the United Arab Emirates' ambassador to London and Paris, who in turn tapped Zayed for a $90-million advance to Egypt. Boeing then turned to Adham, who intervened at the highest levels of the Egyptian government to ensure that Zayed's money was deployed toward the purchase of the Boeing planes.[31]

That and other similar transactions had led to a three-year investigation of Boeing's commission payments by the U.S. Securities and Exchange Commission, whose goal in part was to figure out exactly who Boeing was using to accomplish these sleights of hand. Curiously, in the words of a 1976 *Wall Street Journal* article, Boeing's efforts to suppress those names, particularly Adham's, "has been accomplished with significant help from the State Department, which entered a court fight between the SEC and Boeing to argue that disclosure of Boeing's 'highly placed' consultants abroad could harm U.S. foreign policy interests."[32]

How could the mere disclosure of Adham's name affect U.S. foreign policy? In two ways. First, Adham was the head of the Saudi internal security service—arguably the most important agency of the government, since it protected the royal family—and the General Intelligence Directorate of Saudi Arabia. In that role he was the principal liaison between the CIA and European intelligence agencies, and he even had an agency code name: Tumbleweed. In geopolitical terms, Adham was the five-hundred-pound gorilla of Saudi intelligence, an outfit known and feared for its merciless hunts for dissidents and brutal methods of repression. In its early years its role was to assist the royalists in the bordering country of Yemen in their civil war against insurgent Marxists. But as time went by, it began to wield wider influence, which extended to the surveillance of Saudi citizens and political enemies of the king. (According to several human-rights organizations, Adham's intelligence network had become more of a conventional secret police, and under his leadership political opponents of the ruling al-Saud family were tortured or killed.[33])

But the second and more important foreign policy concern was that Adham was the kingdom's key link to Egyptian President Anwar as-Sadat in the years leading to the Camp David accords in 1979—the years following the 1973 war, when the Saudi-Egypt axis acquired key strategic importance. Egypt required Saudi subsidies to survive, and it was Adham's role, among others, to distribute hundreds of millions of Saudi dollars each year to his close friend Sadat. When Sadat expelled Soviet advisers and severed relations with Russia in 1972, it was a direct result of King Faisal's anti-Soviet campaign. The agent of that campaign was Adham, who, as historian Robert Lacey wrote in *The Kingdom*, "distributed Saudi cash lavishly in Egypt to buy support for Faisal's anti-Russian push."[34] That was not all. In 1978 and 1979

Adham ran cash directly from Zayed and the CIA to Sadat personally and is credited with having applied at least some of the pressure needed to bring Sadat to the table at Camp David. (It should be noted that this was going on during Abedi's run at Financial General, where he used Adham as his principal front.)

While Abedi would deftly tap Zayed and the money-glutted Abu Dhabians for real money, he needed Adham for the same reason he needed Clifford: diplomatic stature, influence, and connections. Documents would later show that Adham never had to front cash in his role as nominee shareholder for Abedi. The first instance of Adham fronting for Abedi was a stunning piece of work that blocked socialist Prime Minister Ali Bhutto's attempt to nationalize Pakistan's nascent oil industry. The other front men in the deal turned out to be the very same ones that Abedi was using to buy his American banks: Adham, Fulaij, and Darwaish.

The second major transaction that Abedi and Adham worked together was BCCI's secret acquisition of Financial General Bankshares. By using Adham as a nominee, Abedi and BCCI were able to control between 12 percent and 19 percent of the shares of CCAH, the Netherlands Antilles shell company that Clifford chaired and that owned First American Bank. In 1982, when Adham acquired 19,050 shares of CCAH, he paid $13 million in cash. In spite of his direct representations to the Fed, the source of the cash was a loan from BCCI. After similar transactions in 1983, BCCI controlled 26,319 CCAH shares—16 percent of the company—in Adham's name, and in 1986 BCCI's Cayman Islands branch advanced another $19 million to him for the purchase of more shares. As the millions flowed out of the Caymans in "loans" to Adham, his legal liability increased, and in 1987 he asked Abedi for reassurance that he would never be forced to make good on the phony loans. In August of 1987 a lawyer from the Caymanian ICIC wrote to Adham to assure him that he would carry no personal liability for the loans.[35]

What did Adham get out of all this? According to investigators at the Fed and elsewhere, he was paid tens of millions of dollars during his tenure as a CCAH shareholder. The other fronts were paid somewhat less. For Adham, this was perhaps just another clever agency arrangement, commissions in exchange for services.

Yet as devious as Adham was, for sheer duplicity in the service of Abedi and BCCI he paled beside another portly, jovial Saudi with impeccable connections in the kingdom: Ghaith Rashad Pharaon.

.   .   .

The year was 1983, in the heady early days of Reaganism's rising arc, of a decade of greed, ostentation, and corruption not seen in the United States since the 1920s. The place was Richmond Hill, Georgia, an obscure little town just outside of Savannah. The occasion was a soiree thrown by Ghaith Pharaon, the smiling and gregarious face of the Arab "invasion" of the United States, a sort of Jay Gatsby in burnoose. He had invited three hundred of his closest friends.

This was no ordinary party, no ordinary place. Though Richmond Hill itself looks like many small Georgia towns—a few modest homes, white-steepled churches, a police station, and a firehouse—the Pharaon residence is among the most splendid mansions in the South. The house was built on an 1,800-acre estate as a winter home by Henry Ford in the 1930s, fell later into disrepair, then was purchased and renovated by Pharaon in 1981. Renovated is perhaps not the proper word. Each of the five hundred windowpanes in the old Ford house was refitted with beveled glass. Italian marble was flown in to replace stairs and patios, faux marble was created with paint on wood throughout the house. From gold-plated bathroom fixtures to millions of dollars' worth of sculpture and art, the house had been spectacularly remodeled. Guests who arrived that night saw before them a Greek Revival mansion of light-colored brick with monumental white columns and ornate staircases surmounting a bluff high above the Ogeechee River, fifty-five acres of landscaped gardens and sculpture-filled glens, a black-bottomed swimming pool, an eighteen-hole golf course larger than the one at Augusta (though Pharaon himself did not play golf), and extensive stables for Pharaon's Arabians and Argentine polo ponies.[36]

This was what the locals called "the Pharaon Zone." Shut out as they were from such affairs, they would never arrive at much of an understanding of what exactly was going on inside the house. (The mayor of Richmond Hill once observed, "Nobody's going down there unless you're a retired secretary of state or something like that."[37]) Pharaon had given the residents some recreational land and a drug-sniffing Labrador retriever named Duke but hadn't invited them to his parties. What was going on that night behind the huge gates tended by armed guards was Pharaon's first big event, a society benefit for the nearby Savannah Symphony Orchestra and Savannah Ballet. No expense had been spared. Pharaon had flown in for the event in his personal 727 jet, monogrammed on the tail with the initials GRP. He had rented, it was said, every available limousine between Jacksonville, Florida, and Charleston, South Carolina, for his guests. Flowers had been flown in from Europe. A society orchestra played softly while guests wandered the enormous balcony with a view of the river below and of the small marina Pharaon had built to accommodate his friends' yachts.

Among the guests that night were former President Jimmy Carter and his wife, Rosalynn, who would be in frequent attendance at Pharaon's Richmond Hill mansion in the coming years, especially as Carter's relationship with Pharaon's close friend Agha Hasan Abedi deepened. The short (five feet eight), stout, bewhiskered, and elegantly dressed Pharaon greeted them in typical fashion at the door, drink and cigar in hand, a broad nervous grin on his face. They were his special guests that evening, the highlight of which came shortly after it was discovered that there was a conspicuous shortfall in the charitable monies donated. With equally typical flourish, and in the presence of the Carters, Pharaon pulled out his billfold and wrote a check for the balance.

Charity, in fact, provided Pharaon and Carter grounds for a happy and practical relationship. In exchange for Pharaon's donations to several of Carter's favorite charities, Pharaon got bragging rights to Carter and even got Carter himself at occasions such as the Savannah Symphony benefit. According to former Pharaon business associate Dale Murray, Pharaon bragged constantly about knowing Carter. At one point, said Murray, "Pharaon had reported to me that he and [savings and loan mogul David] Paul had attended a meeting with Carter. They were arranging to put a great deal of money in some foundation that Carter had. . . . If you ask me for a number, I would say a million [dollars]. One hundred thousand dollars didn't impress anybody much."[38]

In the years to come, Pharaon would throw at least two such parties each year. The ambience he created in the tiny Georgia town was perhaps best described by Peter Applebome in *The New York Times.* "Until recent years," wrote Applebome, "Richmond Hill was best known as a wide spot in the road near Chico's Monkey Farm, a roadside menagerie now out of business. In the 1980s the rich and famous—Saudi princes, Pakistani financiers, Chinese TV stars, and American politicians from Alexander Haig to Andrew Young—flocked here to an improbable social whirl that updated the Great Gatsby to the era of Eurodollars, international trade, arms dealers, and drug cartels."[39]

The parties indeed attracted a motley assortment of celebrities, including F. Lee Bailey and Fess Parker, to name just two jarringly dissimilar characters. And they were conspicuously populated by young, well-endowed women. "The women who were the wives or girlfriends of these international men, especially the Pakistani and Saudi men, would just be loaded with jewelry, you know, the real stuff," former *Savannah News-Press* society columnist Julia Jones Williams told the *Times*. "And every single one of them had these silicone chests that were way out to there. You know, you could balance your cocktail glass on their chests."[40] Pharaon himself, it was said, had six passions: money, beautiful young women, Johnnie Walker Black, expensive cigars, fine art and antiques, and deep-sea fishing.

The putative billionaire and major BCCI shareholder, who served as the pivot in Abedi's secret acquisition of three American banks, fronted for Abedi as chairman of Attock Cement, KIFCO, and Attock Oil Corporation, was one of the luckiest men of his generation. The sweep and depth of his empire in that year called to mind an image from Walt Disney: Scrooge McDuck performing joyous dolphin dives in his prodigious money bin. Pharaon was that rich. His very name means "pharaoh" in Arabic, and his pharaonic good luck began with his birth in 1940 as the son of one of the most influential figures in the history of Saudi Arabia: Dr. Rashad Pharaon.

Rashad Pharaon had the good fortune to serve as physician to the founder of modern Saudi Arabia, King Abdul-Aziz ibn Saud, who happened to be a hypochondriac. The hypochondria led the elder Pharaon to the royal inner circle, which he never left, becoming in time the king's closest adviser and a confidant of four successive Saudi kings. From 1948 to 1954 Rashad Pharaon served as Saudi ambassador to France, and his son Ghaith attended the very best French schools. For his college education Ghaith went to the United States, receiving an undergraduate degree from Stanford and an M.B.A. from Harvard.

Ghaith Pharaon launched himself into the construction business in Saudi Arabia in 1965 with $150,000 given to him by his father. The company was called Saudi Arabian Research and Development Corporation, or REDEC for short. Like Abedi, who in those years was chugging around the Gulf in his chartered plane, trying to cultivate the new oil barons, Pharaon's timing could not have been better. By the time of the 1973 Arab oil embargo and the trebling of oil prices, Pharaon was positioned to be one of the prime beneficiaries of the $150-billion Saudi building boom that took place in the 1970s.

Pharaon's bases of commercial power were the cities of Jedda and Mecca. Jedda was a sweltering, chaotic, and decidedly time-warped boomtown on the coast of the Red Sea whose historical raison d'être was its role as the point of debarkation for pilgrims on their way to Mecca—many of whom were traditionally fleeced by the good merchants of the city. The Jedda of Pharaon's era was a place where shiny new Mercedes limousines and Bedouin goats often competed for passage through the steamy streets. It was the big merchant city in Saudi Arabia where nothing worked; phones, electricity, water, and sewerage operated intermittently at best. Roads tended to end abruptly and for no apparent reason. Pharaon's Jedda was an ancient crossroads forcibly dragged into the Twentieth Century by a surfeit of petrodollars; when he got through with it, it was noticeably more modern but still nothing worked.

Abedi had come across the young Pharaon in 1967. Though he was never allowed to open his own bank in Saudi Arabia, never got his hands on the huge Saudi royal deposits he dreamed about, and never gained a strong entree to the more powerful members of the royal family, Abedi did rather better with the lesser princes and with the kingdom's wealthiest commoners, most notably Kamal Adham, whom he had met the year before. And it was Adham who introduced Abedi to Pharaon, whose newly minted REDEC was just beginning to flex its muscles. The three would soon become partners in the Hyatt Regency Hotel in Jedda and close associates.[41]

By the mid-1970s REDEC had become one of the largest companies in the kingdom, with revenues exceeding $1 billion. Pharaon had secured two hundred $1-million-plus contracts for the sewer and storm drainage systems in Jedda, Mecca, and Dammam. He operated a network of forty different companies, including joint ventures with such giants as South Korean Daelim and the Ralph M. Parsons Company of the United States. He owned pharmaceutical companies, steel-fabricating plants, and water-bottling plants.[42] He owned an international hotel in partnership with Kamal Adham and Khalid bin-Mahfouz of the National Commercial Bank of Saudi Arabia—a project financed by Agha Hasan Abedi and BCCI. In 1979 REDEC had income of $2.5 billion and employed 17,000 people. By the end of that same year REDEC had imported for its own account 5 million tons of cement, making it the biggest mover of cement in the world.[43] Pharaon already had holdings all over the world and had demonstrated an uncanny talent for recruiting famous and powerful people. In Canada, to take just one example, he purchased a company called Miron Cement in Montreal in 1979. Within a year the company's board boasted the speaker of Canada's senate, the former president of the country's biggest bank, the former Canadian finance minister, and a former Quebec cabinet minister.[44]

Pharaon, who was not yet forty, was rolling in cash. He owned the palatial Château de Montfort in the Dordogne region of France, Henry Ford's mansion in Richmond Hill, a London town house on Berkeley Square, opulent homes in Hong Kong, Saudi Arabia, and Malaysia. For each of his homes he had a yacht, and for short hops he would forgo his 727 in favor of the more convenient Learjet. His main office in Paris occupied the choicest location in the city, on Place de la Concorde, flanked by the American embassy and the Hotel Crillon on one side and the Tuileries gardens on the other. Titian's portrait of Philip II hung behind his desk. (Like many other things about Pharaon, the painting turned out to be a fake.) He was, to many, an impressive man, full of constant nervous energy, chewing his nails while he switched from flawless English to flawless French to flawless Arabic to take calls coming through his office. Withal, he said proudly that he was not addicted to his work. He worked, he said, from 8:30 A.M. to noon, took two hours for lunch, then a three-hour siesta, followed by work from 5:00 P.M. until 8:30 P.M. He took two to three months off each year, including at least six weeks of vacation on his yacht in the Mediterranean with his wife and children.

With all of his shamelessly displayed wealth, Pharaon stands as a symbol of the 1980s: an apparently modestly talented individual feeding off the oil boom and the greatest transfer of wealth in history. Yet Pharaon as metaphor for the Me Decade is even more apt. For he was, in addition to all of that, a fraud of titanic proportions, a poor businessman who eventually failed at almost everything he did and much of whose money came from elsewhere than his own coffers. In the end, $500 million of it came from BCCI's unwitting depositors through the careful hands of Abedi. In the grand scheme of things, convicted New York financier Ivan Boesky is a penny-ante player compared to the global machinations of the man who insisted on being called "Doctor" Pharaon, even though the highest degree he held, honorary or otherwise, was a Master of Business Administration. As this book goes to press, he is cruising the Mediterranean on the *Pharaoh,* a gleaming white yacht that is one of his relatively few assets that has not been seized or sold.

What happened to bring such a high-flying tycoon so low? The first and easiest answer is the collapse in oil prices, which similarly destroyed Abedi by closing down the pipeline of funding that kept both of their rickety empires afloat. While Abedi and Naqvi turned to intelligence, espionage, weapons dealing, and the drug trade to brake the financial skid, Pharaon turned increasingly to Abedi and Naqvi, emerging eventually as their most audacious and useful front man,

particularly in the United States. Also driving his spectacular fall were
Pharaon's own limitations as a businessman. He was notoriously
wrong as a stock investor. Even at the height of Pharaon's success in
the late 1970s, many of his investments had gone sour. His purchase
of Commonwealth Bank of Detroit in 1975, which had gained him
instant recognition as the first Arab to buy a billion-dollar U.S. bank,
was such a bad investment that he liquidated it almost immediately at
cost. In 1979 two *Forbes* magazine reporters interviewed Pharaon in
a luxurious suite at the Regency Hotel, jammed with Pharaon's traveling entourage of Frenchmen, Arabs, and Americans, all of whom, the
reporters noted, seemed to be smoking large cigars. The writers estimated that he had spent over $150 million on acquisitions in the
previous eighteen months, making him one of the largest cash buyers
in the world, but noted skeptically:

> Pharaon would like to be thought of as a contemplative, astute
> investor who finds good assets that have been undervalued by the
> market. . . . It's a good thing Pharaon isn't worried about stock
> prices because, by that standard, he has taken a hell of a licking
> on his U.S. investments [in public companies], now valued at
> $17.9 million, down from the $28.8 million he paid. . . . So far
> Pharaon, the consummate, urbane multinational investor, still
> hasn't made it to the head of his investment class.[45]

He never would. One of his less than perspicacious acts as investor
was to organize a group of wealthy Arab investors—including the king
of Saudi Arabia and Khalid bin-Mahfouz, for whom he was acting as
agent—to finance the Hunt brothers' disastrous attempt in the late
1970s to corner the silver market. Though Pharaon apparently
managed to squeeze a commission out of the deal, his syndicate of
investors lost untold millions.[46]

REDEC, which flourished while the oil revenues rolled, disinte-
grated with alarming speed in the petro-bust of the early 1980s.
Pharaon had never had to manage a company under adversity, let
alone a company he had loaded with a colossal debt, and the task was
patently beyond a man who preferred cruising the Mediterranean to
spending long hours in unpleasant and thoughtful work. By 1985 the
bust in oil prices resulted in a sharp drop in demand for cement and
construction, and the company was deeply in debt, owing some fifty
Western banks a staggering $330 million, and in deep trouble. The
loud and constant complaints of those creditors, who wanted to move
against Pharaon and force him to liquidate his assets, were aired at

last through royal circles. When the finance minister of Saudi Arabia told King Fahd that Pharaon was sullying the kingdom's good name, the king revoked Pharaon's passport while investigators hired by the Western banks started digging into his finances. Though Pharaon would get his passport back and manage to reschedule his debt in 1987 and thus stay a step or two ahead of his creditors for several years, he would never recover his honor in his own country. A year later he officially applied for citizenship in Argentina, where he was still regarded as a glamorous Saudi billionaire. What was left of his company went into an orderly liquidation in early 1989.

Pharaon's meteoric fall was tainted with yet another badge of dishonor: a long, fruitful, and frequently criminal relationship with Agha Hasan Abedi and BCCI. It is difficult to say who took whom for the bigger ride: Pharaon, who used BCCI depositors' money to pump himself up long after his business affairs had gone definitively south; or Abedi, who successfully employed Pharaon to spearhead his assault on the U.S. banking market. Either way, it was a marriage of extreme convenience.

Abedi and Pharaon, the ascetic and the sybarite, were very different people. Abedi was religious and deeply ideological. Pharaon was neither. Pharaon had been raised in the international beaumonde, while Abedi had never ventured farther than Lucknow and Bombay as a young man until his forced migration to Pakistan. While the two did share a taste for fine clothing and expensive colognes, Abedi—who was far, far wealthier than Pharaon ever was—it could be said, was all about power; Pharaon was about money. (Adham, Abedi's other main front, neatly united the two.) But Pharaon's eventual selection as Abedi's key front and nominee made perfect sense in terms of Abedi's own ambitions. For him Pharaon was the new face of the Third World, an intelligent, cultivated figure who reversed all the clichés about poor backward brown people living somewhere to the south of real civilization. Like OPEC itself, Pharaon embodied the bold, unapologetic ethos of the new order, the very same image Abedi sought to project through BCCI. Pharaon was moreover a palatable commodity in the West, a man who spoke refined English and bore the imprimatur of Parisian society and two leading American universities. Such nonroyal Arabs were hard to come by in the early days of the oil boom.

Pharaon's purchase of Bert Lance's stake in the National Bank of Georgia in early 1978, orchestrated entirely by his friend Abedi, was his first act as Abedi's front man in the United States. By 1979

Pharaon, acting as a front for Abedi, had bought out the bank's other investors, making BCCI full owner of the bank, even as the bank was being sued by the SEC and Financial General Bankshares in Washington for attempting the same sort of nominee purchase there.

In Georgia all anyone knew was that a spectacularly rich Arab had rescued Bert Lance and had bought a modest $400-million Atlanta bank. No one had ever heard of Agha Hasan Abedi. But behind the scenes Abedi moved to assure himself of a permanent beachhead. In the years following that acquisition he befriended two of Georgia's most famous political players: Jimmy Carter and Andrew Young. Abedi had recruited Young, who was also a close friend of Jimmy Carter, shortly after Young left his post as United States ambassador to the United Nations (he later became mayor of Atlanta). Young was interested, as was Carter, in philanthropy in Africa; and Abedi was interested both in the marquee value of an association with Young and in getting from Young names of potential clients in southern Africa and Central America. Abedi promised to give Young's trading company an annual retainer of $50,000. Meanwhile, in 1981, Abedi—through Pharaon—set Young's company up with a $74,000 term loan and a $125,000 line of credit, even though it was considered by the bank's own analysts to be uncreditworthy. "Andrew Young Associates, Inc." wrote an internal auditor at National Bank of Georgia, "is a small, illiquid, unprofitable, infinitely leveraged company which has not yet achieved the revenues [sic] levels that it had expected. As a result of the aforementioned and NBG's under-collateralized position, the analyst believes that unwarranted credit risk may have been undertaken in extending credit to the company."[47] In 1985 BCCI formally took over the loan and later decided that Young did not have to pay off the remaining $160,000. A gift, basically, though Young's partner Stoney Cooks would later say that the forgiven loan was really the accumulated "consulting fees" Abedi had earlier promised them. Like Carter, and often with Carter, Young flew all over Africa on Abedi's plane, and Young himself said that there was scarcely a charitable idea he and Jimmy Carter had that Abedi was not willing to fund.

Abedi also cultivated another powerful black leader: Jesse Jackson. The two met on a number of occasions, usually in London at Abedi's offices. As with Carter and Young, their common interest was in the health and development of the Third World, especially Africa. In 1985 Abedi instructed his bank officers to give Jackson the royal treatment when he traveled to Paris on his way to Africa. A BCCI officer told authorities that the bank had also given Jackson cash "contributions," but Jackson told *Time* correspondent Sylvester Monroe that he did not remember any such contributions or other favors from BCCI. Jackson's finance man said that Jackson frequently received cash contributions, but he had no memory of money from Abedi's men. However, Nazir Chinoy, then BCCI's general manager for France, remembers Abedi's orders that Jackson be feted. Chinoy put Jackson up in Abedi's usual suite at the Paris Hilton and paid some $11,000 for his accommodations there and later at the Hotel George V. What Jackson did in return is not clear, though Chinoy says he asked him "if it would be profitable for BCCI branches if the central banks for different countries banked with BCCI." Chinoy said that it would. Jackson then told Chinoy that he would take this up with Abedi when he visited him in London.

Once he had consolidated control at National Bank of Georgia, Abedi reconfigured it along the lines of his own bank. In 1979, shortly after Pharaon had bought up the remaining stock, Abedi summoned to his Leadenhall office both Pharaon and a man named Roy P. M. Carlson. Carlson was the Bank of America executive who had set up that bank's purchase of 30 percent of BCCI back in 1972. Carlson had entertained Abedi when he came to the United States to negotiate the deal, and the two had become friends. They remained in contact when, in 1975, Carlson left BofA to become president of Rahim Irvani's giant Melli Group in Iran.[48] Abedi and Irvani too were close associates and partners in the bank Abedi started, Iran Arab Bank, and Abedi had lined up Irvani to be one of his front men in the Financial General acquisition. To complete the circle, Irvani and Carlson were also partners in former CIA Director Richard Helms's consulting firm, Safeer, which he had started after leaving his post as U.S. ambassador to Iran. The three men chatted amiably in Abedi's office, remembering old times, shaking their heads in dismay at the terrible events that were transforming Iran—events that had cost Abedi his bank and Carlson his job in Tehran. Then came the moment for which Carlson had been summoned: Pharaon offered him the top job at National Bank of Georgia. Carlson accepted.

Thus began Abedi's "Southern strategy," in which Ghaith Pharaon would play a key role. Under Abedi's and Pharaon's guidance, Carlson moved quickly to reconfigure the bank and to bring it into the BCCI family. Its logo was changed to mimic the distinctive hexagonal design of BCCI's own corporate symbol. Three BCCI executives, including one high-ranking official named Tariq Jamil, were hired as senior vice presidents charged with transforming a sleepy Southern retail bank into an international operation. Meanwhile, BCCI officers around the world were being retrained to market the services of NBG as BCCI's American affiliate, and NBG officers in Georgia were handing out BCCI annual reports along with those of their own bank. Carlson led delegations of the bank's officers to Abedi's annual BCCI conventions, where they would be feted as members of the family. All the while Pharaon was pumping up the bank's capital with BCCI money: Under his tenure NBG's assets quadrupled from $400 million to $1.6 billion.[49]

The result of all this effort was the creation of a financial institution unlike any other in the United States, one that operated less like a U.S. bank than as an international branch of BCCI. NBG existed primarily as a clearinghouse for BCCI funds in the United States, as a primary destination of BCCI letters of credit, and as a bank that provided loans and other services to BCCI's international clientele. In the process of molding itself along the lines of the Third World bank, NBG neglected its traditional retail deposit base. By 1987 the bank's share of the Atlanta retail market had dropped precipitously to 5 percent. And that same year the bank began to suffer a disastrous string of loan losses that would require huge new capital infusions to keep it solvent. Ghaith Pharaon and BCCI ran National Bank of Georgia into the ground, leaving behind them an unprofitable operation and a deeply scarred balance sheet.

Ghaith Pharaon's relationship with Abedi and BCCI deepened in other ways during the early 1980s. Pharaon was buying up BCCI stock in those years at a rapid rate—so much so that by 1985 he was listed as BCCI's single largest shareholder, with 16 percent of the company. But this holding, like NBG, was a sham, the result of Abedi's infamous circular loan scheme. To buy the shares in BCCI, Abedi arranged for loans to Pharaon from ICIC. Pharaon used the money to "buy" BCCI stock, which he then placed with ICIC as collateral for the loans, which were never meant to be repaid. From $75 million to $100 million moved this way, the effect of which was to fatten Abedi's share of the bank by using money from his own depositors.

In 1986 Pharaon, acting as Abedi's nominee, acquired yet another bank: Independence Bank of Encino, California, for which he paid $23 million. The true nature of the transaction was concealed when Swaleh Naqvi secretly funneled money to Pharaon through the Parisian Banque Arabe et Internationale d'Investissement, a bank run by a member of BCCI's board. Banque Arabe then informed California bank regulators, using precise language supplied by BCCI, that Pharaon had clear funds on hand to make his acquisition. As he had done at NBG, Pharaon quickly installed BCCI personnel, including another high-ranking BCCI officer named Kemal Shoaib, whom he made president. And as with NBG, Pharaon ran Independence quickly out of capital. The bank had to be rescued in 1991 with funds seized from BCCI.

At the time he purchased Independence Bank, Pharaon looked to the regulators like an extremely wealthy man. He listed his personal assets at $584.2 million. His yacht alone was worth $10 million, his collection of antiques and fine jewelry, $25 million. But much of this alleged wealth was not his own. According to Ali Mirza, Pharaon had borrowed as much as $500 million at one time from Abedi's Caymanian accounts. Though the full amount of his borrowings by 1986 was something less than that, this meant that a substantial portion of his wealth was not his own. All of which was made considerably worse by REDEC's severe losses.

By 1986 Pharaon's creditor banks were circling ever closer, demanding that he sell off assets to pay down his $330 million debt, and in Leadenhall Street warning flags went up. Creditors typically hired investigators, and any investigator who got close to Pharaon's BCCI-related holdings—National Bank of Georgia, for example—would realize that they were false assets. Even more important, they included Pharaon's sham stake in BCCI itself. Because Pharaon was by that time BCCI's largest single shareholder, any probe into the nature of those holdings would expose Abedi's larger fraud and would likely bring down the entire house of cards. On top of all those concerns, BCCI was suddenly bleeding cash. That same year the bank suffered what accountants now estimate to be a $450-million loss on commodities trading. Without their customary safety net of incoming petrodollars, Abedi and Naqvi were suddenly, and for the first time, running scared. They had to deal with Pharaon, and they had to plug the gaping holes in their profit-and-loss statement. And they had to do it very quickly.

The idea they hit upon neatly solved all three problems. They instructed Pharaon to put the National Bank of Georgia up for sale. Meanwhile, Abedi told Clark Clifford, on behalf of the CCAH shareholders, to put in a bid. According to testimony by Abdur Sakhia, Clifford and Altman participated in a November 1985 meeting with Abedi during which Abedi informed them of his decision and gave them instructions on how to carry it out. To ensure that the sale looked something like a free-market transaction, Pharaon also put out feelers to one of the biggest banks in the South, North Carolina National Bank (NCNB), which had shown earlier interest in acquiring NBG.

In the meantime, there was the problem of U.S. interstate banking

laws. At the time Abedi decided to sell off NBG, Georgia law prohibited out-of-state banks from buying local banks. Solving this problem
led to the million-dollar influence campaign waged against the
Georgia legislature by Pharaon and local attorney Charlie Jones,
which in turn led to an FBI investigation and, ultimately, the indictment of Abedi, Pharaon, and former NBG officers for fraud.

Still, the Georgia legislators (who, as Bert Lance later noted, would
have relaxed the state's banking laws *without* persuasion) were wined
and dined, invited to Pharaon's Richmond Hill soirees, and flown to
vacation resorts. The bill was rammed through in a single session of
the legislature. The vote was unanimous in the State Senate, and 155
to 4 in the House.

That cleared the boards for the sale of the bank—a transaction that
was a lock virtually from the beginning, since Abedi himself had
ordered it up and had told Clifford and Altman to do it. The only
problem was that the price Abedi wanted far exceeded what National
Bank of Georgia was worth. First American's own financial analysts
put the value somewhere between $120 million and $180 million.
Independent bank analysts Keefe Bruyette & Woods said it was worth
$130 million to $144 million.[50] But First American, spearheaded by
Altman, came in with an offer of $220 million.[51]

Since this was so far off the market and so imprudent on its face,
First American's banking executives, who normally ran the bank itself
for Clifford and Altman, had to be cut out of negotiations from the
start. Clifford and Altman alone handled that, and Roy Carlson ran the
negotiation for National Bank of Georgia. This inspired more than a
little grumbling among First American officers and prompted one to
observe that the bank they were buying was a "dog"—a correct
observation, as it turned out. A year after the purchase NBG began
running up large loan losses, and in 1991 alone $35 million had to be
infused to keep the bank alive.[52] Even more suspect was the "due
diligence" review conducted by Altman—First American's internal
assessment of the value of what it was buying. "Unlike a normal due
diligence review, conducted in order to determine the price to be paid
for a company," reads the Federal Reserve System's civil action
against Clifford and Altman, "this review was ordered by Altman to
determine what First American had acquired. . . . Despite the significant and at times suspicious expenses . . . and the evidence of significant mismanagement and hidden liabilities, [First American] did not
exercise its legal right to withdraw from the transaction."

The bailout money would come from Khalid bin-Mahfouz—the

chairman of the largest bank in Saudi Arabia and financial adviser to the king—in a transaction that was also targeted at removing Pharaon as a BCCI shareholder. In late 1986 Abedi arranged for Mahfouz to buy out all of Pharaon's shares. Instead of being spent to pay down the loans Pharaon had taken to buy the BCCI stock, however, much of the money went directly to BCCI, which then gave it to Pharaon as the purchase price of NBG, who in turn remitted virtually all of it to pay off the loans he had taken out to buy NBG. The now-dangerous Pharaon was removed as the major shareholder in BCCI and the owner of NBG, BCCI replenished its cash coffers, and its two largest U.S. assets were united in one big interstate bank. The transaction was perfectly circular: Abedi raised the money by persuading Mahfouz to buy Pharaon's shares in BCCI, which Abedi himself secretly controlled. This was paid in to Abedi-owned First American, which then remitted it to Abedi-owned National Bank of Georgia, whose owner, Abedi front Ghaith Pharaon, gave it back to Abedi's ICIC. Thus did things happen in the upside-down world of Abedian finance; it will take years for investigators to parse this transaction alone.

Clifford and Altman had thus proved themselves vastly useful to Abedi. Once again their presence and their attention had kept the regulators at bay. By almost any measure they were doing a spectacularly good job for their shareholders. By 1986 the two men had decided that the time had come for them to receive some of the stock that Abedi, on behalf of the shareholders, had long ago promised them. They had used more than $500 million in capital funds from their shareholders to inflate the bank's assets, buying new banks and aggressively marketing loans and deposits. They believed—this was in the days before the real estate portfolio collapsed—that First American was worth $1 billion, and now they wanted a piece of the action. In July 1986 Clifford borrowed $9,960,920 from BCCI, under what is known as a nonrecourse note, in order to buy 4,495 shares in CCAH. "Nonrecourse" meant that, as with all the other front men, the shares of CCAH would be held as collateral for the loan, and that the bank could not go after Clifford's personal assets if he failed to pay it back. Clifford had also managed to borrow 100 percent of the value of the stock, a practice that is not legal in the United States. (BCCI was a foreign bank, and thus not subject to those laws.) In August 1987 Clifford borrowed another $2,310,930 from BCCI on the same terms to buy an additional 951 shares. Altman had gotten identical terms for half of the amounts Clifford received.

After holding most of their stock for only a year and a half, Clifford and Altman suddenly decided in February 1988 that they should sell a large chunk of it, enough to liquidate their debt to BCCI. There was indeed a good market in bank stocks just at that moment, and this may well have figured in their decision to sell, as they claimed it did. But there were other events in February 1988 that might have suggested that it was a propitious time to sell.

That month, for the first time since the Financial General takeover, BCCI was again in the news. Senator John Kerry and Jack Blum at the Senate Foreign Relations Subcommittee on Terrorism, Narcotics, and International Operations had been pushing forward with their investigation of drug dealing in Latin America, and in February they heard remarkable testimony from three sources. José Blandón, the former Panamanian diplomat, placed BCCI at the center of a diagram of drug-money flows and testified that it had close relations with Manuel Noriega. Two other witnesses, marijuana smugglers Leigh Ritch and Steven Kalish, made strong public statements to the effect that BCCI was a major drug-money laundry. On February 23 Clifford and Altman, wearing their hats as corporate counsel to BCCI, summoned Noriega's personal BCCI banker, Amjad Awan, to meet with them in Washington to discuss their concerns that the bank might be implicated. That same month, Agha Hasan Abedi suffered a major heart attack.

For someone unfamiliar with the inner workings of BCCI, those events would have raised no special alarms. But for anyone with an inkling of how badly the bank had deteriorated and how deeply involved in corruption it was, Blandón's testimony alone would have raised horrifying prospects. What was said in the meeting among Altman, Clifford, and Awan is not known. What is known is that within days of that meeting Clifford and Altman decided to sell a large portion of their stock.

They approached Naqvi, now running the bank in the absence of the convalescing Abedi, telling him they would like to sell stock. Could he find an interested buyer? Indeed he could, and quickly: A man named Mohammed Hammoud was ready and willing to buy stock from them at $6,800 a share, more than three times what Clifford and Altman paid for it. Keep in mind that there was no "market," so to speak, for the shares of CCAH. There were never more than two dozen shareholders, and all of them lived in the Middle East and were wholly or partially in thrall to Abedi. BCCI held most of their shares as collateral and was in a position either to set the price it wanted or to manipulate the price as it desired—a conclusion reached in Price

Waterhouse's June 1991 audit. Share prices were thus highly subjective.

Contrary to assertions put out by the PR firm of Hill & Knowlton that he got only a couple of million out of it, Clifford made many times that amount. In early March 1988 he sold 3,200 of his 5,446 shares for $21.76 million. He used the money as follows: He paid off his entire debt of $12,271,850 to BCCI, leaving him as owner, free and clear, of 2,246 shares of BCCI worth exactly $15,272,800 on that day. He then repaid $1,411,831 to BCCI in interest and $1,500,000 in "commissions" to BCCI on the deal. The latter payment is highly questionable. Although it might be regarded as a standard broker's fee, no broker came anywhere near this transaction, which amounted to nothing more than some paper shuffling by Naqvi, who held all the shares as collateral anyway. As such, the $1.5 million looks very much like a kickback. Whatever it was, Clifford could afford it. After paying off these items, he was left with $6,576,319 in cash, which when added to the value of the remaining stock he now owned free of all debt created value for him personally of $21,849,119 (compared to $2,310,930 in the Hill & Knowlton memo). He had invested none of his own money and, because his loan was nonrecourse, could not ever be forced to pay it back. And yet he had made this profit in a mere nineteen months. Altman got exactly half what Clifford got, making the total value of the transaction to the two men $32,773,679, one of the sweetest of sweetheart deals in an age famous for outsized corporate bonuses.

For investigators, the problem was to figure out what this was, or what it meant. Was this a shakedown, however subtle, by two men who knew a great deal about the bank, and who sensed that the Blandón testimony might be the beginning of serious problems for the bank? Or was it a payoff for having done something on behalf of the bank? Or, possibly, was it a routine form of compensation, albeit extremely generous, to two men who had in fact boosted the value of First American well beyond its shareholders' investments, as they claimed? The payoff theory holds that it is direct compensation for having engineered the National Bank of Georgia deal, which was in fact negotiated in private between Altman and Roy Carlson, and had the effect of removing Pharaon and boosting BCCI's balance sheet.

Two separate pieces of evidence suggest that Clifford and Altman were not anxious for the U.S. authorities to know about either BCCI's role as midwife in the First American purchase of National Bank of Georgia or about the loans they took for their stock deal. The first was a highly curious letter sent in May 1986 to Swaleh Naqvi under Clifford's and Altman's names prior to the purchase of National Bank of Georgia. The subject was BCCI's role as middleman in the transaction, acting as pledge holder in the exchange of stock for cash. The letter contained the following sentence that neither Clifford nor Altman has explained satisfactorily: "In addition the proposed structure may focus unwelcome attention on the relationship between CCAH and BCCI and raise questions whether BCCI has acquired control of NBG."

The second came to be known as the "Ryback letters." In December 1989 Fed officer William Ryback wrote Altman and asked him to "provide information on any loans extended to the original or subsequent investors, either directly or indirectly by BCCI or any of its affiliated organizations." Altman replied on February 5, 1990, "We do not have access here to information regarding any financial arrangements that might exist between shareholders of [CCAH] and other financial institutions." This was, in the words of the Minority Report of the House Banking Committee, "a misrepresentation of material fact." Clifford and Altman did not disclose the $18 million in loans they themselves received.

Similarly, their actions as lawyers for BCCI over the years suggest that they knew of the real relationships between the two banks. Altman had blocked damaging memoranda on BCCI from Bank of America as far back as 1978. In 1988 he and Clifford orchestrated the $20-million defense of BCCI in Tampa, which included lobbying hard against a RICO (Racketeering Influenced and Corrupt Organizations) Act suit that might have brought down BCCI. When Kerry's subcommittee began investigating BCCI that same year, Altman was alleged by Amjad Awan and Ali Mirza to have told Awan to flee the country. Kerry's staff, particularly Jonathan Winer, believe that Altman deliberately stonewalled their query, denying the existence of documents in BCCI's U.S. offices relating to Manuel Noriega, for example, when it later came out that such documents had been there all along.

First American's purchase of National Bank of Georgia had another effect as well. By the end of 1987 Pharaon had managed to reschedule his debt, and he and Abedi were again operating as a team in the United States. This time they set their sights on an American institution truly worthy of partnership with BCCI: David Paul's CenTrust Savings Bank of Miami, Florida, one of the largest and most corrupt of all the thrifts that went down in flames in the late 1980s and early 1990s. The volatile Paul had put CenTrust on a staggering growth curve fueled by brokered deposits that he funneled into high-risk real estate loans, junk bonds, and offbeat investments. Paul was playing his own version of the financial Ponzi: As long as deposits roared in from around the country, no one was going to look too closely at what he was doing with them, which was quite remarkable indeed. As the centerpiece of his new empire, Paul built a gleaming postmodernist skyscraper that dominated the Miami skyline and was featured in the opening credits of *Miami Vice*. The building cost $180 million and boasted acres of marble, as well as gold-plated bathroom faucets and sinks. Paul spent another $29 million on art and delighted in showing visitors his $13-million Peter Paul Rubens painting, *Portrait of a Man as the God Mars*, which he had purchased with depositors' funds and had hung in his home. Another $7 million went to purchase a ninety-five-foot yacht complete with a marble fireplace.

Paul also had the best political contacts of any of the new breed of savings and loan tycoons. In the 1980s he gave $300,000 to Democratic politicians and raised far more. This had led Senator John Kerry, then chairman of the Democratic Senatorial Campaign Committee, which collects and distributes contributions at a national level, to appoint Paul financial chairman of the committee in 1987. Paul's appointment book is a veritable index of Washington politics, showing frequent meetings with seventeen different senators, including Kerry, who also availed himself of Paul's corporate jet.

In 1987, however, CenTrust began to unravel, the victim of its wildly imprudent investments and of Paul's de facto looting of depositors' funds. He began to unravel personally as well. A Miami magazine proved that his own official biography was a lie. Like Pharaon, Paul claimed to be a doctor—of urban planning, he claimed—which was patently false. Nor was it true, as he claimed, that he had gone to Harvard Law School. (He did, however, attend Columbia Law School, where he was Jack Blum's classmate.) But Paul was far from down and out. He had his well-connected friends in Washington, who could and did lobby regulators to give CenTrust easy treatment in spite of its deteriorating balance sheet. And he had his new associates Ghaith Pharaon and, by proxy, Agha Hasan Abedi.

The desperate condition of Paul's thrift would have prompted regulatory action much sooner had it not been for the intervention of a fascinating confluence of interests: Agha Hasan Abedi, BCCI, Ghaith Pharaon and Pharaon's lawyer and lobbyist Charlie Jones, Federal Savings and Loan Insurance Corporation Chairman M. Danny Wall, and Georgia senators Wyche Fowler and Sam Nunn. The survival of CenTrust depended upon an elaborate two-part deception. First, the Atlanta regional thrift supervision of the FSLIC had to be neutralized. That was accomplished when Charlie Jones pulled in a favor from Fowler and Nunn and arranged a meeting between Paul, Pharaon, and Wall. According to Pharaon's former business partner Dale Murray, Pharaon told him, "I shut those boys up in Atlanta."[53]

That kept the regulators from seizing or shutting CenTrust but did not prevent them from insisting that Paul come up with more capital in order to shore up his deposits. In 1987 he was finally told to raise capital in the form of subordinated debentures (a form of long-term bonds). To do that, he went to yet another infamous institution, Drexel Burnham Lambert, where he quickly ran into trouble. CenTrust's reputation on the street was such that few investors believed that purchasing CenTrust debt was a good risk. The regulators had told him to raise $200 million. Drexel told Paul that was not possible, and Paul was able to get the amount reduced to $150 million. Still not possible, said Drexel's investment bankers, who themselves were unwilling to underwrite the balance. The best they could do was $125 million. Paul was cornered. If he couldn't raise the capital, he would provoke a nasty confrontation with the already suspicious savings and loan regulators.

The solution, engineered by Paul, Pharaon, and Abedi, was a sham purchase of CenTrust debentures. Pharaon, acting as a front for BCCI and using BCCI money, "bought" $24,668,750 of CenTrust's bonds in 1987, which enabled Drexel to fully subscribe its offering and satisfied the regulators. Yet less than a year later, by prearrangement, Paul secretly repurchased the bonds from Pharaon/BCCI through another subsidiary for $25 million. As a commission on the deal, Pharaon kept the $331,250 difference. The bonds had also dropped substantially in value since Pharaon bought them, and so Paul in effect had to loot his depositors' funds again to make good on his deal with BCCI.

Their cooperation had worked so well in deceiving the regulators that Abedi and Pharaon began to buy up CenTrust stock in large quantities in 1988. Over two years Pharaon, using Abedi's money, bought up 28 percent of CenTrust. Like most of his other investments, this too turned sour: Pharaon and Abedi lost everything when CenTrust was seized in 1990. But that was not all Pharaon lost in his dealings with Paul. In 1987 Pharaon and Paul had teamed up to purchase one of the U.S.'s oldest manufacturers of munitions, Hercules, Inc., of Wilmington, Delaware. Together with an Italian partner they pumped in $43 million for 2.6 million shares of Hercules stock.

Pharaon, the contemplative investor, was wrong yet again—all three were badly burned by the 1987 stock market crash and took huge losses. They also tried, unsuccessfully, to gain control of Jim and Tammy Faye Bakker's PTL television ministry, mainly to get hold of Bakker's huge donor data base, which Pharaon planned to use to solicit business for a Georgia insurance company he had recently purchased.

David Paul was a perfect mark for Abedi and Pharaon, very close to the archetypal BCCI client around the world. He was wealthy and unscrupulous, and at the time of his recruitment his company was in financial trouble. More important than any of those things, however, were Paul's stellar political connections. The year he began working with Pharaon was also the year Kerry appointed him to run the finances of the Democratic Senatorial Campaign Committee. His personal calendar, later made public in congressional documents, reveals that he had frequent contact with key players in the Democratic party: lunch with Jimmy Carter and with Florida Senator Bob Graham; dinners with Louisiana Senator John Breaux and Colorado Senator Tim Wirth; cocktails with Massachusetts Senator Ted Kennedy; several meetings with John Kerry aboard the CenTrust plane; meetings with Michigan Senator Don Riegle, Delaware Senator Joseph Biden, and House Ways and Means Committee Chairman Dan Rostenkowski; and a retreat at a Georgia resort with California Senator Alan Cranston. To name just a few. The lobbying effort to keep CenTrust afloat, long after the Federal Home Loan Bank Board (FHLBB) sought to enforce compliance, was in fact a masterpiece of politicking into which both Pharaon and Paul put considerable effort. Paul, Pharaon, and attorney Charlie Jones toured Washington complaining to their influential friends about Paul's mistreatment. They met on several occasions with M. Danny Wall, then the nation's top thrift regulator, and Pharaon used his Atlanta connections to lobby the Atlanta office of the FHLBB on the subject of CenTrust debentures. In 1992 Pharaon and Paul were indicted together by the Justice Department in Miami for the bond-swap conspiracy. Their collaboration, said the indictment, had delayed regulatory action on CenTrust, a delay, it is now estimated, that will cost the U.S. taxpayers as much as $5 billion over the next thirty years. Pharaon, Abedi, Naqvi, and BCCI were indicted on November 15, 1991, by the Justice Department for their roles in the bond manipulation at CenTrust and the secret ownership of Independence Bank of Encino, California.

·   ·   ·

Because so much came to be written about BCCI, so much sheer tonnage of words, certain clichés came to be repeated thousands of times. Preeminent among them was the notion that Clark Clifford and Agha Abedi were the strangest of bedfellows. How ironic, it was observed, that this starched collar from Washington's sanctum sanctorum had become partnered with this diminutive, ethereal Pakistani banker. But there was really nothing odd about it. Though their meeting was an accident of fate—with a gentle nudge from a rotund Georgian huckster named Bert Lance—their friendship and partnership was logical, and even predictable. Stripped to their bare essentials, both men were masters of the ancient art of wielding public influence—or the appearance of influence—for private gain. Clifford, the perennially private man, was seen differently from the outside: He was viewed as a statesman, and his access was as good as his legend said it was. Abedi, too, was intensely private, and though he had never served government the way Clifford had, his own legend grew out of his connections to command and control. A hemisphere away, Abedi's Rolodex was every bit as good as Clifford's. Though separated by several continents and moving in very different circles, the two men were selling the same essential commodity. Clifford's magic lay in his ability to walk through closed doors in the corridors of American politics and industry. Abedi's derived from his position as power broker between the moneyed states of the Middle East and the military dictatorship in Pakistan.

There were other similarities. Both men spoke a highly precise and often metaphorical version of the King's English; both had manners so courtly—so old-worldly, in fact—that few who met them came away unimpressed. ("I found Mr. Abedi to be a man of considerable charm," Clifford said later. "A man of slight build and stature; a very attractive manner; spoke perfect English, nothing of the promoter type about the man at all."[54]) And both were accustomed to thinking in very large terms. What Abedi offered Clifford was something he already believed in: a clear and uncompromised vision of global influence, far removed from the world of nattering bureaucrats, whose strictures both men had made careers of deftly avoiding.

Though Clifford and Abedi had enjoyed huge success moving fluidly between public and private sectors, what they pulled off in the United States was nothing less than a grand jeté, performed under the relentless scrutiny that accompanied one of the longest and most hostile bank takeovers in history. It is both a how-to manual for the fine art of disguising financial manipulation and an object lesson in how easy it is to hide things from authorities in the modern global financial market. Exactly how much Clark Clifford knew and how large a role he really played are points to be hashed out in a New York City courtroom. Innocent or guilty, he will not be able to change history, which shall record that he was the vanguard of Abedi's cyclonic rush at the American market.

CHAPTER 9

THE BLACK RAJ

In our philosophy, it is not only material success that counts but
also the moral objective, to give as much happiness to as many
people as possible.

—AGHA HASAN ABEDI

From on or about November 1, 1972, through July 22, 1992,
there existed a criminal enterprise, the BCC Group, which was
a group of persons sharing a common purpose of engaging in
criminal conduct . . . in more than seventy countries around the
world, the purpose of which was to acquire money and power.

—FROM DISTRICT ATTORNEY'S INDICTMENT OF BCCI, JULY 1992

Though Abedi had managed to recruit the likes of Clark Clifford and
Bert Lance in the United States, he had much less success ingratiating
himself with most institutions of U.S. government. Banking regulators
had remained overtly hostile to him. He was able to acquire three U.S.
banks and a large chunk of a fourth only by cloaking himself in a thick
veil of secrecy, by using false nominees to sustain a large and intricate
lie.

The reverse was true in the developing world. There BCCI had
rooted itself so deeply in the culture, politics, and business of individual countries, and had forged such strong ties to the ruling establishment, that it often became indistinguishable from that establishment
and even from agencies of the official government itself. More than $2
billion disappeared from the cash-starved continent of Africa alone
into BCCI's financial oubliette; individual countries lost as much as 30
percent of their sovereign reserves.

The modus operandi was simple and straightforward, duplicated in every country in which BCCI did business. BCCI quietly and efficiently helped the ruling class illegally expatriate its wealth, whisking it off into a network of untraceable offshore accounts; BCCI made fast and easy loans; BCCI made a point of hiring and promoting the children of the rich and powerful; BCCI accommodated the needs of the government with dazzling efficiency, in the form of both deposits and loans; and BCCI paid off whomever it needed to pay off to expedite any of the above. It was the frenetic intensity and startling efficiency with which BCCI's officers pursued the bank's goals that moved it so decisively into sovereign inner circles.

Nowhere was the grand design more perfectly executed than in the West African country of Nigeria. That was because Nigeria was a ready-made paradise for the sort of business BCCI did and for the sort of bank BCCI was. First, and perhaps most important, Nigeria was floating in oil. Perennially among the world's top ten producers, Nigeria also sat at the head of OPEC's table for much of the 1980s. Abedi's original vision was to build the world's largest bank out of oil. To his conquests in the Middle East he could add a new source of precious petrodeposits in Nigeria. Second, Nigeria was devoutly Islamic, a perfect mark for the bank supposedly built on the primary concept of total submission to God. Finally, Nigeria was and is prodigiously corrupt, and large-scale corruption in the developing world requires the help of a large-scale, corrupt financial institution somewhere along the line.

BCCI began its operations in Nigeria in 1979, with oil prices rocketing past $30 a barrel and the non-OPEC world reeling in shock. So abundant were the money flows that year that BCCI gained fast notoriety as the first bank ever to make a profit in its first year. Within a decade BCCI's Nigeria operation would boast a growth rate of 200 percent to 300 percent, and nearly half a billion dollars in assets. By the time of the bank's seizure it was the second-largest bank in Nigeria, with forty-five branches throughout the country.

This was due in large part to the man Abedi personally recruited to run that operation: the immensely influential Alhaji Ibrahim Dasuki. To say that Dasuki was well connected is something of an understatement. He was a member of the powerful royal family of Sokoto, the Muslim capital of northern Nigeria, the sultan of which is acknowledged to be the spiritual leader of Nigeria's 55 million Muslims. In 1988 the reigning sultan died, and Sokoto's military governor named Dasuki as the new sultan. His connections to the government of General Ibrahim Babangida were impeccable as well. Dasuki's son was one of Babangida's chief aides, and the country's minister of finance is a close relative. The appointment of the spiritually irreproachable Dasuki, who was paid millions for his efforts, meant that BCCI had immediate and unique access to an enormous Muslim deposit base. In Dasuki, Abedi neatly merged the allure of the Islamic bank with the phenomenal drive to build assets.

BCCI was considered one of the key players in the foreign-exchange market in Nigeria, which meant the black market, and though black money and flight capital were arguably BCCI's stock in trade, its Nigerian operation stands out as a stunning example of how useful a bank could be to foreign nationals trying to get money out. Nigeria was one of BCCI's great success stories, and according to a number of sources, the bank became the principal conduit for capital-flight money from that country. Capital flight is a very simple idea. Let's say you are a Mexican citizen, and the year is 1983. You have accumulated a small fortune in pesos, but skyrocketing inflation, political uncertainty, and a huge national debt are eroding the value of your pesos. You are quickly becoming poor. If you are even remotely intelligent, you will try to convert those pesos into a "hard" currency, like the U.S. dollar, the Swiss franc, or the deutsche mark. To do that, you have to go to a bank and get the bank to change your money—just the way you would at an airport coming into a foreign country. The problem is that the Mexican government owes 90 billion or so in dollars to the rest of the world and it needs every dollar it can lay its hands on because no foreign bank will accept a peso in repayment for anything. So the Mexican central bank has set severe limits on how much you can change. Capital flight is the process whereby you are able to convert your worthless pesos illegally into a nifty dollar account in an offshore haven like the Caymans or in the United States. The neat part is that you have managed to get your hands on a valuable, interest-earning foreign asset while sticking your government with the task of repaying dollar debt to Western banks. That is the magic and beauty of capital flight.

The most common trick in Nigeria involved overinvoicing of imports: A Nigerian citizen, with the help and collusion of BCCI branch bankers, would import products whose real value was, say, $100,000. But on the shipping documents and letters of credit—all handled by the bank—the amount listed would be $150,000, thus enabling the importer to change that amount in Nigerian currency. The $100,000 true debt would be paid off, and a $50,000 deposit would appear at

BCCI Cayman Islands. Then there was the underinvoicing of exports, such as oil, which had the same effect of creating a shadow surplus of hard currency that could be skimmed off. A very large amount of money left Nigeria this way, most of it with BCCI's help. In 1987 the Nigerian government itself estimated that at the apogee of the oil boom in 1978, political officials were transferring $25 million a day out of the country. This had some interesting macroeconomic effects. In 1979, for example, Nigeria's oil exports were some $4 billion less than the actual data showed.[1]

In Nigeria BCCI came up with wildly creative ways to generate new deposits, the least conventional of which was a loan-and-oil barter scheme in the early 1980s. At the time Nigeria was engaged in a dispute with its creditor banks, to which it owed $5 billion, and the government desperately needed a new loan. In exchange for an unprecedented $1 billion credit—no bank in history had ever lent that much to a single borrower other than the U.S. government—Nigeria agreed to pay back BCCI with crude oil, delivered to its shadowy Pakistan subsidiary, Attock Oil. So while the rest of Nigeria's global lenders became increasingly nervous, BCCI not only went ahead and disbursed the money but appeared fully confident that, having passed it into Nigeria's notoriously byzantine bureaucracy, it would be repaid. Which it was, with tankers of oil, while the other creditors still dickered with Babangida's finance men. Such reassurance was not coincidental. According to one of BCCI's top executives, he saw BCCI officers handing out cash to the staff of the Central Bank of Nigeria during a meeting of the World Bank in Seoul, Korea, in 1985.[2] Such payoffs, combined with BCCI's smoothly efficacious bailout, won the bank considerable favor, which took the form of $300 million in Nigeria's hard-currency deposits, most of which were lost when the liquidators took over BCCI in July 1991.

Elsewhere in Africa the pattern was repeated, albeit on a smaller scale. The effect was the same: to drain hundreds of millions of dollars out of economies that could ill afford it, causing tens of thousands of small-business people to lose their savings. Indeed, BCCI's demise is seen as the cruelest of blows to a sub-Saharan Africa that was already in abject poverty, with a plummeting gross domestic product that has shrunk 10 percent in the last five years, leaving the average rural African with a lower standard of living than at the time of decolonialization in the 1960s.[3] The scale of the loss, relatively speaking, is huge: The countries of Zambia, Zimbabwe, and Cameroon together lost some $200 million in national assets.[4]

In the country of Cameroon BCCI's general manager was a former state governor and longtime crony of Cameroon's rulers, and its chairman was the former inspector general of the finance ministry and former head of customs.[5] As in neighboring Nigeria, the bank picked up thousands of customers through sheer efficiency in banking services, such as the transfer of funds across borders. It would take most banks months to repatriate funds from Nigeria. BCCI would do it in days. So efficient was BCCI that it soon accounted for 80 percent of Cameroon's export financing. It was in this area that the bank's seizure caused the most harm, effectively freezing shipments of key commodities and parts for months. One palm-oil refinery, for example, was forced to shut down and lay off its workers in July 1991. It was waiting for $2 million in spare parts from overseas, financed by BCCI. The parts would never arrive. The refinery, at least, made out better than the government, which lost one third of its meager hard-currency reserves.[6] Even the U.S. government was affected, losing the $10 million of U.S. Agency for International Development funds it kept in accounts at BCCI.

In Zambia Abedi had personally cultivated close ties to President Kenneth Kaunda, and the story of his arrival on a visit there in 1987 speaks volumes about the way he brought business to his far-flung banking empire. That year plunging copper prices had thrown Zambia into a sharp recession, and the country badly needed a bridge loan to meet its obligations. Abedi had personally approved the loan on the eve of his visit. When he landed in the capital city of Lusaka, where he would be greeted personally by President Kaunda, he emerged from a BCCI 727 in the company of former British Prime Minister James Callaghan, who happened to be a paid consultant to BCCI. According to one account in the *Financial Times*, Kaunda announced to Abedi and Callaghan, "The money arrived just in time."[7] The next day Lusaka's newspapers prominently featured Agha Hasan Abedi, friend of the country's president, who had not only made a crucial loan, but who, with his friend Lord Callaghan, had come to donate money to a charitable trust. Carefully stage-managed acts like these contributed mightily to Abedi's reputation as a champion of the Third World. They also proved to be a powerful engine for deposit gathering, which was, after all, Abedi's real ambition.

Callaghan was not the only recruit in Pakistan's global PR circus. A far more important connection was to Jimmy Carter. Abedi had met Carter—as he had met Clifford—through Bert Lance. Sensing an opportunity, Abedi had visited Carter at his Georgia home in 1982.

Switching on his 1,000-watt charm, Abedi played his old themes of charity, philanthropy, and financial and technological assistance to the poor countries of the developing world. Not coincidentally, this was precisely what interested Carter in the years following his defeat by Ronald Reagan in 1980. Nor was it coincidental, in retrospect, that the Abedi-owned National Bank of Georgia was the largest single lender to the Carter family's peanut farm in Plains, Georgia. Like Abedi, Carter and wife Rosalynn were occasional guests at Pharaon's parties.

The two men became friends. In the early 1980s Abedi made a striking demonstration of his sincerity, donating $500,000 to help establish the Carter Center at Emory University in Atlanta, and began pumping millions into Carter's Global 2000 Foundation, which was founded in 1985 to provide health care to the Third World. During the 1980s BCCI gave $8.1 million to Carter, and Abedi orchestrated the donation of another $2.5 million from his friend Zayed through the Abu Dhabi Investment Authority. Carter spokesmen said that $1.5 million was given by BCCI to Global 2000 in 1990 alone.[8] Abedi then went one better, offering Carter the use of the BCCI jet for his travels around the world in support of charitable causes and offering Global 2000 office space at BCCI's London headquarters. Carter took him up on both.

Thus began a bizarre alliance that was to bring huge benefits to both men. During the 1980s the Carters became genuine friends with Abedi and his second wife, Rabia, spending brief holidays together in Switzerland. Carter introduced Abedi to some of his distinguished acquaintances, including Lord Callaghan. Abedi's Boeing 727, on which the Carters traveled, was luxuriously furnished with spacious lounges, a dining room, and a private bedroom. For Abedi came the stature of close association with a former U.S. president whose relatively enlightened policies toward the developing world had made him enormously popular there. For Carter there was an apparently unlimited source of money to fund his new global philanthropies.

As with Lord Callaghan in Zambia, Abedi and Carter would arrive in various countries on missions of mercy, bringing with them donations to foundations that provided care for victims of the guinea worm, prostheses for children, and programs to develop farming technology. In Pakistan they met and spent time with President Zia, discussing progress toward a cure for the guinea worm disease. In Ghana Carter was present when Abedi announced to President Jerry Rawlings that he was placing 25 percent of the bank's profits into a charitable trust. There is no way to estimate the public-relations value of Abedi's joint appearances with Carter in Kenya, Ghana, Pakistan, Bangladesh, China, Thailand, and the Soviet Union—all key targets of BCCI business development. These trips also seemed to make things happen for Abedi. In Kenya, for example, where in 1987 three BCCI officers were arrested in a major foreign-exchange scandal, Abedi's visit with Carter to hype a prosthetics foundation led to settlement of the charges against those officers. (At one point *Time*'s deputy Washington bureau chief, Stan Cloud, toured Africa with the two while working on a story about Carter, adding yet another fillip of prestige to Abedi's debarkations.)

Though the sums he received were huge by any standard of measure, Carter claims to have had no idea either that he was being exploited by Abedi, or that his benefactor was deeply corrupt. Still Carter went ahead and took at least $1.5 million from BCCI after the bank was indicted and convicted in Florida. Later, as press criticism mounted, his foundations stopped taking money from BCCI and began to get similar contributions from Sheikh Zayed, who by then controlled BCCI. Said Carter in an interview with ABC Television: "There was never any insinuation that we had until the Panama revelation that there was anything wrong with BCCI. We were quite concerned when that revelation was made."[9] But not concerned enough to stop taking money, even though his foundation was apparently fastidious in choosing from whom it accepted contributions. The Carter Center, for example, recently decided not to accept donations from tobacco companies because it opposes smoking. Carter's judgment was similarly flawed when his foundations accepted more than $11 million from a Japanese gambling magnate named Ryoichi Sasakawa, who had once spent three years in jail awaiting trial as a war criminal and was later convicted in a vote-buying scheme. Carter denies that he personally profited in any way from such transactions.

Whether or not Carter was a witting accomplice, he was highly useful. Former BCCI chief of U.S. operations Abdur Sakhia put the relationship into perspective: "You have to understand the culture of the bank and the global picture of the bank," he said in later U.S. Senate testimony. "Mr. Carter travels with Mr. Abedi to so many parts of the world. He goes to Pakistan, he goes to Kenya, he goes to Zimbabwe, he goes to many other places with Mr. Abedi on Mr. Abedi's plane. What the Kenyans and Pakistanis see is very different—that he is the former most important man in the world, he's a friend of Mr. Abedi. He visits BCCI offices in those countries. The media in those countries are seeing that. So although it does not give him any foothold in this country [U.S.A.] per se, around the world it's a different picture."[10]

By the mid-1980s joint efforts with people like Carter and Callaghan and other current and former heads of state made Abedi and BCCI famous the world over for their charitable acts and for their enormous and apparently selfless donations to everything from rural hospitals to the training of young engineers from underdeveloped countries. Almsgiving is one of the most strictly enjoined tenets of the Muslim religion, and Abedi's good works made him the most visible nongovernmental almsgiver in the Muslim world.

Abedi's charity machine was most active in his own backyard: Pakistan and Bangladesh. These countries were said to be centerpieces of the empire: perfect, profitable, humanitarian scale models of the radical Third World bank.

Bangladesh in particular, an economic basket case whose 100 million citizens annually ranked among the poorest of the poor, needed the pragmatic, charitable help of the prominent Pakistani philanthropist. As in many other countries, Abedi was revered by many Bangladeshis for his generous donations to the poor. But two events have blown that carefully constructed image apart and set the Bangladeshis howling for revenge. The first was the popular revolt in 1990 that overthrew and imprisoned the president of Pakistan, Hussain Mohammed Ershad. The second was the global seizure of the bank. Taken together, they offered a rare glimpse into the extraordinary role BCCI played in helping Ershad loot his own country, and into how BCCI used a charitable foundation as a front to conceal profits and avoid taxes.

"They have plundered this country, both of them," Bangladesh's attorney general, Amin ul-Haq, said of Abedi and Ershad in November 1991. "They were the bankers to all the smugglers and the corrupt people here. . . . And of course they helped ruin us." Haq has charged Ershad with taking kickbacks of more than $1 billion, equal to the annual budget of Bangladesh—money that BCCI helped him illegally channel out of the country.[11]

BCCI gained its inroads there in typical fashion, currying favor with the ruling class by hiring its children and relatives. One of its first moves was to hire three of President Ershad's in-laws. That was just the start of the patronage. Over the next few years BCCI hired no fewer than fifteen people with key family connections, children of prime ministers, finance ministers, foreign ministers, and central bank governors.

But the nepotistic coup de grace, one that effectively erased the line between BCCI and the official government, came in 1985. That year Abedi, who had long had his eye on the oil-rich sultanate of Brunei and its estimated $25 billion in petrodeposits, convinced Ershad to appoint a top BCCI officer in Paris to become the first Bangladeshi ambassador to Brunei. The man, Iftekhar Karim, also happened to be the son-in-law of Ershad's foreign minister. The flamboyant Karim was dispatched to Brunei, where he opened a lavish embassy, threw sumptuous parties, and could be seen cruising the sultanate in a Rolls-Royce Excalibur. In between the lavish parties and expensive cars, Karim also operated the embassy as an informal branch office of BCCI, a bank to which he returned when his embassy was finally closed down. He has the distinction of being the first and last ambassador from Bangladesh to Brunei and the only sovereign ambassador in the direct employ of BCCI.[12]

Meanwhile, BCCI had set up a huge charitable foundation, whose ostensible purpose was to fund rural medical centers, scholarships for the poor, and school libraries. In spite of the grandiose claims, the foundation was really nothing more than a brilliantly devised scheme to avoid government taxation and had been put in place only when the Bangladeshi government tried to clamp down on banks, like BCCI, that were taking their profits out of the country. The foundation became the recipient of all BCCI's profits, which thus became tax-free.

But of all the profits that went in, less than 10 percent actually found its way to charitable works, and BCCI made more tax-free interest alone off the foundation each year than it gave out to charities. The biggest recipient of the foundation's largess turned out to be a private commercial bank in which President Ershad and his financial advisers became one-third owners. That bank received $1.5 million from the foundation, while the foundation's showcase program, a scheme to give interest-free college loans, donated just $10,500 in a single year.[13]

The upshot of this was that BCCI, which made millions from its Bangladesh operation, paid virtually no taxes in a desperately poor country whose average citizen makes an annual income of $100. While it danced around the tax codes, BCCI cemented its relationship with Ershad, helping him to ferry out of the country hundreds of millions of dollars that were earmarked for large development projects. As a capper on a decade of financial depredations, the life savings of some fifteen thousand Bangladeshis were frozen when the bank was seized.

In Pakistan the bank's MO duplicates so precisely that used in

Bangladesh as to seem like official corporate policy. Which may in fact have been the case. BCCI's principal tool of manipulation, ICIC in the Cayman Islands, was owned 35 percent by the BCC Foundation and 35 percent by a Staff Benefit Trust, both of which were used as tax shelters. In Pakistan, too, BCCI ran a de facto employment program for children of the rich and powerful; there too BCCI set up a mostly bogus foundation, with the help of the country's president, to shelter itself from taxes; and there too the foundation's funds were routed into a private company owned by Abedi's cronies.

Despite everything the bank did wrong in Africa and South Asia, it would not be accurate to say that BCCI did nothing more than bank the elites and buy its way into the centers of power. BCCI's relationship with the developing world was far more complex than that. Since he founded United Bank in Pakistan, Abedi had clung tenaciously to the idea of providing the small-business operators of the Third World with banking services, especially loans for the export or import of goods. BCCI officers were exhorted to bank the little people, and they did so enthusiastially, stepping in where the more traditional colonial banks and American multinationals refused to go. BCCI banked hundreds of thousands of such people and was a powerful engine of economic growth in dozens of poor countries. Its very success in banking the small or medium-sized trader or manufacturer made its demise excruciatingly painful for the small and struggling middle classes in much of the developing world. In addition to having lost their savings or their businesses, those same people also came to believe that they had been betrayed.

In other countries—especially in Latin America—BCCI focused directly on the heart of the political establishment. One of the most successful of BCCI's many practitioners of this particular art form was its Panama branch. Like the Cayman Islands, Panama is one of the most opaque financial centers in the world, offering virtually untraceable secrecy in the form of bank accounts and shell companies. In two of the more elegant corruptions of the wide-ranging scandal, BCCI Panama assisted Manuel Noriega in the complicated and risky task of looting the coffers of the Republic of Panama, and bribed its way into the hearts of Peruvian central bankers.

The Noriega-BCCI connection offers one of the most thoroughly documented examples ever of how a corrupt head of state steals money. As was the case with Bangladesh's Ershad, the story would never have become public were it not for the fortuitous combination of Noriega's ouster and imprisonment and the subsequent seizure of the bank. (It seems this is the only way information like this about the bank ever gets out.)

It started in January 1982, when Noriega opened an account at BCCI's Panama branch with funds from Panama's National Guard.[14] This was no ordinary government account. Though the funds belonged to the National Guard, Noriega was the sole signatory. That was prima facie illegal, yet BCCI officers agreed to it without even blinking and took the initial deposit of $1.3 million. From here the funds moved discreetly through BCCI's Miami branch and on to BCCI's branch at Cromwell Road in London, where they now appeared only as numbered accounts. Making the trail ever more difficult to follow, the money was then blipped into other numbered accounts at different branches. One of those numbered accounts, at BCCI's Edgware Road branch in London, became the principal funding mechanism for the Noriega family's London shopping sprees. According to documents in the possession of the Republic of Panama, $223,281.73 was charged at various stores over a two-year period and paid off with funds from the Panama National Guard.

Yet that was small change compared to the tens of millions Noriega was actually moving out of Panama, and the larger money had to be literally made to disappear. In February 1988, for example, a series of transfers from other accounts left $14,877,667.86 in a single account at the Edgware Road branch. BCCI then moved those funds to two accounts at two different banks, one in Zurich and one in Hamburg, from which points they returned again to London under the name of a company called "Finley," controlled by Noriega. The same year, documents show another $12 million following the same sort of circuitous path. These are frighteningly efficient mechanisms of concealment. The effect of the transfers, account switching, and name changing was to camouflage both the money's source and its user. Such a labyrinth is far beyond the capacity of most regulators to trace, even if they know what they are looking for. And yet it is child's play for any international bank that chooses to play the game. Only the forcible opening of BCCI records allowed the Republic of Panama, which has brought suit against the bank for assisting in Noriega's theft, to trace the money.

Most of those machinations were orchestrated by BCCI's Panama branch manager Amjad Awan, the man who later brought BCCI to the attention of the world when it became known that he was Noriega's "personal banker." Awan developed another important account during his years in Panama: Peru.

In 1986 the country of Peru had a very serious problem. The leftist government of President Alan García Pérez had unilaterally suspended all payments on its formidable international debts. With a host of angry and frightened Western banks hovering and uttering veiled threats, the Peruvians were naturally worried that those banks might seize their assets. What they needed were offshore dollar accounts that would be invisible to the raptors of Wall Street.

Enter BCCI Panama officers Amjad Awan and A. M. Bilgrami, who convinced Peruvian authorities to place central bank deposits with them. The Peruvians moved with startling dispatch, even though BCCI ranked, by their own reckoning, as a 4 out of 5 on a sliding risk scale, and even though all the Peruvians had in the way of financial information on the bank was a three-page report. There were also plenty of branches of major banks in Panama that would have been happy to take the business. But before the year was out, $250 million in such deposits—25 percent of the total deposits of Peru's central bank—had moved into BCCI's Panama branch, effectively hidden from the eyes of Peru's creditors and from the International Monetary Fund.[15] The arrangement was hugely profitable for BCCI. Of the total deposit, $50 million sat in a non-interest-bearing account. Meanwhile, BCCI offered lines of credit to Peru of only $85 million—highly unusual, since BCCI was sitting on collateral of $250 million.

What had happened to guide the Peruvian central bank to BCCI, even though it was clearly being taken for a fiscal ride? The answer emerged in the July 1991 indictment of Abedi, Naqvi, and BCCI by New York District Attorney Robert Morgenthau. Among many other items, Morgenthau charged Abedi and Naqvi with authorizing payment of $3 million in bribes to two senior officials of the Peruvian central bank. Though Morgenthau did not mention Peruvian President García in the indictment, the Peruvians themselves opened a full-scale investigation of his close ties to the bank, including charges that he maintained a huge secret account with the bank.

The bribes moved in typically clandestine fashion. From BCCI in the Grand Caymans the money was transferred to Security Pacific Bank in New York, from which it was routed to Swiss Bank Corp. in New York and then on to an account at Swiss Bank Corp. in Panama. They are the subject of an ongoing investigation and have created a minor scandal in Peru.

For all of the corruption, bribery, and financial manipulation that went on in Peru, Panama, Cameroon, Bangladesh, Pakistan, and Nigeria, these countries represent only a fragment of BCCI's global puzzle. At its zenith the bank operated in seventy-six countries, and in most of them the same patterns of criminality emerge. Former BCCI officers say that some of the worst plundering occurred in Southeast Asia, where the bank had branches and subsidiaries in Hong Kong and Bangkok, yet not a single law enforcement probe has been launched in either place. Allegations have been made concerning the bank's close relationship with the family of Deng Xiaoping in China, where BCCI was the first foreign bank to receive a license, but no investigation has been opened, even though the Chinese government lost an estimated $400 million in the collapse of BCCI.

Except for the Bank of England probe and a subsequent government investigation by Lord Bingham, Western Europe showed no interest in pursuing the bank, which had had significant operations there for more than a decade. In the wake of BCCI's shutdown, the French simply pretended that nothing had happened. There were no government calls for an investigation of BCCI's activities within the country, and the French press, far less inclined than the American media to be shocked or intrigued by evidence of commercial bribery, remained uninterested in the scandal. Yet any probe of the wreckage of BCCI's French operations would have quickly revealed that Abedi maintained one of his largest bribery slush funds in the Paris branch. According to reports from former Paris-based BCCI bankers, the slush fund was held in a constantly growing multimillion-dollar ledger account innocently labeled "Miscellaneous & Sundries." It was a fund swollen from profits that couldn't be declared, such as the revenues from BCCI's massive illicit overnight trading in the French franc. This so-called Euro-franc lending netted BCCI as much as 80-percent interest and was expressly forbidden by French law. One of the Paris bankers described those currency transactions in detail to Beaty and Gwynne and then confided that the miscellaneous account was regularly used to pay off French government officials. The banker—who was willing to testify but was never questioned by authorities in either France or America—was able to provide a firsthand account of two of those payments, since he had made them himself. However, he said, Abedi personally flew to Paris to handle the really big money transfers to relatives of high government officials. One of the Paris branch manager's duties was to ensure that Abedi's Rolls-Royce (the green one once owned by the shah of Iran's brother) and a chauffeur would be ready twenty-four hours a day should Abedi arrive in France unannounced, as he usually did. And it was no coincidence, the manager added, that BCCI's top marketing executive in France was the son of a prominent government minister.

It is a testament to the bank's ability to forge intimate political ties that in all those countries, only a handful of BCCI officers have ever gone to jail. With the stories many of them could tell about the financial affairs of key political leaders, it is perhaps not surprising that they remain free.

One of the best glimpses ever into the way BCCI worked with its corrupt clientele around the world came from Miami attorney James Dougherty's pursuit, on behalf of Lloyd's of London, of the Jordanian coffee smuggler and arms merchant Munther Bilbeisi. Like the other U.S. investigators, Dougherty had stumbled upon the bank while tracking something else. In this case, it was insurance fraud that unlocked the door to the criminal machinations of BCCI in Florida, one of the bank's most successful and corrupt operations in the world.

Of the many obsessive hunters of BCCI, none was more zealous than James F. Dougherty II, a fifty-four-year-old lawyer who made his living defending insurance companies against dubious or fraudulent claims—a rough-and-tumble business for which he was perfectly suited. Dougherty was a startling character: a theatrical, hyperactive bundle of aggression who could not sit still. His sun-baked office was festooned with icons of naked aggression: dozens of statuettes of snarling lions and tigers stood atop tables and cabinets, and photographs of warplanes covered the walls. He kept automatic pistols in several drawers in his office and in each room of his Miami Beach home. He was ex–Notre Dame, ex–U.S. Army in Vietnam, and was definitely not someone you wanted to cross. He had first picked up work with Lloyd's on an insurance claim involving Colombian drug cartels and shipments of diamonds from Antwerp. Dougherty had been one of the few insurance lawyers in the United States willing to travel to Colombia to argue insurance claims with associates of the Medellín drug cartel. Dougherty had thought that was fun.

Surrounding him in his chaotic suite of offices on a typical day were a handful of regular attorneys and a highly irregular band of others that included three coffee smugglers from Central America, an expatriate Cuban coffee merchant who doubled as Dougherty's coffee "coyote," and a Haitian who had boxed professionally under the name "Tiger Jones" and had recently been indicted for fraud by the government of Guatemala. Also present were several harried secretaries and a bedraggled-looking fellow named George, who claimed to have personally photocopied four million documents in the past three years. As strange as this group seemed, this was Dougherty's informal task force in his quest for the heads of Munther Bilbeisi and Bilbeisi's personal bankers at BCCI. The irregulars were, implausibly, mostly former associates of Bilbeisi.

Dougherty had built the most comprehensive data base anywhere on the activities of a BCCI branch. There were reams of it, rooms full of it, most of which had been scanned into a gigantic computerized file. All of it was targeted at one man, and one bank. For reporters covering the BCCI story—many of whom eventually got access to Dougherty's files—it was nothing short of miraculous.

Munther Bilbeisi was, as Dougherty liked to say, "a real piece of work." He was born in 1930 in Amman, Jordan, into one of the country's four wealthiest families. His father, Ismail, made a fortune in oil and real estate, and at one time owned Royal Jordanian Airlines. Ismail died in 1977, leaving Munther a large inheritance. The flamboyant Munther Bilbeisi, who maintained lavishly appointed residences in England, Spain, Jordan, and the United States, was part of a breed of all-purpose agents and brokers common in the Middle East, particularly in Jordan and Lebanon. His family acted as general agents for the likes of Toyota, British Petroleum, and Panasonic. Bilbeisi bought and sold many different goods, anything with profit in it. He sold, for instance, twenty thousand tons of sugar to the Jordanian government in one deal, and cement clinker to the Kuwait Cement Company in another.[16] By the mid-1970s he had become involved in illegal arms dealing. His first major transaction had created a scandal in Britain. In 1974, in defiance of a British national policy to inderdict arms sales to South Africa, Bilbeisi had brokered British-made Centurion tanks and Tigercat missiles from Jordan to South Africa. Other Bilbeisi deals included retrofitting Jordanian tanks, the sale of small arms to Honduras and El Salvador, and the sale of U.S.-built F-86 Safra jet fighters from Yugoslavia to Honduras.[17]

Flush with inherited wealth and profits from his arms and commodities sales, Bilbeisi moved his primary residence to Boca Raton, Florida, in the late 1970s, and in the early 1980s decided to get into the coffee business. In those years an accord known as the International Coffee Agreement had set up a two-tier price structure for coffee. Coffee bought or sold in countries that had signed the agreement was propped up by a tariff, thus making it far more expensive than the coffee from "nonagreement" countries. This opened the door to smugglers, and this was the opportunity Bilbeisi saw. He would buy nonagreement coffee at cheap prices and sell it illegally to "agreement" countries like the United States, thus pocketing a huge spread.

From 1982 to 1986 Bilbeisi ran a formidable smuggling operation out of Boca Raton. He did this in concert with his bank, BCCI, which became a full partner in the fraud, financing his purchases and helping him falsify documents in order to fool Customs officials. So valuable was Bilbeisi's business, and so profitable to the bank, that BCCI opened a Boca Raton branch in 1983 specifically to service his account. The bank provided $105 million in financing and letters of credit in support of Bilbeisi's operations during those years. Bilbeisi was an ideal BCCI client: a wealthy Middle Easterner with close ties to the rulers of Jordan and other countries, who was willing to cut the bank in on some of his illegal action. It also happened that Bilbeisi's first cousin Fakhri was manager of BCCI in Amman, Jordan. It was BCCI's Amman branch that assisted in one of Bilbeisi's first American enter- prises, putting up $18 million in 1982 to finance a transaction involving Bilbeisi and members of the New Jersey mob. Though the deal did not go through, it concerned the sale of a parking lot from Philadelphia mob boss Nicodemo "Little Nicky" Scarfo to a partnership consisting of Thomas "Corky" Vastola, reputed leader of New Jersey's DeCaval- cante family, and Munther Bilbeisi. Bilbeisi was getting a fast start.

From all accounts Bilbeisi's relationship with his BCCI bankers in Florida was a cozy one indeed. He lived with his American wife and two children in the opulent Sanctuary section of Boca Raton. There he was visited daily by officers from BCCI, particularly the bank's branch manager, a Pakistani named Nadim Hasan whom he considered his best friend. According to a contemporaneous account by Bilbeisi's wife in a petition for divorce, the scene at the house sounded like an extended fraternity party; the house was continuously full of people smoking and drinking and staying up late into the night. The guests included several young women with whom Bilbeisi had affairs and whom he purveyed on several occasions to officers of BCCI. The guests also included, on at least one occasion, Agha Hasan Abedi. While the guests partied and the smuggling profits rolled in, Bil- beisi was paying off his good friends at BCCI by means of cashier's checks cashed without account debit numbers by a secretary at the Boca Raton branch. Between 1984 and 1985 the cashier's checks alone—which amounted to straight bribes and kickbacks—came to $100,000.[18] At the peak of his collaboration with BCCI, Bilbeisi and his associates had seventy-eight different accounts with BCCI in Boca Raton, Miami, London, Nassau, and Panama. He enjoyed instanta- neous access to all officers at the larger Miami branch.

Bilbeisi might never have been caught and later indicted if he had not tried yet another scam that he had worked successfully in the past:

insurance fraud. He made two false claims against Lloyd's in the 1980s, one for supposed theft of art and one for a shipment of coffee he said had been illegally "switched" to inferior brands and therefore rendered valueless. Lloyd's adjusters in London, correctly suspecting a pattern of similar claims dating back to the 1970s, had hired James Dougherty both to defend the huge insurance syndicate against Bilbeisi's claims and to countersue.

Thus in 1988 Dougherty began to investigate Bilbeisi's business activities. Fortuitously, Bilbeisi had cheated most of his old partners, and Dougherty quickly found a small group of them who were willing to become witnesses for Lloyd's against Bilbeisi. It was not long before Dougherty encountered Bilbeisi's principal partner. In dozens of depositions, in which witnesses detailed the methodology of the smuggling operation, the same name kept resurfacing: BCCI. Dougherty's discovery of the bank had been quite accidental—as was Jack Blum's earlier the same year during his probe of Manuel Noriega. It seemed that BCCI's Boca Raton and Miami offices not only banked Bilbeisi, but were also full partners in the smuggling operations.

The problem was proving it. That meant, among other things, getting hold of BCCI records. Dougherty began deposing BCCI officers and filing court motions to force an adversarial BCCI to show records of its dealings with Bilbeisi. Meanwhile, Bilbeisi's former partners had told Dougherty in detail how the smuggling operation worked. One of them, a Haitian named Louis Altemar—who had been Bilbeisi's chauffeur, house manager, and eventual business associate—told Dougherty about an illegal weapons sale Bilbeisi had made in Guatemala. Altemar had given Dougherty a pile of documents detailing two deals: one for Sikorsky S-76 helicopters and one for F-5 jets. The helicopter deal—for which there were no end-user certificates, thus making it illegal—had been consummated. The seller was the government of Jordan, the buyer the government of Guatemala. The price was grossly inflated and suggested a political fix of the first magnitude.

Dougherty thus concocted a plan. He needed to be able to prove that Bilbeisi and BCCI were defrauding Lloyd's by using Lloyd's insurance to cover shipments of smuggled goods. The Guatemalans, who themselves had been cheated out of millions of dollars in duties and tariffs, could give him the sort of proof he needed, assuming they were motivated to investigate a man who had just sold them weapons at a huge markup. Dougherty, who had the names and roles of all Guatemalan officials involved, decided he would use this information to bludgeon the Guatemalans into cooperating with his investigation.

Dougherty's plan constituted major interference by a private citizen in the affairs of a foreign country.

Dougherty traveled to Guatemala, where his first contacts were with the president's chief of staff, Roberto Mata Galvez, and Army Colonel Marco Antonio Vargas Espinoza, whom he promptly accused of taking part in the helicopter deal. A screaming match ensued, whereupon Mata put Dougherty under arrest while an aide de camp fled down the hall in search of Guatemalan President Marco Vinicio Cerezo Arevalo. A few minutes later Cerezo entered the room.

"So I made my case," recalls Dougherty, who did not hesitate to invoke the powerful influence of Lloyd's of London, which insured much of Guatemala's export business. "I said, 'I want proof that coffee smuggling has been going on.' I threatened them and said, 'Look, if you don't cooperate, you're not going to ship a single bag of beans out of here. I want the freedom to investigate and the freedom to take sworn testimony. How would the people who elected you like it if they knew you were in a deal to buy helicopters from the man who cheated Guatemala out of all this money?' "

Dougherty, needless to say, is not a subtle man. He was packed off to lunch with the country's attorney general, who mollified him with assurances that Guatemala would help him.

Back in Miami, Dougherty made a breakthrough. Among the many documents Altemar had given him were details of the "assignments" of profits from the helicopter deal. They showed that Bilbeisi had purchased the helicopters for $2.1 million in Jordan and sold them, supported by a BCCI letter of credit, to the Guatemalans for $5.175 million. Of the $3.075 million in profits, it turned out that $400,000 had gone to BCCI, some $500,000 had gone to accounts in Luxembourg and the Isle of Jersey to pay off members of the Jordanian military, and $270,000 had been paid by BCCI Miami into a numbered account with the Israeli Bank Leumi in Florida. Dougherty discovered that that account belonged to Milton David Cerezo García, the brother of Vinicio Cerezo, the president of Guatemala.

Vinicio Cerezo quickly found out that Dougherty knew about the account, and suddenly Lloyd's of London was getting a lot of cooperation in its investigation of Munther Bilbeisi. A meeting between high-level Lloyd's executives and Cerezo and his staff took place in New York, and full cooperation was pledged. Dougherty soon had affidavits from Cerezo and other Guatemalan officials testifying to Bilbeisi's corrupt activities. And Guatemala issued formal charges against Bilbeisi himself.

Dougherty's pursuit of Bilbeisi was relentless in other areas as well. In 1990 Bilbeisi was required to appear in Miami for a deposition, which he had been avoiding for months with the claim that he was suffering rectal bleeding and needed to go to his hospital every day. "We nailed him on that one," said Dougherty, chortling. "I hired a woman named Vivian, Jordanian by birth and ex-FBI. She's a redhead, a knockout. For $5,000 and a leather jacket she went to Amman and surveilled him. She had photographs of Bilbeisi looking perfectly healthy, cruising around the town. We blew their lawyers out of the water."

In early 1990, after two years of constantly badgering BCCI for documents on the Bilbeisi account, Dougherty and his associate Richard Lehrman got hold of a set of these letters of credit. With them came the incontrovertible proof that Bilbeisi was smuggling and that BCCI was helping him do it.

The results of Dougherty's efforts were disastrous for Bilbeisi. In the United States Bilbeisi was indicted in August 1991 for failure to pay $840,000 in taxes, and a warrant was issued for his arrest. He was charged with corruption in Guatemala and there, too, a warrant was issued for his extradition and arrest. According to officials at the attorney general's office in Guatemala, *Time* magazine's June story on Bilbeisi's smuggling and weapons deals prompted Guatemala's new administration to open an investigation of the matter and a probe into what is still a mysterious $30-million loan from BCCI to the Republic of Guatemala. As a consequence of that investigation, criminal charges have been brought against a wide range of Guatemalan officials, including former President Marco Vinicio Cerezo Arevalo and his brother Milton David Cerezo García, former head of immigration; Hector Alejandro Gramajo Morales, former minister of defense; Roberto Mata Galvez, former chief of staff; Mauricio Coronado Laura, former Guatemalan consul in Florida; and Colonel Marco Antonio Vargas Espinoza. There is no word yet as to what became of BCCI's $30-million loan.

BCCI's entire Florida operation, including its Caribbean regional office and branches in Miami and Boca Raton, was closed down in early 1991, never to reopen. Munther Bilbeisi, whose claims against Lloyd's were dismissed by a Miami court in November 1991, remains free in Jordan. There is no extradition treaty between Jordan and the United States, and given the power of the Bilbeisi family and its close connections to the ruling establishment, it is unlikely he ever will be returned to face charges.

Nor did he ever bring the $100 million lawsuit he had threatened against *Time* magazine. Shortly after the threat was made in June 1991, John Stacks had decided, against the advice of *Time*'s lawyers, to visit Bilbeisi in Jordan and hear him out. Even though Bilbeisi's charges were false, *Time* neither likes nor appreciates $100-million lawsuits, which can drag on for years, consuming massive amounts of time, money, and resources. Stacks had no intention of backing off the article, but he believed that if he took the time to go talk to Bilbeisi, they might be able to reach an understanding.

Time's lawyers had warned Stacks that Bilbeisi was so influential in Jordan that there was a strong possibility he would have Stacks arrested. Stacks had other ideas. Before he went to Jordan he set up two appointments, back to back. The first was at the home of Munther Bilbeisi. The second was with Jordan's King Hussein at the royal palace. With him Stacks brought *Time*'s Cairo bureau chief, Dean Fischer, and a stringer from Beirut. If Bilbeisi tried anything, Stacks was determined that it would quickly become an international scandal.

In the first meeting Bilbeisi told Stacks in an agitated voice that *Time*'s article was 90-percent wrong, that it had ruined his reputation, that his children could not hold up their heads at school. When it became clear that Bilbeisi was not prepared to say where the *Time* article was wrong, Stacks lapsed back into his irascible mode, and the meeting ended with chilly politeness. Beaty and Gwynne would learn later from Dougherty that what had most infuriated Bilbeisi was something none of them had expected: The *Time* article reported that Bilbeisi had claimed to be friends with King Hussein during his years in Boca Raton. The truth was that Bilbeisi had been in disgrace in those years. From his point of view, claiming friendship with the king was far worse than having been caught smuggling or committing tax and insurance fraud.

Dougherty's investigation of Bilbeisi showed why BCCI's services were so important to its corrupt clientele. And it showed, in particular, the devastating effectiveness of two of those services: commercial letters of credit, which provided cover for smuggling operations, and international money transfers, which enabled clients to hide money from sovereign authorities.

There are untold billions of dollars of illegal shipping transactions that BCCI supported with its letters of credit. Letters of credit (or "LCs" in banking jargon) are the grease that makes international trade work, bridging the gap between a buyer in, say, the United

States, and a seller in, say, Argentina. LCs solve the two principal concerns in any sale: the seller's desire to be paid and the buyer's desire to receive the exact goods he paid for. To reassure the Argentine seller, the American buyer goes to his bank, where he has good credit, and asks the bank to "open" a letter of credit for a certain amount of money in favor of the seller. The bank thus puts its credit between the two parties to the transaction. The bank then sends the letter of credit to the seller's bank in Argentina, which verifies the American bank's creditworthiness and advises the seller that he can ship his goods. When the goods arrive in the United States, they are checked for their contents and condition, and the shipping documents are forwarded to the buyer's bank. The bank and buyer then review these documents, and if all is in good order, the American bank remits funds to the Argentine bank for credit to the seller.

Almost all international trade—licit and illicit—is covered by LCs of one sort or another, underscoring the key role played by banks in the world's business. Munther Bilbeisi's coffee-smuggling operation offers a classic example of how the same sort of LCs can be used to aid and abet international fraud. One of the main methods of smuggling was to buy nonquota coffee in Guatemala or Honduras and create shipping documents showing that the ultimate destination was Jordan, also a nonagreement country. That coffee would then be shipped to Miami, where it was supposed to be transshipped to the Middle East. But the coffee never left Miami. Instead, Bilbeisi had it transported to warehouses, where the bags were relabeled to disguise the coffee's origin, and from there it was sold to American brokers and roasters. Over time, Bilbeisi discovered that the U.S. border was so porous that he could ship virtually any amount of coffee through such techniques as "short shipping" and "overstuffing." According to his former associates, they were all surprised at how easy it was. (Which suggests, among other things, how frighteningly easy it is for any commodity to cross our borders, including drugs.)

The only real problems were financing the shipments and doctoring the shipping documents themselves—which were the services supplied by BCCI. BCCI's own letters of credit specified the exact amounts and weights of coffee to be transshipped through Miami to Jordan. This was what the Central American governments believed was really happening. Under the terms of the LC, BCCI, together with Bilbeisi, would agree to pay the seller only if the correct weight of coffee arrived in Jordan. Yet once the coffee arrived in Miami, Bilbeisi would waive the usual staggering inconsistencies in the amounts of coffee and the destination. BCCI officers, who were fully aware that "nonagreement" coffee had just magically become "agreement" coffee, would sign off on it and pay the seller, thus closing the loop on the smuggling operation.

Those were not the only services BCCI provided to Bilbeisi. One of the fastest, easiest, and least traceable ways to pay bribes is in the form of cashier's checks. They cross borders easily, can be endorsed to third parties, and are as good as cash. As time went by, BCCI issued more and more of these instruments to Bilbeisi, his partners, and his clients. In one instance, thirty-one cashier's checks totaling $765,000 were issued on a single day out of BCCI's branches in Boca Raton and Miami.

Bilbeisi also availed himself of the bank's ability to move and hide money. When Bilbeisi's wife first petitioned for divorce in 1984, he decided to conceal as much of his wealth as he could. Bank officers at BCCI's Miami branch initiated a series of transfers of Bilbeisi's funds to secret numbered accounts at their Nassau and Panama branches, effectively concealing them from his wife or her attorneys. At a May 1984 meeting at Bilbeisi's home, BCCI officer Nadim Hasan explained how he could set up three London accounts in the names of phony Panamanian coffee companies expressly for the purposes of helping Bilbeisi and his partners evade U.S. income tax. Bilbeisi thus could make what appeared to be "payments" to these accounts, which were then deducted from his taxable income.

The services offered to Bilbeisi by Hasan (who was later indicted) were typical of what BCCI officers were doing all over the world. They were by no means exclusive to BCCI. In most offshore havens such as the Cayman Islands and Nassau, similar services are available through some of the world's largest and most reputable banks. Someone looking for secrecy in, say, Panama, would do quite as well at various Swiss banks as he would at BCCI. In the words of a high-level BCCI executive, when asked about his bank's reputation for helping people avoid financial laws, "To be honest, all foreign banks try to work around the controls. BCCI did it more blatantly."[19] BCCI, again, was merely mimicking the state-of-the-art practices in the respectable West. The difference was BCCI's aggressive marketing strategy, which targeted not only the millionaire who wanted to hide his profits, but criminals: drug lords, arms dealers, and smugglers. Within BCCI these banking services were highly systematized, were coordinated from the top, and constituted the primary engine of the bank's deposit growth. The marketing strategy was known within the bank, variously, as the "dollar deposit mobilization program" or the "external marketplace program" (EMP).[20]

EMP began with a reference from a customer or a BCCI officer. EMP was never offered to people off the streets. Once referred, the customer would then be shown, in precise detail, how he or she could bury his or her wealth so deeply in offshore tax havens that no governmental authority anywhere would ever be able to find it. This was not an empty promise. And it demonstrates with alarming specificity the mechanism by which billions of dollars flee the United States each year. Though much has been made of the fact that BCCI's U.S. agencies were not allowed to take deposits from U.S. citizens or corporations—the idea being that, because of the diligence of U.S. authorities in not granting BCCI a full banking license, U.S. citizens were not harmed by the bank's failure—BCCI in fact took hundreds of millions of dollars from Americans who wanted to hide their funds from the IRS. Though the bank's agency might be located in Florida or California or New York, thus barring it from accepting U.S. deposits, its officers would simply "book" the deposits into an offshore branch, thus sidestepping the U.S. law. That these same American depositors are not clamoring for their lost funds is hardly surprising, for to make a claim is tantamount to an admission of tax fraud. Though no official estimates exist of how much U.S. deposit money flowed into BCCI, the number may well approach $1 billion.

What Hasan described to Bilbeisi at that meeting in May 1984 was a comprehensive system of tax evasion, one-stop shopping for the likes of smugglers, currency restrictions violators, arms dealers, corrupt politicians. In this case, the Florida offices of BCCI marketed offshore deposits. To maintain secrecy, the bank provided confidential courier services, numbered accounts, false offshore addresses to which account statements could be mailed. Bank officers could also provide, within a matter of days, "nominee" corporations based in Panama or Europe, creating "loans" that were really just transfers of money backed by false collateral. Once given their false addresses, Panamanian front companies, false loans, and numbered accounts, the customers were assured that no more than two BCCI officers would ever know their real names and that their accounts would be kept apart from the regular accounts of the bank, literally locked in a manager's drawer. Customers were told that no authorities anywhere would even learn of the existence of those accounts, let alone the names of the persons holding them.[21] Only the unprecedented global seizure of the bank allowed a glimpse into these "hot money" accounts. The suggestion here is that, as long as you keep your offshore money at a solvent bank, there is little chance that investigators will ever be able to follow the paper trail.

Such was the marketing strategy that kept BCCI pumped full of deposits in the years after the fall in the price of oil in the early 1980s. Because of EMP's wild success, BCCI took pains to establish its own internal controls. First, "local" employees were never allowed to conduct such transactions. This role was reserved to "men of confidence," all of whom were Pakistanis and all of whom spoke Urdu. These men kept few tangible records of their transactions, rarely wrote down anything, relying instead on telephone conversations conducted in Urdu and on private, handwritten (again, in Urdu) notes kept locked away in personal safes. They were pointedly not trained to comply with U.S. laws, so that they could claim ignorance of those laws. When a leak of any kind occurred, the retribution from above was swift and severe. BCCI even maintained a corps of internal inspectors whose job it was to travel to branches and make sure that the proper levels of secrecy were maintained.[22] EMP was taken very seriously, and throughout the 1980s the performance of these "men of confidence" was measured mainly by their success in generating EMP accounts. The EMP program was made possible by the financial magic of the Caymans.

This branch-level secrecy abetted by lax or nonexistent regulation made it possible for BCCI, through its extensive network of offshore accounts, to run its scams for so long without being caught. All of the worst manipulations were booked through opaque havens like Luxembourg and the Cayman Islands. BCCI actually did have two buildings in the Caymans, in which several dozen people worked. But they had little to do with "booking," which was done from London.

The complexity of BCCI's organizational chart was made possible by yet another easy fiction in which the Caymans and the Bahamas specialized: the "shell" company. It was not all that difficult, even for offshore novices, as Abedi and Naqvi were in the early 1970s.

In the late summer of 1991 Beaty and Gwynne decided to try to find out just how hard it was to set up an offshore network that in microcosm would look very much like Abedi's own organizational gem. The system is shockingly simple and not very expensive to work. For the price of about $1,000, anyone can set up a corporation in a perfectly invisible offshore haven, complete with corporate officers and directors (front men, just like Abedi's), offshore trusts, and offshore bank accounts. (One such place is Ireland, which recently reduced its corporate tax rate on nonresident corporations to zero.) For that fee, the customer establishes an official "office" with a shingle on the door. Income is received directly into the company, which pays no taxes to any government and is virtually invisible to the IRS. To make sure that the IRS will never see it, another $1,000 or so buys a blind trust in Panama or Hong Kong, which means that the company is now nominally owned by equally phony "trustees" there. This provides nearly perfect cover from snooping national authorities. In Panama, for example, "the state has no knowledge of who is using these structures. The user does not appear in any written agreement. Local professionals who form the company . . . do not even know the identity of the true owner."[23]

Now let's say that the individual who has set up all this is not content just to pay no taxes on his offshore income. He wants the money paid into his U.S. bank account, and he still wants to pay no taxes on it. This is a bit more involved but still not very difficult. For $5,000 it is possible to have one's very own offshore bank in the Netherlands Antilles.[24] Though this is really nothing more than a "paper bank," the secrecy laws in the Antilles will prevent anyone from ever finding that out. To get the money back into the United States without having to pay taxes on it, the individual need only transfer funds from the offshore Irish account to the offshore bank in the Antilles. From there a "loan" for the same amount is created, and the funds are transferred to an American bank. The IRS, or anyone else who cares to look, sees only a loan and no income. Meanwhile, the individual can pay his own offshore bank interest on the fictitious loan, which is deductible from our U.S. taxable income, while the interest itself shows as profit in the tax-free offshore haven. This is business as usual for countless thousands of companies; in fact, offshore "captive" banks and insurance companies have been common practice for years among the Fortune 500. (Bermuda insurance captives were all the rage in the 1970s, for example, and were especially favored by midwestern manufacturing companies such as Firestone Tire & Rubber in Akron, Ohio. They were thus able to deduct their premiums from their U.S. income while booking the revenue offshore; the same game exactly.)

All of this could be put together within a week or so and would create an untraceable network of offshore companies, blind trusts, and banks that would enable anyone to evade all taxation. Abedi simply did the same thing on a grander scale, funneling money from his operations all over the world into the Caymans not only to avoid taxes but to siphon it off for his own projects, such as the acquisition of American banks.

BCCI is a paradigm of the way much of the world works, and nowhere was this more true than in its activities in the Cayman Islands. Long before it was shuttered in July 1991, BCCI had come to be the world's leading "underground" bank, performing services and making its money off the underground economies from Pennsylvania to the Pacific Rim. There are several definitions of "underground," but they reduce mainly to those parts of the economy that, in response to regulation, taxation, or law enforcement, have managed to remain invisible to the authorities. This can include everything from money running through offshore banks and cash payments to construction crews to cash from illegal drug transactions. Everyone has by now heard of or read about the black market economies of the former Soviet Union and Eastern bloc. But even the most advanced First World economies are bursting with black money.

In the United States, that model of responsibility and active government enforcement, the size of the underground economy is estimated to be $350 billion to $500 billion a year, equivalent to more than 10 percent of the U.S. gross national product (and $100 billion or more in lost revenue for the government). Economists at the World Bank and the International Monetary Fund estimate that a similar 10 percent of the Western European economy and 70 percent to 80 percent of the economies of the former Soviet Union and Eastern Europe are "black." In the developing world the black numbers are also remarkable: Peru, 60 percent; India, 50 percent; Taiwan, 40 percent.[25]

Most of this money is completely untrackable. "In general, no one has even a remote idea of the precise size or direction of global secret money flows, or of the identity of those involved," wrote Ingo Walter in his excellent 1990 study, *The Secret Money Market*.[26] To illustrate how completely off in the stratosphere and beyond the purview of anyone all of this activity is, one need only consult the tables that track the world's balance of payments. These simply track global deficits and surpluses—a minus in the U.S. balance sheet is balanced by a plus in the Japanese ledger, and so forth. By definition, the world must be in balance with itself. Yet from an approximate balance in the early 1970s, an inexplicable black hole—a deficit of $20 billion—had developed by 1978, and in 1982 the deficit hit $110 billion. As Walter observed: "Either the world as a whole had a transactions deficit with the man in the moon, or something is wrong."[27] Yet what is wrong is wrong only in theory; black markets and offshore tax havens are the way of the modern world, and nothing is going to change it.

Nothing illustrates this better than the phenomenon of capital flight, at which BCCI was one of the most adept practitioners in the world, and for the facilitation of which, it can be argued, the Caymans were expressly designed.

How damaging was capital flight to the Third World? In the years 1976 to 1985 $200 billion was transferred offshore by citizens of developing countries. Of that, $53 billion moved out between 1983 and 1985, the worst years of the debt crisis, from the countries that had the hardest time paying off their debt: Mexico, Venezuela, Argentina. It has been estimated that as much as 96 percent of dollars borrowed abroad by these three countries—for things like infrastructure projects, and factories—ended up in the accounts of private citizens abroad, many in the very same banks that had lent the money in the first place. In 1986 Morgan Guaranty Trust estimated that of $375 billion in new debt taken on by the ten major Latin American countries between 1975 and 1985, almost half vanished forever as flight capital. Though comparatively little has been written about it, this amounts to one of the greatest pure rip-offs of all time. The wealthy in places like Argentina protected and enriched themselves, while the poor and the middle class had to bear the brunt of the brutal "austerity" programs foisted on them by the International Monetary Fund to deal with their indebtedness.

Once the money moved into Cayman accounts, of course, the islands' secrecy laws prevented anyone from looking at it. If there was concern, BCCI could give the client a numbered account, as the Swiss have done for years. The Caymans were not BCCI's only global repository for such funds. But the Caymans would hold the bulk of them, and most of the money in need of immediate and total disguise ended up there. There was, of course, always the risk that someone, some real person who knew the accounts, would go to outside authorities. By the late 1970s this was already a sensitive point for Abedi and Naqvi. In 1978 a man named Masood Asghar, an associate of Abedi's who had worked in the BCCI offices in the Cayman Islands, among other places, decided to leave the bank. At the time he left he claimed that Abedi owed him $3 million, but Abedi offered only $250,000 plus a Mercedes-Benz. Infuriated, Asghar threatened to expose BCCI in a book. But the day he returned to his house in the affluent Defense Officers' Society section of Karachi, there was a knock on his door. He was summarily beaten and raped, and, according to reports in the British press, never threatened Abedi again.

Thirteen years later, as authorities picked through the wreckage of a $20-billion bank that had been cleaned of almost all of its assets with demonic thoroughness, they would have agreed that the Caymans are every bit as good at hiding things as their Panglossian PR says they are.

PART THREE

BANKERS, GUNS, AND MONEY

CHAPTER 10

ROCK AND ROLL

"You are never going to understand BCCI if you persist in
thinking of it as a bank."

—JOHN MOSCOW, ASSISTANT D.A., MANHATTAN

—"HEINRICH," BCCI WEAPONS DEALER, WARSAW

—SAMI MASRI, BCCI OPERATIVE, KARACHI

—JACK BLUM, SENATE SPECIAL COUNSEL, WASHINGTON, D.C.

—IRS INTELLIGENCE AGENT, MIAMI

For Beaty and Gwynne, reporting the detonation of BCCI had been
an exhilarating but exhausting experience. The month of July 1991 had
seen the seizure of the bank, the indictment by Morgenthau, the Fed's
civil action, and the publication of *Time*'s cover story. That story took
weeks to put together, and "closing" it at *Time*'s New York headquarters required three sleepless nights. When the two reporters staggered
out of the Time & Life Building on Saturday morning, the sun was just
coming up. They peered, molelike, at the outside world and waved at
a taxi slowly cruising up the deserted Avenue of the Americas. Neither
man felt a trace of either triumph or elation. Both were numb with
exhaustion and emotionally drained after putting together what
seemed, at that moment, the riskiest story either had ever produced.

They were aware there might be an element of personal risk: After
all, they had just written about BCCI's highly dangerous Black Network operatives; and weren't most of the former BCCI bankers they
had interviewed convinced that some of the men running the bank
would go to any ends to protect themselves?

But the risk they worried about was professional, not personal.
They had just put their reputations on the line by making assertions—

astonishing assertions at that moment in time—based on information from sources they probably could never name, in the face of strong denials from the government. As reporters they were out there alone, and the magazine had trusted them enough to climb out on a limb with them. *Time* magazine did not lightly accuse the United States government of cover-up.

However, even that was not the reason for their apprehension. They couldn't help worrying that a mistake lay imbedded in the article that might discredit their argument—that BCCI was a global criminal empire protected by its hidden ties to governments. The *Time* article was sure to be picked up by the wire services and would be quoted in other media. But at this point the concept they had introduced was too fragile to survive even a relatively minor mistake. The opposition, if that was the word for it, could be counted on to pounce on any error. A multimillion-dollar lawsuit, for example, could easily scare the rest of the press away from the story's larger implications and even cause *Time* to rethink its decision to expend every resource to stay out ahead on the story.

Gwynne was headed for La Guardia Airport and a plane to his family on Cape Cod for a brief vacation. Beaty, lugging heavy suitcases full of notes and documents, was bound for Kennedy and a flight to Los Angeles, and then on to his home in Hermosa Beach. He planned to take vacation time, but it was first imperative that he get himself organized, a cliché the partners had repeated to each other so often that it had become blackly humorous. And they needed a place to get organized in. They had been traveling for five months, living mostly in hotels and writing in borrowed offices in *Time* bureaus in New York, Washington, and London. They were overwhelmed with barely assimilated information and documents, many only hastily read; data and allegations that hadn't fit immediately into whatever segment of the ever-widening story they were working on at that moment.

Few investigative reporters will relinquish control of their notes and research as a story progresses, but in this case things were out of hand. The BCCI scandal was not one neat financial story waiting to be packaged: Here were dozens of complex stories, each spiraling off in a different direction. In the beginning the reporters each carried a bulging briefcase from city to city, then two, and then eventually suitcases and duffels weighted with documents. Somehow all these records—any one of which might (one never knew) contain an invaluable clue—had to be gathered together, studied, and sorted out. They were looking at serious volume here. For example, on one four-day sweep through Houston and Dallas, Beaty, who gathered documents compulsively, shelled out $2,500 for State Corporation Commission and SEC reports on every Texas-based company he could think of that might have links to BCCI. And then he literally had to drag one-hundred-pound black plastic trash bags of printouts back to New York because the bean counters at *Time* had refused to pay for the last suitcase he bought to haul documents.

Beaty's answer was to convert the back room of his home into a temporary headquarters, link it to *Time*'s computer system in New York, and sit down and read. The slightly down-at-the-heels Spanish-style stucco had been built as a weekend cottage in 1927. Its sole claim to distinction was that a narrow slice of white sand and green Pacific Ocean was visible from the front yard. You could hear the waves.

The dusty home workshop was hastily dismantled. Table saws and woodworking tools, untouched for months, were packed away, and three computers were installed, perched on plywood tables supported by sawhorses. New telephone lines, one listed under a fictitious name, were augmented by two cellular phones. Using a satellite-beamed telephone-paging service linked to a telephone that taped messages and then hung up and automatically dialed another telephone—in this case one of the unlisted numbers—and replayed the message, the reporter cobbled together a simple phone cutout system. Most of Beaty's sources were paranoid about telephone taps, and while he doubted that his system would foil a government-installed tap, his most anxious sources could take comfort in the illusion of electronic sophistication. Were his lines being tapped? Beaty didn't know—the strange echoes and clicks on his calls might well have been lousy telephone service—but he did think it significant that his law enforcement sources didn't want to talk over his phone. "When an FBI agent wants you to call from a pay phone, what do you think?" he asked Gwynne plaintively.

By midsummer there were two good reasons to worry about the security of telephone lines. In late July and early August two reporters who had been working on the BCCI story were killed. The first was a reporter for the *Financial Times* named Anson Ng, who was found dead in his apartment in Guatemala City, Guatemala. The story was recounted by Senator Alan Cranston before the Kerry subcommittee:

> First, according to people who talked by phone with Ng in the days before his death, the British journalist mentioned that he

was working on a quote, big story, unquote, related to BCCI and Guatemala. Second, although officials in Guatemala have sought to characterize Ng's assassination as the work of common criminals, the murder seems to be the work of professional hit men. . . . Apparently a silencer was used in the killing, which was done by a single bullet wound to the head. . . . I am told that Ng's head was wrapped in a towel and his body left in the bathroom, something consistent with efforts to keep the murder secret for a period of time. According to those closest to Ng, a set of documents were stolen from his desk.

Less than two weeks later a similar story hit much closer to home. On August 10, a Washington, D.C., freelance writer named Danny Casolaro, who had also been working on BCCI as part of a larger story, was found dead in a Martinsburg, West Virginia, motel room. He was discovered in a bathtub surrounded by a pool of blood. Though it was immediately ruled a suicide, there were enough unanswered questions that the press jumped all over the story. He had supposedly killed himself by slashing his wrists—except that the cuts had been phenomenally deep, all the way through the tendons. There was also evidence that someone else had been in the room with him. "It looked like someone tried to wipe up the blood on the floor and slid the towels under the sink," one of the motel's housekeepers said in a magazine interview. "It looked like someone threw the towels on the floor and tried to wipe the blood with their foot, but they didn't get the blood, they just smeared it on the floor."[1]

Casolaro's death led to a strange interlude for Beaty in Hermosa Beach. By coincidence a last entry in Danny Casolaro's calendar read: "Call Jonathan." Ten days prior to his death Casolaro had met with Beaty at the Jefferson Hotel in Washington, D.C. Casolaro had wanted to compare notes and get advice on how to sell his idea for an investigative story about a conspiracy called "the Octopus" to book publishers. The two had discussed BCCI at length. When reporters covering the story discovered the entry in Casolaro's calendar, Beaty began to receive several telephone calls a day; the reporters wanted to know what Casolaro was working on, and Beaty was one of the last people to talk to him about his work. He had not been able to provide much help, since Casolaro's project had seemed extremely complex and was difficult to follow, and he had told Beaty nothing about his upcoming trip to Martinsburg.

Though no one could be sure what to make of the deaths of Casolaro and Ng, they suggested that there might at least be some danger in covering the story. That had led Beaty and Gwynne to take further steps to secure their telephone conversations. Beaty had developed his cellular cutout system a year before, based on the techniques used by the Colombian cocaine cartels, not to avoid taps but to confound the *Time* Los Angeles bureau chief to whom he nominally reported. Beaty disliked having to appear regularly in the Los Angeles bureau—where a hapless reporter could be handed an unwanted minor assignment just because he was standing there when a warm body was needed— unless it was unavoidable. Jordan Bonfante, the bureau chief, traveled a good deal and tended to keep track of correspondents by telephone. Even when he was in the bureau he would buzz reporters on the interoffice system once or twice a day from his corner office rather than walk down the hallway to chat, so the solution was obvious. Beaty set up things so that whenever the telephone in his office rang he could answer it, even if he happened to be working at home at the moment. Or sitting on the beach. In Hermosa or Miami.

Since Beaty usually worked special assignments and reported directly to the chief of correspondents in New York, few people at *Time* ever knew exactly what he was working on. With his telephone lash-up even fewer knew exactly where he was while he was doing it. He considered this to be a major career achievement. So did most of his colleagues.

Other electronic equipment linking Hermosa Beach to the world crowded the tiny back room, including a fax machine, various tape recorders, and a TV set and video recorder that constantly monitored CNN. But the major new addition was a powerful 486 computer capable of storing tens of thousands of documents on its hard disk. Gwynne and Beaty had returned from James Dougherty's Miami law office with a carton full of floppy disks containing virtually every newspaper story printed in English since 1972 mentioning BCCI or any individual even remotely connected to it. The lawyer had spent a small fortune gathering the thousands of clippings and feeding them into a computer, and it was a 40-megabyte information bonanza. The news clips were valuable not for any particular overlooked revelation—there had been precious few critical or decently analytical stories written about BCCI before its indictment for money laundering in Tampa—but for the incidental mentions of names of BCCI bankers and associates and the enumeration of corporate acquisitions that could be gleaned from the innocuous and long-forgotten business-page stories. Each name, each reference from the past, could provide a new lead. *Time* magazine, the global communications giant, had no computers or programs available to the edit staff sophisticated enough to store and sift through this much data.

Getting organized was obviously a good idea. It even worked for a few days—until Beaty had another good idea and decided that since he was tied to one spot while doing research, he should fly in sources to be debriefed, working on the theory that it didn't cost the magazine any more to bring sources to him than it did to send him to interview them in their home cities. Almost instantly, "Surfside Central" became a three-ring circus, crowded with spooks, weapons dealers, and conspirators, some of whom revealed information that escalated the story beyond anything yet imagined. Getting organized was quickly forgotten.

Within days of closing the cover story, Beaty had flown in Bill White, a Houston businessman who alleged that his former business partner was a CIA agent with strange ties to both BCCI and President George Bush. Beaty stashed White in a room in the nearby Hotel Hermosa. Another visitor was Gene Wheaton, a former U.S. military-intelligence type who knew some of the BCCI players from his days as an intelligence security chief in Iran and more recent connections with Ollie North's Contra supply crew. And then, as if to ensure there was action in all three rings at once, "Heinrich," a major weapons dealer from Germany who had extensive business dealings with BCCI, flew in from Europe and was also put up at the Hotel Hermosa.

Beaty kept juggling his debriefing schedules so the three men would never meet, and this added a certain Marx Brothers flavor to the comings and goings at Surfside Central. Beaty's wife, Linda, an editor at the *Los Angeles Times*, was quite used to strange visitors who might, or might not, be willing to give their names. She would knock on the door of the rear room and announce: "There's someone at the front door for you: I think it's that spy from Orange County," and Beaty would wince and then apologize and ask his guest of the moment if he would mind leaving through the back door. Linda always went along with the program, but she exhibited her distaste by calling a spade a spade. On Wednesday of that week, when she answered a call from Karachi placed to the family phone, she walked into the room and announced dryly: "There's a terrorist that wants to talk to you on my phone."

In the case of the trio in hand, Beaty had a couple of reasons for trying to keep them separated. One was professional courtesy. White was an amateur player, an outraged citizen, and pros like Heinrich and Wheaton were uncomfortable around "civilians." The other involved elemental trade craft, and it had to do with the two professionals. Heinrich and Wheaton had never met and worked different sides of the street, but they each had a piece of knowledge about the same event. Beaty wanted to check one version against the other: Objective truth, in the world of winks and nods, is very difficult to come by.

Coherence is also a difficult to maintain in a sprawling investigation, as both reporters learned and relearned as they followed trails that branched, crossed one another, or came to unexpected dead ends. Beaty's effort to simultaneously check out the stories of White, Wheaton, and Heinrich was another example of the three-dimensional chess game.

Bill White, from Houston, was the All-American Boy, even if he was middle-aged. Athletic, clean-cut, size extra large, hair neatly parted, White was as earnest as a minister and friendly as a puppy. He had been a star football player in high school, graduated from Annapolis, and became a naval flight officer. After the navy he put away his combat decorations, earned a Harvard Business School graduate degree, and returned to Texas to become a well-paid investment point man for a lot of heavy-hitting Republicans. Patriotism is real in Texas: White paid his dues and was admitted to the club by the good old boys who run things.

He was sponsored by another Harvard M.B.A., Lloyd Bentsen, Jr., the son of the distinguished Texas senator. The younger Bentsen had discovered White when he returned to campus on a very specific job-recruiting trip. The senator's son, who had been a Harvard classmate of George Bush, Jr., ran on the inside track and was looking for someone who could handle discreet private investments. The boyish-looking, personable former navigator had just the credentials he was looking for. As White explained it, Bentsen had suggested that when White returned to Texas he should look up a Houston businessman named James Bath, who was in real estate and aircraft sales and represented some of the richest Arab sheikhs. Bath, also a friend of George Bush, Jr., was looking for a business partner. Bentsen thought that since Bath was also a former fighter pilot, the two men would have a lot in common.

White sat in the brown leather chair in Beaty's back room, wearing khaki pants and a sport shirt, surrounded by pilot's suitcases and boxes packed with documents to support his story. He had so many documents that he couldn't carry them all and had shipped ahead several boxes to Beaty via Federal Express. The two had conferred earlier in Houston, and the reporter had agreed to help with his research. Now Beaty looked at all the boxes of papers covering his floor and suppressed a groan. He didn't want to have to assimilate all this, but BCCI was surely involved in White's complicated tale of intrigue and duplicity.

White had gone into business with Bath and they had done quite well for a while, especially in land development deals. White was the amiable front man, while Bath, who shunned publicity of any kind, quietly rounded up the investors. But they had had a falling-out, and now White wanted to explain why he believed his former partner had been a front man for Arabs connected with BCCI who were buying influence in America.

"You have to understand that they thought I was one of them," White said earnestly. "Bath told me that he was in the CIA. He told me he had been recruited by George Bush himself in 1976, when Bush was director of the agency. That made sense to me, especially in light of what I had seen once we went into business together. Bath and George, Jr., were pals and flew together in the same Air National Guard unit, and Bath lived just down the street from the Bush family when George, Sr., was living in Houston. He said Bush wanted him involved with the Arabs, and to get into the aviation business." White began pulling documents out of his cases as he talked.

"That's how Bath, who didn't know anything about the aviation business, became one of the biggest jet aviation dealers in the country within a couple of years. Look, here's a Boeing he's leasing to the Abu Dhabi National Oil Company. That's a multimillion-dollar jet. And that's how he became a representative for Sheikh Khalid bin-Mahfouz, whose family controls the National Commercial Bank of Saudi Arabia."

He handed the reporter a legal document attesting that Bath was the representative of Mahfouz, empowered to act in his name for "all U.S. business activities." Beaty nodded thoughtfully. Mahfouz really was one of the richest men in the world, and he was a controlling shareholder in both BCCI and First American Bank.

He took notes as White continued rapidly. White's story was cogent and well organized. It was also off the wall. He talked about Mahfouz's investments and his early venture into Texas banking in partnership with Ghaith Pharaon and former Treasury Secretary and Texas Governor John Connally. The three had been principal investors in the purchase of tiny Main Bank in 1976. Beaty looked at the newspaper story White handed him. Main Bank had made the news when a bank examiner discovered that it was purchasing $100 million in hundred-dollar bills each month from the Federal Reserve, an amount that dwarfed its minuscule asset base. That was strange, but there was nothing illegal about it on its face. Except that according to White, Bath was investigated by the DEA while the two men were partners. The DEA, he said, had suspected Bath was using his planes to fly the currency to the Cayman Islands, although they didn't know why, since drugs didn't seem to be involved.

White also spilled out a tangled tale of Sheikh Mahfouz's more recent Texas investments, including the alleged sweetheart purchase of the Texas Commerce Bank Tower for some $200 million during the mid-1980s Texas oil-business crash. That purchase, White indicated, greatly benefited the fortunes of the Baker family, who were founders and principal holders of Texas Commerce stock. That Baker family included James Baker, President Bush's confidant and secretary of State, who had been forced to put his Texas Commerce stock into a blind trust after questions about potential conflicts of interest arose while he was secretary of the Treasury.

From there, White launched into an account of George Bush, Jr.'s, business ventures. He described how Bush's storefront energy company, Arbusto (Spanish for "Bush"), had been purchased in 1988 by a little-known Dallas firm, Harken Energy. Harken was primarily in the business of buying up old refineries, and George, Jr., had been named a director of the company. Then Harken's threadbare fortunes had zoomed when the company—which had no offshore drilling experience—unexpectedly won an offshore drilling concession from the Gulf kingdom of Bahrain that was potentially worth billions.

White suspected that Mahfouz, or other BCCI players, must have had a hand in steering the oil-drilling concession to the president's son. He thought it was part of a pattern, since Bath—who made his fortune by investing money for Mahfouz and another BCCI-connected Saudi, Sheikh bin-Laden—had once confided that he was an original investor in George Bush, Jr.'s, oil exploration company. In fact, White said, Bath had bragged he had put up $50,000 to help George, Jr., get started in the oil business.

White pulled out more documents that seemed to support his contentions, legal papers from James Bath's contested divorce. There, in a list of his assets, was a $50,000 investment in Arbusto oil, Bush's original company. White's point was that Bath had no substantial money of his own at the time he made that investment. Most of Bath's investments, including his main holding—a Houston company named Skyways Aircraft Company that held Middle Eastern contracts—were really fronts for Mahfouz and other Saudis connected with BCCI.

Much of White's tantalizing paper trail had come from four years of legal battles with Bath, the result of an admittedly adversarial relationship. Adversarial might have been too weak a word. According to White, his falling-out with Bath had come after Bath had "borrowed" $500,000 from funds supplied by his Saudi/CIA backers to invest in a sure-thing real estate deal. When Bath lost the money in the Texas real estate and oil crash, according to White, the desperate Bath had come to him and insisted that he help cover the hole in the books. When White refused, Bath vowed to ruin him. Whether White's version was true or not, the records showed Bath indeed had driven White into the ground with an onslaught of ruinous lawsuits. Legal fees alone had bankrupted White, who said Bath had bragged that his problems would never end because of Bath's CIA connections and friendships with judges in Houston.

Beaty had the sudden feeling that he was entering yet another hall of mirrors. He promised again to help White in his quest for evidence. White, so broke that all the furniture had been hauled out of his offices, was trying to search Federal Aviation Administration (FAA) records and aircraft manufacturers' logs in order to prove Bath, BCCI, and the Saudis were running a CIA-connected international air freight business. Beaty phoned a Houston computer store and gave his credit card number to authorize White's rental of a 486 computer and an optical data scanner. He tried not to think about his *Time* expense account as he maneuvered White out the door, promising to review the records and fly to Houston as soon as possible to begin checking out White's story. It all seemed too preposterous to be true, and he didn't have time for this, but White's documents were too convincing to walk away from. (Beaty and his *Time* colleague Richard Behar eventually published a story on the strange affair of George Bush, Jr.'s, Bahrain oil concession award and a companion story on the mysterious James Bath's ties to Arab millionaires linked to BCCI, but they were unable to find hard evidence that any of the BCCI players had a hand in the windfall business deal dropped in the president's son's lap. Knowledgeable oil company sources believe that the Bahrain oil concession was indeed an oblique favor to the president of the United States but say that Saudi Arabia was behind the decision.)

.   .   .

Gene Wheaton's off-the-wall contribution centered on the former military intelligence officer's investigations into the real cause of the crash of a plane carrying 248 American soldiers returning from the Middle East in Gander, Newfoundland, in December 1985. Even though Islamic Jihad terrorists had quickly boasted they blew up the jet, chartered from Arrow Air, a CIA-connected company, both the U.S. and Canadian governments insisted the plane had plunged to the ground because of ice on the wings. There was abundant evidence to the contrary.

Wheaton, serving as a private investigator for the Families for Truth About Gander, Inc.—an organization formed by the relatives of most of the soldiers who perished in the crash—believed that Iranian terrorists blew up the plane out of anger after they received a shipment of defective Hawk missile parts from the United States. That missile equipment was part of the then-secret arms-for-hostages deal authorized by the White House and orchestrated by CIA Chief William Casey and Lieutenant Colonel Oliver North. Wheaton thought the government refused to acknowledge the real reason for the disaster because it would have threatened the ongoing clandestine negotiations.

The reporter took notes as Wheaton, sitting in the brown leather chair, described the federal investigation at the crash site. Beaty wasn't really interested at the moment in Wheaton's conspiracy theory. He was waiting for a fragment of information relating to something the military investigators had found when they first reached the crash site. Wheaton had mentioned it in passing some months ago. At the time it hadn't meant anything to the reporter, but now Beaty wanted to hear it again, in context and without prompting.

"The scene was a mess," Wheaton explained. "Even though the government later said there were no explosives aboard, fire fighters heard small arms popping all over the place and saw debris flying into the air from delayed explosions. There were six heavy wooden crates aboard that probably contained contraband arms that had been loaded into the jet's cargo in Cairo without military customs clearance."

Beaty was reminded of the heavy wooden crates put aboard the CIA plane out of Karachi, as described by Sami Masri, and dropped his eyes to his notes so his sudden interest wouldn't show. The BCCI link was coming.

"The military got those crates out of there fast, and since they were never on the manifest, they were never referred to again. And neither was the money that was taken out."

Bingo. "What money?"

Wheaton didn't hesitate. "Nobody, except the people who removed it, knows how much there was, but a thirty-two-kilo army-issue duffel bag stuffed with U.S. currency was found in the wreckage. How many hundred-dollar bills does it take to fill a seventy-pound duffel? Two men in civilian clothes, men that the military personnel on the site believed to be from the CIA, took custody of the money and departed immediately after that."

"Gene, how public is that information, about the money? It figures to be millions. Has that ever been reported in the press?" Beaty asked.

"No, not to my knowledge, and I've read just about everything on the subject." Wheaton sounded a bit defensive, automatically assuming that the reporter was questioning what he had said. "But there is no dispute about the fact that it was found. There are references in records, but you have to know where to look. There are transcripts."

"No problem," Beaty said. "I was just wondering."

Wondering just how a German weapons dealer named Heinrich, who operated out of Europe and had almost no American connections, would have known that a large amount of money—unaccounted-for cash money at that—was being carried on that flight. Especially if it hadn't been reported in the press.

Yet Heinrich, who was close to high-level people in BCCI, since they financed many of his sub-rosa deals, had also recently mentioned the Newfoundland crash. Heinrich didn't sell surplus military rifles for a living: He did multimillion-dollar deals with the governments of Second and Third World countries looking for tanks, sophisticated fighter planes, and tactical missiles, and he worked with the top echelon of the BCCI apparat who specialized in weapons procurement and financing. He had been describing a particular conversation with some of his BCCI contacts. Beaty remembered every word of Heinrich's offhand comment. "They were complaining about losing a lot of money in the Gander crash. It was BCCI money, and they thought it was being, perhaps, stolen from them."

Beaty ended the session with Wheaton as soon as he could and called Heinrich at the hotel.

Half an hour later the neatly dressed, bespectacled German was sitting in the leather chair—the only decent chair in the room, really—looking bemused and a little worn. He looked, Beaty thought, like an accountant who had lived a very hard life. The reporter could never decide how old Heinrich was—direct questions about Heinrich's personal life were verboten—but Beaty thought he was younger than he appeared. He asked his question.

"I've told you this before."

The reporter aborted a sharp retort. Heinrich reminded him of a testy university professor who expected students to remember every precious word he uttered. "I don't have your kind of mind, Heinrich. You're pretty unusual, you know. There aren't many people who can retain as many details as you do; if I don't write it down, I forget it. Especially when I don't understand what I'm being told. And a lot of what you told me when we first met was going over my head."

Placated, the arms dealer relented slightly. He was not so smart that he couldn't be appealed to on the basis of his superior intellect. (After years of interviewing everyone from captains of industry to Mafia hit men, Beaty was still amazed by how far a little flattery could take him. He tried to resist it when someone used it on him, but it worked almost every time.)

"You still don't comprehend this, I see. Perhaps it is difficult, but I have told you that you are never going to understand BCCI if you persist in thinking of it as a bank."

Beaty nodded. He must have heard that line from Sami a hundred times.

"This money on the plane was money that Abedi, money that the bank, had provided U.S. Intelligence for covert operations. The money was being used by the American military. I have no idea what for. You don't ask these kinds of questions of these people. This was not my business there, and I was just listening to them talk. But money of this sort is always cash—unlimited cash sometimes—and there is never any paperwork, so there is never real accountability. And that means, does it not, that it does not always go for the uses that it was intended." Heinrich smiled one of the humorless smiles that made him look older.

"One of the bank men—perhaps I should call him an associate of the bank men—was a little angry about this money. He believed it was being, ah, appropriated, by some of the special-forces soldiers. Someone else thought perhaps it was being diverted to another operation. Who could tell? I know only that the subject of the Gander crash came up, and these people talked about BCCI money going down with it."

Beaty rubbed his eyes. He was having a difficult time accepting this even though Heinrich so far had been consistently accurate about BCCI. At least as far as he could check. He had fastened on Wheaton's description of the mysterious duffel bag full of money found in the wreckage because it was evidence, of a sort, that Heinrich hadn't simply made up a tale. He was intent on establishing Heinrich's credibility, not the puzzle of the Arrow Air flight. But now, once again, Heinrich was leading him into deeper waters.

"Let me get this straight. You're saying that Agha Hasan Abedi, BCCI, was providing big-time operational funds for the American spooks, even military covert ops, in the Middle East and in Europe? I remember what you said about them being CIA and DIA paymasters in Latin America."

Heinrich gestured impatiently. "Jonathan, I have already told you. It's not that you don't remember; there is nothing wrong with your mind. You didn't believe me. Abedi was close to Bill Casey. They met many times. BCCI financed operations, BCCI brokered weapons and supplies, BCCI acted as a paymaster. You yourself told me that American operatives in Wiesbaden were using BCCI credit cards."

The telephone rang. It was Bill White announcing that he was on his way to the airport but that he wanted to stop by for a moment to show Beaty another important document.

"Jesus, Heinrich. I've got somebody else I've got to talk to and you probably don't want to meet him. Can we talk later tonight?"

Heinrich, no stranger to parleys where some of the participants avoided meeting face to face, was courteous as always. "I can walk to the hotel and you can call when you're ready. Please tell your lovely wife that I was sorry to have missed her." Beaty watched Heinrich walk up the alley soldierly erect, and shook his head as he closed his back door. He was going to have to get Linda to quit calling him Attila the Hun.

For reasons still best known only to him, Heinrich had come in out of the cold voluntarily and quite early in the game and was one of the decidedly nonestablishment sources for a small piece of the cover story. In a way it was a little astounding that anyone had listened to him and passed him on to the two reporters working the story, but that it had happened was a credit to the *Time* magazine machinery.

Each *Time* story, especially in the beginning, had produced its share of would-be informants and commentators who wrote or telephoned the magazine. Heinrich was one of several exceptions, but such volunteers, especially the letter writers, tended to be loosely wrapped conspiracy buffs who filled their margin spaces with cramped afterthoughts and drew arrows connecting the names of the players in whatever plot they were describing, lest the reader miss the point. The telephone callers usually had more immediate concerns: They would breathlessly announce inside information that would make BCCI dwarf Watergate and then ask how much the magazine might pay for it. In the general practice of journalism, especially at the national news level, few such callers or writers would be given more than a polite brush-off, even if they sounded rational. The news desk staff in New York knew that Beaty and Gwynne wanted anything that sounded credible passed on, but most of the calls about BCCI sounded zany.

Time's original contact with Heinrich, an overseas call from a nervous-sounding man who wouldn't give his name and wasn't sure he wanted to talk, had been fielded by Ann King, the very astute assistant to the two deputy chiefs of correspondents. She had somehow caught a ring of authenticity in Heinrich's voice and pulled Beaty out of a meeting to talk to him.

The reporter blew it the first time around. Heinrich sounded real enough on the phone that Beaty to offered to pay his airfare from Europe to New York for a meeting, but after they spent a day and an evening talking in Beaty's hotel, the correspondent was ready to bail out. For one thing, he couldn't get a handle on Heinrich's motivation. All the German would say was that Agha Hasan Abedi was an evil man and that the way things were going, the full story of BCCI was going to be buried. And the BCCI empire that Heinrich described was too outrageously dramatic to be believed. It sounded like a movie about an international conspiracy. The only person who had ever described the bank in terms anything like this was Sami Masri, whom Beaty had at that point just taken under his wing, and he was having too much trouble remaining serious about Masri to take on another conspiratorialist. This man, Heinrich, was talking about a bank that was a world-class weapons dealer; a bank that bribed presidents, including a president of the United States. Beaty thanked him for coming, and Heinrich, who was having second thoughts about talking to a reporter, headed back to the airport. He didn't bother to give Beaty a phone number.

Within a month Beaty had learned enough to regret dismissing Heinrich. It was coming in bits and pieces that didn't necessarily connect, but others were saying some of the same things. He asked John Moscow to help check out Heinrich.

"He said that if I tried to check up on him I wouldn't learn anything," Beaty told the assistant D.A. "I'm not even sure what his real name is, but here is the name he used on his passport." Moscow was willing to help. Heinrich's reports of BCCI-orchestrated weapons deals didn't help the case Moscow was building against Clark Clifford and Robert Altman, but the prosecutor knew BCCI was a bigger criminal conspiracy than anyone had imagined.

Moscow called a few days later. "You've got a strange friend here." He wouldn't say specifically to whom he had talked, but Beaty gathered he had been in touch with Interpol and one or more European intelligence agencies. But the information that came back on Heinrich was gibberish. Two agencies showed two different birth dates, both wildly improbable. There was apparent uncertainty about his country of birth, even his citizenship. He was reported to be wealthy, his associates were questionable, and there had been investigations. But in sum the official records read to Moscow contained little real information. There was no explanation of his wealth, and even more surprisingly, there was no mention of his real occupation.

Heinrich telephoned Beaty from Europe a short time later to tell the nonplussed reporter that although he understood Beaty's motivation in checking up on him he wished that "Mr. John Moscow" would cease making telephone calls and inquiries because it was occasioning unwanted attention.

"I told you that you would find nothing helpful, but a certain agency called me in yesterday and asked a number of questions, including why the Americans are interested."

That particular agency posed no problems for him, Heinrich said calmly, because he had a protector there, but he worried that the agency itself wasn't secure. There had been reports of leaks. Beaty—and Gwynne, who had been hurriedly waved over to listen on another phone—were impressed that Heinrich was so inside that he had been able to learn the name of the law enforcement official asking the questions. Inside somewhere. And Heinrich's uneasiness about "leaks" from one of the most respected intelligence agencies in Europe sounded like the grumblings of every spy type Beaty had ever known. The deeper into the trade, the more universal the suspicion. Heinrich was clearly a professional, but Beaty wasn't sure what kind. However, Heinrich accepted his invitation to come back to America for another conversation. He would think over the proposition that he also have a chat with Mr. Moscow, but he sounded very doubtful.

There had been other meetings since, but Heinrich, worried about exposure and retaliation, limited the information he gave to careful bits and pieces. He, Beaty, and Gwynne talked philosophy, religion, economics, and history, taking one another's measure. But Heinrich did open up in one remarkable way after the magazine printed a couple of major BCCI stories and he was unable to easily identify himself as a source of any given piece of information. He proved absolutely that he was who he said he was.

The German took Beaty inside a multimillion-dollar weapons deal. The two met in Paris, flew to the Middle East and then onward to meet with bankers and other participants in a clandestine government-to-government deal originally crafted by BCCI. In negotiating sessions Heinrich introduced Beaty as one of his aides and once delighted himself by presenting the American as the man who took care of the payoffs in a third country in the transactions. Heinrich had a sense of humor, even if it didn't usually show. Beaty relished the cover he was given, listening as an international banker handling a major slice of the financing described how the "distributions" to various generals and government officials would be made. He knew he would be unable to write about it: He wouldn't pretend to be someone other than a reporter in order to get a story. It wasn't just journalist's ethics: He thought such practice was too much like shooting fish in a barrel. Besides, writing directly about what he was seeing with his own eyes could get Heinrich killed. However, there was no longer any doubt that this mysterious man who liked to quote Teilhard de Chardin and Nietzsche was a major player in the Eastern European weapons market and enjoyed a close business relationship with BCCI.

Now, back in Beaty's dimly lit workshop, Heinrich was being asked to start again from the beginning and connect the bits and pieces he had divulged. He didn't stop talking for a long time. At first Beaty kept his head down, his fingers flying over the keyboard balanced on his lap, avoiding direct eye contact as if he were afraid to break the mood. But the arms broker had made up his mind to get specific. His memory was phenomenal. With only occasional references to the tiny handwriting in his diaries, he reeled off names, street addresses, phone numbers, even bank account numbers as he ticked off which weapons transactions the reporter could pursue and those about which he must keep silent. He began to expand on Abedi's role in brokering technology to the Soviets.

"The supercomputer deal ran through India about fifteen months ago. It was E. S. Vijayakumar who handled it, but I don't remember whether this is the son or the father. It was the father who handled the deal. That's Mala Export Corporation, 31 Kothari Road, Madras, India. They have offices in London and Abu Dhabi, and they do a lot of high-technology stuff with BCCI and Russia."

Beaty looked up. "This reminds me of something else, Heinrich.

Sam Gwynne and I have a source from Pakistan. I can't tell you who it is, but you probably know him, at least by reputation. He's in your line of business. Anyway, he's given us quite a bit on Abedi's support of Pakistan's nuclear bomb program, and he's talked about Abedi getting communications technology from the U.S. and peddling it to the Soviets. I gather this was fairly secret satellite stuff the U.S. gave Pakistan under the table, but BCCI was in the middle of it somehow."

Heinrich looked very interested.

"He talked about BCCI, or Pakistani intelligence, which he says is the same thing, being involved in obtaining satellite communication and surveillance technology. He mentioned Glosnass, the Soviet satellite navigation system, said Pakistan was getting help from the French, and claimed Pakistan could download our surveillance satellites. He said BCCI had helped build a processing center near Karachi for Landsat imagery that could process raw data with amazing resolution. Have you heard anything about any of this?"

Heinrich stared at his polished gentleman's boots. "I know not much about Pakistan except that there is a large German company in the country right now providing scientific and technical assistance for their nuclear program, and BCCI is, or had been, paying the bills. I won't give you the name: They're not doing anything Westinghouse hasn't done for Pakistan through its Canadian subsidiary." He paused for a long beat. "But I do know something about BCCI and your American Navstar System.

"BCCI sold it to the Russians."

That tore it. Beaty tossed his keyboard on the desk with a thump and stood up abruptly. "And how do you know that?"

The reporter, who had learned a little about navigation because he owned a boat, was familiar with Navstar, a global positioning system operated by the Department of Defense. The Navstar system had approximately a score of satellites circling the globe, beaming down radio navigation information. It provided hair-splitting accuracy, giving three-dimensional positioning in latitude, longitude, and altitude anywhere in the world. Commercial ships and planes navigated by the signals. But because the military also used it to guide intercontinental missiles to their targets, or cruise missiles screaming down the streets of Baghdad, it was very sensitive technology. The Defense Department system degraded the information beamed to commercial receivers by distorting the signals so that it would not provide positioning closer than 100 feet or so from an actual location. At the flip of a switch the Defense Department could, and often did, distort the commercial band signals even further so that users couldn't position closer than 1,000 feet from actual position. That was close enough for mariners and pilots. Military receivers, like those in jet fighters, received another set of coded signals from the same satellites, called the P-code, which gave dead-bang accuracy.

Heinrich stood up too, and stretched. He was tense.

"Jonathan, I saw Navstar plans in a safe in the Kremlin, in the offices of the Soviet space agency, Glavkosmos. They have been trying to upgrade their own GPS [global positioning system], which was less reliable, and they had many U.S. technical documents, secret manuals from the United States. One of the Glavkosmos directors bragged to me that they had been obtained for them by BCCI."

"Damn, Heinrich! Why do you tell me things like this? It's important, but there's not a way in the world we can prove this. Who would believe it?"

Beaty watched the German's expression grow cold. Heinrich couldn't be reasoned with if you questioned his veracity. The first time he had suggested that Heinrich was exaggerating—a standard enough interview technique—Heinrich had frozen up and dropped out of sight for weeks.

"No, I believe you," Beaty said. "It's my editors that would choke if I tried to put this into print." When in trouble, blame your editors. They didn't teach that in Journalism 101 either, but every reporter learned it quickly enough. Beaty added a twist. "After all, you yourself are such a secret I haven't even been able to tell my editors who you are, and they're not about to take my word on something like this."

A white lie. Except in extraordinary circumstances, Beaty's "editors" never asked who his sources were if he didn't want to name names. He was paid a fair salary because he was trusted to separate the wheat from the chaff. When it came to sources who couldn't be quoted by name, it was his word that was accepted, not the source's, whether the source was of high or low reputation. Beaty, like most reporters, had to be convinced he was being told the truth and that there was some way to prove it if push came to shove.

Heinrich looked thoughtful and raised an eyebrow. "It is important that this information be known. The American intelligence agents who have worked with BCCI will not talk to you because they believe it would be disloyal, even those who think it has gone too far. If they knew that Abedi was working with the Soviets, it would put things in a different light for them. They might talk to you then."

He tapped his fingers together rapidly, revealing a sudden tension.

"There is a way, of course: I could get into the safe at Glavkosmos, where I saw the satellite manuals." Heinrich explained rapidly how and why he had access to the Soviet space agency and the office where the documents were kept.

"This is not the big Glavkosmos office on Krasnoproletarskaya next to Red Square," he continued. "This one is near Space City, and from the outside it appears to be just another office building. But there are still guards—soldiers with AK-47 automatic rifles—and you must have a pass and go through metal detectors. But if I could get a camera in, I could take pictures of the documents—the secret American manuals. I have seen the safe opened many times: So often that I have the combination and I could arrange to be left alone in the room. I have done research there to work up proposals."

Beaty tried not to blink, then decided that keeping a poker face wasn't appropriate to this sudden exposure. If he was telling the truth, Heinrich had just revealed information about himself, and his business dealings, that could get him dead or in even worse trouble. Beaty blinked.

He realized that Truth was very relative here: Who could say what is exactly true in the shadow world of arms deals and the clandestine services? Heinrich's explanation of how he, a man who negotiated and helped consummate deals between Soviet bloc countries and Third World nations—deals greased with commissions paid to politicians and generals on both sides—had come upon this information was utterly plausible. If Beaty published the story he had just heard about Heinrich's dealings with the Soviets, underwritten by BCCI, it certainly would be believed by all the principals, and Heinrich would find himself in very big trouble. That was truth. No wonder he had friends to protect him in Western, and probably Eastern bloc, intelligence agencies: In order to continue operating, the man had to give up a little information to every side. A very dicey way to make a living.

His plan to photograph the purloined documents seemed impossible on the face of it: If the Russians caught him, he would be accused of spying and hauled off to a Lubyanka Prison interrogation cell. Or he would be shot.

"When could you do it?"

Heinrich looked at his watch. "I still have to catch the 7:00 A.M. plane; I have to be in London tomorrow for a meeting that I can't postpone. I can go the next day. You will have to provide a suitable camera and pay for my expenses. You know I am a businessman: I won't ask for a profit, but I'm not going to pay for a . . . a chance to be put in front of a firing squad out of my own pocket." He laughed a little nervously. Sangfroid apparently had its limits.

"How would I get a camera to you? The only thing I own is a cheap automatic-everything Nikon a *Time* photographer got for me. The photogs call them 'drunk cameras.' They carry them in case something happens when they've had too much to drink to focus a real camera. Artie Grace took one of his most famous pictures with one. It was—" Beaty cut himself off abruptly; he had been trying to lighten things up. It had gotten awfully heavy in the small room.

"What kind of a camera would you need?" the reporter asked.

"I know little about photography. You're resourceful. Just find something suitable and send it to me in Warsaw. I will go there from London because it will look more natural if I come into Moscow from Warsaw. I have made that trip many times. I will give you the name of a company there, and the name of the vice president for research. This is a machinery firm that I have done business with, and they will not think it strange to hold a package for me. But you must send it via DHL tomorrow or the next day, without fail: I cannot wait long in Warsaw."

They were still talking details as the sun came up and the time came to take Heinrich to the airport. Beaty wasn't sure all this was really happening, but whatever was happening was moving fast. Driving to the airport in his big Chevy four-wheel-drive pickup truck, taking Vista Del Mar to skirt along the ocean's edge, a calm turquoise in the morning light, Beaty wondered about his mental health. The whole idea seemed so far out that he decided to just keep moving ahead until something derailed the plan. That way he could tell himself that he hadn't yet made an irreversible decision. After he dropped Heinrich in front of the international terminal, he got out of the pickup and they shook hands. They were a little stiff about it.

He wondered what to say and the words came unbidden: "Good luck, Heinrich. You're a damn good man. And a brave one." Embarrassed at sounding sincere, he gave half a wave and climbed back into his truck and gunned it into the airport traffic.

On the way home he parked and stared at the ocean for several minutes. He had already begun worrying about getting *Time* embroiled in an international incident. But if there was evidence that BCCI had brokered American secrets to hostile nations, he wanted it. And there was more to it than than a scoop. He didn't need Heinrich to tell him that the American intelligence community and the Bush administration in general were dummying up on the BCCI scandal.

Other reliable sources were giving clear indications that the government knew a lot more about BCCI than it was saying, and that within some circles there were mixed feelings about protecting BCCI. Proof that Abedi had double-crossed CIA Director Casey and was helping the Soviets could push some of the fence sitters over the edge. Maybe. BCCI wouldn't have been able to obtain such secrets to broker without high-level cooperation from someone, maybe a lot of someones, in the U.S. government. Which meant either treason on the part of individuals or some sort of clandestine policy . . . which might explain the government's strange reluctance to pursue the BCCI prosecution.

But none of this would ever be known unless Heinrich could carry out his plan, and to do that he needed a camera. Finding the right one, however, proved to be more difficult than Beaty expected. He called two, then three, *Time* photographers. "I need something that can take pictures of documents, but my person can't afford to be discovered. He'll have maybe thirty minutes, and there may be a couple of hundred pages. He's got to get the camera past a metal detector." These experts, mildly intrigued, offered a variety of suggestions that all foundered as soon as they learned that a novice would be taking the pictures. Tiny spy cameras easily used by a nervous amateur existed, apparently, only in the movies. In the end, they decided on a top-quality Japanese nearly-all-plastic fully automatic camera: It wouldn't be small, but at least it would look like a tourist's camera if Heinrich got stopped going in.

A dozen frustrating phone calls into the afternoon, Beaty learned it was impossible, despite perestroika, to ship a camera directly into Poland. DHL, the international package delivery service, required a sheaf of forms and permits and estimated it would take four to five days to get it through, and then it would have to be picked up at customs. And a friendly clerk at the Polish legation in Los Angeles casually advised against mislabeling a camera: packages from the States were certain to be opened and inspected.

Heinrich called that night from London. He was set to leave the following afternoon: Where were his tickets and his traveling money? Was the camera on its way?

At 3:00 A.M. Beaty was still up, talking to Europe. He called Adam Zagorin, *Time*'s man in Brussels, and asked him to go to a travel agency and pay for Heinrich's tickets to Warsaw on his personal credit card. Zagorin was anxious to learn more about the operation in progress.

"The less you ask the better, Adam, but we don't want this to show on *Time* expense and bureau reports." Beaty was uneasy at the thought that he must sound like a little like Ollie North, but he was worried about the caper causing an international embarrassment if it went wrong. He could see the headline in his mind's eye: "TIME" CAUGHT SPYING ON SOVIETS. Zagorin asked no further questions, but there was a rather strangled response from Bill Mader, the London bureau chief, when Beaty called to ask him to have £2,000 cash in an envelope ready for an unknown courier to pick up for uses that couldn't be divulged.

Mader was a gentleman and a veteran of the old *Time* school. He was also precise and fussy about details, which made him perfect for London but less than cooperative in shaving regulations or bending protocol. Over the phone Beaty could hear him puffing on his pipe, a sound of agitation.

"Look, Bill," Beaty pleaded, "just charge it as an advance to my expense account." The reporter silently winced.

Mader knew Beaty had the right to draw money for expenses. He gamely agreed to go to the bank to withdraw the cash but was distressed at the idea of handing that much money over to a stranger.

"You say this is to be picked up by a person named Heinrich. Will he have identification?"

"No, Bill. He won't because that's not really his name. Nobody's using their right name in this." Beaty hung up quickly before Mader could think of a reply. Mader was okay; he just wanted to dot all the *i*'s.

It was 2:00 A.M. in Rome when Beaty finally reached Rudi Frey. Calling Rudi was an inspiration born of desperation. The silver-haired, Austrian-born photographer had been with *Time* for years, valued as much for his special skills as his photography. Rudi was a natural fixer. He lived alone in a stylishly shabby high-ceilinged penthouse apartment that was distinguished by a sunlit *terrazzo* and a massive safe filled with cameras and good wine. Rudi traveled the world at a moment's notice, acting as *Time*'s advance man for the pope's trips and as a man for all seasons for traveling *Time* brass. He was an expert in the black markets on both sides of the Iron Curtain and could talk his way into, or out of, anything. Back in his drinking days, Beaty had shared with Frey a couple of adventures, caroming around Italy in pursuit of Mafiosi and terrorists. On one all-night barhopping stint in Venice they had solemnly decided to quit *Time* magazine and go gold prospecting in outback Bolivia, in partnership with the son of a local cocaine czar with whom Beaty had become friendly. Beaty knew that at this hour of the morning Rudi would be ready to listen to any outlandish proposal that offered excitement.

Rudi was cordial on the phone and only slightly sloshed. No problem, he said. He could buy the camera first thing in the morning and then fly to Warsaw. He would wear it on a strap around his neck with his other cameras and give it to Heinrich along with a crash course in photography. Frey had taken *Time*'s Man of the Year cover portrait of Lech Walesa. Everything in Warsaw, he said, was his for the asking.

"He's not going to use the camera in Poland," Beaty said. "I don't want to say his destination on the phone, but I want you to wait in Warsaw for him to return and then bring the camera and his film back out. You may need to take the film to Paris to put it on the Concorde. I'll be waiting in New York to catch it."

Beaty was acutely aware that the National Security Agency monitored all overseas calls and explained that he was calling from a pay phone. "If you have to call me, watch what you say: I'll send you details about what hotel my man will be at, and the name he'll be using, by Telemail." The magazine's computer modem messages were more difficult to unscramble so they weren't routinely intercepted. Except in paranoid countries.

The telephone rang again. It was Sami Masri calling from Karachi. Tilt. Beaty had managed to forget him for a few days, but the hot-headed Palestinian had resurfaced after the debacle in Abu Dhabi. James Dougherty, who still coveted the BCCI documents Masri claimed he could obtain, had sent Masri back into Karachi, at Lloyd's expense. Somehow IRS intelligence was in on this deal, but nobody had told Beaty the details. And of course, nobody was sure whose side Masri was really on. Beaty doubted if Masri himself knew. Now Masri was agitated. He said he had gotten inside BCCI's vaults and collected documents that could blow things open, and that he had to escape from Karachi fast.

When Beaty had last seen Masri in Abu Dhabi more than a month before, the man was surrounded by tough-looking security men. Beaty was told Masri was about to be expelled from that country, and he had tried to make sure he would be forewarned if his former source tried to get back into the United States. He wanted to be prepared if he answered the doorbell some night and saw Masri standing there. Over the years Beaty had managed working relationships with some dangerous men, had even become friendly with some of them, but the volatile Masri worried him because of his unpredictability.

Beaty had consulted with John Moscow, and the prosecutor had asked Immigration and Customs to put Masri on the terrorist watch list and to notify the New York district attorney's office if Masri landed back in the country. It wasn't strictly a favor: Now that Masri had blown his status as a confidential source for *Time* magazine, the D.A.'s men had some questions they wanted to put to him.

It was now late August. In June Khalfan al-Mazrui had called Beaty from Karachi and in his halting English asked the reporter if he would talk to Masri. He said he understood there had been some kind of misunderstanding in Abu Dhabi. Beaty was not surprised that Masri was back in Karachi, apparently in good stead with BCCI and His Excellency's Private Department, but he was surprised that the cautious sheikh had stepped back into the picture. Who was on what side here? Beaty refused the overture in spite of his curiosity. Then, in early July, Masri had called Beaty, who was in New York, and said he wanted to meet.

"I'm in Philadelphia."

Beaty almost laughed. He didn't know whether to credit Masri's reinsertion into the United States to the quality of forged travel documents or to the ineptness of the border watch, but he had to admit that Masri had balls. Masri sounded repentant: He was drunk when he threatened the reporter, he said, and it had been a mistake to try to change sides. He had been in Abu Dhabi with Beaty for only a night, he claimed, when he was visited by members of the Black Network, one of whom was a high-level officer in Abu Dhabi intelligence. They wanted to know what he was doing traveling with a *Time* magazine reporter. To save himself, he told them he was pretending to work with *Time* as part of an operation to learn how much the magazine knew. After all, he said, it was the *Time* stories that were doing so much damage.

"To tell you the truth," Masri explained, "I did go back to them. I was afraid to talk to Zayed. I was afraid of BCCI, the BCCI that I knew in Karachi. And what was in it for me, risking my life and you weren't even paying me any money? But now they are suspicious of me. Listen to me, Jonathan: I can get the documents you want out of the safe in Karachi. I have to get enough money to go away, to start a new life. Do you think that Dougherty would pay me?"

"Sami, it's over. You're not reliable. I don't know about Lloyd's of London, but I couldn't get the magazine to pay for a bus ticket to get you to the other side of Philadelphia, let alone a plane ride to New York. If you want to help yourself, you should go tell Morgenthau's people everything you've told me. We have no bargain anymore. Our agreements are finished."

To Beaty's amazement, Sami agreed—provided the reporter would go with him to the district attorney and provided the district attorney would promise not to arrest him on sight. Beaty called Jim Dougherty in Miami, and, grumbling, the lawyer arranged for the ticket and expenses for two days.

"You've got to baby-sit him," Dougherty told Beaty. "I'm on my way to Los Angeles to take depositions from some BCCI executives. Do you know there are tons of bank papers out there that nobody has even looked at? But that little shit has been right about too many things to ignore. If he actually talks to Moscow's people and tells them anything worthwhile, you send him on out to me in Los Angeles. Tell him if there are really documents that prove anything, I'll set him up anywhere in the world he wants to go. But tell him if he's lying, I'm going to have his legs broken."

John Moscow didn't attend the interrogation session in a grimy basement room in the district attorney's office, but five of Morgenthau's hardest men did. Beaty didn't see it all, since he was asked to step out of the room while particular questions were asked—Morgenthau's men were protecting the integrity of their grand jury probe—but he caught enough to get the flavor of it. It looked pretty much like a back-room session in an old black-and-white movie, except there was no good cop/bad cop routine: The dicks, three of them hefty men from the street, were all bad.

"You couldn't say they weren't polite," Beaty told Gwynne later. "They carefully called him Mr. Masri, but on the other hand they treated him like a terrorist. I'd hate to be questioned by those guys. At one point they're pumping questions at him about whether BCCI ever murdered anyone, and Sami is dodging around saying he's only heard stories, and then Fred Ghussan, who has been sitting there looking sleepy, asks him in perfect Arabic why he's lying. I thought he was going to stop breathing."

Detective Ghussan was one of Morgenthau's secret weapons in the BCCI investigation: He had formerly been a cop in Jerusalem.

"They tossed me out at that point. Sami told them going in he wasn't going to talk if I wasn't in the room, but after Ghussan pounced, he ran out of bravado."

Beaty hadn't seen Masri since. After the session with the district attorney he was put on a plane to Los Angeles, where he was met by Dougherty. And two IRS criminal intelligence investigators. According to Dougherty, Masri agreed to talk to the feds, who held a subpoena from a Florida grand jury. An agreement was reached postponing his testimony, and Masri was put on a plane bound for Karachi. Dougherty picked up the tab.

Now, in late August, Masri was calling to announce that he had the documents he had promised: four hundred pages of BCCI memos, some in English, including, he said, communications between Robert Altman and Sani Ahmed, the head of BCCI's protocol department.

"Jonathan, you've got to send somebody to Karachi to pick them up. I can't wait long."

Beaty agreed to make the arrangements and then picked up another line that was ringing. It was Rudi Frey, calling from Warsaw. He had found Heinrich and they were together at the Grand Hotel. Frey was drilling him in the photographic techniques he would need and thought it was all great fun. Heinrich was to leave for Moscow aboard an early-morning Aeroflot flight.

The phone rang again. It was the news desk in New York. Beaty was working on a follow-up story to the BCCI indictments of the previous week, and the business editor wanted to know when he could expect his copy. It was getting close to deadline. Beaty promised to file soon.

The next call was from Bill White, who was back in Houston. The FAA headquarters in Oklahoma City didn't release certain records to the public, but he could go there personally and review the files. Could Beaty pick up expenses for the trip? He promised to stay in an inexpensive motel. Beaty shook his head, trying to clear it, and said okay.

Beaty looked at the clock. It was still daylight in New York, and he called John Moscow, who had been recruited to find someone who could go into Karachi, rendezvous with Masri, and take possession of the documents.

"Call this number," Moscow said. "This is someone from State Department intelligence. Don't give them your name; you're just an intermediary and he's expecting the call. I think they can be trusted, and they have people on the ground over there."

"Damn it, John, I've been learning more as we go along: I'm not sure about asking for State Department help on this. The BCCI ties to the government are more complicated than we've thought. I'll talk to him, though. Thanks."

Then Beaty called Dean Fischer, the Cairo bureau chief, getting him out of bed, to ask if he could set up accommodations for Masri if he got out of Karachi.

Working through time zones on the West Coast, East Coast,

Europe, and the Middle East, Beaty began to lose himself in space and time. He no longer knew whether it was night or day; he was unaware whether the plates of food Linda brought him were breakfast or dinner. He hadn't shaved. The phone would ring; he would talk briefly, then, as often as not, trot down the alley behind his house to the corner pay phone to return the call. Moscow phoned again, his call bounced to one of the cellular telephones.

"Jonathan, I don't like to tell you this, but you were right. You're better off not to trust the man in State Intel. I have a bad feeling about this." Beaty told him he had already scrubbed that idea, that he too had a bad feeling after talking to the man. Dougherty was trying to locate a private detective in Karachi who sometimes worked for Lloyd's. Beaty watched the hands on the wall clock. Heinrich had been in Russia for eighteen hours and was due out any time. If he was coming out. Beaty's stomach felt uneasy.

The phone rang. It was a triumphant Rudi Frey. "He's back! He has the merchandise! It was hairy, but he got it!" Heinrich came on the line briefly. He sounded giddy with relief, trying to be nonchalant but not quite making it. Beaty would later hear the story of his and Rudi's celebratory dinner at the Grand Hotel. Rudi, whose idea of inconspicuous was parading through the hotel wearing a black satin jacket with the words DESERT STORM embroidered on the back, had been buying drinks for everyone at the bar. Nothing like a *Time* expense account.

Hours later Rudi called in to say he had made it back to Rome, the camera containing the crucial film slung around his neck. He had decided to ship the film via DHL because it would be faster than sending it by commercial pilot packaging. Beaty immediately made reservations to New York and headed for the shower. He felt a hundred years older.

Joelle Attinger tried to look stern, but her eyes sparkled as she listened to Beaty's briefing. They were waiting in her office in the Time & Life Building for the photo lab to develop the three rolls of film Rudi Frey sent from Europe. Beaty had his detractors at the magazine, but this deputy chief of correspondents was not one of them. She regarded him as incorrigible, but then she had plenty of establishment-type correspondents to cover the establishment point of view. She had championed the idea of teaming the unorthodox Californian with the Yankee Sam Gwynne (even though *Time* correspondents didn't, as a rule, work in teams), and it was working well. Gwynne was a fast, organized writer, and his presence gave comfort to the editors who deplored Beaty's deadline-pushing habit of reporting a story until there was little time left to write it. The edit staff had been surprised at how well the seemingly mismatched partners meshed: They were inseparable on the BCCI story, and the news desk had taken to calling them 007 and 007.5. Attinger looked at Beaty, who was sitting on her couch wearing his twenty-fourth-floor corporate gray suit. He was smoking her cigarettes and jiggling one foot impatiently as he talked.

"Did it occur to you to tell anybody what you've been up to?" she asked.

"Well, you knew I was still running Sami with Dougherty's help. It was Lloyd's money, but several other people were in on it. Like some feds and Morgenthau's people. We couldn't get anybody into Karachi to make a pickup, so Sami sent the material out, or so he claims, to Prague, with one of the airline crews he uses. Sami got to Cairo. Naturally he wanted to stay at the Nile Hilton, and Dean Fischer got him on a plane to Czechoslovakia. As of last night he had missed the rendezvous set up with one of our stringers there, but they heard from him. I asked Rudi this morning to go in and meet him and not to mess around. I think he liked the idea; he took his bulletproof vest. But who knows if Masri is playing straight with us?"

"Jonathan, that's not what I was talking about."

"Well . . . the thing with Heinrich just unfolded too fast. I didn't see any sense giving everybody heartburn until I found out whether it was possible, and by then it was running. I did call Stacks just before Heinrich went in and there was still time to abort. I got him out of bed."

"What did John say?"

"Well, basically, he said if we weren't paying Heinrich a fee to do this, what Heinrich did was his own business, so why was I waking him up?"

Attinger could read between the lines. No doubt Heinrich had been climbing on the plane to Moscow before Beaty called in. He wasn't giving anyone time to think it over or discuss it. That was his standard method of operation, yet the chief of correspondents' grumpy dismissal was really an unqualified expression of confidence in Beaty. She conceded she was glad the decision hadn't been handed to her in the middle of the night.

Michele Stephenson, the chief of photography, knocked and stepped in with a large stack of eight-by-ten glossies. Some news desk staffers could be seen casting quick looks inside before the opaque glass door closed again. It was obvious from the flurry of calls and hasty meetings that morning that something exciting was happening. The desk knew word had gone down to photo early in the morning that some special film had come in, that it had to be developed in-house, and that the contents must be very closely held.

They spread the hastily processed prints on the desk and stared. The resolution wasn't very good: Even blown up, the English text on the pages was hard to read. There were technical drawings of trajectories and orbits, wiring diagrams, isometric illustrations of optical systems, and whole pages of mathematical equations. There was little doubt they were looking at Rockwell International's technical manual for the Navstar Global Positioning System satellite.

Heinrich had even taken positioning photos of the gray stone building with armed guards posted in front, and two or three photos of Red Square. One close-up of a newsstand showed the day's newspapers, and Beaty was sure that further enlargements or computer enhancement would reveal the date. Heinrich may not have been a photographer, but Rudi had coached him well on how to authenticate his work.

Beaty picked up the last picture and began laughing out loud. It showed a large canvas-topped army truck, a red star on the door, full of Russian soldiers all smiling and waving back at the camera.

"The man has brass balls. He had a camera full of film that would have gotten him shot, and then to get this picture he must have shouted something funny, in Russian, at these troops passing by."

"So what does all this mean, Beaty?" Attinger asked.

The reporter shook his head and shuffled through the photos. "I don't know how secret all this is, or was. GPS technology is evolving rapidly. Our man says he thought the Soviets got this in 1989. But our man"—Beaty couldn't bring himself to use even Heinrich's code name in front of Michele, even though she was part of the inner circle at *Time*—"has just shown us the Soviets have a safe full of sensitive American technical documents, and he says the Russians bragged they came from BCCI. And we know from two or three sources that Abedi himself had been traveling to Moscow in the late '80s, just before his heart attack, trying to persuade them to let him open up BCCI banks throughout the Soviet Union. Maybe this was trade goods, so to speak. One spook type I know had an interesting take: He didn't know anything about Navstar, but he suggested that what Abedi knew about American politicians was more valuable to the Soviets than military or technical secrets.

"And we have two BCCI-connected sources who say that Abedi and one of his top weapons merchants were meeting secretly with Bill

Casey in the mid-'80s, cooking up cooperative deals. John Moscow over at Morgenthau's shop has a BCCI witness who has said the same thing, and so does Ira Silverman at NBC News. Our best source on this says that General Zia came with Abedi a couple of times, so that raises the possibility that this may have something to do with our aid program to Pakistan. The Reagan administration was slipping them a lot of military and technical goodies in addition to the hardware Congress approved. I'm going on the assumption that if Pakistan had it, Agha Hasan Abedi had it."

Beaty started packing the photos into his metal Haliburton. "In summary, I don't know what in the hell it means. I'm catching the shuttle to Washington. Gwynne's meeting me there and we're going to start asking questions." Beaty was out the door and almost safely to the elevators before he was accosted by Sheila Greene Charney, his nemesis from *Time*'s business department.

"When are you going to turn in some expense accounts, Beaty? We haven't had anything from you for months, and you owe more than sixty thousand dollars in advances." The reporter was grateful for the stainless-steel elevator doors closing in front of him. Sheila was a very nice person, but she was too easily horrified.

Though Beaty had gotten a stern warning, the next day he and Gwynne found themselves meeting Jack Blum for lunch at one of the more elegant Washington restaurants. Blum had brought their guest, a man of ample girth who loved fine dining and who was arguably the top private attorney in the world of weapons-and-technology regulations. He was also a veteran of State Department intelligence, and he didn't want his name used, a refreshing change from the typical Washington lawyer. After the main course Beaty, having explained the background, handed him the Kremlin photographs.

The lawyer looked at them closely, with Blum peering over his shoulder. "These aren't stamped 'top secret' and there are no paragraph-by-paragraph classification codes, so I imagine this is the commercial Navstar version. There's no way I can tell whether there is enough here so that one could decipher the encrypted P-channel from these formulae. The military P-code is transmitted on a different frequency than the commercial and carries more information so it produces more accurate results—down to a few feet. And the Defense Department has nightmares about terrorists obtaining NAV system receivers that can pick it up."

He paused, his expression judicious. "With a safe full of technical documents to choose from, your man shouldn't have used up his time taking pictures of every page of one document. The accepted technique is to take pictures of a few pages of as many documents as you can. You're going to have to send him back in."

Beaty spit his mouthful of Perrier back into his glass and started to sputter. Gwynne laughed, recognizing a joke when he heard it.

"I don't want my name involved in this," the lawyer said. "I have to keep working in this town, and you fellows look like bearers of bad news. However, I'll give you a list of people you should talk to and make a couple of calls on your behalf. Military encryption codes or not, there is absolutely no way the USSR should have had this in its possession if your man is roughly correct about the date they got it. They've been trying to update Glosnass, their own satellite navigation system, which is inferior to ours, and Gorbachev made a big pitch to the administration to share our commercial technology. As usual, the Commerce Department and the Pentagon and State all had opposing opinions about transferring the technology. Commerce is willing to sell anything, the Pentagon doesn't want to let go of anything, and State dithers. But Congress mooted the discussion by voting against it about a year and a half ago. You won't be allowed to look at the technology transfer records, since they're not public, but I can guarantee that this didn't go through as an approved technology transfer."

Starting from the list of names provided by the lawyer, Beaty began moving through the strange Washington world of mirrors and double-speak called arms control. Within a couple of days he could see it was going to be impossible to get an official answer to any of his questions from the bureaucracy.

It all came under the Office of the Under Secretary of Defense, but the vast bureaucracy was riven with internal disputes and contained a warren of agencies operating at cross-purposes. There was the Center for Defense Trade (CDT), headed by an assistant secretary of state for politico-military affairs, who directed the Center for Defense Trade (PM/CDT), which in turn directed the Office of Defense Trade Controls and the Office of Defense Trade Policy. But then there was also an under secretary for export administration, who directed Export Enforcement and the Office of Export Intelligence, as well as the assistant secretary for export administration, who directed the Office of Export Licensing and the Office of Technology and Policy Analysis.

It was even more topsy-turvy than it looked: Until recently the Center for Defense Trade had been named the Office for Munitions Control. The change of names had marked the Bush administration's behind-the-scenes maneuvers to transform the government from a regulator of international arms sales into a virtual partner of the American arms industry in promoting weapons exports. Hawks clashed with doves, and entrepreneurs drove tanks and fighter planes through the loopholes.

Nor was it a good time for any reporter to be asking questions about stolen or diverted American technology: A hunt was on for leakers within the arms-control bureaucracy who had just disclosed that Saudi Arabia had engaged in unauthorized transfers of American-made military equipment to Iraq, Syria, and Bangladesh. Another leak concerned Israeli transfers to Iraq, and yet another exposed new revelations of American transfers to both Iran and Iraq during their bitter eight-year war. Heads were going to roll, it was rumored, which was ironic, since the United States' use of Israel to pass American arms to various Middle Eastern countries without approval by Congress had been going on for years. BCCI, Beaty had been learning, was in the middle of much of it.

He had hoped to get some straight answers from William Rudman, head of the Defense Technology Security Administration. Rudman had come from Customs' strategic investigations section, the only group other than the Defense Intelligence Agency, the National Security Council, and the CIA that tracked illegal diversions to the Soviets. Since his sources all agreed that the CIA, the NSC, and the DIA had been involved at one time or another with the Bank of Credit and Commerce International, Rudman seemed to be his best bet.

Interviewed alone, on deep background, Rudman might have leveled with Beaty, but because of the national security implications, Rudman couldn't shake his own assistants. His staff insisted, over Beaty's vigorous protests, on having a watchdog attend and tape-record the interview. The reporter realized there didn't have to be a sinister implication. If *Time* magazine calls up and says they have evidence that the notorious BCCI has been selling U.S. secrets to the Kremlin, what did he think was going to happen? But on the other hand, it was clear that Rudman would have said more if a transcript of the interview wasn't going to be read all the way up to the under secretary level. When Rudman indicated, with a nod of the head, that he was familiar with BCCI's weapons-trading operations, his watchdog cut in and cited national security reasons that preempted any answers to questions about BCCI and classified U.S. technology.

Other knocks at the front door were equally fruitless. When Beaty tried to go over Rudman's head, the hawkish high-level officer in the Office of the Under Secretary of Defense for Technology Security

Policy wanted to use the Navstar evidence Beaty had acquired as an internecine political weapon. The strangest thing, Beaty thought, was not that the top-level people didn't want to talk about BCCI—it was their singular lack of curiosity. No one even asked to see the photographs. And it wasn't just the issue of whether Navstar technology was still a relevant secret. In frustration Beaty began to ask about allegations he couldn't prove, such as his information that the Pakistanis were capable of downloading the KH-11, America's most secret intelligence satellite. That was the one that could provide a real-time image of a golf ball hundreds of miles below. Nobody, including Israel, was allowed nondegraded KH-11 product, let alone a bellicose nation like Pakistan. But the question produced the same lack of interest. It was clearly cover-your-ass time.

By contrast, two old sources Beaty had talked to, much lower-level intelligence types, freaked out at his descriptions of what he had seen and heard.

He went underground, although that meant he wouldn't have anyone to quote by name or even generic title. Nobody had admitted curiosity, but word of what he was looking for had gotten around quickly, and an intermediary set up a very private meeting with the deputy director of one of the relevant agencies. This time there would be no watchdogs.

The official's apprehension about talking to a *Time* correspondent was remarkable. Beaty waited for him outside the State Department, knowing that the official had been given his description. The man walked past him, giving the slightest nod to follow as he descended the broad steps. Beaty followed for two blocks before the man acknowledged him. As they threaded through the lunchtime crowd on the street, the man took off his hat and light coat and looked over his shoulder.

"The only reason I wore the hat was to take it off . . . in a crowd even the best tail tends to follow the hat." He led the way quickly into a store and out the side door. They ended up in a packed mall cafeteria with glass walls that revealed the pedestrians walking by. For Christ's sake, Beaty thought, this man is right up there at the top of the government and he's worried about being tailed. After a few minutes' conversation Beaty understood why.

The man spoke quickly and in a near whisper, looking around and past the reporter's shoulder as he talked. "You're onto something and you're correct about there being no separation between Abedi and Pakistan's intelligence agency, the ISI [Inter-Services Intelligence]. A number of Pakistan's generals have been on Abedi's private payroll for years. You might not be aware of it, but several people in the State Department have resigned over the years in protest to the extent of our tilt to Pakistan. We gave them unauthorized satellite and communications technology as well as authorized sophisticated technology like the F-16 fighter plane sale. We ignored the drug trading and their nuclear bomb program, and your friend Abedi and BCCI were in the middle of all of it.

"I don't how your Navstar documents got to the Soviets. But if the Pakistanis obtained Synthetic Aperture Radar, as your source says, somebody stole it from us. We gave them the Landsat processing equipment you talked about, but that was more or less aboveboard. They could see everything India was doing. Why do you think India built up such a massive army?"

Beaty decided he was on a roll and tossed out one of the big questions he was holding. "I haven't told this to anybody in Washington yet, but one of our sources said that a couple of years ago BCCI had three Columbine Heads and they were selling them to Iraq. I got the impression this was one of our biggest secrets, but I can't even find out what a Colombine Head is. Apparently even the name is classified top secret. Do you know?"

The man pursed his lips and appeared pained. When he spoke he looked away from the reporter and talked from the side of his mouth. "It might be the trigger for the fuel-air bomb. I think we better end this conversation."

He stood up. "Why don't you finish your cappuccino before you leave? If you need to talk to me again, ask the same friend who suggested I talk to you. Don't try to call me at home. My phone has been tapped before." The deputy under secretary picked up his hat and disappeared into the crowd.

Beaty took out a notebook and wrote down everything before he lost the exact wording. Sweet Jesus, the fuel-air bomb? No wonder nobody wanted to talk. Iraq's bombardment of Israel during the Gulf War—with Scud missiles financed by BCCI—had created panic because it was feared Saddam possessed the fuel-air bomb and that he might be able to deliver some of them with the Scud rockets. It was called the poor man's hydrogen bomb, and it worked by exploding a large cloud of vaporized gasoline. The resulting explosion rivaled atomic blasts. It was almost primitive technology, but it took an extremely sophisticated triggering system to ignite the gas cloud. Sweet Jesus.

Beaty headed for a phone to try to find Gwynne, who was in South Carolina interviewing a former partner of Ghaith Pharaon. They couldn't abandon the mainstream BCCI story, but Beaty was beginning to feel like Alice in Wonderland again. BCCI was news, but he could count on his fingers the number of people in the media and law enforcement who weren't narrowly focused on whether Clark Clifford and Robert Altman knew they were working for BCCI. Why wasn't more of the truth about BCCI coming out? It dawned on him that more information about Abedi's secret empire was being held at the highest reaches of the American government than anywhere else.

Gwynne had checked out of his hotel, so Beaty left a message for him with the bureau switchboard. They had to catch a plane to the Caribbean tomorrow. They were going to meet the Pakistani on neutral ground. The Pakistani was the source who had told them about the Columbine Heads.

CHAPTER 11

THE BANK THAT
CAN GET YOU ANYTHING

They converged on the Caribbean island that Monday afternoon on
separate flights landing within an hour of each other. Beaty, conspicuous in a gray business suit, was standing in the long line of color-
fully dressed tourists at immigration and customs when Gwynne,
dressed in khaki wash pants and a faded maroon golf shirt, debarked
from a Washington plane and, grinning, waved at him. The older
reporter had grabbed the last shuttle flight from Washington to New
York the night before, to make an early-morning meeting with John
Moscow. In his luggage was a wrapped parcel containing the eight-
by-ten photos of the Navstar satellite system manual that Heinrich
had taken in the Soviet space agency. After clearing immigration,
the two men stuffed their baggage into a pint-sized taxi and waited
cheerfully in the baking heat for Ali Khan, who was traveling several thousand miles to join them. None of them had been to this
island before, and they were pleased with themselves for arranging
a clandestine conference in an idyllic setting. It was almost like getting away with something.

"We've got to meet offshore because our man isn't about to step foot
in the United States with a full-blown investigation of BCCI under
way," Beaty had explained to Attinger. "This is the source we call Ali
Khan. Stacks still won't let us go to Pakistan, so we offered to meet
Khan anywhere else in the world. He was worried about being seen

with us in London or Paris, since the top BCCI people know him, and our pictures were in the magazine. He says they're following our stories closely. I suggested this island, and that tipped the scales."

Khan showed up on schedule, and Beaty introduced the diminutive Pakistani to his colleague. Beaty had met Khan once before, in London, and they had been talking by phone ever since. They had grown to trust each other: Khan's identity had been protected and the reporters had found his information reliable. Khan was an educated, well-traveled man highly placed in Pakistan, and what he said about the bank's operations had helped convince the reporters—and their editors—that Sami Masri was telling them the truth. He was much more sophisticated than Masri and had a wider perspective, but his information dovetailed almost exactly with the Palestinian's story of the bank's Black Network. The three men crammed into the taxi, and it set off at breakneck speed along the narrow, winding roads to an isolated resort near one end of the island.

They talked for two days and two nights, spending the days on the beach. In the evenings they walked along the shore, absorbed in their talk. To avoid sounding like a police interrogation, the reporters took turns taking notes so that one of them could keep up their end of a civilized conversation. Without realizing it, Gwynne and Beaty had grown skilled at working as a team.

On Tuesday they rented swim fins and diving masks and drifted down the rocky coast until they found a large crevice in the high volcanic cliff. Inside the narrow cove, sitting on the sand, they felt hidden from the rest of the world. Khan had towed along a Thermos of gin and lemonade, his favorite drink. He told them a little about Pakistan's nuclear, satellite, and communications programs, and how BCCI had played a pivotal role in locating, financing, and shipping much of the equipment. Khan had had a hand in some of that supply and wasn't anxious to go into specifics.

"Just think of it as if BCCI is the owner's representative for Pakistan's nuclear program," he said. "In the West Abedi presented one face, but in the Muslim world he and his bankers have always promoted themselves as a Third World Muslim bank that would eventually dominate global finances by using oil dollars and Abedi's network of influence. And Abedi whispered in the ears of the sheikhs and the generals that he would bring them the Muslim Bomb."

If Khan was loath to reveal too many details about supplying nuclear technology to Pakistan, as well as to Iraq and Libya, he was positively voluble about BCCI's services in conventional-weapons deals.

"It's just like the the rest of the bank's, ah, unconventional business," Khan said. "Their unbooked letters of credit provide documentation for shipments of anything. It's described as agricultural equipment or whatever you like. They handle everything: brokering, financing, letters of credit, false end-user certificates, shipping, spare parts, technicians, training, and even personnel. You can order a bomb, a plane to deliver it, and somebody to drop it. The Gokal brothers handle most of their shipping. Since the Gokals' money all comes from Abedi, that means Abedi owns, or owned, one of the biggest shipping fleets in the world. He even has his own insurance company to insure the cargoes."

Khan sipped the gin and looked at Beaty. "Did you tell Sam about the Kuwaiti tanks in Desert Storm?"

Beaty shook his head. He had, but he wanted to hear Khan describe it again.

"You remember the victorious allied march to retake Kuwait City? It was spearheaded by a contingent of Kuwaiti tanks, which was considered a political rather than military necessity. However, there was a difficulty executing the plan. The Kuwaitis had no tanks. BCCI was able to solve the problem: They already had a factory order in for new and retrofitted Yugoslavian M-84 battle tanks—that's an upgraded version of the Soviet T-72—for another contract, but they shifted orders to supply the Desert Storm request. BCCI supplied, I think it was, sixty-four such tanks, financing the package and handling the shipping to the coalition forces. And since the Kuwaitis weren't familiar with this tank, they supplied East European personnel to maintain and drive the tanks—I believe most were Czechoslovakian. The Kuwaitis rode on top of the tanks and waved."

Gwynne smiled at the image. "How did you learn that?"

"My business associate had the factory contract that was deferred. There was negotiation."

Like Heinrich, Khan seemed to be able to remember everything about weapons deals, down to specific nomenclature of equipment, how it was financed, and its terms of delivery. He described a current BCCI effort to obtain MIG 29s and four hundred T-72 Soviet tanks for Pakistan's military: "The tank price, as it stands at the moment, is $790,000 for two hundred of the T-72 models; those are the tanks in storage that are to be rebuilt to specifications with the new night-fire-control system. One hundred of the new tanks are available immediately. Those are $1 million each, plus another $90,000 for the Commander version, which have extra radios and other bits and pieces. The 72s are from a Communist bloc country; a lot of the rest of the equipment would come from the Soviets directly."

Beaty and Gwynne were fascinated: Khan was describing a major BCCI arms connection with the Soviets and the hard-cash-starved Eastern bloc countries that wanted deals in dollars rather than rubles. "At least before the last year it was always easy to win the heart of the manager of a Soviet production facility. Because of the nature of his system, he may make less money than the factory foreman on the floor, so he is easy to bribe. BCCI spent a lot of money on entertainment, throwing parties, and bringing women into the hotels for top officials in order to get things done. Of course they did that in Beijing too."

BCCI seemed to be the intermediary of choice for the Middle East. Khan had a seemingly endless list of examples: the sale of OF-40 Mark 2 main battle tanks from Italian arms manufacturer Oto Melara to Abu Dhabi; a dozen S-23 180mm artillery guns from North Korea for Dubai; and the sale of ASTROS II battlefield multiple-rocket launchers from Brazil sold to both Iran and Iraq. BCCI, he said, had arranged for the sale of Argentine TAM battle tanks to Iran in 1989, and supplied Iraq with French-made Roland antiaircraft missile systems and with G6 mobile artillery units from South Africa. He described Chinese ballistic-missile sales to Pakistan, Iraq, and Saudi Arabia, all brokered by BCCI, as well as Scud missiles from North Korea.

Khan told them of BCCI's substantial business dealing over the years with one of the world's preeminent makers of military aircraft, Dassault Aviation, the French producer of the Mirage jet fighter. "Asaf Ali has always handled the Mirage sales, he's probably Dassault's biggest Third World broker, and he nearly always uses BCCI to finance the transactions. If Ghaith Pharaon is Abedi's front to buy banks and businesses, Asaf Ali is his front man for major weapons transactions. He's a good friend of 'Happy' Minwallah and he's very close with the Pakistani air marshal."

Ticking off items on his fingers, Khan detailed BCCI-backed Mirage sales to Pakistan, India, Peru, Iraq, Libya, and the Arab Gulf states. The French had shot themselves in the foot when BCCI had brokered a batch of Mirage 2000s to Iraq for use in the Iran-Iraq War. The French air force was all but grounded during Desert Storm for fear that allied jets would mistake French Mirages for the Iraqi Mirages over Kuwait and shoot them down.

Then a look of concern crossed Khan's smooth features. "You must promise me not to mention anything about Asaf Ali's transactions unless you can find this out from another one of your sources who can be surfaced. He is an extremely rich, extremely powerful man, and he represents what you might call the darker side of the bank. If you use this information, he would know immediately that I have been talking to you."

Gwynne spoke up. "You have our word that we won't use anything you tell us without your permission; you know that. But if even you are afraid of him, I don't like our chances of finding someone to go on the record." The reporters knew they would need at least one other reliable source on this before they could publish the Mirage connection. Preferably more: Dassault Aviation was virtually an arm of the French government. If that second source had to be willing to allow his name to be used, to provide cover for Ali Khan, it was going to be tough.

Beaty, drawing pictures in the wet sand with a stick, had been listening intently. "Ali, we have some information from another source who knows something about Abedi's weapons business. He says that around 1985 or so Abedi was trying to make some kind of a deal with Moscow."

"Yes, he was going to Moscow. More recently than that: Before his heart attack he was quite interested in the idea of opening offices of the bank in the Soviet Union. And Pakistan was interested in obtaining the capacity of Gorizont, a satellite system they wanted to tap into for military and civilian use. They were even exploring purchasing, or trading for, launch space on the Proton or Tsyklon rocket systems. And of course, the Soviets had oil, which always interested Abedi."

Beaty looked a question at Gwynne, who nodded his head. Beaty quickly described finding the Navstar technical manuals in Moscow. "Our man is close to one of the directors of the Soviet space agency, who told him the Russians had been buying U.S. technology secrets from BCCI. What do you know about BCCI's stealing and brokering military secrets? What about those Columbine Head things you told me about?"

The Pakistani was silent for a minute. "I think that this subject is dangerous for me to talk about. Perhaps we can return to it someday. Yes, I did mention the Colombine Heads to you, but I told you I don't know what they are. Only that BCCI had three of them, this was perhaps two years ago, and they were being sold to Iraq. This wasn't Asaf Ali, but it was BCCI men of the same group. All I heard was that it was American technology and that it was something very secret. 'A weapon that could alter the balance of power in the Middle East,' was the way it was referred to. I think it must have something to do with a nuclear warhead or a nuclear delivery system. I have no idea how they obtained them."

Beaty resisted an impulse to tell Khan what he had learned in Washington about Columbine Heads. This was getting complicated. "I know you have to protect yourself, Ali, but this is important."

Khan stood up. He waded into the water, then walked back into the tiny cove.

"What you called in your story the Black Network. I never heard that name, but there was all the activity you described. To fathom this, you would have to understand how it was in Pakistan, and in Karachi, during the Afghanistan War. BCCI was working with your CIA. Abedi and the bank are interwoven with Pakistan's intelligence agency, and Inter-Services Intelligence was in charge of supplying the Afghan fighters. Abedi was dealing directly with William Casey. I know he met with Casey in Washington, several times, I think. He was there with General Zia at least once. Asaf Ali also was in meetings with Casey; he talks about staying at Casey's house. They were all great friends. Pakistan received a great amount of military technology from the United States that was under the table. You would have to understand how it was."

Beaty shook his head. Sami Masri had told him Abedi and Casey knew each other, but he had thought Sami was exaggerating the importance of the Black Network's connection to the CIA. Condor had confirmed that Abedi and the bank provided services for Middle Eastern intelligence agencies, but now Khan was taking it a step further, saying Abedi was also working with the French, the Americans, the English, and the Israelis.

"Jonathan, I once told you about a small company in North London BCCI worked with. That company is an MI5 front company, British intelligence. It would get end-user certificates from the Israelis, and BCCI would coordinate with American companies to get F-14 and F-4 Phantom aircraft parts for Iran. You have much to learn yet."

Khan looked up at the sky above the cliffs. "It's going to get dark. Perhaps we should make our way back to the hotel." The two reporters stared at him, speechless.

Khan went to bed early, forestalling further questions. Gwynne and Beaty got little sleep. While the three men had spent the day in splendid isolation, the hardliners in Moscow had staged a coup, and the fate of the Soviet Union hung in the balance. Heinrich, unable to reach Beaty, had called Ann King on the news desk: He was on his way to New York to meet them. It was urgent. Sitting in Gwynne's bungalow with the Navstar photos spread on one of the beds, Beaty finally reached the German at one of the numbers he had left with King. Heinrich was leaving for the airport in minutes. Ann had given him the reporters' flight schedule, and his plane would arrive at JFK International Airport not long after Gwynne and Beaty were due to land. Would they meet him at his terminal?

Gwynne was tapping away on his laptop computer, trying to get down everything Khan had told them. On his desk were pictures of various tanks, rocket launchers, and jet fighters that Khan had obligingly provided to show the scope of BCCI's weapons dealing. "What does Heinrich want?"

Beaty looked around the cluttered room. "I can't decide whether we still work for *Time* or we're in the middle of a spy novel. Heinrich wants to see the pictures he took. He's freaked over what's happened in Russia, and he kept talking about all his deals that have just gone down the drain because of the coup. I think he's in shock: He said he's changed his mind, and he's ready to talk to Morgenthau. We better not miss our plane connections tomorrow evening. We're going to pick him up at the Lufthansa terminal."

Beaty picked up the phone again, glancing at his watch. "I think this justifies getting John Moscow out of bed, don't you? Why should he sleep?"

Gwynne took off his glasses and rubbed his eyes. "You might as well call Attinger too. I don't know what we're going to do with this spy-meets-spy stuff. This is too incredible. Abedi and William Casey were pals? If that's true, no wonder nobody ever busted BCCI. But we've got enough to do the story on BCCI as a weapons broker. I think little Mr. Khan has put us over the top. If Heinrich is going to be in New York, he can help. The least he can do is answer questions for the lawyers." They both laughed at the thought.

Ali Khan left at noon the next day, and the reporters flew to New York that same afternoon. While they waited for Heinrich's plane, Beaty called Condor, hoping he was not out of the country, as he was most of the time. He found him at home and told him what he and Gwynne had learned about the weapons deals. Beaty hadn't decided whether he dared tell Condor about the Kremlin photography caper, and he certainly wasn't about to mention the alleged Casey connection. At least not yet. Condor listened and answered a couple of questions briskly. He agreed to meet the reporter on Thursday and hung up.

"Khan's on the money," Beaty told his partner. "Condor confirmed the Chinese Silkworm missile sale to Saudi Arabia and said BCCI had handled it. And he added a twist that Ali didn't mention: The missiles were retrofitted with a more sophisticated guidance system supplied by Israel."

Gwynne looked at him. "I don't think we're in Kansas anymore, Toto. There's Heinrich."

As the three men greeted each other in front of the terminal, a scruffy-looking cab driver solicited them and started gathering up their luggage. Without paying much attention, they followed, engrossed in conversation. The reporters' pleasant trip from the Caribbean was about to turn into a nightmare.

In the cab Heinrich was bursting to talk about Navstar; he still didn't know what Beaty had learned on his fact-finding trip to Washington with the photos. But as they started to talk, the German noticed the cabbie's credentials in their plastic cover on the dashboard and nudged his companions. The driver had a Russian name. Heinrich asked him a question in Russian, and the two made small talk about how the immigrant liked life in America. Beaty smiled to himself at Heinrich's caution, but nothing more of substance was said during the trip into the city.

Beaty was checking in at the desk of the Parker Meridien when Gwynne, counting their bags, realized that Beaty's computer was missing. They rushed back out to the street. The computer was gone, vanished into the city in the trunk of the battered yellow cab. The three men fought down panic: Stored in that Toshiba 1200 was information that could blow Beaty and Gwynne's most guarded sources out of the water. It was bad enough to lose weeks' worth of notes, but the loss of these could get Heinrich killed three times over. The reporters could see by his chalk-white face that he knew it.

What had seemed perfectly innocent suddenly seemed strange: Heinrich pointed out that they had not found the cab in the taxi line; the driver had approached them. They had assumed he was just a gypsy driver. Both Heinrich and Gwynne had checked the trunk when the bags were taken out and seen nothing left behind. Had the driver secreted it? Had he been sent to pick them up? It was difficult to believe, but still, Beaty's computer was abroad in the streets of New York.

In his hotel room Beaty hustled to get ready for an interview he couldn't postpone, while Gwynne and Heinrich set about trying to find the computer. They phoned the police, the airport, the taxicab companies, the New York Taxi and Limousine Commission, and the licensing bureau. Most of the time they got tape-recorded messages. Gwynne remembered most of the letters in the driver's last name but was told that without the number of his cab it would be impossible to trace him. No one remembered the number of the cab.

Gwynne called John Moscow at the district attorney's office and asked how he should go about trying to find the cab. Did Moscow know anyone who could help? He'd ask around and call back, he said.

An hour later Moscow was back on the line. His own people were trying to track down the driver. For five hours Gwynne heard nothing. Then Moscow called back.

"We've got it," he said. "Don't ask how. Just don't ask how."

"Okay, I won't ask," said Gwynne.

"Put it this way: They found the guy in Staten Island, and the guy didn't want to give it back. I think maybe it got a little exciting. The detectives will be coming by tonight. They wanted to know if you were buying the beer."

"That, or anything else they want!" said a jubilant Gwynne, and he immediately phoned Heinrich to tell him the news.

A couple of hours later three of Morgenthau's finest arrived at Gwynne's hotel room with Beaty's laptop. It was immediately clear why they had gotten the computer back so fast. They were Moscow's enforcers and street-level investigators, the ones who tracked the leads and squeezed the sources: Andy Finan, the lead investigator under Moscow; Fred Ghussan, the former Jerusalem beat cop; and Terry Hayes, a Brooklyn-raised detective on temporary assignment to the BCCI case. They were polite and deferential, shrugging off Gwynne's and Heinrich's effusive thanks.

No one had a clue as to why the cab driver had taken the computer. When the detectives had peered in through his apartment window, the unshaven driver was punching buttons on the laptop. The detectives were quite sure, however, that the driver wasn't going to make a complaint about the sudden force by which he had lost his find. What surprised Gwynne was how seriously the D.A.'s men had taken the mission. Though they eventually cracked jokes about the look on the cabbie's face when they showed up at his door, it was clear that they felt they had done very important police work. The reporter called room service and ordered up a couple of six-packs of beer and a bowl of peanuts.

What Gwynne hadn't considered was the urgency John Moscow had attached to finding the lost computer. By any standards, Beaty's notes had reached national security status. It might have been happenstance, but Moscow hadn't had to read *Time* magazine to learn about Abedi's Black Network. He had his own concerns about BCCI's operatives and their intelligence connections.

Morgenthau's men had a darker view of the bank than any yet revealed in print. By the D.A.'s count, sixteen deaths around the world were related to the BCCI investigation. Some were undoubtedly coincidental, but potential witnesses, and some of the players, had been murdered or had died in mysterious circumstances. This was the reason John Stacks was keeping Beaty and Gwynne out of Pakistan. Word had come to Stacks from Morgenthau's office that Beaty had become one of two or three people who would be worth the risk of elimination.

The detectives were under orders not to discuss the BCCI case itself—at least the parts not yet made public—so the conversation in the hotel room was desultory. More beer was consumed. Fred Ghussan reminisced about the interrogation of Sami Masri. More beer was ordered. Each time the doorbell rang, Terry Hayes leapt to his feet and moved in behind the door, one hand on his revolver. Whatever else might happen that night, Hayes was clearly determined that no one was going to harm Gwynne or Heinrich. Not on his watch, anyway.

Beaty called in from Connecticut and was told his computer had been found. He was exultant. He had been worried that if it wasn't found, Heinrich might bolt for a hole and never surface again. He wouldn't have blamed him. Beaty was in Hartford to talk with the imprisoned Arif Durrani, a Pakistani arms dealer convicted of selling to Iran parts for the U.S.-designed HAWK missile system. BCCI was the banker. Beaty, and an ABC News team, were going in to interview Durrani at nine in the morning.

Into the third round of six-packs, the conversation took a sharp right into Catholic metaphysics. Gwynne was not a Catholic, but he had read the Revelation of Saint John. He soon realized that the High German Catholic weapons dealer and Terry Hayes, the Irish-Catholic cop from Brooklyn, were talking seriously about the antichrist. Specifically, about Agha Hasan Abedi as the antichrist. Heinrich, the pragmatic international weapons dealer, was convinced that Abedi's power and influence were the manifestations of pure evil.

"You know, I have heard about some strange things that Abedi was supposed to be able to do," said Gwynne, struggling to keep up with the dialectic. "BCCI employees were quoted describing a sort of trick Abedi would do at training seminars. He would hold a piece of paper in his hand and tell them to concentrate on an ink spot in the middle of it, making it grow and shrink in size. As it turned out, there was no ink spot, but he made them believe it."

Everyone considered this in its new context. They had all heard stories about Abedi's mesmerizing aura. Then Heinrich said, "I'll tell you something. I've never told anyone this before. I saw him do something. I was in Lahore. He had some sort of office there, and the day I was visiting he happened to be in, so my client suggested we meet him. Just a brief hello. When we walked up, the door to his office opened by itself. We went in and I turned, expecting to see whoever opened the door, but the only person in the room was Abedi, seated at his desk. When we left, the door closed silently by itself. I don't think it was anything mechanical. I've never seen anything like it."

He and Hayes then began to discuss the nature of evil and God's purpose on earth. The detective continued to go on alert every time room service showed up. Gwynne was thinking about the implications of Heinrich's story, but not about whether Abedi could or could not do some spooky things. This was the first time Heinrich had indicated that he knew, or had even met, Abedi. Both Beaty and John Moscow believed the German knew a great deal more about BCCI than he had revealed so far, and perhaps they were right. They all had been reserving judgment on a couple of things Heinrich had told them about high-level bribes BCCI had paid and his assertions about BCCI's involvement in narcotics trafficking.

At midnight the party broke up, and Gwynne went to bed. It had been a very long day. It had been a very, very long time since that day in February when Beaty had called him to say he had a story to tell him.

The doors at the Federal Penitentiary at Hartford opened promptly at 9:00 A.M., and guards led Beaty and the TV crew down corridors into a steel cage in the middle of a barred room. A steel table was bolted to the floor.

"Your prisoner will be here in a few minutes," one of the guards said, and the doors clanged shut.

The correspondent introduced himself to the ABC producer, Jay Lamonaca. Beaty and Gwynne had been working informally with the network's investigative news team since Beaty had appeared on two *Nightline* shows to talk about BCCI. It was a friendly but uneasy alliance, since both were holding information they didn't want to share, but both *Time* and ABC wanted to question Durrani. It had taken weeks and the combined pressure of both news organizations to win permission for this interview. The authorities weren't eager to have the press talking to prisoner No. 09027-014.

Durrani's case was both obscure and tantalizing. At his trial the federal prosecutors had painted him as a wealthy arms merchant, proficient in the art of deceit, who had traveled the world in luxury with a mistress. The prosecutors said he was an agent for the regime of Ayatollah Khomeini intent upon the illegal purchase and sale of weapons on behalf of Tehran.

Durrani admitted being an arms merchant supplying Iran, but he insisted that he was part of a joint operation conducted by the U.S. and Israeli governments, which, at the time, were trying to win release of American hostages in the Middle East. He said he had met in London with a U.S. official named Ollie North, who was part of a team trying to obtain the HAWK parts. Durrani's arrest, on October 3, 1986, came one month before the U.S. government's secret arms-for-hostages deal with Tehran was revealed.

ABC's interest had been sparked by the Iran-Contra connection, and information developed by Lawrence Lifschultz, a former correspondent for the *Far East Economic Review*. Lifschultz and a research team had developed information that showed that Durrani was part of a group that illegally delivered "hundreds of millions of dollars" worth of armaments, much more than ever revealed in the Iran-Contra investigation, to Iran from the United States and other NATO countries in the 1980s. The suppliers appeared to have high-level protection.

Beaty's interest in Durrani was focused on BCCI. Sources had said Durrani was part of the BCCI group, that he knew Abedi personally, and that his operations were financed by the bank. Durrani was also close to Mustafa Gokal, the director of Abedi's mysterious shipping company. Beaty was also intrigued by one uncontested fact that had emerged at Durrani's trial: Until his arrest, Durrani had been the managing director of Merex, a California arms firm that was a main supplier of the Israelis.

Durrani, a smooth-featured man in his mid-forties wearing a prison-orange jumpsuit, was ushered into the holding cell and the doors clanged shut again. Everyone shook hands. Beaty and Durrani murmured together for a moment, and both agreed that the cameras could roll while they talked. An intermediary, one of the reporter's sources, had already explained to Durrani why *Time* wanted the interview.

Durrani described his connections to BCCI readily: He had grown up in Karachi with many of the men who were now BCCI executives and had worked with them from the beginning of his career as an arms dealer.

"What's the biggest arms deal that you have heard of BCCI being part of?"

"BCCI basically . . . part of it was funded on instructions of the government of Pakistan. They would pay out . . . they built that Mirage factory, and a lot of money came from BCCI bank. They also . . . I do not know if you heard rumors, or you met the person who is the agent for, basically, the Mirage factory—he lives in London. And he is very close to BCCI, so he uses BCCI to arrange transactions . . ."

Beaty held his breath. "And what's his name?"

"Asaf Ali."

"And he is an agent?"

"For Dassault. For the French Mirage factory. This whole setup is like a little nest in London. And he manipulates . . . Pakistan was one of the largest customers. And because of Pakistan, Mirages were sold into Abu Dhabi. They were sold to Libya, and so on."

"How do you know he is with BCCI?"

"Well, I know Asaf, and I know those people."

"And Asaf Ali has the Ariadne rocket franchise for Pakistan?"

"Right. Most of the major French aerospace industry basically relies on him."

Beaty let out his breath. Durrani continued, outlining some of BCCI's and Ali's weapons deals throughout the world, from Bulgaria to Nigeria. Beaty now had his cover for Ali Khan, not only on the record, but on videotape. He was ready to turn the interview over to the ABC people and leave. But Durrani had more to say. He described BCCI's methods of clandestine weapons purchases and shipments, and Abedi's relations with the generals who controlled Pakistan. It all fit with the descriptions Khan and Heinrich had provided. Then unexpectedly, Durrani's explanations swerved to Clark Clifford and First American Bank. He said BCCI had steered some of his business to First American in New York. Durrani had his money in BCCI, but he said the two banks were interchangeable and he could obtain his money through First American as readily as he did through BCCI.

"As far as I was concerned, it was just another branch of BCCI."

Beaty caught a commuter plane for New York, where he and Gwynne met with Stacks and Attinger in Stacks's corner office. It was late in the week. Deadline was approaching, but the BCCI weapons story was on. Outside Stacks's office, Gwynne and Beaty shook hands and grinned at each other. "You keep reporting," Gwynne said. "And I'll start writing."

On Thursday Beaty rented a conference suite at the Parker Meridien for a meeting between Heinrich and Morgenthau's people. This was a far cry from the detectives' grilling of Marsi: Morgenthau sent a team of his top prosecutors and investigators, and everyone was exceedingly polite. Moscow's investigation of Heinrich's background had convinced him this was a man with high-level connections. Beaty had showed him the photos of the Navstar documents. Heinrich was a bit nervous and insisted that Beaty be present. But once Beaty saw things were going smoothly, he excused himself and raced to the *Time* offices five blocks away. He came back often enough to keep a handle on what Heinrich was telling them, and his absences gave Morgenthau's men an opportunity to ask questions they didn't want him to hear.

That was all right with Beaty: He was as close to the scene of action as any reporter was likely to get.

It was a marathon session for Heinrich. The reporters kept him up most of Thursday night and throughout Friday, using him as their technical expert. They didn't confront *Time*'s lawyers with Heinrich—his presence and name were closely guarded secrets—but he frequently supplied the answers it took to satisfy the lawyers. It was a hell of a way to put together a story. The researcher for the BCCI articles from the beginning was Sue Washburn, who was unflappable under deadline pressure. This time she became an instant arms-transfer expert, delving through obscure military periodicals, United Nations reports, and the published military budgets of a dozen countries to confirm Heinrich's descriptions of particular transactions.

On Friday there was a glitch. François Prigent, the Dassault spokesman, was reached at home on holiday and denied any knowledge of the deals. The article sought to describe a complicated deal in which Mirage fighters, sold to Peru, had been diverted, presumably by Asaf Ali, for a more urgent sale to Pakistan. Ali had brokered the sale of forty-nine Mirage 2000s to India and then, to maintain parity, had to find a similar number of new and used Mirages for Pakistan. A political scandal had already erupted in Peru over BCCI, in part because of the financial transactions in the on-again-off-again Mirage deal. A large amount of government money had disappeared.

Prigent dismissed the story. "The shipment to Peru is the business of Peru; what happens to planes after we make a delivery is up to them." Prigent also brushed off any knowledge about BCCI: "Banks are chosen by clients, not by us." Even more critically, he denied any connection to Asaf Ali. "We don't know that man," he said.

The reporters by now had multiple sources who said otherwise, but *Time*'s lawyers were still nervous. Better safe than sorry. In the end Adam Zagorin succeeded in finding an unassailably knowledgeable source. In the story, Beaty and Gwynne referred to Zagorin's source as a French businessman who had worked on arms deals in Pakistan and quoted him as saying: "Asaf Ali has been an important Dassault agent for years, and everyone knows that." The reporters regretted that they couldn't use their source's further statements about kickbacks BCCI paid French high officials. Condor had told Beaty the same thing about kickbacks and had said BCCI made payments to a relative of one official on every transaction involving French arms sold to Africa. The man Condor named was so important that the reporters knew they would have to have ironclad proof, and since neither Condor nor "the French businessman" was in a position to appear in court if a libel suit was filed, they had to let it pass.

The story, published the first week of September 1991, was headlined: "Not just a bank. You can get anything you want through BCCI—guns, planes, even nuclear-weapons technology." The article spiraled the BCCI scandal one notch higher.

Finally Beaty and Gwynne had been able to publish their concept of BCCI:

> Though the discovery of irregularities led to the shutdown of BCCI's banking operations last July, Abedi's $20 billion "bank" is in fact far more complex. It is a vast, stateless, multinational corporation that deploys its own intelligence agency, complete with a paramilitary wing and enforcement units, known collectively as the Black Network. It maintains its own diplomatic relations with foreign countries through bank "protocol officers" who use seemingly limitless amounts of cash to pursue Abedi's goals.

Those goals included development of a "Muslim Bomb" as well as transactions "that have often upset the uneasy technomilitary balance sought by the United States and other major powers engaging in government-to-government [weapons] sales." The article described BCCI as a middleman in weapons deals involving the United States, China, Israel, Iran, Iraq, Saudi Arabia, the Soviet Union, and Pakistan. It said Abedi was providing financial and technical support for Pakistan's acquisition of nuclear weaponry.

Five months later an extraordinarily authoritative voice from within BCCI would express much the same concept. Sheikh Kamal Adham had inexplicably decided to give an insider's defensive appraisal of BCCI to an Arab audience. Adham, who shuns publicity, broke his own rule of silence in a radio interview in Cairo on January 5, 1992, which was later translated into English by the Middle East News Network. He said, in part:

"This bank, as it is, is not any bank. It is a bank that owns sixty-nine banks around the world in sixty-nine countries. . . . This is not very much appreciated by the big powers, who were somehow like the guardians to the younger students in a school. They always, in the past, used to monitor what the Third World used to do.

"For example, if you want to buy arms, they [the Western powers] know exactly how the deal is made. If you want to make a venture in atomic energy, which they don't want anybody to do, they monitored all that. Suddenly, a new vehicle appeared on the scene which belonged to the Third World, and this vehicle was spreading so fast that it had branches all over the world. This somehow made them feel that the Third World, instead of using the vehicle they usually assign us to use, have their own vehicle now so the money that came from the oil business went to this vehicle instead of the banks of the Western World.

". . . If you look around in the banking world, you will see that most of the Arab banking organizations with international branches are being hit one after the other, and it cannot appear to be coincidental. I believe some of it is intentionally done because the New Order does not allow anyone to have his own vehicles and to do with it as he wants. There are so many things that were done through the bank [BCCI] that are regarded by the Third World as an achievement, like funding the Pakistani atomic energy program.

"To the world this is a dangerous game the young people are playing and they are not part of the [nuclear-bomb] club, but for the Pakistanis, the one that helped them is a hero—since India has an atomic bomb, so why can't Pakistan? This is the only way it can defend itself."

That was an astonishing statement by any standard, although not intended for Western ears. Indeed, the Western press never caught wind of it. One of the most powerful and knowledgeable players on the Middle Eastern stage had acknowledged that the Pakistanis had their own atomic bomb and that Abedi and BCCI had helped them get it. Moreover, Adham was defining BCCI not so much as a bank as a geopolitical entity designed to siphon petrodollar deposits away from Western banks, a force certain to confound U.S. efforts to maintain a technomilitary balance of its own design among Third World nations. Such an entity could forward the Islamic cause unfettered by the dictates of any superpower's foreign policy. Or law.

It was precisely the picture that Beaty and Gwynne had been laying out in their *Time* articles—although government spokesmen scoffed at the concept and the rest of the media largely ignored it.

At the moment he made this speech, Kamal Adham was anticipating being indicted in the United States in connection with his involvement in BCCI's frauds and bribery. So why would he want to call attention to all of this? The Western press aside, the wily old spy master certainly knew that the intelligence agencies of the United States and elsewhere would pick up his remarks and pass them on. He may have been sending a message directly to George Bush, reminding the president that Kamal Adham knew far too much to be trifled with.

To put Adham's message in perspective, we have to go back to September 1991, when Adham decided to take steps to deal with the attack being mounted by Robert Morgenthau. The New York district attorney, free of the diplomatic and national security constraints apparently hampering the Justice Department investigation being run out of Washington, had drawn a bead on the powerful Saudi as one of the main culprits of the BCCI scandal. But Morgenthau, on the advice of friends in Washington, had been keeping quiet about his intention to indict Adham and Sheikh Khalid bin-Mahfouz. Morgenthau hoped to avoid State Department intervention.

Then Kamal caught wind of what was happening and quietly hired himself an unusually well-placed attorney: White House Chief of Staff John Sununu's former executive assistant, thirty-three-year-old Edward M. Rogers, Jr., who had just—unexpectedly—quit his White House post to open a private law practice.

Rogers's contract with his very first client was gold-plated: Adham was to pay him a staggering $600,000 over a two-year period. An official familiar with both men suggested to *Time* White House correspondent Michael Duffy that Adham was merely trying to execute what Arabs call *wasta*, a sort of well-placed personnel fix, similar to Libyan Colonel Muammar el-Qaddafi's hiring of President Carter's brother, Billy, as a foreign-trade representative in the 1970s.

But like the Billy Carter episode, Adham's Rogers ploy backfired and dragged the Bush administration into the BCCI scandal for the first time. The Adham-Rogers story led the evening news shows on TV, and American political reporters, who had generally ignored the BCCI affair, had a brief field day with its implications.

"Too Many Questions," *Time* headlined its story of the affair: "But few answers about a shameless attempt to buy favor with the White House and the Justice Department's reluctance to investigate BCCI." The tone was almost strident by *Time* standards, but the magazine's top editors were growing a trifle indignant. Beaty and Gwynne had learned that the White House was closely monitoring the BCCI investigation, insisting that a representative of the administration sit in on congressional and Justice Department interviews with some potential BCCI witnesses. FBI agents had complained to some of the reporters' sources that the FBI probe was spinning its wheels "because it was deemed too political" and decisions were being held up in Washington. And another *Time* correspondent had gleaned this explanation from someone high in the Justice Department:

"There is a feeling that somebody in Washington is trying to cut a deal on BCCI; that they really don't want the U.S. Attorney's offices to actually return indictments because that would muck up their ability to do some kind of an overall package deal, where we cut off the hands of a few Pakistanis and paint it as if they were really all the big folks. They'll all get out their charts and graphs to absolve [Sheikh Zayed] and then let the bank reopen overseas" to repay its foreign debts.

Rogers hastily backed out of the contract with Adham, but he had already embarrassed George Bush. When a reporter asked what Rogers might be selling Adham that was worth so much money, President Bush snapped, "Ask him. I don't know what he's selling. I don't know anything about this man [Adham] except I've read bad stuff about him. And I don't like what I read about him."

Beaty and Gwynne, writing *Time*'s story in the Washington bureau, went off the wall when they heard Bush's reply. Beaty, who had been talking to Condor and his other intelligence-world sources about Kamal's background, was sure the president had just told a certifiable lie, although he wasn't sure why. They asked Dan Goodgame, who covered the White House for *Time* with Michael Duffy, to ask Bush's press spokesman, Marlin Fitzwater, if Bush had meant to say that he didn't know, had never before heard of, Sheikh Kamal. Goodgame and Duffy were writing a book about George Bush, and Goodgame had to explain that because the book was critical of Bush, he and Duffy were at that moment personae non gratae at the White House. Fitz-water would not talk to them, but Goodgame said he would get someone else in the White House press corps to ask the question. The word came back promptly: The president knew nothing about about Kamal Adham.

The reporters were incredulous. Adham had been the director of Saudi Arabia's equivalent of the CIA in 1976, when George Bush headed the CIA. The American agency had been helping to modernize Saudi intelligence during Bush's tenure, and Kamal had been Saudi Arabia's main liaison with the CIA. Even without that connection, the chances were slim to none that George Bush, who was known throughout the Middle East as "the Saudi vice president" and had more firsthand knowledge of the Middle East than any previous U.S. president, didn't know the sheikh. "Flat impossible," State Department and intelligence sources told Beaty. Kamal Adham had been a main man in Saudi Arabia for the past two decades, whether you were making business deals or policy.

Adham apparently thought the same thing. In the January 1992 Cairo radio interview, Adham was asked about Bush's denial and the "alleged derogatory comment about Adham made by President Bush," since it was well known they had headed their respective intelligence agencies at the same time. Was Adham going to sue *Time* magazine?

"No. There was a period of overlap, but whatever the case, it is not possible for a president to say that. The next day nobody mentioned [that] the White House spokesman came out and said that the president knows Mr. Adham and he did not like what was written in the papers. But nobody wrote this . . . the papers only want bad news. No, no legal action was taken against the *Time* article."

Adham had been cautious enough not to directly contradict Bush. But he had managed to say the politically correct thing to one audience and send a reminder to another. (If Marlin Fitzwater "came out" the next day, it wasn't to the White House press lounge to say the president hadn't liked what was written about his friend Kamal. One can only wonder what statement was made to pacify Adham and soothe Saudi sensibilities. Something face-saving, certainly: Adham's nephew, Prince Sultan bin-Bandar, is ambassador to the United States and a frequent guest of his close friend George Bush. Another nephew is Prince Turki, the current head of Saudi Arabian intelligence.)

What about Adham's dramatic assertion that Pakistan had the atomic bomb and that Abedi was a hero in the Third World for helping obtain it? If this was a message, it was even more oblique. It's not exactly a secret that Pakistan has nuclear-weapons capacity, but the political realities are such that no government has ever fully admitted it. It is the classic case of the unclad emperor. An admission of the obvious would, at the very least, upset delicate power balances and open the myth of nonproliferation to question.

The Reagan administration, intent on continuing military aid to Pakistan during the Afghanistan War, turned a blind eye, since U.S. law prohibited aid or military sales to nonnuclear countries known to be developing nuclear weapons. The situation was even stickier for the Bush administration: In 1988 and 1989, in the face of overwhelming evidence to the contrary, President Bush was constrained to certify that Pakistan still did not "possess a nuclear explosive device" to justify continuing massive U.S. support for Pakistan, which was by then the third-largest recipient of American aid, after Israel and Egypt. The officially concocted excuse was that Pakistan had only the unassembled components of a bomb. In 1990, with the Soviets pulling out of Afghanistan, it was declared that possession of unassembled components violated the rules: Bush refused to give Pakistan another clean bill of health, and U.S. aid was abruptly shut off.

Time was the first publication to assert that BCCI was instrumental in Pakistan achieving unofficial Nuclear Club membership when it described BCCI as "the owner's representative for Pakistan's nuclear bomb project," but it was no secret in the Middle East. It simply wasn't talked about. That Kamal Adham should say publicly that Pakistan had the bomb and that Abedi had been the financial angel of its development was puzzling on the face of it. As he noted, the West was not pleased with the idea of BCCI helping to spread nuclear technology. And to speak of such clandestine acquisitions implied criminal behavior, since supplying nuclear-weapons technology to Pakistan was illegal in most countries.

Perhaps Adham was hinting that he knew a real secret. His term "atomic bomb" in this context is quaintly old-fashioned. No government wants to confront the question of Pakistan's exact nuclear capacities because the actuality is that Pakistan is known to have modern thermonuclear devices, along with midrange ballistic missiles that can deliver nuclear payloads, sophisticated navigation and guidance systems, satellite surveillance technology, and other electronic intelligence capabilities. It had received sophisticated American military technology that Congress never authorized. Adham may have been suggesting that it wouldn't be in the Bush administration's self-interest to probe too deeply into how Pakistan, and BCCI, came to possess such military capacity.

The sheikh, more than almost anyone, was in a position to know that BCCI was the creation of a real-life Dr. No, whose empire brokered ballistic missiles, satellites, illicit pharmaceuticals, stolen military secrets, heroin, and hot money, leaving a trail of corruption across two decades and seventy countries. And of all people, Adham had reason to know that the White House knew it too, and had known about it for years.

CHAPTER 12

THE HIDDEN ALLIANCE

"I'm going back to Karachi, where I will be safe because it is
a completely lawless society."

—SAMI MASRI, 1991

It is not possible to comprehend Agha Hasan Abedi's empire without
understanding Pakistan—a country that defines political turbulence—
and how he built his most enduring power base there. The goals,
fortunes, even the administrations of both Pakistan and BCCI have
been inextricably interwoven since the bank's creation two decades
ago. It was a partnership that went far beyond banking, although
Abedi's financial support of Pakistan's frequently shaky central bank
was an important element of the codependent relationship. Abedi and
his bank, working in the shadows, implemented Pakistan's foreign
policy and critical domestic programs, such as its clandestine drive
to build a deliverable hydrogen bomb. BCCI operated as a quasi-
governmental ministry, particularly during the eleven-year reign of
General Zia ul-Haq, reaping extraordinary private profits in the process. Abedi's protocol department in Karachi helped to maintain Pakistan's official diplomatic relations with Saudi Arabia and the Persian
Gulf emirates and to expand Pakistan's important ties with China.

BCCI hired many of its managers from the highest government
ranks, and, in turn, Abedi got his people appointed to key government positions. The revolving door between the bank and the government was so extensive that it becomes difficult to separate national
initiatives from Abedi's commercial ventures. Abedi, for example,
managed to get Mustafa Gokal, whose vast family shipping business

was completely underwritten by BCCI, named Pakistan's minister for shipping. It was a handy connection, especially when Abedi was awarded an unprecedented contract to finance and broker the sale of Pakistan's entire rice harvest.

Another example of blurred interests involves Sultan Mohammed Khan, Pakistan's former ambassador to the People's Republic of China, who helped arrange Henry A. Kissinger's historic secret trip into China in 1971. Khan helped Abedi win permission to open his bank in China in 1982 and then became a director of BCCI's China operation. Similarly, Mohammed Khan served as Pakistan's ambassador to the United States (1979 to 1980) and later became a principal figure in BCCI's mysterious agency office in Washington, D.C.

The symbiotic relationship between Abedi and the government was multifaceted, and unspoken, but one dimension of it is easily described. From its birth, Pakistan has been run by a handful of powerful families—most of them connected to the military—and Abedi always made sure that the important generals and politicians were cut in on some of the wealth passing through BCCI. Records uncovered in the investigations of BCCI show that in May 1985, BCCI's Dubai branch issued a check payable to General Zia personally for 40 million rupees (nearly $3 million). The ties between Abedi and Zia were so strong that it is difficult to separate the intelligence operations of BCCI and those of the much-feared ISI, which Zia used to control the military and keep himself in power.

The profits that accrued to Abedi through these connections, however, may have been incidental to a larger truth: The hidden alliances in Pakistan—and within other Islamic states—provided Abedi and BCCI the kind of sweeping immunity from laws and regulation that is assumed by sovereign nations when they take action in the name of "national security." Pakistan's single-minded drive to transform itself into a militarily mighty Islamic state, supported in part by its enormously wealthy Muslim cousins in Saudi Arabia and the Emirates, neatly fit Abedi's overarching vision of BCCI as a Muslim Third World power that would transcend political borders. BCCI, fueled by petrodollars, was going to forge the shining new sword of Islam. It would be a terrible Nuclear Age sword that would give Pakistan—and other Muslim nations—parity with the Zionists and would lessen their military dependence on either of the global superpowers of the Infidel world. The crucial underground alliances Abedi would forge with intelligence agencies from Washington to Riyadh were built, in large part, on the basis of BCCI's role as arms broker to the Middle East.

Abedi headquartered his bank in London, his fashionably decorated door to Western banking, and created the illusion that BCCI was backed by the oil wealth of Saudi Arabia and the Emirates, while the real heart of the Bank of Credit and Commerce International remained in Karachi. Abedi's thinking, and the bank's culture, were shaped by the economy of Karachi, where corruption is regarded as an integral part of commerce, and commerce is dominated by narcotics trafficking, arms dealing, fraud, and smuggling.

Three historical events created the hothouse climate that nurtured BCCI in Pakistan and catapulted Abedi to global power: the partition of India, the arrival of the Bedouin princes from the Persian Gulf, and the Soviet invasion of Afghanistan. The Afghanistan War would bring BCCI into the narcotics trade and at the same time provide Abedi a secret alliance with the United States that would shield him from criminal prosecution in America. To see this we must step back to the creation of Pakistan.

When India's Muslim-majority provinces and princely states were given the choice of remaining in India or joining Pakistan in 1947, the provinces of Sind, the North-West Frontier, Baluchistan, and three fifths of the Punjab combined to form what became Pakistan, a nation that extends from the Arabian Sea a thousand miles northward across eastern plains to the Hindu Kush and the foothills of the Himalayas. Pakistan, however, became a boiling cauldron rather than a melting pot. The 100 million Muslims of British India, slightly more than a fourth of the population, have little in common other than their religion. There are vast differences in language, culture, and social and economic backgrounds between, say, the Muslims of the Punjab and those of the central provinces. Urdu, which became the official language of Pakistan, is spoken by only 11 percent of its people.

Nowhere were these differences more pronounced than in Karachi, which had been a sleepy fishing port on the Arabian Sea since 2300 B.C., the time of the Indus civilization. In 1947, when Abedi moved to Karachi, the capital of the newly created nation, it had a population of less than 200,000. The city at once was riven by schisms. The native Sinds, who were the countrified landed aristocracy, were rudely eclipsed by the flood of better-educated Urdu-speaking *mohajirs* seeking jobs at the seat of the new government. By 1951 Karachi had 1.1 million residents, half of whom were *mohajirs*, like Abedi. During the next decade the *mohajirs*, who at first controlled the bureaucracy, were buried by waves of newcomers from the Punjab and the North-West Frontier who came to work in the textile mills and on the thousands of construction sites as the city grew by haphazard leaps and bounds. The tribal Pathans and the Punjabis, with their own languages and customs, founded their own colonies on the outskirts of Karachi.

As a capital, Karachi did not suit the military regimes that ran Pakistan: It was seven hundred miles from Rawalpindi, the general headquarters of the army. Furthermore, unlike Karachi, Rawalpindi was predominantly rural, tribal, clannish, and inward-looking, and many of the military leaders were products of this culture.[1] Thus construction of a new capital, to be named Islamabad—the City of Islam—was begun in 1961, just north of Rawalpindi.

The sprawling port city of Karachi became a teeming metropolis of more than eight million people with the addition of hundreds of thousands of Afghan refugees in the 1980s. Animosity among the cultures doomed any political cohesion, and open warfare has been been further exacerbated by the decade of unrestricted trafficking in guns and narcotics that flourished while Washington used Pakistan to provide clandestine support for the Afghan rebels. Bombing, riots, assassinations, and gun battles between "drug mafias" transformed Karachi into one of the most violent and lawless cities on the planet. It is no wonder that Abedi and his ideas also flourished in this particular mix of cosmopolitan affairs and open anarchy. Karachi is a city of political fragmentation where personal and family alliances are vastly more important than institutional allegiances.

Most accounts of Abedi's career begin with his forced departure from Pakistan in 1972, after President Zulfikar Ali Bhutto nationalized Abedi's United Bank and placed him under temporary house arrest. It was this turn of events that spurred Abedi to London and Abu Dhabi to create BCCI. It is less well known that Bhutto's action provoked a personal and political feud that still divides the country.

Zulfikar Bhutto, schooled in Bombay and polished at the University of California at Berkeley and at Oxford, was named president and chief martial law administrator of Pakistan in 1971, in the turbulent days after the civil war that led to the independence of Bangladesh. The founder of the People's Party of Pakistan (PPP) and heir to vast estates in the Sind, he had launched a socialist-style government with aims far broader than the takeover of Abedi's United Bank. Abedi's were not the only capitalist toes on which Bhutto stepped. In 1972 thirty-one large-scale industries, including all the banks and insurance companies, were nationalized, and state enterprises were set up to manage them. External trade in rice and cotton, the country's main exports, were also brought under government control.[2]

Abedi, however, took the loss of his bank personally. He had anticipated the socialist action but believed Bhutto timed it to foil his move into Iran, where he intended to launch his vision of world banking. The wealth of the shah of Iran and his country's oil revenues beckoned, and Abedi had chosen his entry point carefully. In 1971 he began negotiating to take over Asnaaf Bank, a private Iranian bank that had collapsed. True to form, he entertained Iranian officials lavishly—operating out of a palatial suite at the Hilton on London's Park Lane—to recruit the right nominee shareholders. Iran limited foreign bank investments, so Abedi's United Bank could own no more than 40 percent of Asnaaf Bank. Thus Abedi needed to find friendly and powerful Iranians to front for him so that he would have actual control. He had visited Tehran, along with his United Bank associates Swaleh Naqvi, Velayat Abedi, and Dildar Rizvi, and eventually found the Iranian partners he needed.[3] The ambitious Agha Hasan Abedi had woven an elaborate web of under-the-table understandings (cutting in the head of the appropriate Iranian ministry, according to one of *Time*'s BCCI sources) and walked away with the license to begin a bank in Iran. It was to be named Iran-i-Pak.

When Bhutto heard about Abedi's successful venture in Iran, he was reported to be furious. He publicly rebuked his ambassador to Tehran, and the nationalization of Pakistan's banks followed almost immediately. Iran's finance minister was constrained to ask Abedi to return the banking license he had just been granted, since a bank owned by a foreign government could not be allowed to do business in the shah's empire. In one stroke, Abedi had lost not only United Bank, which he had built into Pakistan's largest and most modern financial institution, but also Asnaaf, which was to have been the first jewel in Abedi's international banking crown.

Bhutto was close to the shah of Iran and had his own idea of a Pakistani-Iranian relationship that obviously didn't include Agha Hasan Abedi. Even so, Abedi continued to spin his webs in Iran. After the aborted takeover, he ensnared the shah's brother, Prince Mahmood Reza Pahlavi, to be one of BCCI's first glittering phony shareholders. Later, convinced that members of the royal court were sabotaging his commercial ambitions in Iran (which included, according to some sources, the transshipment of heroin), Abedi would connive in the shah's downfall and make profitable oil-trading alliances with the fanatical government of mullahs who replaced him.

Abedi's enemies in Pakistan and London whisper today that Bhutto's move against Abedi eventually cost the prime minister his life. There is no proof that Abedi conspired in the coup against Bhutto or that he later helped persuade General Zia that Bhutto should be hanged, but the theory is an article of faith among Bhutto's followers today. Bhutto's daughter, Benazir, who became prime minister after Zia's own violent death in 1988, has privately said she believes Abedi conspired with others against her father and was as responsible as Zia for his execution.[4] Whatever Abedi's role in determining Bhutto's fate, however, there is no doubt that Zulfikar Ali Bhutto greatly underestimated the ambitious banker, and in doing so created a powerful enemy.

It is characteristic of the calculating and completely pragmatic man behind the façade of a philanthropic visionary that Abedi didn't allow that enmity to show. As he began to expand his banking empire in Europe, the Middle East, and Africa, Abedi worked assiduously to ingratiate himself with Bhutto and his military-dominated government. All the while he was building an unassailable power base in Pakistan.

The banker soon found ways to profit from Bhutto's determination to create a socialist economy. BCCI quickly became a main conduit of capital flight, ushering hundreds of millions of dollars out of Pakistan as the affluent class—the industrialists and entrepreneurs—sought safer havens for their money. BCCI, with new offices on Leadenhall Street in London as well as in Abu Dhabi, was also able to help influential Pakistanis who wanted to go into business abroad after having their enterprises seized by Bhutto. One such was Nawaz Sharif, the current prime minister of Pakistan, whose family's holdings, including a steel plant, were seized by Bhutto. The Sharifs relocated the plant in the emirate of Dubai, where Abedi loaned them start-up money, arranged for the local investor required by Dubai regulations, and then, when the foundry later became unprofitable, found someone to buy them out and forgave the balance of the original $2-million loan. As reported by *The Wall Street Journal*, BCCI had made a lasting friend of the future prime minister.[5]

There were other reasons Abedi's influence was growing in Karachi and Rawalpindi. He was staffing his BCCI offices around the world with the cream of Pakistan's commercial banking community, stealing away the very directors Bhutto had placed in charge of the nationalized banks. Abedi could offer salaries that were handsome by Western banking standards and simply awesome in Pakistan's state-controlled economy. Operating from London, Abedi could still make loans at favorable rates to members of Pakistan's military clique and arrange for them to be included in sure-thing business deals. Most gratifying of all, Abedi was able to offer the generals' sons—and even occasionally their daughters—well-paying banking jobs abroad.

From the beginning, BCCI's Pakistani managers were afforded a kind of life-style they had seen only in movies. Abedi encouraged them to live beyond their means. "We were told: 'Think rich, act rich, and you will be rich, and so will be the bank,'" Muzaffar Ali Bukhari, at one time a top BCCI manager in Pakistan and the bank's regional manager for Southeast Asia, told *Los Angeles Times* reporter Mark Fineman.[6] "In the beginning everybody used to stay in five-star hotels. Mr. Abedi said, 'It doesn't matter.' He said, 'You must build up your stature.' He believed that you must dress well, you must live well, you must mix in high society so that you gain confidence."

One of Abedi's most successful tactics was to offer extraordinarily well-paid positions to relatives of leaders in whatever country he was doing business. Nowhere was Abedi more intent on nepotistic alliances than in his own Pakistan. A glance at the names of some of the BCCI officers who ran afoul of the law in the United States in 1988 is sufficient to make the point. Amjad Awan is the son-in-law of a Pakistani air marshal. Another BCCI man convicted with Awan in the Tampa case is the son of a former head of Pakistani military intelligence. And Arif Durrani, the BCCI client imprisoned in the United States for selling arms to Iran, is the son of an army general.

Abedi didn't have to leave his own neighborhood in Karachi to recruit these sons of the influential. Durrani, interviewed in prison, told Beaty of those early days when Zulfikar Ali Bhutto was in power: "I've known Amjad Awan from childhood. I know Agha Hasan Abedi. He lived a stone's throw from our house. Sheikh Zayed is our neighbor in Karachi; when he first came to Pakistan he wanted to buy our house, [my father wouldn't sell] and now our house sits in the middle of property which Sheikh Zayed owns. It is just a very exclusive enclave in what is called the Defense Officers' Society. Across from us used to be a general living in the president's house, and on the other side of the fence is the navy chief of staff. It was through all that that the government of Pakistan kind of arranged . . . Abu Dhabi purchased Mirage jets, which the Pakistan air force was maintaining for Abu Dhabi. Abedi helped arrange it."

A case can be made that within the realpolitik of the country, the Defense Officers' Society *is* Pakistan. It is not a pluralistic society. The army governs Pakistan, and Bhutto, and later Zia, controlled the army. Abedi needed to make alliances with relatively few people to consolidate his power.

It was Bhutto who began Pakistan's unending drive to modernize and expand its military capacity. Driven by fears of Indian domination and a desire for prominence in the Islamic world, Bhutto entered into military protocols with Kuwait, Iraq, Oman, the United Arab Emirates, Libya, Saudi Arabia, and the P.L.O. (Palestine Liberation Organization). Under these agreements Islamabad provided training facilities in Pakistani defense institutions for members of the armed forces of the contracting states and posted contingents from Pakistan's military to the same countries. More than ten thousand men were posted to Saudi Arabia, and Riyadh paid for such assistance, in part, by obtaining sophisticated weapons systems from the United States that it refused to provide directly. Bhutto's anti-American rhetoric, his alliance with China, and Pakistan's war with India had all combined to freeze American military aid.

Bhutto also launched a nuclear development project in 1972, coincidentally the same year Abedi opened BCCI's doors offshore. (Bhutto's paranoia over India only increased two years later when India exploded a nuclear device.) Abedi, through his financial resources and ever-expanding business contacts around the world, found himself in an ideal position to help Pakistan with both its conventional-weapons buildup and the development of nuclear-weapons technology. While there is no direct evidence that Abedi played a role in the first step of the latter program—the acquisition from France of a large reprocessing plant to extract plutonium from spent reactor fuel—Abedi's fingerprints are clear from that point on. (As Durrani indicated, those fingerprints can be seen on the flow of goods between France's nuclear, military, and aerospace industries and Pakistan. France's first sales of Mirage jet fighters to Pakistan in the late 1960s and early 1970s were brokered by Asaf Ali, the multimillionaire Pakistani businessman closely associated with Abedi and BCCI, as were similar Mirage sales to Abedi's mentor, Sheikh Zayed of Abu Dhabi, during the same time period. Abedi played a direct role, according to his weapons-business associates. That flow would increase through the 1980s to include other nuclear technologies and sophisticated satellite communications and photography technologies.)

Zayed's arrival in Pakistan, along with other Bedouin sheikhs, provided Abedi his trump card. Attracted by falcon hunting—as well as the wide open pleasures of Karachi—the Gulf-state Bedouins built palaces, hunting lodges, and homes in Pakistan. Increasingly Abedi and BCCI managed Zayed's holdings and business affairs in Pakistan, and soon Abedi was handing out the sheikh's money, guiding the generous Bedouin's magnificent philanthropies, and handling his local investments. It gave Abedi enormous clout in Pakistan and allowed him to play the intermediary for Arab loans and grants for Pakistan's military procurements. In Saudi Arabia and the Emirates, Abedi's manner was deferential, as was proper for a merchant, but in his own country he was emerging as the man with the Arabs in his pocket.

Even while Bhutto kept BCCI out of Pakistan, Abedi's fortunes there flourished. If some people wondered why, there was a very simple answer: Abedi was paying the prime minister millions of rupees under the table.

Bhutto was greasing his own skids for a slide out of power. His PPP had promised democracy, or at least elections, but Bhutto kept the country under military rule and relentlessly used his Federal Security Force to discourage political opposition. Corruption had been rampant throughout the bureaucracy during Bhutto's tenure, which offended the Pakistani middle class. His foreign and domestic policies drifted, and Pakistan's conservative Muslims no longer believed he was dedicated to placing the nation under Islamic law. As opposition mounted, Bhutto unexpectedly called for a national election to be held in March 1977, trying to catch his disorganized opponents unprepared. He won by such a comfortable margin that nobody believed it. There were mass demonstrations protesting what was perceived as government-orchestrated election fraud. The protests turned into riots, and Pakistan was once again riven by armed skirmishes in the streets.

Abedi's fortunes at home were about to improve decidedly. The army was called in to restore order, and when the dust had settled, General Zia ul-Haq, the army chief of staff, had deposed Bhutto. It was the country's third military coup. General Fazle Haq clapped Bhutto in prison to "protect him" while the army tried to figure out what to do with him.

Zia, who had received training in the United States, was known in Pakistan as a professional soldier with no strong political views. There is evidence that the other generals had to coax him into leading the coup. He was, however, a devout Muslim, and once in power he conceived it to be his duty to bring about a full-fledged Islamic state. He would maintain martial law for eight and a half years and hold the presidency in his strong grip for eleven years, until he was assassinated in 1988. His aggressive vision meshed perfectly with the plans of Agha Hasan Abedi, who quickly became a trusted confidant. This time Abedi would have no problem making himself, and his bank, indispensable. So indispensable that Pakistan would soon appear to be a subsidiary of BCCI.

One of the first signs that Abedi was back in the catbird seat came almost before the ink dried on Zia's appointment as chief administrator of martial law. Bhutto's plans to nationalize Attock Oil—the prize of Pakistan's small petroleum industry—were scrubbed, and Abedi was given the go-ahead to purchase 51 percent of the company from its British holders. Coveting the company, he had already purchased Pakistani-held shares. Typically, Abedi disguised his ownership by using KIFCO, his secretly controlled Kuwaiti investment company, and Ghaith Pharaon as his fronts for the purchases.

Banking licenses were no longer an insurmountable problem for Abedi. Zia had named Ghulam Ishaq Khan finance minister and would leave economic policy in his hands for the next ten years. Khan was one of Abedi's closest friends, and Abedi was soon back in the banking business in Pakistan. In early 1978 Abedi opened a gleaming BCCI office in Karachi.

The banker was on a roll. At the same time his bank's doors opened in Karachi, Abedi was finalizing his purchase of the National Bank of Georgia from Bert Lance—again using Pharaon as straw man—and was poised to take over Financial General Bank in Washington, D.C. Abedi's operations in America and Pakistan were intertwined from the beginning, and the connection would become crucial both to the earnings of vast profits and to Abedi's ability to turn aside criminal investigations.

By early fall 1978 Abedi opened bank branches in Lahore and Islamabad, and his choice of the young Nazir Chinoy, from the Bank of America's Lahore branch, to head them and to "devise marketing strategies to enhance the business of the bank in Pakistan"[7] illustrates another link in the shadow alliances he was forging in America. Abedi orchestrated a similar cross-fertilization move by directing Pharaon to fire the incumbent CEO of the National Bank of Georgia and replace him with Roy Carlson, the former head of Bank of America's Middle East operations. (Carlson had other valuable connections: After twenty years with Bank of America he had gone to work for one of Abedi's Iranian associates, Rahim Irvani, and Irvani's American partner, Richard Helms, the former director of the CIA and U.S. ambassador to Iran.)

Abedi already knew that he and the Bank of America were going to have to part company publicly. Under U.S. banking regulations his international bank couldn't take control of Financial General, a multistate bank holding company, while having another U.S. bank holding company as a major investor. There were other reasons on both sides for the coming public divorce of Abedi and Bank of America, but

neither envisioned actually parting company: They would live together without being married. Five of Bank of America's senior officers were either on BCCI's board of directors or helped to manage
Abedi's bank. For the next decade the two banks would move billions
of dollars a week through each other's international offices, and the
Bank of America would be an invaluable, if hidden, ally, since it would
continue to accept BCCI's letter-of-credit business after virtually no
other Western bank would touch it. Indeed, it can be argued that Bank
of America became the single most important financial institution
helping BCCI stay afloat. In the United States alone, Bank of America
transferred more than $1 billion a day for BCCI until the moment of
BCCI's global seizure in July 1991. And BofA was a key player in
Abedi's deposit-gathering scheme. According to Yakoob Wadalawallah, a former officer in BCCI's Los Angeles office, Abedi exhorted his
remote branches to pay high premiums for deposits, as much as 1
percent over the going market rate. But that, of course, put the
branches in the position of paying more for their deposits than they
were earning from them. Abedi's solution was to have officers like
Wadalawallah place those deposits in BCCI accounts at Bank of
America, where BCCI would compensate the branch for the high rate
that it was paying its own client. Thus Bank of America acted as a sort
of global vacuum cleaner, sucking up many BCCI branch deposits and
thereby providing the fuel Abedi needed to keep his Ponzi scheme
alive.

Meanwhile, a great deal of money was also routed through Bank of
America's Pakistan branches, perhaps one reason BofA hired a son of
General Zia in 1978. A shareholder's lawsuit against BofA alleges that
Zia's son was employed by BCCI, "even though he was completely
unqualified for the position," as a way of helping "BCCI bribe important Pakistani officials."[8] Bank of America spokesmen have dismissed
the allegation as outrageous. Still, in 1991 a bank spokesman told
Beaty that the last Bank of America office still handling large BCCI
transfers was the one in Karachi.[9] The spokesman denied allegations
of a BCCI insider that the electronic money flow between that branch
and BCCI's secretive Cayman Islands branch was so extensive that
the two offices were linked by ten dedicated telex lines. The favors
granted to Abedi were not a one-way affair. What was good for
Pakistan was also good for Abedi. He was building up a remarkable
latticework of favors done and favors owed, while adeptly disseminating the benefits coming back his way. As usual, Abedi's routes to
profits had little to do with commercial banking. His most effective ally

in Karachi became something called the protocol department, headed by his confidant Sani Ahmed. Ahmed had worked for Abedi at United Bank but by all accounts had little technical banking knowledge.

Abedi established the protocol department in 1975, while United Bank was still in business, to look after the needs of his wealthy clients who came from the Middle East to visit Pakistan. When BCCI opened its doors in Karachi in 1978, the protocol department was in place with a staff of more than one hundred and a $1.5-million budget. Sani Ahmed had a bigger staff than the bank itself. Ahmed built and looked after the Pakistan palaces and homes of royal families. He hired gardeners, cooks, and servants, and acted as tour guide and factotum to major depositors who came to hunt or to party. The protocol department kept more than one hundred limousines at the disposal of important guests.

Just as Ahmed hired hundreds of helpers to beat the bushes in advance of falconing expeditions, the protocol department was also responsible for sweeping the countryside in search of another kind of prey: very young girls for the entertainment of the sheikhs and Middle Eastern businessmen.

Begam Asghari Rahim, the wife of a Pakistani doctor, was in charge of rounding up the girls and bringing them to Karachi to be outfitted in proper clothes before being presented to the princely clients. Often she would shepherd more than fifty girls at a time through a department store, shopping for jewelry and dresses. This practice was so successful—far more effective than giving away microwave ovens or toasters—that the bank would spend as much as $100,000 on such an evening's entertainment. According to the Senate testimony of Nazir Chinoy, Madame Rahim would also "interview girls, women, and take them . . . to Abu Dhabi for a dancing show or arrange some singing shows." Throughout the Middle East, "dancing girls" and "singing girls" are euphemisms for prostitutes; Chinoy chose to be tactful before the TV cameras. Eventually, he said, Begam Rahim became interior decorator to the royal family of Abu Dhabi.

The protocol department continued to grow: By 1988 it employed nearly five hundred people and was prepared to supply benefits more exotic than the "young beauties from Lahore" Sami Masri mentioned in telling Beaty about the gifts dispensed to Senator John Tower.

According to Masri, the protocol officers directed by Sani Ahmed were also responsible for moving money to pay for illicit operations and for luring businessmen, military officers, and politicians into Abedi's web of intrigue through a combination of favors, money, blackmail, and intimidation. BCCI officers showed up at the most unusual, high-level places: They were there for Henry Kissinger's first secret mission to China; they accompanied Jimmy Carter on visits to both Pakistan and China.

Abedi had money to spare to underwrite the protocol department: In 1981 Ghulam Ishaq Khan granted BCCI a special tax-free status allowing Abedi to avoid tens of millions of dollars in taxes and to pour his huge Pakistan profits into one of his front companies and into Pakistan's atomic bomb project. When Abedi formed the BCCI Foundation in Pakistan in 1981, he named Khan chairman and announced that 85 to 90 percent of all the bank's profits would be donated to charity, a claim that greatly enhanced his reputation as a philanthropist.

Abedi made sure that his charitable contributions—for pilgrimages to Mecca, cancer research, leprosy hospitals, and a slum-renovation project—were highly publicized, and he gained a lasting reputation as a generous supporter of the poor. When BCCI's doors were closed by international regulators in July 1991, former Pakistani Prime Minister Ghulam Mustafa Jatoi defended Abedi as "an angel in the form of a human being." Jatoi didn't mention that an audit of BCCI Pakistan showed a long-overdue $1.6-million loan to Jatoi's family business. (Jatoi has said that any loans outstanding are adequately secured.) Another influential Pakistani who praised Abedi's humanitarianism was Jam Sadiq Ali, chief minister of Karachi's province of Sind, who recently vowed he would never permit Abedi's extradition. Ali didn't mention that Abedi had supported him through several years of exile in London.

Nor did Abedi ever mention that the BCC Foundation in Pakistan existed, as it did in many other countries, as a tax dodge, or that less than 10 percent of BCCI's declared $60 million in profits went to charity. Or that the foundation's investment in tax-free government bonds allowed it to earn more in interest than it gave away. Or that most of the money actually given to hospitals and slum projects came from the generous Sheikh Zayed.

Most of the millions that flowed through the foundation went to two uses: first, to investments—patently noncharitable—in a company called Attock Cement, owned by Abedi's associate and U.S. front man Ghaith Pharaon. The second beneficiary was something called the Ghulam Ishaq Khan Institute of Engineering Sciences and Technology. In 1983, for example, the foundation's investments in Attock were five times the amount donated to its fifty charitable causes[10], which included Jimmy Carter's Global 2000. And in 1987 the foundation's single largest donation, $10 million, went to the Khan Institute.

According to its brochures, the Ghulam Ishaq Khan Institute trains young scientists and engineers. The reality is a little more ominous, at least from a Western point of view. The director of the institute is Dr. Abdul Qadeer Khan, the man most closely linked with Pakistan's efforts to develop nuclear weapons. Khan, a German-trained metallurgist, once worked at a classified enrichment plant in the Netherlands, where he gained access to key plans. So important is he to the Pakistani national interest that even his whereabouts are considered a national secret.[11] Another foundation branch is the New and Emerging Sciences and Technology (NEST) Institute, chaired by Pakistan's leading nuclear physicist and the father of its nuclear program, I. H. Usmani.

It was little wonder that during the early 1980s Abedi believed he was on an American intelligence "watch list." During those years, he told associates, he was frequently harassed crossing borders and searched many times. Through the foundations it funded and controlled, BCCI was carrying out a key element of Pakistani national policy: shopping the world for nuclear technology and material. Bhutto himself had acknowledged the motives behind an attempt in the mid-1970s to purchase a French plutonium extraction plant. "All we needed," he wrote, "was the nuclear reprocessing plant."[12]

When the United States blocked the French sale, Pakistan began acquiring hardware and technology for a uranium enrichment plant. Virtually an entire uranium conversion plant was smuggled out of West Germany between 1977 and 1980 and set up in the Pakistani town of Dera Ghazi Khan. Critical equipment was brought in from Switzerland, as were engineering plans from China.

Abedi and BCCI were involved in much of this, most often as financier of export shipments of materials, which involved elaborate falsification of documents and phony letters of credit. In 1991 German authorities jailed retired Pakistani General Inam ul-Haq, whom U.S. authorities had sought since 1987 in connection with the purchase of nuclear-weapons-grade steel for Pakistan's bomb project. It came as no surprise to U.S. officials that Inam's financier was BCCI. The U.S. intelligence community had in fact been tracking the money behind those nuclear deals for years as part of a program to determine who was financing international terrorism. BCCI's role in prohibited nuclear technology deals for Pakistan, Iraq, Iran, and Libya was prominent in the reports delivered to the National Security Council at the

White House from 1981 on. The NSC official who analyzed those reports, Dr. Norman Bailey, had worked closely with Bill Casey, whose agency provided much of the information.

With his coffers in the Middle East and Africa flush with deposits generated by steeply rising oil prices, Abedi's most obvious contributions to Zia and to Pakistan came in the form of money. After five years under Bhutto—during which many of those in power enriched themselves rather than their nearly impoverished nation—Pakistan was facing a ragged balance sheet. By then Abedi was in a position to bail out Zia, the military government, and Pakistan's central bank. In that order.

The loans and phony central-bank deposits Abedi would make to the Zia government were critical. Pakistan was short of hard currency and was under World Bank pressure to devalue the rupee, so Zia had no way to prime the economy. The World Bank and the International Monetary Fund (IMF) were monitoring Pakistan's central bank closely and insisted that Pakistani banks could extend the government no further credit unless the country increased its U.S. dollar reserves. Zia's escape route was the hidden, and illegal, infusion of cash from Abedi, beginning in 1979.

The New York grand jury that indicted Abedi thirteen years later made this charge: "The BCCI Group, through defendants Abedi and Naqvi and others known and unknown to the grand jury, used a bank from the BCC Group to issue a $1-million loan to the government of Pakistan and aided and abetted officials of the government of Pakistan in not reporting the $1-million loan as required. Rather, the proceeds were falsely represented to the World Bank and the IMF as an increase in Pakistan's dollar reserves. This resulted in the IMF deferring the imposition of further restrictions and a threatened devaluation of the rupee."

In another 1979 dodge "to aid and abet government officials in Pakistan to evade other requirements of the World Bank and the IMF,"[13] Abedi used KIFCO to make a $100-million deposit in BCCI's Karachi branch. Then he transferred half of it to the Pakistani State Bank. It was a wonderfully cooked deal, especially since KIFCO got the $100 million for its "deposit" from a loan from BCCI's Cayman Islands division.

The central bank held the $50 million as part of its hard-currency reserve for three months—before returning it to Abedi—in order to fulfill a bargain it had struck with the IMF. The international regulators had agreed that if Pakistan increased its reserves by at least $50 million for ninety days, the State Bank could raise the lending limits for commercial banks. In turn Pakistan's central bank had agreed to increase by 50 percent the lending limits of any bank bringing in such a deposit (not a loan). Abedi, whose new Pakistani banks had been limited to $750,000 loans, needed the elbow room. According to the Senate testimony of Nazir Chinoy, Abedi eventually pumped enough phony deposits into Pakistan's central bank to raise BCCI's lending limits from $750,000 to $100 million.[14] In Western banking circles, $100 million isn't that much of an investment portfolio, but in Pakistan's economy Abedi had a very large stack of rupees to distribute.

The two examples cited here are those the Manhattan district attorney's office filed in its indictments of Abedi, his top officers, and the bank. But according to former BCCI officers, Abedi's bailouts of Pakistan's central bank were far more extensive. Muzaffar Ali Bukhari has described the "numerous times" when Pakistan's finance minister or central bank governor called him with pleas for help in averting a foreign-exchange crisis. On such occasions Bukhari would call Abedi, who would then transfer $100 million or $200 million from BCCI to the government's account, "charging full interest but never specifying a repayment schedule."[15]

Nineteen seventy-nine was a watershed year for Abedi. It was the year Zia finally hanged the troublesome Zulfikar Ali Bhutto, thereby clearing the way for Abedi's unimpeded access to the top of the Pakistani political establishment. The Middle East was about to ignite in war and revolution, and Abedi, and his bank, would become major—if hidden—players in an historical restructuring of power and alliances in the Islamic world. In January America's greatest non-Jewish ally in the Middle East, the shah, fled Iran, leaving his country to Ayatollah Ruhollah Khomeini and his Revolutionary Council. Later that spring the Camp David accords, fostered by President Carter to bring peace to the Middle East and luster to his faltering administration, fell apart as Saudi Arabia severed diplomatic ties with Egypt, joining the general Arab boycott of the Sadat regime. Crown Prince Fahd ibn Abdul-Aziz had decided that if the United States couldn't save the shah, it couldn't save Saudi Arabia from the fundamentalists either. In the aftermath of Camp David, Crown Prince Fahd concluded an agreement with General Zia to finance two battalions of Pakistani commandos to be on permanent standby in case of trouble in the Gulf.[16] In Iraq, Saddam Hussein seized power. And on November 4 the Iranian revolutionaries stormed the American embassy at Tehran and seized sixty-six hostages, an event that would ultimately remove Jimmy Carter from the White House and usher in Ronald Reagan.

In all of this, Agha Hasan Abedi's position was strengthened and his profits enhanced. In Iraq BCCI was immediately used to hide and manipulate the large sums Saddam Hussein was skimming from his nation's oil revenues. In Iran, where Abedi had been setting up alliances in anticipation of the shah's ouster, Attock Oil was in place to begin receiving oil from the revolutionary government. (According to a reliable BCCI source, Abedi and his Iranian associates had traveled to Washington to lobby at the highest level of the Carter administration for the United States to end its support of the shah. Beaty and Gwynne were never able to confirm this, but it is a matter of record that Abedi's associates included the first oil minister of the ayatollah's government, and that Attock Oil, operating out of a New York office, immediately began brokering Iranian oil after the shah's downfall.)

Abedi had been brokering arms for Pakistan (as well as for other embargoed nations, such as South Africa), but now a vastly larger marketplace beckoned: Quite suddenly, the Middle Eastern weapons business, which had been dominated by the United States and the Soviet Union, was thrown open to competition. The coming war between Iraq and Iran would accentuate this, since the United States, the Soviets, Israel, other Middle Eastern nations, and European powers would all find it in their cynical national interests to aid and abet both sides in the bloody war. Yet because they all had to keep their support clandestine, what better broker could they find than Abedi's bank, which worked so well in the shadows?

None of this, however, would affect the fortunes of BCCI as much as the events that boiled up on the other side of Pakistan's northwest border in December 1979. On Christmas Eve Soviet helicopters landed in Kabul, and the Afghanistan War began. Pakistan would be cast in the role of America's "frontline" state in the battle to contain communism.

The staging ground for the resistance movement within Pakistan was the North-West Frontier Province and neighboring Baluchistan, a rebellious territory that craved autonomy and had traditionally defied any central government control. The Pathan tribesmen and the Baluchis in the lawless frontier were under the nominal authority of Zia's friend Lt. General Fazle ul-Haq, commander of the famed Khyber Rifles. By 1983 about two million Afghans were camped along the Pakistan side of the border in hundreds of tent-and-mud-hut camps. The refugees, mostly women, children, and old men, subsisted on foodstuffs and clothes paid for by the American relief program. The aid passed through the hands of Pakistanis who demanded payment for ration coupons and identity papers. Corruption within the agency distributing the supplies was pandemic.

The border region became a vast base for the Jihad: the Mujahedin came there for arms, for training, for rest, and to settle their families in the refugee camps. Seven factious and ill-disciplined Mujahedin political parties—three of them Islamic moderates and four controlled by fundamentalists—were headquartered in the territorial capital of Peshawar, just twenty-five miles east of the Khyber Pass. Each party had its leader and commanders who competed for the American-supplied arms. Some of the commanders also competed to control opium poppy production in their regions as a means of paying for guns.

Poppy cultivation boomed in Afghanistan during the war years, as did Pakistan's own opium crop in the remote frontier area. Traditionally, opium had moved out of Afghanistan through Pakistan, Iran, Turkey, and India, but because of a drug crackdown in Turkey, the Islamic revolution in Iran, and the Soviet invasion of Afghanistan, virtually all west-flowing opium was being diverted through Pakistan. With the war as a cover, it also became profitable to process the opium into heroin before it began its journey, and hundreds of small laboratories sprang up on the frontier. Soon the Pakistani market was glutted with cheap narcotics, and drug barons penetrated the politically unstable and economically weak society. (In 1979 Pakistan's drug addiction rate was neglible; by 1992 addicts numbered at least 800,000.) By 1984 an estimated forty drug syndicates were flourishing, and Pakistan was the origin of 70 percent of the world's supply of high-grade heroin.

The guns-and-drugs trade in Pakistan, protected by army officers and businessmen close to Zia, was out of control. When in 1986 local authorities sought to close the Bara market, a bazaar on the edge of Karachi famous for open trafficking in weapons and narcotics, riots broke out, leaving 170 people dead and thousands more injured. The government had to send in troops to regain control of the area.

The lawlessness along the frontier worsened as secret police and paramilitary units from Afghanistan, seeking to discourage support for rebels, began bombing bazaars from Peshawar to Karachi. The terrorist campaign was carried out amid open warfare among competing drug gangs. Meanwhile, the U.S. arms supply line to the Afghan rebels, stretching seven hundred miles from the port of Karachi to Peshawar near the border, had become intertwined with the narcotics route from the tribal areas to ships waiting at Karachi.

The CIA sent the Inter-Services Intelligence agency enormous quantities of cash to keep things moving through Pakistan; the secret arms-procurement branch of the agency spent billions of taxpayers' dollars on guns, ammunition, and equipment for the Mujahedin, but the CIA officers in Islamabad could do nothing more than complain about the corruption and drug running that marred the operation. The CIA was responsible for obtaining the arms and ammo (until 1985 only Communist bloc weapons were purchased, to maintain the appearance that America was not involved), but once those were delivered to Karachi, it was the ISI's job to move the tons of equipment by truck and rail to ISI headquarters in Rawalpindi. It was a round-the-clock operation. The CIA money paid for hundreds of trucks that made their way, with Afghan drivers and Pakistani army guards, from Karachi to Rawalpindi loaded with arms and returned, all too often, loaded with drugs. This was possible because the supplies were moved in secrecy. The license plates were changed often on the trucks, which always appeared to be privately owned commercial vehicles. The drivers carried passes that gave them virtual immunity to police checks of any kind.

According to Sami Masri, the Black Network was employed, in part, to unload the incoming weapons shipments destined for the northern border and to facilitate the movement of narcotics back out of the port of Karachi. Private contractors in the two-way traffic, the thugs employed by BCCI provided muscle and guns to protect the operations.

The Herald, an English-language magazine published in Pakistan, once noted: "If you control the poppy fields, Karachi, and the road which links the two, you will be so rich you will control Pakistan." In its September 1985 issue, *The Herald* carried this eyewitness report: "The drug is carried in [trucks owned by the Pakistan army,] which come sealed from NWFP [North-West Frontier Province] and are never checked by the police. They come down from Peshawar to Pipri, Jungshahi, Jhimpir, where they deliver their cargo, sacks of grain, to government godowns. Some of these sacks contain packets of heroin. . . . This has been going on now for about three and a half years."

Masri spoke of BCCI cargo flights given air escort by the Pakistani air force and described operations involving the Pakistani army. Beaty and Gwynne learned they didn't have to rely on his word to conclude that the Pakistani military was involved in the black operations. There is little doubt that the army contained one or more major heroin syndicates. In two separate incidents in 1986, an army major and an air force officer were arrested while driving from Peshawar to Karachi. Each was carrying 220 kilos of heroin, which had a street value equal to twice the U.S. budget for the Afghanistan War. As reported by Lawrence Lifschultz in a groundbreaking 1988 article in *The Nation*, both officers escaped under "mystifying circumstances" before an investigation could be undertaken.

There were indications that Zia was involved. In 1984 Pakistani police, acting on a complaint from the Norwegian government, arrested one Hamid Hashain, who was suspected of managing the drug traffic from Pakistan to Norway. In his briefcase, officers found checkbooks and bank statements for accounts of General Zia, and Zia's wife and daughter. Hashain, a vice president of the state-controlled Habib Bank, handled Zia's personal finances and those of a number of military officers in Zia's inner circle.[17] Hashain eventually was convicted, but authorities in Pakistan and Norway have said that evidence leading beyond Hashain was covered up. Although Islamabad was crowded with U.S. agents from the DEA, narcotics-suppression officers from the State Department, and covert agents from the Defense Intelligence Agency and the CIA, the Americans were unable to break a single major narcotics case during the war years. Their police work and intelligence was top-notch, but Washington wasn't listening.

This, then, was the Karachi in which Abedi was building his most enduring power base. This was the state of affairs the United States had to ignore to maintain its supply lines through Pakistan and its crucial partnership with the Pakistani army. But it didn't bother CIA Director Bill Casey at all.

CHAPTER 13

MR. CASEY'S BANK

"I think at some point in time . . . I would say in 1984 . . . I think there was obviously an overt effort by our intelligence agency to, for lack of a better term, to co-opt Mr. Abedi and BCCI and, in effect, turn them into the bank of the CIA."

—T. BERTRAM LANCE
SENATE TESTIMONY, OCTOBER 28, 1991

"There was an impression in the bank that [Abedi] was being on a watch list [of U.S. intelligence agencies] . . . and he had a lot of ambivalence about expansion, travel to, doing business in the United States. . . . From mid-1985 his attitude changed completely. He was then freely coming. He decided about the expansion into California, Florida . . . the merger of First American and NBG, et cetera. . . . My own impression is that some deal had been struck somewhere."

—ABDUR SAKHIA
FORMER HEAD OF U.S. OPERATIONS FOR BCCI
SENATE TESTIMONY, OCTOBER 22, 1991

Some deal struck somewhere. Was this the reason for Abedi's otherwise inexplicable immunity from criminal and regulatory investigation in the United States? Or was he flourishing under the same kind of corrupt protective umbrella that he had fashioned in so many Third World countries? This was the puzzle that most fascinated Beaty and Gwynne: They had a flickering picture of the global criminal empire Abedi had built, but they weren't coming up with any answers about how he had managed to hold it together in the United States.

In other countries Abedi had bribed his way in, and certainly he had spent millions buying the favor that got him into the United States in the first place. But all of that—the favors, loans, jobs, charitable contributions, lucrative consulting and legal fees, and outright envelopes of cash—had gone to the Democrats who were then in power. Beaty and Gwynne had no reports, even from their most knowledgeable sources, of serious money being siphoned to individual Republicans. Yet it was the Reagan and Bush administrations that had extended de facto immunity to Abedi for so long. Several sources said Abedi began meeting with CIA Director Casey in 1984. Maybe Abedi had made a deal with the CIA, but that couldn't be the whole explanation.

Beaty and Gwynne debated this point endlessly. How and why Abedi got away with operating illegally in the United States had become the Gordian knot of their investigation.

"Look," Beaty told Gwynne in exasperation one day, "even if Abedi came over here and personally shook hands with Bill Casey on some private understanding, how much protection would that buy him? The CIA isn't omnipotent: We all know the agency has used national security arguments to persuade investigators, or maybe even a U.S. attorney here or there, not to pursue some weapons dealer on a particular transaction. . . . It isn't just weapons deals, the operative phrase is 'particular transaction.' Abedi was being given blanket coverage; he was dancing between the raindrops with lots of U.S. attorneys, the IRS, the DEA, the stuffy straight arrows at the Federal Reserve, Treasury. . . ."

Gwynne agreed. The pattern was clear. Whenever a police agency, local or federal, started looking into criminal activity involving BCCI, the reports were duly sent up the chain of command, but somewhere—way at the top of the heap—the reports were sent back down again, and the investigation was shelved.

"That's what I'm saying," Beaty went on. "The CIA just couldn't put out that many fires by itself. It's dicey for them to get involved in a domestic criminal case in the first place."

The reporters turned again to Condor, the only source they could count on for a coherent overview of U.S.–Middle East relations. But Condor seemed increasingly uneasy about the unfolding BCCI story. In the beginning he had been candid and had gone out of his way to help Beaty, calling others to find answers to some of the reporter's early questions when he didn't have an explanation or didn't want to give it himself. Part of it was friendship, but Beaty knew Condor also was using him to keep track of the progress of all the investigators.

As the weeks passed and the scandal spread, Condor's mood turned somber. From the beginning he had hinted that the answer to BCCI's success in the United States was bigger and more complicated than the reporters had envisioned.

In September Beaty and Gwynne visited Condor at his home outside of Washington. It was the first time Gwynne had met his partner's most closely held source, and as Beaty and the government man poured coffee and chatted, he wandered about the Nineteenth Century study and paused before a wall covered with framed photographs and testimonials. It was impressive, he thought. Lots of Washington biggies and would-be biggies had an autographed photo of the president, but here was this man smiling next to presidents and kings, and the testimonials were handwritten thank-you notes from . . . some very important people! He could see that Condor had held some significant government posts. In taking telephone messages for Beaty from Condor, Gwynne had decided some time ago that Condor was probably the only man in the world who could casually call his six-foot, 210-pound, fifty-five-year-old partner "Kid." Beaty could get his back up when he felt he was being patronized, but Gwynne could see now why he thought nothing of it when it came from Condor.

The three men talked for a long time. Beaty wanted to go over the Pakistani end of things from the beginning and had brought along a now-tattered copy of Ali Mirza's debriefing by the unidentified "former" CIA agent.

"Jonathan, you asked me once why nothing happened after the CIA sent that memo on BCCI—the one that said BCCI controlled First American Bank—over to Treasury in 1985, when Don Regan was secretary. Actually, it went over just as Regan was trading the Treasury spot to Jim Baker for his job as Reagan's chief of staff. . . .

"I told you this involved the White House. Where Abedi really got his strategic relationship with the U.S. was with the Reagan people. Abedi could buy his way into the Carter administration, but when the Republicans came in they had a different take on things. Reagan believed deeply that the Evil Empire could be made to collapse . . . but he had problems with Congress, which wouldn't permit or fund several parts of his USSR 'destabilizing programs,' really what the old man felt to be God's work. So Reagan and Casey turned to the outside for help. This was the Saudis' game when Congress cut off funding for the Contras. Prince Bandar sets up King Fahd's last state visit to see Reagan, and he tells the king, 'Our friend in the White House has a problem with the black tent.' "

Beaty, playing the good student, cut in to explain to Gwynne that in Saudi Arabia the women's tent is usually black colored, so the Saudis called Congress "the black tent" because of all the bickering and turmoil that Reagan got from the Congress on covert operations.

Condor shot Beaty a look: He had stolen his line. "Yes. So the Saudis began underwriting the Contras. It worked, and Casey began to use the outside—the Saudis, the Pakistanis, BCCI—to run what they couldn't get through Congress. Abedi had the kind of money to help."

The reporters were silent. Ali Khan had told them BCCI was helping run black ops for the CIA in Africa, Central America, and elsewhere, but it was quite something else to hear Condor say it. Casey had used the bank in operations he wasn't telling the oversight committees about. They also caught the nuance: Condor was subtly drawing a distinction between Casey and the CIA proper.

"It was common knowledge in the late '70s, certainly by 1980, that BCCI was criminal, but it was also the bank that, from a transactions point of view, did business with *all* the players in the Middle East. So what does the U.S. government do with this knowledge? You look at it and say, 'Do I really want to stop this?' No, you allow it to operate, and you study it and take information out of it. But next someone thinks, 'Why don't we use it?' BCCI was operating the way we did forty years ago, the way the OSS [Office of Strategic Services] guys used to operate. The way Casey wanted to operate in Afghanistan."

Condor ended the session graciously but firmly: "I told you that Karachi had a halo around it. People couldn't be touched. Go take a look. And do your homework on Bill Casey."

Beaty and Gwynne, busy with their thoughts, didn't talk a lot on the long drive back into Washington. Once again the story had sprouted new legs. They would have to have to track Abedi's activities in Pakistan during the 1980s and try to learn what was happening at the CIA during that period. If they understood Condor correctly, one mystery was cloaked in another. The government was turning away questions about its knowledge of Abedi's operations in Pakistan because, somehow, that was connected with wide-open drug trafficking to which the United States had turned a blind eye. That was an understandable reason for a reluctance to explain things, but beneath that there seemed to lie a bigger secret. If Abedi and Casey had struck a bargain, just what services had the CIA director purchased?

General Muhammad Zia ul-Haq was not a popular man in the United States. His bad press began with the overthrow of Bhutto and got worse as he began to enforce a new set of *shariat* (Koran-based) laws, imposing Islamic punishments—lashing, amputation, public hanging, and death by stoning—for crimes such as adultery, theft, and drinking. American newspapers carried photos of the army administering the punishments, and when Zia refused pleas for mercy and hanged Bhutto, his reputation took a further plunge. So when eighty thousand Soviet troops landed in Kabul to quell a brewing Afghan rebellion, there was little immediate reaction to Zia's request for American help guarding Pakistan's 1,200-mile border with Afghanistan. President Jimmy Carter was preoccupied with the Iranian hostage situation and still incensed that Zia had taken no action to keep Muslim fanatics from sacking the American embassy in Islamabad earlier that year.

When Carter offered a grudging $400-million aid package, Zia spurned it as "peanuts." If Pakistan was to become the chief bulwark against a Soviet menace to the subcontinent, Zia wanted the Pakistani military upgraded dramatically. He refused to tangle with the Soviets otherwise. The already poor U.S.-Pakistan relationship deteriorated further. Carter was not about to alarm India's new government under Prime Minister Indira Gandhi by providing Pakistan with attack air-craft and electronic surveillance systems. The rush of events, how-ever, dictated that the United States take some action. Hundreds of thousands of Afghan refugees—the first of three million to come—were crossing into Pakistan, and the border area was being trans-formed into a rear staging area and headquarters for the Mujahedin resistance forces.

The White House decided to go underground with aid to the rebels. Early in 1980 Carter signed a presidential "finding" on Afghanistan, a classified directive authorizing the CIA to aid the Afghan rebels in "harassment" of the Soviet occupying forces through secret supplies of light weapons and limited funds. Nothing further was envisioned, since the consensus at the Pentagon was that the Russians had arrived in such large force that they could not be dislodged by a resistance movement. Nor could the United States intervene directly: In real-politik, Afghanistan was a Soviet buffer state, and Moscow claimed that Kabul had requested its intercession. What was to be America's last Cold War battle would be fought in secret, though it would become the largest covert-action program since World War Two.

Carter envisioned a limited role for several reasons, not the least of which was a lack of faith in his own intelligence community. The CIA that director George Bush had turned over to Carter's appointee, Admiral Stansfield Turner, had been the subject of congressional inquiry and a source of scandal since Vietnam and Watergate. The investigations shed light on rogue agents, profiteering, plots to assassinate foreign leaders, and allegations of condoning drug trafficking, and of spying on Americans who opposed the Vietnam War. With Carter's approval, Turner had decimated the agency, eliminating the jobs of nearly 1,300 employees and operatives and drastically curtailing covert operations.

Thus the undertaking in Pakistan was planned as a hands-off operation for the CIA—day-by-day contact with the Mujahedin would be left to the Pakistani Inter-Services Intelligence agency. The United States could then deny any involvement. The CIA would supply the weapons and the money: weapons purchased from Third World countries so they would not appear to have come from America and untraceable cash money. Arrangements were also struck with China and Saudi Arabia. China agreed to sell the Mujahedin arms, and Saudi Arabia was to match U.S. financial contributions and send the funds through clandestine channels to the ISI. The accord with China—which viewed the Soviet muscle flexing with as much unease as did America—would be one of the most closely guarded secrets of a secret war. To be sure, General Zia wanted more than a trickle of aid for Pakistan itself, but he agreed completely on the need for secrecy. He was about to declare a Muslim holy war against the Soviets, and he could not afford to be seen in the Islamic world as a mere puppet of American interests.

Ronald Reagan saw the Afghanistan situation differently than Carter had: There were few shadows in the new president's black-and-white view of the Communist menace. He came into office with a natural sympathy for the fledgling Mujahedin resistance forces, whom he viewed, in his simple way, as brave freedom fighters. More important, the whole Middle East had erupted into a "Crescent of Crisis," as the phrase makers had it. Reagan and his advisers were convinced the Russian Bear had to be contained at every point, lest it increase its influence amid the shifting alliances. The CIA was already involved in Afghanistan, but the Reagan forces wanted a revamped, more aggressive CIA to confront both the Russians and the international terrorist organizations they were certain the Kremlin was supporting.

One of Reagan's early perceptions of the CIA he was about to inherit came to him from a French spy master with a reputation for ruthless efficiency. Late in 1980 the Count Alexandre de Marenches, director of France's Direction Générale de la Sécurité Extérieure

(DGSE), met privately with the president-elect in the Los Angeles home of Reagan's friend and adviser Alfred Bloomingdale.[1] The DGSE and its predecessor agency had fallen into ill repute—agents running drugs and guns and engaging in murder and kidnapping in the name of national security—but De Marenches was known to have curbed the worst excesses. And, like Reagan, he was an implacable anticommunist. The two men pored over maps of the world as they discussed Afghanistan and other countries where the Russians pressed for advantage. Before the meeting was over, the French intelligence director offered one piece of advice that Reagan didn't forget: "Don't trust the CIA. These are not serious people."[2] De Marenches disdained the CIA for its inability to keep a secret and for its universal practice of giving agents cover as diplomats in American embassies, which made them transparent to practically everyone.

The warning made a deep impression on Reagan, and in an oblique way, it led to William Casey's appointment as CIA director and head of all U.S. intelligence. The obvious choice for the director's spot was Admiral Bobby Inman, former head of Naval Intelligence and then director of the supersecret National Security Agency. Senator Barry Goldwater, then chairman of the Senate Intelligence Committee, argued strenuously for Inman, citing the respect congressional intelligence panels held for him. A consummate professional, Inman also had the backing of the intelligence community. But Reagan spurned Goldwater's pleas; he was determined to have an intelligence chief he knew and personally trusted. Casey, Reagan's sixty-seven-year-old campaign chairman, had served in the CIA's predecessor, the OSS, during World War Two, and he was going to be the man.

"Casey wanted to be secretary of state, but Nancy vetoed that," one highly placed U.S. intelligence source said, "so Reagan offered him the job of director of covert ops and, because he was embarrassed that Casey would take it as a slight, he told him that he would be free to run intelligence as he saw fit, without any interference."

That interpretation of events is still widely believed within the CIA, and if the politics behind Casey's appointment was slightly more complex, the simple version is close enough. The mumbling, corner-cutting multimillionaire may have been thirty-five years past his last brush with espionage, but the president trusted him. And while Casey was an unorthodox choice by anyone's standards, OSS alumni still formed the "old boy network" within American intelligence, and they gave him the nod for obvious reasons. Richard Nixon had banished director Richard Helms to be ambassador to Iran when Watergate became embarrassing, and Turner—openly scorned as ineffectual by National Security Adviser Zbigniew Brzezinski—never found a way to get Carter's ear. The agency was adrift, and only a director with real access to the president, a man the president trusted, could remake it. And Casey's reputation as a devious and secretive businessman who cut deals too sharply for comfort didn't work against him.

The cowboy-style covert operations that evolved out of that trust were not long in coming. One bizarre plan for undermining the Soviets in Afghanistan, hatched in the first days of the administration, illustrates the inclination to Hollywood solutions that entered the White House with Ronald Reagan. It also shows Casey's willingness to make end runs around the cautious bureaucrats at Langley.

It was Count de Marenches who proposed the highly unorthodox operation when he and Reagan met again soon after the inauguration, this time in the Oval Office. "What do you do with all the drugs seized by the DEA, the Coast Guard, the FBI, the Customs Service?" De Marenches asked the president.

The count, according to his published memoirs, suggested that the confiscated narcotics be put to use as bait for the Russian troops in Kabul. He said that addiction within the ranks would soon pressure the Soviets to leave Afghanistan to avoid their army's "moral and physical disintegration." He suggested that "Operation Mosquito" could be organized for $1 million and carried out by a few trusted people.

"This is great!" Reagan replied, according to De Marenches. "No one has ever told me anything like that." The president immediately placed a call to Casey, told him of the plan, and said he must talk with De Marenches about it. De Marenches met Casey at Langley two days later and made his pitch. "He loved it," the French spy master wrote in his memoirs. "A bear of a man, he leaped from the chair and sliced at the air with his fists."

Casey knew he would have serious problems explaining the idea to Congress, yet he "desperately wanted to do it," De Marenches wrote, and he asked if the French agency would carry out the program for him if the CIA provided the funds. De Marenches agreed, on the condition that no Americans would be directly involved.

According to De Marenches's account, the planning went forward and "Pakistani operatives and Afghan freedom fighters would be responsible for infiltrating the country with the contraband . . ." But just before the action was to begin, De Marenches became "worried about the growing number of Americans who had become aware of the operation" and flew to Washington to seek Casey's promise that, should the caper be exposed, his name would be kept out of the press. When Casey replied that he couldn't make such a guarantee, De Marenches says, the drugs-to-Afghanistan project was scrubbed.

Nonetheless, the Pakistani army, Abedi's bank, and—according to reliable sources—a few American intelligence operatives were deeply enmeshed in the drug trade before the rebel war ground to an end. Of course, sending the Soviet troops drugs seized from the vast American marketplace would have been hauling coal to Newcastle, since Afghanistan and Pakistan were already awash in heroin and hashish. De Marenches and Casey might have envisioned a flow of drugs into Afghanistan to destabilize the Soviets, but the final reality was that, under the cover of the war, heroin and hashish flowed out of Afghanistan and Pakistan, with little official interference, into the United States. During the war years kilogram-size bricks of hashish began appearing in the United States stamped with a distinctive seal: crossed AK-47 rifles encircled by the legend SMOKE THE SOVIETS OUT. And heroin addiction in the United States increased 50 percent in the years between 1982 and 1992, with the number of addicts rising from 500,000 to 750,000.

De Marenches, a very serious man, undoubtedly had his own reasons for revealing his vignette of a credulous American president, an amateur espionage chief, and a Pakistani military-intelligence arm that apparently saw nothing but advantage in narcotics trafficking. However, the tale also sheds light on Casey's immediate willingness to operate beyond the limits observed by the career professionals at Langley, and, secondly, Casey's inclination to go outside the agency to accomplish something the intelligence bureaucracy—or the congressional intelligence oversight committees—might deny him. Those proclivities would eventually lead Casey to to Agha Hasan Abedi, whose bank would perform any service for a client. Any service in any country, if the price was right.

The Reagan administration, less inclined than Carter to worry about offending India, had no problem accommodating Zia on military and economic aid. Zia played "the American card," and the administration promised to rearm Pakistan. In December 1981 Congress authorized $1.6 million in economic assistance and sales of Patton tanks, self-propelled Howitzers, and attack helicopters worth $1.5 billion. Saudi Arabia gave Pakistan the money to buy the hardware. The sweetener in the deal was Reagan's agreement to sell Pakistan forty F-16a jet fighters, one of the most sophisticated weapons in America's arsenal. Amid rumors that Pakistan was building an atomic bomb, Congress (and the State Department) balked at supplying advanced electronic fire-control and navigation systems for the fighters. But Reagan dug in his heels. In order to push the bill through, he declared an exemption to the Symington Amendment, which prohibited U.S. military sales to any country producing weapons-grade nuclear material.

Meanwhile, the president handed Casey the job of increasing clandestine weapons supplies to the Afghan resistance. Before it was over, the United States and Saudi Arabia would pump more than $4 billion into that pipeline. To understand the matrix that included Casey, Abedi, drugs, nuclear-weapons projects, and the emergence of BCCI's Black Network, one must understand something about the heart and mind of William Casey and how he pursued his covert wars against the Evil Empire. A central fact: Casey disliked and distrusted most of the professionals who manned the agencies over which he had been given control. He preferred end runs using his own ball carriers and had no compunction about stiffing the regular CIA apparatus. The question to be answered is not whether Casey made an alliance with Abedi and BCCI to further his goals in Pakistan, but when. The answer has a direct bearing on the larger question of how much the upper reaches of the Reagan and Bush administrations knew about BCCI's criminal activities and whether, under the rubric of national security considerations, both administrations sought to protect, rather than prosecute, the Bank of Credit and Commerce International.

There is one further question that has not previously been raised by any law enforcement agency probing the BCCI affair, yet it is one of considerable importance: Did Casey's hidden alignment with Abedi allow BCCI access to American military and technological secrets? Secrets that Abedi, or BCCI associates, either gave to potentially hostile nations or sold to the highest bidder? If the answer is yes, we have one more explanation for the reluctance to fully probe the affairs of BCCI in the United States.

Precisely when Abedi and Casey first met isn't known, but several sources have spoken of meetings in Washington between the two men that began in the latter part of 1983 or the beginning months of 1984. In February 1992, NBC News asserted that Casey, as CIA director, had met secretly with Abedi over a three-year period. The network said the meetings took place every few months at the Madison Hotel in Washington, and that Casey and Abedi discussed details of U.S.

arms deals with Iran and the arming of the Afghan resistance forces. Ira Silverman, the respected investigative journalist who produced the NBC report, had obtained his information from two sources: a former BCCI executive and an intelligence agent of a friendly foreign government. The latter source also told Silverman about a meeting in Hong Kong between Abedi and Robert Gates, who later became director of the CIA. The source said Casey was using Abedi's bank operation in China to monitor corruption at high government levels there.

John Moscow, of Morgenthau's office, and Jonathan Winer, of Senator Kerry's investigating committee, had also debriefed a former BCCI officer who talked of the Washington meetings between Casey and Abedi, but because of pledges of confidentiality, neither Silverman, nor Moscow, nor Winer was sure whether they had all talked to the same source. However, Beaty's and Gwynne's own separate sources also reported that Abedi, and occasionally Asaf Ali, the BCCI-connected weapons dealer, had visited Casey in Washington. The *Time* sources also said Casey had met with Ali in Pakistan, and that on another occasion Abedi and Asaf Ali accompanied General Zia on a trip to Washington, where they all met with Casey. Condor indicated that the CIA began using BCCI in the bank's earliest days, which was logical, since the bank was establishing itself in countries in which American intelligence had few assets, but that the cooperation escalated to a multifaceted relationship after the Soviet invasion of Afghanistan. It was a confluence of covert interests.

The CIA has repeatedly denied any links among the agency, Casey, and BCCI, but quite tellingly has left a back door open, as sort of a bolt hole to be used in case of further revelations.

The Kerry subcommittee, in its September 1992 report, neatly summed up the public testimony of Richard Kerr, then acting director of the agency:

"According to Kerr, critical to understanding the contacts between the CIA and BCCI were a number of things the CIA did not do. Kerr testified that, contrary to press reports, the CIA had not been involved with a BCCI 'black network' of thugs and assassins, had not been involved with or had knowledge of any use of BCCI for the sale of arms to Iran or the diversion of funds for the Nicaraguan Contras, had not violated any laws, had no relationship with BCCI's head, Agha Hasan Abedi, and had never placed Abedi on a watch list."

However, at the same time Kerr was making such categorical denials, the subcommittee staff was hearing a slightly different version from the working level of the agency. Said the subcommittee report:

"One possible explanation of the contradictory accounts, according to the CIA's legal department, is that Casey undertook actions in the foreign policy or intelligence sphere, while director of the CIA, outside its record-keeping and operations. The CIA's legal department has described such activity by Casey, including any role he had in the Iran-Contra affair, as being undertaken in his position as an adviser to the President, rather than his position as Director of Central Intelligence. In such cases, Casey would have taken actions which were outside the record-keeping of the CIA, undocumented, fully deniable, and effectively irretrievable."

How terribly convenient.

Condor once painted for Beaty a much more vivid verbal picture of Ronald Reagan's spy master and his technique of wearing different hats. He described Casey's infatuation with the cloak-and-dagger aspects of intelligence and his creation of a band of amateur spies that reported directly to him. Many of them were millionaire business acquaintances whom he dispatched on important missions—missions Casey would not entrust to the CIA in part because of the agency's reluctance to violate established rules of conduct, such as informing Congress of covert activities.

Condor described one such irregular, the man Casey frequently sent to Pakistan on special assignments, as an American patriot who fervently supported efforts to bring communism to its knees.

"When Casey came to the agency," Condor said, "he immediately realized he couldn't trust anyone, and he began to bring in his own operatives, his own cast of characters. 'The Hardy Boys,' we called them. It drove the agency people crazy. The Hardy Boys didn't have clearances, yet they had their own back door, so to speak, into Langley. They would ride upstairs in Casey's own elevator, and he would give them top-secret gadgets and send them off."

Then Condor made bubbling sounds, mimicking Casey poking at buttons and pulling wires on some electronic device.

"Casey never was very good at mechanical things. He'd poke at something like that and then thrust it out, and say, 'You make the damn thing work.' Some of these were very secret devices—and out the door they would go. Nobody knew what these guys were up to or exactly what they were supposed to be doing. They were mostly men his age, businessmen friends like Max Hugel and Bob Anderson, or old OSS cronies like John Shaheen. And there was Bruce Rappaport. You should be familiar with those names. Casey liked to meet the Hardy Boys in little out-of-the-way delis and greasy spoons. Or he would drive himself out to meet with them at night somewhere along the turnpike and give them their assignments."

The Hardy Boys were picked more for their loyalty to Casey than any proven abilities in the world of intelligence, and some of them got so tricky that they self-destructed. In 1987 Casey's friend Anderson, who had been secretary of the Treasury in the Eisenhower administration, was sentenced to prison for tax evasion and illegally operating an offshore bank. Hugel was an old business pal of Casey's who had made a fortune peddling Japanese-made typewriters and sewing machines; he had also helped in Reagan's presidential campaign. To the horror of almost everyone in the intelligence community, Casey had picked this five-foot-five, tough-talking entrepreneur from Brooklyn for the agency's most sensitive job: deputy director of operations. ("The KGB chiefs in Moscow will find it incredible . . ." wrote one CIA alumnus.) Hugel, however, didn't last long enough to make any mistakes: He resigned after being implicated in an illicit insider stock transaction involving his former company. Shaheen, a former navy captain who worked under Casey in the OSS, was perhaps the most professional of the lot. After the war Shaheen went into the oil business and stayed close to Casey.

Condor's view of the Hardy Boys wasn't all negative. "Casey knew the Arabs," he said. "He did a lot of deals in the Third World. He was a true international businessman, and he picked these guys because they all had done business overseas. They knew the ropes and could blend in, unlike some of the agency 'diplomats.' They were wealthy and spent their own money on operations. One of them once told me, 'I spent hundreds of thousands, but I never took a tax break.' They thought that Casey was saving the world for capitalism. But not all of them worked out so well."

It had been an interesting lecture, but Beaty wasn't sure why he had been reminded of all this. "So, was a Hardy Boy running things in Pakistan?" he asked.

"Not exactly. Casey did have a personal representative he sent out there, but I wasn't talking about Pakistan in particular. You just want to look around. Not everything is as it appears."

Until 1984 Casey had been content, as one former intelligence officer put it, to run the Afghanistan operation out of his hip pocket. The CIA's role had been limited to purchasing arms and shipping them as far as Karachi, as well as supplying money to Pakistan's Inter-Services Intelligence to keep the hardware flowing. Abedi had his fingers in the pie from the beginning, but the links are disguised by Casey's irregulars, who acted as cutouts.

Take the example of Rappaport, an Israeli-born Swiss businessman, who was a Hardy Boy archetype. He frequently played golf with Casey at the Deepdale Golf Club in New York's affluent Nassau County, one of Casey's favorite spots for meetings with his irregulars far away from the curious eyes at Langley.

Like the elusive Abedi, Rappaport appeared again and again just in the background of events. He was involved, for example, with the National Bank of Oman, which channeled millions of dollars supplied by the CIA and by Saudi Arabia to Pakistan for the Afghan freedom fighters. The Bank of Oman was a major affiliate of BCCI, which held a large chunk of its stock. According to the report of Senator John Kerry's subcommittee investigating BCCI, "There is substantial evidence that both BCCI and the CIA have played a major role in the foreign policy and economic affairs" of Oman. "The National Bank of Oman and its CEO, Qais-Al-Zawawi, also did business with CIA Director Casey's associate, Bruce Rappaport."

Rappaport and the Bank of Oman's managing director maintained key contacts with the Saudis, who were pumping money through the bank for the Afghan rebels, at Casey's request. Rappaport was evidently in charge of keeping officials in Oman happy with the situation: He once flew Zubin Mehta and the London Philharmonic Orchestra to Oman to give a private concert for the sultan and his royal court. Records also show that BCCI had made many multimillion-dollar loans to companies and government agencies in Oman, as well as to the Bank of Oman director and his business associates. The bottom line: Hundreds of millions of dollars in clandestine funds flowing to Afghanistan passed through Abedi's hands before they even got to Pakistan.

Rappaport's other activities on Casey's behalf sometimes touch BCCI, but it is difficult to pinpoint those connections, since they were designed to remain in the shadows. He allegedly controlled Swiss bank accounts that received $10 million that the sultan of Brunei secretively donated to the Contra forces at the request of Elliott Abrams, then under secretary of state for Latin American affairs. (Rappaport was investigated by the Iran-Contra special prosecutor for representing Casey in that transaction, but no charges were made.)

Rappaport had a close business relationship with BCCI shipping magnate Abbas Gokal, and he placed Alfred Hartman, the BCCI director who also headed BCCI's secretly held Swiss affiliate, Banque de Commerce et de Placements, on the board of directors of his own Intermaritime Bank of Geneva and New York. (Hartman was also on the board of the soon-to-be-notorious Banco Nazionale del Lavoro in Atlanta; the Georgia branch of the Rome-based bank had given Saddam Hussein hundreds of millions in "unapproved" loans for his military buildup, and the Bush administration has been accused of trying to stifle a criminal investigation of the bank. Much of the money that flowed out of BNL to Iraq passed through BCCI.) It was Rappaport who visited Bert Lance in 1984 and asked so many questions about Abedi that Lance concluded, as he later testified, that Casey planned to recruit Abedi for the CIA.

Investigators are also trying to discern a connection between another company, Tetra Tech, of Pasadena, California, whose operations in Oman were managed by a former CIA agent, James Critchfield,[3] and Tetra Finance, one of two Hong Kong banks created by Casey's friend and associate John Shaheen in 1981.

Shaheen, one of the primary Hardy Boys, founded his two Hong Kong banks within days of Casey's being named CIA director. Another founding director of Hong Kong Deposit and Guaranty and Tetra Finance: Ghanim al-Mazrui, Sheikh Zayed's longtime liege man. (Another founding director was Hassan Yassin, a former Saudi Arabian official who has been described as a close business associate of Kamal Adham and a confidant A. R. Khalil. Yassin, a cousin of arms broker Adnan Khashoggi, was named by Kamal Adham as the man who brought him into the First American Bank deal.)

Although there is no direct proof, it is likely that the two Hong Kong banks were part of Casey's earliest efforts to set up offshore banking mechanisms for covert activities. According to Senate investigators, the Hong Kong banks were mirror images of BCCI, and they "made use of the identical structures for doing business . . . including creating numerous holding companies, shell entities and nominee relationships and made use of back-to-back lending to hide the actual nature of financial arrangements and to inflate corporate books."[4]

The two banks collapsed after two years, causing several hundred million dollars in depositor losses. According to closed-door Senate testimony, Casey's friend Shaheen received a top intelligence medal from the CIA for his important services to the agency shortly after the banks failed.

However, even though the Hong Kong banks' activities remain shrouded in mystery, one thing is clear: They represent a 1981 link between Casey—through his much-used cutout man, Shaheen—and

BCCI in the person of one of its most powerful shareholders, Ghanim al-Mazrui.

Casey himself would soon move closer to the action, reducing the number of "unofficial" cutouts between the agency and operations in Afghanistan. In the fall of 1984, the Soviets deployed an additional 40,000 troops in Afghanistan, many of them close to the Pakistan border, for a total occupation force of 120,000. And the Soviets were increasingly bellicose about Pakistan's support of the Mujahedin: Soviet planes were crossing the border to bomb refugee camps. These moves reinforced intelligence reports that Moscow had decided to resolve the Afghanistan problem by escalating the conflict enough to crush the resistance. Casey and other leaders in the Reagan administration were determined to back up the rebels to match the Soviet moves. As far as Casey was concerned, Afghanistan was going to be the Soviet Union's Vietnam.

If the situation in Pakistan had been somewhat surreal before Casey stepped in, it would soon resemble a scene from *Apocalypse Now*. Way up the river. The tough, ragged Mujahedin warriors, who shouted *"Allah o Akbar!"* as they charged, were fighting a Holy War—a crusade against unbelievers. So were Ronald Reagan and Bill Casey. There would be much more money, more and better weapons, and an outpouring of under-the-table, out-of-congressional-sight military and intelligence aid to Pakistan. Some of the operations would be just as bizarre, dangerous, and illegal as Count de Marenches's aborted plan to smuggle American cocaine to the Soviet troops. And Casey's irregulars, Abedi included, would be in the middle of it all as the operations, and the players, spiraled out of Pakistan and Afghanistan, around the world, and into the United States.

The huge black C-141 Starlifter arrived in darkness, as it always did, after flying the ten thousand miles from Washington nonstop, refueled in midair by KC10 tankers, to touch down at Chaklala Air Base, a few miles from Islamabad. The forward section of the plane was furnished in luxury; the rear was crammed with sophisticated communications equipment, including the latest in electronic jamming devices to deflect any incoming missiles.

On this night in early 1984, as usual, the landing vicinity was cleared of Pakistani military personnel except for an outer-perimeter guard. Care was also taken that no American diplomatic officers or staff would be in the area: As usual, the U.S. ambassador had arranged a dinner at the embassy to distract attention.

As the plane rolled to a stop, a ground convoy drove out to meet the tall old man about to descend the steps. Pakistanis called him "Cyclone" in recognition of his anticommunist outbursts. It was William Casey, director of the U.S. Central Intelligence Agency, on one of his secretive visits to Pakistan.[5] He was there to kick things into high gear.

Brigadier General Mohammad Yousaf, head of the Afghan bureau of Pakistan's Inter-Services Intelligence and the man directing the Afghan resistance, stood at attention in the dark as Casey deplaned.

Yousaf, in his fascinating memoir *The Bear Trap*, described Casey as well as anybody has:

> He had little patience with politicians. He headed an agency with the fastest growing budget among all the executive branches of the U.S. government. In 1987 the CIA received funds totaling $30 billion, a 200 percent increase over 1980. With Reagan backing clandestine operations in Nicaragua and Angola as well as Afghanistan, Casey was on the crest of a wave. He was contemptuous of Congress's right to know what was happening in covert operations. He fought ferociously with the Senate Intelligence Committee, withholding information if he possibly could and reporting only sporadically. His ridicule of rules and regulations worked to our advantage. Once, when one of his staff tried to explain that the delay in our obtaining sniper rifles was due to some obscure edict classifying them as terrorist sabotage weapons, Casey yelled, "To hell with politicians, we're fighting a war!" It was good to have him on our side. Casey had a flair for innovation, for bright ideas, for the James Bond unorthodox approach.

Unorthodox indeed. On this particular visit to Pakistan, on the eve of the U.S. escalation of the battle in Afghanistan, Casey was full of ideas about carrying the war to the Soviets. The special sniper rifles Yousaf mentioned figured in Casey's plan to have the Mujahedin begin eliminating high-ranking Soviet military officers in Kabul, a plan that cut perilously close to the U.S. Senate's ban on CIA-sponsored assassination. Casey also envisioned Afghan raiding parties crossing the Soviet border to mount terrorist attacks.

In these schemes, as in many others, Casey was opposed by some of the professionals at Langley and others at high levels in the U.S. intelligence community who were correctly concerned about Kremlin reaction to American-backed attacks on Soviet soil. (In fact, the one minor incursion into Mother Russia that General Yousaf mounted provoked such fierce threats of retaliation that Casey was forced to back down.) The opposition only intensified Casey's determination to circumvent his own agency.

On the face of it, the covert Afghanistan supply operation was the nexus that drew Abedi and Casey closer together, and by all accounts their partnership flourished. Asaf Ali represented BCCI's weapons division, and the CIA was covertly purchasing hundreds of tons of weapons in unlikely parts of the world to support the Afghan resistance. Casey had every reason to know that BCCI was highly experienced in providing misleading letters of credit and other false documentation that would facilitate the purchase and shipment of arms around the world.

There is no doubt that Casey knew exactly with whom he was dealing: By 1984 the CIA had amassed considerable information on Agha Hasan Abedi and his bank. So had the White House. "We were aware by the early 1980s that BCCI was involved in drug-money transactions," said Norman Bailey, the onetime National Security Council official who monitored global money movements to track terrorist activities. "We were also aware that BCCI was involved with terrorists, technology transfers—including approved and unapproved transfers of U.S. technology to Soviet bloc countries—as well as weapons dealing, the manipulation of financial markets, and other activities." A primary source of the raw intelligence data flowing to Dr. Bailey at the NSC was the CIA.

For Abedi, stepped-up U.S. support in Pakistan and an understanding with the CIA director couldn't have come at a better time. By 1984 the price of oil had collapsed, along with OPEC. Oil revenues in the United Arab Emirates had fallen by 41 percent, and fifty-one banks in the Gulf region had failed. However, 1984 was a banner year for Abedi: He took over the Banco Mercantil in Colombia and launched major expansions in the United States and Latin America. It was the year he opened representative offices in Washington and Houston and his U.S. assets climbed to $4 billion. And he had the power to bail out Abu Dhabi: Zayed's crimped oil income had left his Private Department temporarily unable to meet the bills. Abedi moved in with cash and loans, and in the process BCCI became an integral part of the shiekh's Private Department.

It was probably not a coincidence that Sami Masri was recruited for the Black Network in 1984: BCCI was on a roll in Pakistan, taking bites of the Afghan and Pakistan support—amounting to hundreds of millions of dollars a year—at every step along the way. Hundreds of tons of arms and ammunition were pouring into Karachi, and BCCI's cadres controlled the port and dominated the Pakistan customs service through bribery and intimidation. Labor crews and heavily armed guards were needed, and BCCI provided them.

The CIA arms-supply effort had been corrupted early on, but it is not clear who, exactly, was benefiting. The Pakistani ISI blamed the CIA for either corruption or ineptitude, while the CIA officers in Islamabad countered with accusations that the Pakistani military was abetting the drug trade. Despite the vast funds the CIA was spending to buy the weapons, the Mujahedin often received rusted junk, such as 60,000 rifles and 100 million rounds of ammunition purchased in Turkey. The arms had been withdrawn from use by the Turkish army thirty years earlier and were virtually useless. Another shipment, of 30,000 82mm mortar bombs from Egypt, was found to be unusable because of age, and rifles—for which the CIA was paying top dollar—arrived rusted together. In one scam described by Mohammad Yousaf, an unnamed Pakistani "merchant" sold the CIA 30 million rounds of .303 rifle ammunition at a highly inflated price. The problem: The old ammo came from discarded stocks of the Pakistani army. To disguise its origin, it was loaded on a ship that sailed out of Karachi for a few days and then turned around and sailed back to Karachi to unload the ammunition for the CIA. Because all the rounds were stamped with an identifying POF (Pakistan Ordnance Factory) imprint, the ammunition was useless, especially in light of the elaborate efforts to avoid sending any weaponry into Afghanistan that would reveal the United States or Pakistan as the backers of the freedom fighters.

BCCI's heaviest involvement in the supply line, however, involved mules. The arms shipments were under the control of the Pakistan military from Karachi to the northern border, but once the munitions were unloaded at the frontier, the war materiel had to be transported hundreds of miles into Afghanistan on mule back. Private Pakistani contractors, many employed by BCCI, handled this end of the supply line.

Ali Khan described it this way: "The BCCI people were responsible for getting the guns into Afghanistan; they often crossed the border and often came under fire. Sometimes they would continue trekking across Afghanistan into Iran, where they would sell the American-purchased guns to the Iranians."

According to both Khan and Masri, the BCCI Black Network was also involved in obtaining and brokering military technology. The Americans were providing the ISI a treasure trove of satellite intelligence and, according to sources in Pakistan as well as within the U.S. State Department, considerable related hardware technology. Said one U.S. official in an interview with Beaty: "One of the basic mistakes we made was underestimating the intelligence of the Pakistanis. We gave them enough that they were able to make breakthroughs."

The situation had its hallucinogenic moments. In May 1984 Vice President Bush arrived in Islamabad to be welcomed with a nineteen-gun salute and greeted by Zia and a high-level military delegation. It was the first visit to Pakistan by a senior American official since Zia seized power in 1977. The vice president's appearance in public with Zia may have been intended to boost the general's image—since he was constrained to maintain martial law to keep himself in power—but Bush had serious matters to discuss privately. Details of the arms pipeline remained to be worked out, as well as Zia's request for $3.2 billion in further U.S. aid beyond the $2 billion for covert support of the Afghan resistance.

Bush was well informed of the situation in Pakistan: He had, of course, headed the CIA and kept close contact with the agency as vice president, and he now presided over the National Security Council and was involved in counterterrorist planning. However, in public Bush played his role as the slightly spaced-out American vice president in charge of his nation's drug interdiction efforts. At a banquet in Zia's honor Bush heaped praise on the general's antinarcotics program, declaring that drug control was a matter of "personal interest" to him and that Pakistan's efforts to control the drug trade were exemplary.[6] Presumably Bush was also informed enough to know that by this time Pakistan was distributing 70 percent of the world's supply of heroin.

Abedi was also benefiting from the sheer volume of cash and aid pouring into Pakistan. There was much more to it than the clandestine deposits the CIA placed in BCCI's banks to bankroll activities in Pakistan. BCCI was virtually a branch of Pakistan's central bank, and BCCI would provide letters of credit and bridge loans to the central bank in anticipation of American aid money.

It may never be known how far Abedi's deal with Casey extended, or how many U.S. intelligence operations were undertaken in cooperation with the BCCI Black Network. Masri's assertion that the Black Network performed such services as locating individuals for the agency was reasonable, given the bank's extraordinary reach throughout the Middle East and the Near East. His further assertion that the network assassinated people for the agency would seem absurd on the face of it, except for the fact that Casey believed assassination was a valuable tool and fretted that it was denied him by law. Soon after 241 U.S. marines were blown up in their Beirut barracks and Muslim extremists began taking American hostages, Casey reacted by ordering the CIA to train and support small units of foreign nationals in the Middle East to conduct "preemptive strikes."[7] These were to be, by any name, deniable assassination teams. In 1985 Casey once again tapped Saudi Ambassador Prince Bandar for help and received $3 million for the operations. (However, in March 1985 the Lebanese hit teams, hired to take out Hizbollah leader Sheikh Fadlallah, blundered and killed eighty innocent people and wounded two hundred others in an attempt to bomb Fadlallah. The idea of using Lebanese "counterterrorist" squads was hastily scuttled as everyone involved scrambled to cover their tracks.)

Nor will anyone be likely to learn—short of a full-press congressional investigation—how far Abedi's alliance with Casey, or the CIA, led to the leakage of U.S. military or technological secrets. It was the spring of 1992, more than a year after Beaty and Gwynne began their investigation of BCCI, when the reporters learned how concerned Condor was with this aspect of the BCCI scandal. In hindsight, they realized, this concern probably explained why Condor had occasionally guided them through some of the twists and turns of their probe.

Beaty, who had already given Condor a look at the photos of the Navstar technical manual secreted in the offices of the Soviet space agency, had arranged one more meeting to discuss what he had recently learned about BCCI's role as a broker of secrets.

But Condor had questions of his own. He wanted the reporter to tell him again, in detail, about Sami Masri's assertions of BCCI cash being transported from Karachi to BCCI's Washington, D.C., representative office. Masri had described how the bank moved some $90 million in cash in the mid-1980s.

"My sources have described the same thing," Condor said. "And my sources on this are very credible," he added dryly.

"It's believed that in one eighteen-month period, ninety-two million dollars found its way to Washington. Cash in those amounts obviously isn't needed for normal commercial purposes; if commercial transactions were involved, they simply would have wired the money. But that is also too much money for normal corruption purposes. That's far too much for any conceivable form of political bribery. I'm afraid I can only think of one commodity that would require outlays like that."

Beaty caught the point. "Espionage? Stolen secrets, stolen hardware?"

Condor frowned as he nodded. "Something like that. The key is to find out where that money went. You should be pushing on that."

Beaty snorted. His efforts to pry into possibly stolen secrets had taken him into a baffling arena of national security taboos and even threats. One knowledgeable *Time* stringer, a newspaper reporter hired part-time to help Beaty on the espionage project, had quit after his intelligence sources warned that Beaty's and Gwynne's probes into this subject were going to get them, and the newspaperman, killed.

"We've all been looking to see where that money went," Beaty said. "Everyone's first thought was that it was a bribery slush fund of some sort, but I don't think that even Morgenthau's people have gotten very far. BCCI's far too expert at passing money without a trail. I'll tell you if anyone finds anything, but you've got to do me a favor. I've really never asked you for anything before, but this is important."

Condor raised an eyebrow.

"I have to know how Abedi or BCCI came into possession of the Columbine Heads. How in the world could they get their hands on the fuel-air bomb trigger to sell it to Iraq and maybe give it to Pakistan? It's got to be one of our most closely guarded secrets. Was treason involved somewhere?"

Beaty paused and then asked quietly: "Or was it some sort of CIA deal, some sort of trade?"

The wrinkles around Condor's eyes deepened.

"Jonathan, I don't know. I don't think it was the agency, but I told you about the Hardy Boys. I'll check for you, but don't burn me on this."

It would be weeks before Beaty heard again from Condor.

PART FOUR

THE COVER-UP

CHAPTER 14

THE BIG SLEEP

"It's almost as if in the 1930s someone discovered bootlegging
in Chicago, and someone discovered bootlegging in New York,
and someone else discovered it in Los Angeles, and they all had
evidence that it was tied to one big Mob and they went to their
higher-ups, and the higher-ups said, 'Well, we don't have the
time to do that.'"

—REP. CHARLES SCHUMER (D-NEW YORK)
PRESS CONFERENCE ON BCCI, SEPTEMBER 5, 1991

Perhaps the most disturbing aspect of the BCCI affair in the United
States was the failure of U.S. government and federal law enforcement to move against the outlaw bank. Instead of swift retribution,
what took place over more than a decade was a cover-up of major,
alarming proportions, often orchestrated from the very highest levels
of government. When the Justice Department finally moved decisively
against BCCI in late 1991, it did so reluctantly, with both Robert
Morgenthau and the national press corps breathing down its neck.

The government knew a great deal about BCCI's criminality and
knew it from a wide variety of sources. Though the public did not hear
about its transgressions until later, BCCI had long been graven into
the annals of U.S. law enforcement, intelligence, national security,
and diplomacy. Authentic, unambiguous information about the bank's
money laundering, weapons dealing, nuclear proliferation, terrorist
accounts, and other crimes had reached the State Department, the
Justice Department, the Treasury, the CIA, and even the White
House's National Security Council years before. The detail of information was exceptional, the failure to follow up on it baffling. U.S. offi-

cialdom had known for years just exactly how bad the bank was, and even that it secretly owned First American Bank. "The government had enough information by the mid-1980s to put BCCI on the most-wanted list," wrote Representative Charles Schumer (D-New York), chairman of the House Judiciary Committee's Subcommittee on Crime and Criminal Justice, in his highly critical report of law enforcement's handling of allegations against BCCI. "It is clear that Federal authorities had scores of contacts concerning BCCI dating as far back as 1983."[1] The authorities offered no explanations other than the now-familiar and specious claim that the government had acted with dispatch once it had hard information.

What finally busted the logjam was not the government but the prodigious buildup of information on BCCI from sources outside federal law enforcement: from Morgenthau, from Blum, from Kerry's maverick subcommittee, from current and former BCCI employees around the world, from sources in the intelligence and weapons communities. All of this had been accumulating, like water behind a fragile dam, while complacent denials were issued in the centers of power. By the late summer and fall of 1991 the center could no longer hold.

One of the first of the high-level close encounters with BCCI took place in 1984. That year Senator Paula Hawkins of Florida traveled to Pakistan with a congressional delegation to visit General Zia. To the surprise of her compatriots, she brought up an unpleasant subject in her brief conversation with Pakistan's military dictator. She told him that she was concerned about a Pakistani bank that was laundering money out of the Cayman Islands. This was a critical time in the new U.S.-Pakistan alliance; billions of U.S. dollars were flowing into the country, and the last thing Zia wanted was to hear complaints from a U.S. senator about Pakistani skulduggery. After her departure, Zia ordered an investigation, which found that there were, in fact, no Pakistani banks in the Cayman Islands. His staff communicated this back to Hawkins's office in Washington. They were then told that the senator had been talking about BCCI. (Of course, BCCI was not a Pakistani bank.) According to Abdur Sakhia, Zia immediately called Abedi, "blew his top, and said, 'Look, you are spoiling our relationship with the U.S.' "[2] Abedi called Sakhia, then the top-ranking BCCI officer in the United States, and ordered him to Washington to placate Paula Hawkins.

Sakhia hustled to Washington from his office in Miami, met with Hawkins, assured her that BCCI was not laundering money out of the

Caymans, and pledged cooperation in finding the culprits. Hawkins ended the meeting abruptly, claiming an appointment with President Reagan, and told Sakhia to return two days later. The senator did not attend that meeting. Instead, Sakhia met with one member of her staff and three government officials: one from Justice, one from State, and one from the Drug Enforcement Administration. They told Sakhia that, to their knowledge, BCCI was not the subject of investigation. Sakhia protested. "Then you have, without telling us what we have done wrong," he said angrily, "already convicted us in the eyes of General Zia."[3]

The reply was simple and direct: "We will take care of it." That was the end of the meeting. Sakhia learned later that the Americans had kept their word. In the weeks that followed the meeting, the U.S. Department of State indeed formally advised the government of Pakistan that BCCI was not the subject of investigation. And thus ended one of the more bizarre subchapters in the BCCI story. This pattern of behavior was repeated many times during that decade: an immediate, logical, and apparently authentic show of concern followed by a rapid denial that there were any real problems at all. It seems likely that Hawkins heard about BCCI's money-laundering circus in the Cayman Islands from the CIA, though why she should have remains a mystery. According to Richard Kerr, the CIA first began producing and disseminating reports on BCCI's involvement in 1984. The net result was that the State Department silenced Hawkins, reassured Zia, and appeased Abedi. And the Justice Department and the Drug Enforcement Administration had been part of the arrangement. Sakhia heard nothing more about the "problem."

Still more disturbing was a report produced by the CIA in 1985. The CIA knew about some of BCCI's criminal activities as early as 1979. In 1983 the agency started distributing information to other government agencies, most prominently Treasury, Customs, Justice, the FBI, Commerce, the Drug Enforcement Administration, the National Security Agency, the Defense Intelligence Agency, the Federal Reserve Board, the State Department, and the Department of Energy (the last suggesting, among other things, that BCCI's role in nuclear weapons proliferation had been the subject of some of the studies.) In 1984, for example, four years before the Tampa indictments of the bank, the CIA was describing BCCI's money-laundering activities in detail to the Treasury Department.

By 1985 the agency had learned so much that it flatly told both the Department of the Treasury and the Department of Commerce that

BCCI secretly owned Clark Clifford's First American Bank. Treasury then informed the Office of the Comptroller of the Currency. Six years before the scandal broke, the nation's top financial enforcement officials—with the exception of the Fed—knew BCCI's deepest and darkest American secret, yet did nothing about it.

Even more intriguing than the report itself, however, was how that information traveled from the agency to Treasury, and what became of it. In January 1985 a CIA agent arrived at the 1500 Pennsylvania Avenue office of Douglas Mulholland, the intelligence liaison at the Treasury Department, with an unusual document. All CIA documents destined for Treasury officials, including Secretary Donald Regan, passed through Mulholland, who had been chosen by William Casey personally to be the CIA's main link with Treasury. That the document was hand-carried by a CIA agent was strange enough. Stranger still, the document Mulholland saw was printed on plain paper—there was no CIA letterhead, no evidence of its source. Mulholland said in Senate testimony that in all his years working in the intelligence community he had never seen an agency report delivered in such a format, which suggested that this was very hot stuff. The subject was BCCI.

Now, in Mulholland's own mind, events become almost comically distorted. In testimony he said that the document disappeared—vanished from the CIA's files. Neither Treasury, nor the CIA, nor Mulholland himself knew what happened to it. He also said that though he personally remembers the contents of the memo, the CIA has in effect classified his memory and he is not allowed to say what he remembers. Mulholland said he could not remember what he did after receiving the memo, even though this part of his memory was not classified by the CIA.

If this was not curious enough, there was yet another memo written by the same CIA agent who had carried the report to Mulholland, describing exactly what Mulholland did. This memo, which the CIA eventually declassified under pressure from Kerry, tells a remarkable tale. According to the second memo, which did not come to light until almost a year after the seizure of BCCI:

> CIA provided this foreign intelligence to the Treasury intelligence community representative [Mulholland] in January 1985, who reported to CIA that he carried it directly to the Secretary for his further disposition. The Treasury intelligence liaison officer also recommended only two persons in the Comptroller

hierarchy see this material, which he described as "dynamite." The liaison officer praised this information, promised to keep the Agency fully informed of Treasury's reaction to it, and provided follow-up collection requirements to the Agency. These included a request for examples of BCCI management encouraging the use of bribery. The Treasury liaison officer also requested the name of the Washington, D.C.–based bank holding company owned by BCCI and the names of any other U.S.-based companies controlled by BCCI.[4]

Mulholland, said the agent, was so impressed by the report that he had hand-carried it to Secretary of the Treasury Donald Regan. And he thought enough of it to ask for "follow-up," which meant that the material was so good that he wanted more. Mulholland not only gave it to Regan, but also sent it over to the deputy comptroller of the currency, Robert R. Bench. Mulholland could not remember that, either, but Bench did. He said that the information in the memo was sufficiently stunning that, even though the issues involved had virtually nothing to do with his job, which was to look after Third World debt, he "took a step." What that "step" was also remains classified.

The CIA memo landed with explosive force on the doorstep of Donald Regan and the U.S. Treasury. It precipitated an immediate response from both Mulholland and Bench, who sent the agent scurrying back to find more information. What happened next would become the trademark U.S. government response to BCCI in the years to come. Suddenly, and for no apparent reason, Treasury lost all interest in BCCI. The agent was mystified by the abrupt silence at Treasury. He visited Mulholland again four months later:

> In April 1985, Agency officers had a curiously unsatisfactory discussion with the Treasury intelligence liaison representative concerning BCCI activities reported earlier by the Agency. The Treasury official explained that the position of the Treasury enforcement offices was that the BCCI activities reported by the agency were not surprising and complemented the general picture Treasury had of BCCI. The Treasury officer stated that although his organization was interested in BCCI's activities to manipulate an international financial market and in the bank's buying into the U.S. along the lines of its acquisition of Financial General Bankshares, Treasury was not concerned enough to levy further collection requirements on the Agency. The Treasury intelligence liaison officer said that money laundering remained the major focus of Treasury's enforcement side.[5]

Something had happened over at Treasury to change everyone's mind about the "dynamite" information that had come into their possession four months before. Mulholland could not remember what that might have been, and Bench's memory on that point has been classified by the CIA. Someone had, in the intervening months, gotten to Regan and Mulholland, and the message had been unambiguous: Back off. Regan refused to be interviewed by Beaty in early 1992 on the grounds that his "memory about that sort of stuff isn't very good."[6] In an ironic last twist, Regan's aides referred Beaty to one Douglas Mulholland, who, as it happened, was by then in charge of State Department Intelligence under Secretary James Baker—the same State Department that professed to know nothing at all about BCCI in Beaty's and Gwynne's early queries.

The Mulholland memo was merely one of several hundred reports on the bank's activities generated between 1979 and 1991 by the agency's directorate of operations, which had even written far longer and more comprehensive reports where "information about the organization was tied into larger discussions of terrorism and counternarcotics."[7] In 1986 the CIA told the State Department in detail about BCCI's link with the terrorist organization of Abu Nidal in the form of multiple accounts at BCCI European branches[8]; in 1987 the CIA reported on BCCI's financing of illegal international weapons sales. Other reports told the FBI about BCCI's role in drug smuggling. In short, every governmental agency that had anything to do with the crimes BCCI had committed had been told about the bank in some manner.

After its involvement in the Paula Hawkins episode, the Justice Department continued to have contacts with BCCI. These were apparently independent of the frequent reports it was receiving from the CIA. In 1987 Abdur Sakhia was contacted by FBI agents who were following the trail of a weapons sale. This particular transaction was an integral part of the covert arms-for-hostages gambit in Iran that would become the centerpiece of the Iran-Contra scandal. The dealer was Adnan Khashoggi. The FBI said that to finance the deal, Khashoggi had received a large loan from BCCI's Monte Carlo office, for which he had paid a $100,000 bribe to a BCCI officer. The FBI said it wanted to see records from BCCI Monte Carlo. In exchange for that, it promised to keep BCCI out of the press.[9] Sakhia said he had "cooperated" with the FBI in the case, which never did surface in news coverage of the Iran-Contra affair. Thus as early as 1987 the investigative arm of the Justice Department knew in detail about BCCI's involvement with a weapons dealer and knew that BCCI had played a key role in Iran-Contra.

That same year the FBI, the U.S. attorney in Miami, and the Internal Revenue Service received a full-scale criminal referral from the Federal Reserve, whose May 1987 examination of BCCI's Miami office identified large-scale money laundering. As with the increasingly desperate attempts by James Dougherty, the Miami attorney for Lloyd's of London, to get the attention of law enforcement, there was no response from Justice. Indeed, even though the C-Chase investigation was in full cry by this time, Customs knew nothing about BCCI until an undercover agent stumbled into it in casual conversation. In 1988 the Fed made yet another criminal referral to Justice, this time about BCCI's New York office. Again, Justice did not follow up, even though, like so much of the other information Justice officials received and disregarded, this would have broadened the scope of the Tampa prosecution considerably.

Even the ballyhooed Tampa investigation was deeply compromised. From the earliest days of the Tampa probe, the actions of Justice officials were counterintuitive, counterlogical, and comprehensible only as either a massive, orchestrated attempt to bottle up damaging information or as one of the late Twentieth Century's great pieces of law enforcement bungling. Among thousands of other incriminating documents, investigators in Tampa were in possession of the tapes from the Ali Mirza debriefing conducted by Jack Blum in early 1989. Mirza had described BCCI's secret control of three American banks, bribes paid to politicians, and systematic attempts to fix a congressional investigation. And yet the same words that later prompted *Time* magazine to launch a no-holds-barred investigation of BCCI brought no response from Justice in Tampa. The case went forward as though the Mirza memo never existed. At the very least this was a dazzling display of incompetence; at its worst a Promethean conspiracy to obstruct justice, funded by taxpayers' money.

The Tampa investigation had been proclaimed as the greatest single takedown of drug smugglers and money launderers in history. Ninety people were arrested, among them eleven officers of BCCI. C-Chase netted not only the likes of Gerardo "Don Chepe" Moncada, one of the kingpins of the Medellín cartel, but scores of smaller smugglers who ran the infrastructure that facilitated shipment, sale, and payment for Colombian drugs sold in the United States. And of course the feds had gotten the bank alleged to be the biggest drug-money launderer in the world: BCCI. That is the way it looked to the public, anyway, when the sting took place in October 1988, carefully timed to coincide with a speech by Vice President (and presidential candidate) George Bush on the war against drugs. And that is the way it looked in 1990 when BCCI pleaded guilty and five of its executives went to jail.

But that was not how it looked to insiders. Among other oddities in the case, the BCCI officers were never treated as ordinary defendants, either by officials of the Justice Department in Florida, or by the bank itself, which insisted that these people represented an isolated instance of criminality in an otherwise pure and wholesome banking operation. As low-ranking offenders, one might have expected them to be thrown into a jail with other common criminals, as were the various Colombian operators who were arrested in the sting.

But this was not the case. By arrangement between the Department of Justice and BCCI's lawyers, the defendants were moved to comfortable condominiums in Tampa, paid for by the bank. By further arrangement, they were guarded in their seclusion by off-duty Tampa police officers. In their comfortable house arrest, all of their needs were provided for. Not only that, but Swaleh Naqvi, who was supposed to be furious that these men had sullied the bank's good name, instructed Clark Clifford and Robert Altman to hire one of the largest armadas of law firms and lawyers ever assembled to defend a handful of low-level crooks. They assembled fifty lawyers from twenty law firms to defend both the bank and the accused individuals. By the time of the trial in 1990, Clifford and Altman had doled out over $20 million in legal fees, paid for by a bank that had no capital at all and was rapidly hemorrhaging cash.

Why such an arrangement, and why such gargantuan legal fees to so many different lawyers? "You have to understand the circumstances," said Jack Blum, whose Senate investigation led him to probe the events that followed the C-Chase takedown in Tampa. "If you put these guys in jail, they get to know the other inmates, and they get to know the jailhouse lawyers. And they learn about things like plea bargains. Now these guys, they're Pakistanis, they know little or nothing about how these things work in the United States. If you keep them isolated, they'll never learn about a plea bargain. I think that was the purpose of the condominiums."[10]

It is incomprehensible, prima facie, that not a single defendant in the money-laundering case against BCCI sought to plea-bargain, nor did the high-priced attorneys make an obvious or an all-out effort to convince them to do so. Here was a bank for which drug-money laundering was, in the words of the Justice Department's own 1988 indictment, "corporate policy," of which the defendants were unquestionably well aware. (Later this notion was somehow buried and forgotten by the very same prosecutors who brought it forward in the first place.) Had the defendants turned state's evidence, undoubtedly they would have received greatly reduced sentences. As it was, five Pakistani bankers from BCCI Tampa received sentences of from three to twenty years in federal prison. For the two who got twenty years, their lives were destroyed. From the wailing that went up in the Tampa federal courtroom from the families of those convicted, and the screams in Urdu in the corridors, it was clear that none of them had bargained for this.

Yet that is what they got, and that is precisely what BCCI, working through its attorneys, wanted them to get. Naqvi's goal was to separate corporate BCCI from the defendants, to create the appearance that the criminality was sharply confined to one of the bank's branches. If Naqvi's public indignation at the indictment of his employees was remotely real, he would never have paid for their defense, nor for their opulent confinement in condominiums within walking distance of the federal courthouse. What he really wanted was to trade the convictions of five minor employees for the freedom of the larger entity. He got what he wanted.

He also wanted and needed something else: a legal deal that avoided a sweeping indictment that could have allowed the Justice Department to seize the bank's assets. This indictment, under the RICO statute, never happened, thanks in part to a massive lobbying campaign, orchestrated by Robert Altman, which employed some of the best legal talent in the United States and was targeted directly at Justice. To offer one example of the sort of muscle that was brought to bear, BCCI's attorneys met several times in Washington with the Justice Department's head of Crime and Racketeering to persuade Justice not to bring the RICO. These were not ordinary lawyers. The lobbying campaign in Washington was led by a firm, subcontracted from Altman, called Laxalt Washington Perito and Dubuc. ("Laxalt" is the former Republican senator from Nevada, Paul Laxalt.) The point men were former Justice Department officials E. Lawrence Barcella and Paul Perito. Barcella had made a national name as the spy-chasing U.S. attorney who caught and convicted rogue CIA agent Ed Wilson. Perito was also a former chief counsel and staff director for the House Select Committee on Crime. Even beyond the bank's guilty plea in January 1990, the attorneys continued to lobby. Senator John Kerry, outraged at the plea bargain, introduced a bill a week later that would allow the government to revoke the license of any bank whose officials had been convicted of money laundering. The so-called "death penalty bill" had frightened BCCI, and so the bank summoned the same group to lobby against it. Two days after Kerry introduced the legislation, Perito and Barcella met with Senator Dennis DeConcini to plead against the "death penalty" law on behalf of BCCI. After the meeting, Barcella wrote DeConcini thanking him, and included a "fact sheet" full of criticism of Kerry and his proposed law.[11]

Altman had made a point to hire former Justice Department officials to defend the bank in Florida and in Washington. He hired John Hume, who had spent most of his career as a top government prosecutor in Washington, to defend former BCCI officer Amjad Awan. And he hired Peter Romatowski, another big-name former Justice prosecutor from New York, to defend former BCCI Paris manager Nazir Chinoy. Circulating aggressively through Washington on behalf of BCCI were yet another former federal prosecutor, Larry Wechsler, top Washington lawyer Ray Banoun, former Senator John Culver, and Hill & Knowlton executive Frank Mankiewicz, a longtime Washington insider who had run George McGovern's presidential campaign. Large, politically powerful law firms like Holland & Knight in Miami and Morrison and Foerster in San Francisco were enlisted and paid handsomely for similar efforts to squelch criticism and allow the bank to stay open.

Though BCCI had retained a high-powered legal team to look after its interests in Washington, two of its most active lobbyists were Senator Orrin Hatch (R-Utah) and his aide Michael Pillsbury. Both made important approaches to Washington officials as part of BCCI's attempt to remove itself from further scrutiny following its plea of guilty to the charges in Tampa. In late 1989 Pillsbury and prominent BCCI shareholder Mohammed Hammoud visited Swaleh Naqvi in London to offer Hatch's help. This was an unusual team. Pillsbury was the former deputy under secretary for defense credited with initiating the effort to obtain Stinger missiles for the Afghan Mujahedin. Hammoud was a longtime acquaintance of Hatch who had purchased Clifford's and Altman's stock in the Naqvi-engineered deal that brought the two men millions in profits. After the plea bargain was announced, Pillsbury was able to arrange a meeting between Hatch and BCCI lawyer Ray Banoun, during which, Banoun told *The New York Times*, Hatch called a Justice Department official to lobby on behalf of BCCI.[12] The result of Hatch's contact with BCCI's lawyers was a speech drafted by Barcella, Wechsler, and Altman and delivered by Orrin Hatch on February 22, 1990, on the Senate floor. It was a ringing denunciation of Kerry and others who had criticized the Justice Department and the plea agreement. Soon thereafter, Hatch received a warm letter from Swaleh Naqvi, who through Altman had simultaneously recruited Holland & Knight in Miami, who cited Hatch's speech to pressure Florida banking authorities into allowing the bank to stay open. Two weeks after the speech Hatch called Naqvi again, this time to encourage him to make a $10-million loan to Hatch's friend and business partner Monzer Hourani, a Lebanese immigrant from Houston, Texas.

Pillsbury also proved quite useful. According to the final report issued by Kerry's subcommittee:

> In order to assist BCCI, Pillsbury met with Treasury Department, Justice Department, and other officials seeking to evaluate their attitudes toward BCCI and to find ways to help BCCI achieve a more favorable outcome in its trial. Memoranda from BCCI's lawyers state he was paid by Hammoud in this period and indicate that Pillsbury was seeking to use political influence on BCCI's behalf in Washington as a means of circumventing the decision-making process in Tampa by the local federal prosecutors.[13]

The "death penalty bill" that Kerry introduced never became law. A RICO case was never brought, prompting Charles Schumer to comment in his House subcommitee report, "Had charges been brought under the RICO act, BCCI may have faced the forfeiture of the operations of its subsidiaries the threat of such a penalty might have had a powerful effect on the terms of the plea agreement."[14] That, in part, was what BCCI got for its $20 million.

Other, inexplicable, events added to the scent of impropriety hanging over the BCCI investigation. There were sudden large withdrawals of cash by drug dealers immediately prior to the C-Chase sting. In the weeks before the bust, at least $10 million moved out of the bank, and daily movements of millions of dollars in deposits came to a halt. The day before the arrests were made, members of a Colombian drug ring moved $2 million from their account at BCCI Panama, closing their account, and agents for Medellín drug lord Gerardo "Don Chepe" Moncada removed another million. All of this suggested to government investigators that somehow the news of the upcoming arrests had been leaked.[15]

Panama was also the scene earlier that year of yet another strange piece of business. In spring 1988 subcommittee staffers were approached by an undercover informant. He said he had a box of documents on BCCI he was trying to remove from Panama. He said if he was caught smuggling them out, he would be killed. So he sealed them up and took them to the American embassy in Panama City, from where they were shipped in diplomatic pouch to the DEA office in Miami. When they arrived, the box had been opened, the contents removed. DEA pursued an internal investigation but found nothing, and no one was prosecuted.

Justice itself had radically curtailed its prosecution. In the words of Clark Clifford himself, in testimony before the House Banking Committee:

> We did look into the matter [of the Tampa indictment]. We learned a great deal about it. And what we learned about it was astounding, that the charge levelled against BCCI for laundering funds was confined only to the money that government agents, performing in a concealed capacity, were passing on through these particular employees. There was no proof of any laundering of any other drug money—just what the government had done for some two years in this planned and concerted action against BCCI.

Robert Altman articulated the same point:

> We were informed [by Justice] that this was an aberration and reflected an effort by a few employees down in Florida. That was not simply the position that we are presenting to you. That was the position of the prosecutors in open court, that this violated the policies of BCCI. . . . So we were hearing from the government that the transactions which were the subject of that indictment did not reflect the policy of BCCI.

So there were at least two leitmotifs operating here: the strange and inexplicable failure of Justice to push for a wider case, with evidence such as the Mirza tapes, and with clear knowledge from other sources that BCCI had been engaged in money laundering on a grander scale. Then, too, there was no doubt that BCCI's high-powered lobbyist-attorneys had tried hard to influence the outcome of the case, and little doubt that they had succeeded in accomplishing at least part of what they set out to do. But the pivotal question was whether Justice's own investigation had been tampered with, whether Justice officials were heeding something other than the call of their consciences—not to mention the letter of the law—when they prosecuted BCCI and its employees in Tampa.

Even the former U.S. attorney who originally brought the charges was critical. Robert "Mad Dog" Merkle, who had indicted BCCI in 1988 but was replaced by Robert Genzman before the plea bargain, said, "My feeling was that this was a beginning indictment, that law enforcement was going to look at this much more closely later on. The thought was that this would not be an end-all cure." Later, when as a private citizen he saw the terms of the plea bargain, Merkle said he was greatly upset. "I was shocked at the time," he said. "My initial reaction was that the plea agreement was too generous."[16]

There was also the problem of a peculiar addendum to the plea bargain, one that seemed to absolve the bank from further prosecution based on the documents and evidence introduced in the Tampa case. Michael Rubinstein, the assistant U.S. attorney in Tampa, stated categorically that this was not the case. He said that this applied only to the Middle District of Florida, and that it did not impede any other efforts to prosecute the bank.[17] Rubinstein's boss, Robert Genzman, reiterated the same position: "The plea agreement relates only to the U.S. attorney in Tampa. It does not bar any other prosecutor, state or federal, from prosecuting BCCI itself for any offense."[18] But Dexter Lehtinen, the U.S. attorney for the Southern District of Florida, flatly contradicted this. According to Lehtinen, he was told by the Justice Department in Washington that he could not bring an indictment on tax fraud against the bank because of "double jeopardy"—the bank's right, based on the plea agreement, not to be prosecuted twice for similar crimes, and the very thing Genzman and Rubinstein insisted would not pertain.[19] William von Raab, the former Customs commissioner who supervised C-Chase, put it more bluntly. "It was unbelievable," he said, "considering all of the loose ends and possible directions in which this could go, to agree to exempt from the prospective scope of any investigation or prosecution all of the information that was available or known to the U.S. attorney there."[20] Obviously, that information included the Mirza tapes.

What Rubinstein and Genzman had said was untrue. Or, if it was true from their perspective, it certainly was not true in terms of the actions of their superiors. There were more untruths to follow. Genzman also maintained that Justice had done its utmost not only to pursue the investigation but also to cooperate fully with banking authorities in Florida, who were actively considering taking away BCCI's license. This may, again, have been their understanding, but Main Justice again proved it a lie.

On February 13, 1990, just weeks after the plea bargain, and following immediately upon the decision by Florida Banking Commissioner Gerald Lewis to close BCCI's branches, Charles Saphos, chief of Justice's Criminal Division Narcotics section, wrote Lewis pleading him to let the bank stay open. Saphos began his letter by reminding Lewis that "BCCI agreed to cooperate with law enforcement authorities in the conduct of certain investigations. That cooperation has already begun." He also added an odd request: "There may be customer accounts at BCCI which the Dept. of Justice would like to open or maintain. We are therefore requesting that BCCI be permitted to operate in your jurisdiction."[21]

On February 14 an apparently mystified Lewis wrote back and reminded Saphos that a felony had been committed, adding, "In making my decision on the renewal, I must consider the fact that Section 663.06(2), Florida Statutes, requires the licensee to have complied with all requirements of the law." He then offered to meet with Saphos. "Your letter indicates that you may have information I should consider in resolving this matter. To this end, I invite you or any other appropriate Justice officials to meet with me in Tallahassee on February 19, 1990 . . ."[22]

To which Saphos replied immediately, using extremely careful language that seemed to anticipate further scrutiny:

> I must apologize if there was ambiguity in my letter of February 13, 1990, which led to a belief on your part that the Department of Justice wished to influence your decision on whether to permit BCCI to retain its license. The Department of Justice is *not* requesting that you permit BCCI to be licensed. The Department of Justice takes no position in that regard. The sole purpose of my letter was to indicate that, if you allow BCCI to continue in business, there may be occasions where the Department of Justice may request BCCI, pursuant to its obligations under the plea agreement, to make or continue a banking relationship with customers who are the subjects of criminal investigations.[23]

Saphos had written to others as well. He sent letters identical to his first letter to Gerald Lewis to the banking commissioners in New York and Florida. He did so after meeting in Washington with the same ex–Justice Department attorneys for BCCI. Mysteriously, copies of those letters were sent to those attorneys but not to the U.S. attorney in Tampa, Robert Genzman, and the subsequent clarifying letter sent to Lewis was never sent to the New York or California commissioners.

In spite of the play given the BCCI indictments, there is little evidence that Justice wanted to pursue the case beyond the narrow definition of a small money-laundering operation. Jim Dougherty, who had stumbled into the bank in his pursuit of Munther Bilbeisi, made repeated approaches to Justice in Florida, without effect. "They never did anything," said Dougherty. "In 1989 and 1990 we already knew about how Bilbeisi worked with BCCI in Boca Raton. We knew about the bank's role in coffee smuggling and weapons dealing and the payment of bribes to the Guatemalans. But we needed documents, and we believe that somebody in law enforcement ought to be looking into a $200-million coffee-smuggling and weapons scam. Not only are they not interested in doing anything about the smuggling, but they refuse to let us see any documents at all. They're sitting on a huge pile of them."

Dougherty saved an extraordinary catalog of letters he had written to law enforcement officials. It went on for pages and pages.

"We wrote our first letter to Customs in September 1989, asking for records. No response. We wrote to the U.S. attorneys in Miami and Tampa later in the fall. No response. In April 1990, when BCCI is about to be shut down, with most of their records shipped out of the country or destroyed, we wrote to the assistant U.S. attorney in Tampa, begging for a meeting. No response. I've never seen anything like it."

The only response he received was from the Criminal Investigation Unit of the IRS—which eventually resulted in the indictment of Bilbeisi on tax charges the day before the statute of limitations on tax evasion ran out but well after the similar statute on smuggling and weapons sales had expired. "I don't know why they did it," he says. "Here was Lloyd's of London offering to open up a whole new front for them. All we wanted was a little cooperation."

That is the backdrop, more or less, against which the aberrant behavior of the Justice Department in 1991 would play out. In 1989 and 1990 there had been considerable love lost between the investigations of Morgenthau and Kerry on one hand, and of Justice on the other. The most bitter points of contention had been the Mirza tapes and the warehouse full of BCCI documents seized from the bank's offices in Florida. Justice had denied the existence of the Mirza tapes and had refused to produce documents.

In 1991 relations worsened, and the debate soon went public, first in *Time* magazine, and then in the May Senate hearing in which Robert Morgenthau was openly critical of the pointed lack of cooperation from the Justice Department. As the summer progressed, the state of investigatory affairs deteriorated still further. By early fall Morgenthau was accusing Justice of instructing witnesses not to cooperate with his investigation. Kerry went public on several occasions with his complaints about Justice, which had been tenaciously blocking his attempts to depose Robert Mazur, the dissident Customs agent and key operative in C-Chase who had resigned in disgust over the handling of the investigation. Justice had also, in its early attempts to "cooperate" with Kerry, produced a series of documents pertaining to the Tampa prosecution. Many of the "documents" were redacted to the point of absurdity: memoranda with every word blocked out except the subject and date, other documents with all trace of subject, date, and author blocked out, leaving only a few paragraphs of disjointed text.

Meanwhile, the head of Justice's criminal division, Robert Mueller, whom Beaty had debated on *Nightline*, continued to insist that the investigations were moving forward. There were grand juries sitting in Washington, D.C., Atlanta, Miami, and Tampa. Justice, Mueller maintained, was pursuing BCCI with utmost diligence. But as time went by, these claims rang less and less true. By mid-August Morgenthau's office had already indicted Abedi, Naqvi, and BCCI. Kerry's open hearings had begun in early August. And as it turned out, Justice had a mere handful of FBI agents assigned to its Washington investigation—the one that was probing the roles of Clark Clifford and Robert Altman.

In the early fall the façade of law enforcement began to crack. Dissidents began to come forward. Kerry received a detailed letter from a U.S. Customs officer complaining that "tons of documents were not reviewed . . . and the CIA put a halt to certain investigative leads" in the Tampa case. "We had drug traffickers, money launderers, foreign government involvement, Noriega, and allegations of payoffs by BCCI to U.S. government political figures. I will not elaborate on who these U.S. government figures were alleged to be, but I can advise you that you don't have all the documents. Some were destroyed or misplaced."[24]

And Justice officials in the field, embittered by their treatment at the hands of Main Justice, now came forward. Several federal attorneys, in fact, said that they were told by Justice Department officials that BCCI was a "political" case and that prosecutorial and investigative decisions must be made in Washington. "We are constantly flabbergasted," said one, who was certain he would lose his job if he did not remain anonymous, "that the Justice Department says we should go forward and yet we never get the permission from Washington." Others complained that applications to subpoena witnesses, suspects, and records had backed up in Washington.

Perhaps the best example of this is the story of Dexter Lehtinen, the U.S. attorney for the Southern District of Florida. Although James Dougherty and his client, Lloyd's of London, had been bitterly frustrated by the failure of justice in Miami and Tampa to cooperate with them, and the apparent utter lack of interest in the documents and information they had gathered, Lehtinen did in fact try, against considerable opposition from Main Justice, to bring a case against BCCI. By late 1990 Lehtinen's office began to move aggressively on a tax case against the bank, issuing subpoenas to BCCI for production of records. Unlike the Tampa investigation, Lehtinen believed that the conspiracy to defraud reached far beyond the confines of BCCI's Florida offices. And so he had issued subpoenas to BCCI branches in ten countries. The problem was that BCCI was not cooperating, not responding to the subpoenas. BCCI claimed, among other things, that it could not produce documents that were in foreign jurisdictions. "We learned in the course of the investigation . . . that BCCI's legal counsel directed BCCI officials not to honor U.S. Senate subpoenas." And now BCCI was evading subpoenas from Justice in Florida. Now, although a subpoena carries with it the full force of the law, it cannot be enforced without a specific court order compelling compliance. In early 1991 Lehtinen wrote a series of letters to Main Justice in Washington.

"Our letters did argue to the Justice Department that Senate subpoenas were being evaded. They argued that the bank was evading its subpoenas, that it had destroyed records in New York, that it was hiding records, that one official had had his records purged, and that they were doing everything to evade, and that they were going to leave the country, and that it was our belief that they were going to leave and take the records."[25] What Lehtinen said he needed, and fast, was enforcement action for the subpoenas to ten foreign countries.

What he got instead was permission to enforce subpoenas only for

Panama and the United Arab Emirates, and he got that only very slowly. Limited though his access to documents was, Lehtinen pressed forward. By August 22 he was ready to bring a tax indictment against BCCI. But when he queried Main Justice officials, he got a strange response in the form of a letter. "Our review of the case," wrote the Justice official, "has revealed that although this case appears to be a potentially viable prosecution, considerable additional work is necessary to bring a prosecution that is legally and factually supportable." The truth of that particular question may have been academic, but the next point was not. The letter went on to say, in effect, that Lehtinen had never done an authorized tax grand jury investigation. This was simply not true. The case had been well known inside Justice, and Lehtinen's investigators had been in frequent contact with Justice's tax division.

Although it did not quash Lehtinen's investigation, the machinations of Main Justice had a chilling, delaying effect. After clarifying his position in another series of communications, Lehtinen bounced back. In mid-September he again informed Main Justice that he wanted to indict BCCI. But now he was told, in direct contradiction to the claims made by Genzman and others, that he could not bring tax charges at all against BCCI because of "double jeopardy." He was told that, even though his investigation had been running more than a year, the plea agreement in Tampa precluded him from indicting BCCI, not only in Florida but in the rest of the world. Blocked again, Lehtinen was finally forced into submission. The indictments he eventually brought were narrowly focused and buried within the large indictments of the bank issued by Robert Morgenthau and the Justice Department on December 19, 1991. Lehtinen's indictment was not even mentioned in the large press conferences held in New York and Washington. If, as Lehtinen forcefully maintains, documents were being hidden and destroyed by BCCI, the net effect of the actions of Main Justice was to buy BCCI many months in which to do so.

The Kerry subcommittee's relations with the CIA were nearly as bad as they had been with Justice, and for the same reasons: Both agencies had known for years about BCCI and were hard-pressed to explain why nothing had been done. After Kerry badgered the agency for several months for a briefing on its relationship with BCCI, the CIA finally agreed to a meeting. The problem was that the person sent to speak with Kerry staff members Jonathan Winer and David McKean was a junior officer. "The guy they sent to brief us was a joke," said

Winer. "He didn't even know who Kamal Adham was. He didn't know anything about accounts with BCCI. He didn't know anything about BCCI. He didn't even seem to know why we were there." Winer said that after the meeting he and McKean had encountered another CIA briefer, who, noting their expressions, said, "You look like you guys just got screwed."

Winer's response: "No, you guys just screwed yourselves."

Meanwhile, Kerry continued to press CIA Director William Webster for CIA reports on BCCI. Finally, on July 23 came the first break. Webster admitted in a letter to Kerry the existence of two documents, both of which he described as "extremely sensitive." When Kerry reviewed them privately, he was astonished to find that one of them, dated 1986, reported that BCCI secretly owned First American (the Mulholland memo would not turn up until several months later). He obtained permission to declassify it and showed it to Virgil Mattingly at the Fed, who, according to Kerry staffers, "expressed shock that the CIA, Treasury, State Department, and Office of the Comptroller of the Currency had possessed this information in 1986 and never provided it to the Federal Reserve." The CIA itself finally went public when Acting Director Richard Kerr announced at the National Press Club on August 2, before an uncritical audience of high-school students who were not allowed to ask questions, that the CIA did have some normal operational accounts with BCCI.

Winer's comment that the CIA had "screwed" themselves was not far from the truth, as it would soon happen. John Kerry is nothing if not persistent, and he was most dangerous to his adversaries on the BCCI case when he believed he had been slighted or taken lightly. About this time George Bush nominated Robert Gates for director of the CIA. That nomination had been thrown into question in July when Alan Fiers, former head of the CIA's Latin American task force, had pleaded guilty to two counts of lying to Congress about when high-level officials at the CIA first learned about the illegal diversion of funds to the Nicaraguan rebel forces. This raised new questions about what Gates himself, who had been deputy director under William Casey, knew about the Iran-Contra affair. With the nomination of Gates—whose confirmation the Republican administration passionately wanted—under fire, Kerry saw his opportunity. He told the CIA that unless he got cooperation, the Gates nomination would be put on hold permanently. (Under the Senate's arcane procedural rules, a single U.S. senator with grave objections to a nomination can in fact hold it up indefinitely.) Okay, replied the CIA, we'll give you another briefing, a better one. No, said Kerry. He would be satisfied with nothing less than the public testimony of Richard Kerr. And so Kerr, greatly against his will, was brought before Kerry's subcommittee in October 1991, where he admitted both that the CIA had known for years about BCCI and that it had maintained accounts there.

Yet another story—this one from inside the Office of the Comptroller of the Currency—showed again just how much had been covered up by the government. One of the more striking parts of the Mulholland-CIA story was that the CIA's information on BCCI's secret ownership of First American had been given directly to the second-ranking officer of the Comptroller of the Currency, Robert R. Bench. This meant that in 1985 it had reached what was, along with the Federal Reserve, the very core of banking regulation in the United States. Yet this was not the first time the OCC had heard about BCCI, nor was it the first time Bench had seen a detailed report on the bank. And here, again, is a tale of documents that disappeared and were later covered up and fiercely guarded against outside inquiries.

In early 1978 Joseph Vaez, a bank examiner with the OCC, was sent out with a team of auditors to look at the books of what was then the largest bank in the world: Bank of America. The man who sent him out, and who later received his report, was Robert R. Bench. Vaez's assignment was to evaluate the bank's six-year-old investment in 30 percent of the shares of the Bank of Credit and Commerce International. The memo he wrote to his superiors was the regulators' first objective glimpse into the world's fastest-growing multinational bank—into what Agha Hasan Abedi and his cohorts had really been up to in the middle 1970s. Writing in the determinate, phlegmatic language of bank examiners, Vaez rolled out a description of a bank that was—even by the go-go standards of those years, when the sudden crush of petrodollar deposits and Third World lending were straining bank balance sheets around the world—dangerously out of control.

The Vaez memorandum provided the OCC with a horrifically detailed summary of the bank that within a decade would boast a huge presence in the United States. What happened at the OCC? When Senate investigators later probed the question, the OCC claimed that it had "lost" that memo. Then, when Vaez graciously agreed in 1990 to send the OCC a copy from his own files, the OCC refused to let the investigators have it. It came to light only after the force majeure of a congressional subpoena. The weird odyssey of Vaez's report was the first of many, many instances of reports of BCCI's activities that were unaccountably buried by U.S. authorities.

The man who directly received that report, Vaez's supervisor Robert R. Bench, later became a partner at Price Waterhouse. By a curious coincidence—one of many in the BCCI saga—it was Bench who in 1989 was assigned to supervise Price Waterhouse's client relationship with BCCI in the United States, and to help the bank "comply" with U.S. banking rules in the wake of the Tampa indictments.

In spite of the specificity of the case against the Justice Department, the State Department, and the CIA, it would be unfair to single them out as the only U.S. governmental agencies that knew much and did little. The Drug Enforcement Administration not only sat in on the Sakhia meeting but had 125 cases in its files mostly linking BCCI with undercover storefront money-laundering operations. According to the Schumer report, "DEA agents in storefronts all over the country knew, as a matter of course, that BCCI is the place to launder drug money."[26] The report also argues that the most shocking failure to follow up occurred at the Internal Revenue Service. "Most startling is the IRS refusal to begin an undercover investigation of BCCI despite persistent requests by Criminal Investigation Division personnel," said the report.[27] According to Schumer, the IRS had identified fifteen major matters involving BCCI between 1984 and 1991, including:

- In 1986 India gave the IRS documents showing a multimillion-dollar laundering scheme involving BCCI in a number of countries. No follow-up.
- In 1987 the IRS received a criminal referral from the Fed regarding cash transactions and irregular activities in BCCI Miami and Atlanta accounts. No follow-up.
- In 1988 the IRS brought a major money-laundering case against defendant Jerry Lee Harvey. Sixty million dollars were laundered, much of it through BCCI Panama and BCCI Cayman Islands. No follow-up.
- In 1989, in Oklahoma City, the IRS indicted and convicted a heroin dealer who had laundered $1 million through BCCI in New York and Hong Kong. No follow-up.
- In 1989 the IRS office in Dallas requested and was refused permission to expand its investigation to Miami after a large undercover operation had fingered it as a key link in money-laundering activities.

When indictments were finally brought against the bank by the Justice Department, they had an odd, hesitant character. Morgenthau had embarrassed the Justice Department by moving first and moving decisively on July 29, indicting BCCI, ICIC, Abedi, and Naqvi. On September 5, Justice in Tampa finally announced the unsealing of an August 23 indictment against six BCCI officers, including Naqvi. But Justice still had not moved against Abedi, and this indictment, though brought under the RICO act, did not mention Abedi and did not name the bank itself. The thing BCCI and its American lawyers feared most still had not come to pass. On November 15, in response to a wave of criticism from Kerry, Morgenthau, and the press, the Justice Department announced that it had finally brought a RICO indictment against BCCI and Abedi, also charging Ghaith Pharaon. Still, the indictment's scope was severely restricted to BCCI's secret ownership of Independence Bank in California and its secret ownership of shares of stock and debentures in CenTrust Savings Bank of Miami. Justice had still not uncorked the big one, the sweeping RICO that would allow it to seize BCCI's assets in the United States.

In December 1991, fully three years after the conclusion of C-Chase, the Justice Department finally used the sweeping RICO powers at its disposal, issuing a "superseding indictment" against the bank. That same day BCCI pleaded guilty and agreed to forfeit $550 million in U.S. assets—everything the authorities could get their hands on.

CHAPTER 15

BEYOND ZERO

"Abedi bought his way into the United States during the
Carter administration, but when the Republicans came back
into power, Abedi offered them strategic alliances."

—CONDOR, 1992

Why Agha Hasan Abedi and his rogue bank went unprosecuted for so
long is the enduring mystery at the heart of the BCCI affair.

The simple answer is that his watch-me-break-all-the-rules act relied upon the near-absolute complicity of many sovereign governments. High government officials and financial regulators around the
world knew what the bank was doing, and yet they created the deep
silence that cloaked BCCI's global operations. In the United States,
for instance, the bank was allowed to operate illegally for a decade,
even though the CIA and the White House—throughout both Ronald
Reagan's and George Bush's administrations—knew about its drug
and weapons deals, its involvement with terrorists and espionage, and
its strong ties to foreign intelligence agencies.

By 1988 so much was known at the highest reaches of government
that undercover Customs agents were risking their lives to learn less
about BCCI than what several top administration officials and a host
of lesser bureaucrats already knew. Those people—among them at
least two cabinet officers—had kept silent. And they blocked further
inquiries. If the press discovered this negligence, a political disaster
loomed. There was no acceptable way to explain why, if the president's advisers had been aware for years that BCCI illegally owned
and controlled a major U.S. bank and that BCCI was laundering drug
money through its Miami and New York offices, no orders were given
to shut it down.

Though neither Reagan nor Bush has been tied directly to the BCCI cover-up, the consistency of response, or lack of response, across a broad spectrum of agencies and a wide geographic area suggests damage control from the top. This was necessary, in part, because of the very large and very deep pool of "guilty knowledge" about the bank. Too many people knew too much about BCCI, and they knew it long before the bank spun itself into bankruptcy and scandal. This, more than anything else, explains the pervasive official silence on BCCI. That Robert Gates could jokingly refer to it in a conversation with Customs chief William von Raab as the "bank of crooks and criminals" three years before the scandal broke merely reflects the run of knowledge around Washington. Indeed, it would probably have been difficult to find very many people with real power who did not know about the bank, based on the wide dispersion of CIA reports. The question of what they knew and when they knew it becomes almost moot. The real question is why—why no one saw fit to tip off either the Federal Reserve or state banking authorities, who had been told virtually nothing. BCCI was being taken care of certainly by Casey, probably by the National Security Council. Somewhere between intelligence gathering and policy making, BCCI disappeared.

The astonishing depth of this official knowledge would not become apparent until much later. Between 1979 and 1991 federal law enforcement agencies received more than seven hundred tips about the bank's criminal enterprises, according to Congressman Charles Schumer's final 1992 report for the House Subcommittee on Crime and Criminal Justice. Taken together, the tips covered almost all of BCCI's lines of business, from promoting political unrest in Pakistan to the smuggling of arms to Syria, Iran, and Libya, to financing terrorist groups and organized crime in the United States and Italy. Concluded Schumer: ". . . At the very least, there was nobody putting together all the pieces. . . . You could make a credible case that somebody told them not to do anything about BCCI."[1]

That somebody remains unnamed. William Casey had something to do with the immunity BCCI enjoyed, but Casey died in early 1987. General Zia had contributed to Abedi's immunity, but Zia was killed in August 1988, as the Soviets were preparing their retreat from Afghanistan. Abedi's usefulness as a hidden ally of American intelligence went away with the Soviet troops. And before the year ended, the charismatic Abedi himself dropped out of sight, sidelined by a heart attack. Yet the mantle of protection that seemed to shield BCCI's American operations remained in place until the bank's rapidly dwindling assets made it impossible to paper over the frauds any longer. In part, this was because BCCI, though it was virtually imploding after 1988, remained a necessary middleman in clandestine weapons deals and other foreign initiatives. "BCCI wasn't finished in 1988," Condor said. "They were the only way we could talk to certain folks, and they were the only vehicle available for some transactions. Who else could wire something together involving Saudi Arabia, China, Israel, and the U.S.?"

To see how BCCI's links to U.S. intelligence compromised law enforcement, one need ask only two questions: If an agency of the government—call it Agency X—had run a serious probe of BCCI at any given point in time, what would it have been likely to find? And what would have been the implications of making the findings public?

In 1982, when BCCI took over Financial General after a three-year struggle, Agency X would have found it intriguing that the CIA neglected to tell the banking regulators who some of the purchasers really were. Based on what was known, there were only two possibilities: Either one of the most influential banks in Washington had just fallen into the hands of the foreign intelligence chieftains of Saudi Arabia, or an international bank of ill repute had just been allowed to buy into the American banking system, illegally, and over the objections of the Federal Reserve. Even a rudimentary background check on such shareholders as Kamal Adham and A. R. Khalil would have revealed those intelligence connections.

Had investigators from Agency X looked at BCCI in 1984 or 1985, they would have discovered the bank's burgeoning relationship with the CIA. Abedi had by then become an ally in William Casey's crusade against the Evil Empire. When Senator Paula Hawkins visited Pakistan in 1984 and upset applecarts by confronting General Zia with her knowledge about a "Pakistani bank" laundering drug money out of Miami and the Cayman Islands, both the State Department and the Justice Department intervened with dazzling speed. The reasons, in retrospect, are obvious. Had the senator been helped with her probe instead of being warned off, she might have uncovered the massive money laundering being run by BCCI through the Caymans-Miami-Tampa nexus. That would have led her to Panama and Manuel Noriega, who happened to be on the CIA payroll at the time. But the Afghan civil war was heating up, and Abedi had bent U.S. foreign policy to his own ends.

After 1986 an investigation of BCCI could have veered at any moment into the most dangerous political mine field of the Reagan-Bush era: Iran-Contra. Though the scandal haunted Bush's reelection campaign, he weathered the many allegations of his involvement by insisting that he had not been in "the loop" on the Iranian arms-for-hostages initiative or the covert support of rebel forces in Nicaragua. (His statements were flatly contradicted the week before the November 1992 election, when the Iran-Contra special prosecutor released part of former Defense Secretary Caspar Weinberger's diary, which revealed that Bush, in a critical meeting, voted to send Iran TOW missiles in exchange for hostages. The potentially damaging evidence in those notes did not, however, prevent George Bush from issuing a full pardon on Christmas Eve 1992 to Weinberger and five other Reagan administration officials who had been convicted of lying to or withholding information from Congress. Special prosecutor Lawrence Walsh, furious at the pardon, said that Bush "has stopped the trial of a confederate.") But the fact was that the arms dealers, former military officers, and Middle Eastern hustlers that Oliver North, William Casey, and the National Security Council had recruited to promote the Nicaraguan rebellion and to arm Iranian extremists had all used BCCI's services in some of their key operations. The president, with all his other political problems, didn't need to hear any more questions about what he knew and when he knew it.

Those questions swirled around BCCI's role as financier to both Saudi arms dealer Adnan Khashoggi and Iranian middleman Manucher Ghorbanifar in the National Security Council's hidden arms swaps with the Iranians; it was full partner in a number of the arms deals. Khashoggi participated in five of the deals for the United States, and BCCI provided the bridge financing through Israel to Iran. According to the Kerry subcommittee's summary report on BCCI: "Khashoggi's business manager Emanuel Floor described Ghorbanifar as stating: 'These are my associates,' and writing down the name 'BCCI.' Floor described BCCI as acting not merely as Ghorbanifar's and Khashoggi's bank for the purpose of these transactions, but as an actual partner in the Iranian arms deals."[2]

In 1985, 1986, or 1987, Agency X would have discovered that two of the highest-ranking officials in the Reagan administration knew about BCCI in considerable detail. In 1985 the CIA sent Treasury Secretary Donald Regan the damning report on BCCI via Douglas Mulholland—damning because Regan, who had sworn to uphold the nation's laws, failed to take action and instead bottled up the information. Then, in 1986 and 1987, Agency X's investigation would have placed BCCI a notch closer to the president even than Regan. In those years, according to former NSC official Roger Robinson, the CIA delivered two more detailed reports on BCCI to James Baker, who replaced Regan at Treasury during Ronald Reagan's second term. If Robinson is right, there was far more at stake than an appearance of nonfeasance at the highest level. No one was closer to George Bush than James Baker, his Texas confidant, business partner, campaign chairman, and cabinet officer. Any hint that Baker had early knowledge of BCCI's criminal side or of its secret purchase of three American banks would raise questions of whether he had consulted Reagan or Bush on the matter and why none of them had taken action.

Still other liabilities arose from the National Security Council's—and therefore the White House's—knowledge of BCCI. "We were aware that BCCI was involved in drug-money transactions," said Norman Bailey, the NSC economist who monitored world terrorism by tracking movements of U.S. money, and who had discovered BCCI's criminal activities in the early 1980s. "We were also aware that BCCI was involved with terrorists, technology transfers—including the unapproved transfer of U.S. technology to the Soviet bloc—weapons dealing, the manipulation of financial markets, and other activities."

Agency X would have found different levels of knowledge about BCCI within the CIA. Casey compartmentalized knowledge of all operations rigorously, which meant that although the agency was using BCCI in connection with covert operations from England to Pakistan, other elements of the agency were collecting information about Abedi and the bank's nefarious activities and forwarding the information to policy makers. Casey's wilder off-the-books operations with BCCI were known to few, although international weapons dealers say BCCI's role in providing private channels for weapons and even mercenaries for some of the world's intelligence agencies, including those of the United States, was well known in their world.

Similar geopolitical considerations had inhibited the U.S. government for more than a decade from simply arresting Abedi and closing his banks in the United States. One of the best examples occurred in 1991, when the Justice Department should have been racing to build its case against the bank. That year the United States was amassing an army in the Gulf, preparing to retake Kuwait from Iraqi President Saddam Hussein. The obvious problem was that the prosecutorial trail led directly to the court of Sheikh Zayed in Abu Dhabi and to King Fahd's intelligence agency and the head of the largest bank in Saudi Arabia, an investment adviser to the royal family. The public unraveling of BCCI's criminal activities would certainly expose both to embarrassment on a world stage. Washington was not prepared to indict principal figures within the governments of its two major allies in the coming war. Humiliating King Fahd and Sheikh Zayed could have endangered the fragile consensus for the American-led invasion that George Bush and James Baker were trying to put together through personal diplomacy.

Moreover, the Saudis had been the generous but hidden partners of the Reagan and Bush administrations in several clandestine ventures, providing the money for operations that the CIA—or the National Security Council—didn't want to tell Congress about. "There was a great deal to be gained by proceeding [with the federal investigation] slowly," explained a former State Department official close to the situation. "The consensus we needed in the Middle East was much more difficult to put together than you imagine. And the bank was going to implode in any case. The Saudis were convinced that Morgenthau's zealousness was part of a Zionist plot, but they expected a certain amount of understanding from George Bush. They thought that if their good friend in the White House couldn't stop Morgenthau, at least he could keep this as low-key as possible. It was a matter of perceptions."

All of this meant there would be no vigorous prosecution of the bank in the United States. And the agency appointed to impede the investigation, or at least to make sure that it moved very slowly, was the U.S. Department of Justice. Perhaps the earliest clue to the Justice Department's undeclared agenda and the Treasury Department's self-applied blindfold emerged at the time of the bank's indictment in Tampa in 1988. Customs chief William von Raab thought it was an enormously meaningful case and announced that BCCI was the most important drug-money bank ever hit. But instead of being lauded by his superiors—he reported directly to the Secretary of the Treasury—he was told to dampen his public enthusiasm. When he persisted, he was cut out of the investigation. When he complained, he was asked to resign. And then the Justice Department let BCCI off the hook, collecting a limited guilty plea and a $14-million fine that scuttled any further significant investigation. And then a senior Justice Department official wrote letters to banking regulators of all the states in which BCCI maintained offices, suggesting they allow BCCI, which had just pleaded guilty to drug-money laundering, to continue operating.

A door to another dimension opened as Morgenthau's men, a few reporters, and Kerry's Senate investigators all began to learn independently how systematically Attorney General Richard Thornburgh had smothered efforts to widen the probe of BCCI. To many, the cover-up appeared to be bigger than the crime, considering the bulk and age of the information various parts of Justice, the intelligence community, and the administration had been sitting on. Partly because of the prodigious amount of such guilty knowledge, and partly because Justice had been warned off, the Justice Department never demonstrated any appetite for pursuing or expanding the BCCI case.

In July 1992, a year after Morgenthau indicted BCCI and its principals Abedi and Naqvi, the district attorney announced that the New York County Grand Jury had indicted Clifford and Altman for taking millions of dollars in bribes from the leaders of BCCI—in the form of sham loans and stock deals for themselves and money conveyed as legal fees—in return for helping BCCI influence the affairs of First American Bank. The bribery charges shocked those who believed the still-powerful Clifford would be charged with no more than a technical violation of banking regulations, if that. But after three years of investigation Morgenthau saw BCCI as a "sophisticated and corrupt criminal enterprise, organized from the top down to accumulate money and power," and Clifford as a principal manipulator. He intended to prove that Clifford, who claimed he had been deceived by Abedi, had actually concocted the plan to use nominee fronts to slip the bank into America.

The New York indictments cataloged BCCI's worldwide criminality: The BCC Group, it said, achieved its ends in the United States and abroad by paying bribes to bank regulators and central bankers in Pakistan, Nigeria, Morocco, Senegal, Tunisia, Ivory Coast, Congo, Zambia, Argentina, and Peru, defrauding in the process the World Bank, the International Monetary Fund, the Nigerian National Supply Company, and the African Development Bank. The bank, it alleged, used front men to become owner of Banco Mercantil of Colombia, the Independence Bank of Encino, California, and the National Bank of Georgia through frauds in which Ghaith Pharaon was involved, and became the owner of First American through frauds in which Clifford and Altman played leading roles.

It came as no surprise that the prosecutors believed that BCCI spent depositors' money on charities to garner favorable public reception and that they hired politicians and government employees as consultants to increase the BCC Group's access and influence in the various countries in which it operated. One aspect of the indictment was particularly startling to the press. "In furtherance of its affairs," the indictment stated, "members of the criminal enterprise made systematic efforts to influence the press by subsidies, payoffs, and intimidation." No further details were given.

The New York grand jury also indicted Ghaith Pharaon and Faisal Saud al-Fulaij, and brought additional charges of bribery against Agha Hasan Abedi and Swaleh Naqvi.

Later that month Morgenthau made the final leap that the Justice Department had, perhaps understandably, balked at for so long. Morgenthau moved against the Saudis. To the surprise of everyone except Morgenthau and his crew—and, belatedly, the State Department— Kamal Adham, one of the most powerful men in the Middle East, had slipped into a Manhattan courtroom and entered a guilty plea to charges that he conspired to conceal the true owners of First American. Facing indictment, he agreed to pay a $105-million fine and cooperate with Morgenthau's still-widening probe. Saudi financier Khalid bin-Mahfouz had already been indicted, and it was known that A. R. Khalil was being probed by the criminal investigators. King Fahd was furious and Saudi-American relations were reported to be strained.

And finally, as if anyone in the Middle East or the White House had missed his message, Morgenthau signaled the fact that he was now taking a tough line with Abu Dhabi. "Abu Dhabi," he said, "has been promising cooperation for a year, but we've gotten nothing out of them." John Moscow and his men had found witnesses who led them into Zayed's palace.

On the same day Morgenthau announced his wide-ranging indictments, the Justice Department announced that the U.S. attorney in Washington had also indicted Clifford and Altman. It was a narrow target, and the case that the U.S. attorney in Washington finally developed against the two men was amazingly thin when compared with Morgenthau's steamroller. In spite of all of Justice's protestations that it had pulled no punches in one of the largest white-collar crime investigations ever, the federal prosecutors told a Washington court they were ready for an immediate trial of Clifford and Altman, since they had only thirteen witnesses. The trial, they estimated, would take no longer than three weeks. Morgenthau, by contrast, advised the New York court that he expected to call more than one hundred witnesses and predicted the trial might continue for four to six months.

Quickly, a behind-the-scenes tug-of-war developed between the state and federal prosecutors as to which would try the two Washington lawyers first. One critical problem: If the federal trial, with its earlier scheduled trial date, took precedence, Clifford and Altman would never be prosecuted by Morgenthau, because New York State law prohibits a second trial for similar charges. Three years of investigation would go down the drain.

The defendants' lawyers appeared more than eager to face prosecution by the feds rather than by the New York district attorney. The aging Clark Clifford deserved a trial at the earliest possible date to prove his innocence, his lawyers claimed. The court, they said, should ignore reports of Clifford's failing health: He was prepared to stand trial immediately in Washington. (By contrast, they later said Clifford was far too ill to be tried in New York.)

However, the climate within the Justice Department had changed when Attorney General Richard Thornburgh resigned in 1992 to run, unsuccessfully, for the governorship of Pennsylvania. Press criticism of how the department handled its investigation had mounted, and the incoming attorney general, former CIA official William Barr, directed his forces to speed up their investigations of BCCI and to end their antagonism toward Morgenthau's investigation. Although the Justice Department's response to this new directive was uneven, the new wind made it seem even more certain that Thornburgh, for unknown reasons, had indeed given orders to limit the BCCI investigation. When the jurisdictional dispute over who would try Clifford and Altman erupted, Barr ultimately supported the theory that Morgenthau's stronger case should be heard first, rather than the case prepared by the U.S. attorney in Washington. A federal judge decided that the district attorney would bring the two men to trial first, in a case now scheduled to begin in February 1993.

A county district attorney stubbornly following a criminal case to its logical conclusion had broken through the gridlock of conflicting goals and fears about BCCI that had plagued Washington for years. Morgenthau's achievement creates a comforting Jack-the-giant-killer image, but the reality is that Robert Morgenthau had undertaken a task that should have been undertaken by the federal government with its far greater resources and authority. Morgenthau's ability to turn the Manhattan trial of Clark Clifford and Robert Altman into a stage for a global drama—a real look at the criminal empire built by Agha Hasan Abedi—is limited, at best. A county district attorney, no matter how imaginative and zealous, can go only so far in pursuit of international criminals, especially if they happen to be ranking officials of a foreign country.

Perhaps the most intriguing aspect of the BCCI affair, circa 1993, is how very few of the perpetrators of the fraud have been brought to justice, and how few of them are likely ever to stand trial anywhere. A $20-billion fraud is almost unimaginable and required the participation of, at the very least, several hundred bank officers. The case record is perplexing. Of BCCI's fourteen thousand employees in its heyday, a mere handful are in jail anywhere.

Abedi remains at large in Pakistan. His still-powerful political contacts will prevent him from ever being extradited or brought to trial anywhere. He is said to spend most of his time in bed, resting in his 4,000-square-foot walled compound in the Defense Officers' Society section of Karachi, entertaining occasional visitors and mumbling his innocence. Seventeen other senior officials, including Swaleh Naqvi and Zafar Iqbal, are under house arrest in Abu Dhabi, living comfortably and no doubt wondering what is to become of them. That there has been no summary justice—even though it is now estimated that BCCI officers embezzled at least $2 billion and possibly much more from Zayed's personal funds—is testament to the extraordinary intertwining of the sheikh's Private Department and the bank. The deeply interlocking relationships suggest that there is a great deal more at stake there than just the fates of the BCCI people in custody. If it was difficult for the United States to separate the interests of Zayed and BCCI, it will be excruciatingly painful for Abu Dhabi itself, since many officials of the Private Department were complicitous in the fraud.

The extent of Ghanim al-Mazrui's involvement is not a matter of public knowledge, but his early involvement with William Casey's men, and his inseparable ties to the president of the United Arab Emirates, suggest that neither the United States nor the Arab states may be interested in a public answer. In hindsight, it no longer seems perplexing that Sandy Martin Zayed's long time United States lawyer—the man who worked most closely with Ghanim al-Mazrui—is a former National Security adviser and consultant to the Pentagon's Joint Chiefs of Staff. As Gwynne and Beaty thought so often: There are wheels spinning within wheels here.

Fourteen of the seventeen former bank officers under house arrest have now been officially charged with crimes, and a trial is expected to take place sometime in 1993. No provisions have been made for the extradition of Naqvi and others to the United States to face charges of fraud and conspiracy. Sani Ahmed, the head of BCCI's protocol department and the man who directed the mysterious affairs of BCCI's

Washington representative office, is safely back in Pakistan. At last report, he is still working with Abedi and has received a license to open a new Pakistan bank.

Of Abedi's once-powerful allies and fronts, the Gokal brothers are bankrupt, and owe the liquidators of BCCI more than $700 million. Ghaith Pharaon is fleeing from several indictments in the United States. His REDEC is gone, bankrupt and sold off at pennies on the dollar. The mansion at Richmond Hill has been seized by the Federal Reserve. He is in disgrace in Saudi Arabia, under investigation in Argentina, and afraid to go ashore in Europe, for fear that he might be extradited to the United States. He is said to be traveling on a Paraguayan passport given him by one of his former cronies and business associates, former Paraguayan strongman Alfredo Stroessner. After pleading guilty to criminal charges in New York, Kamal Adham has pledged to cooperate with the New York investigation. How far that cooperation will extend is anyone's guess. The wily old Saudi intelligence chief knows where bodies are buried, but he didn't rise to his position of influence by revealing secrets.

Though Sheikh Khalid bin-Mahfouz has been indicted by Morgenthau, it is unlikely the United States government will insist he be extradited. A clamor over the Saudi financier would draw attention to his involvement in the purchase of Houston's Texas Commerce Bank Tower in 1985. The seventy-five-story Bank Tower, built at a cost of $140 million at the height of the oil boom four years earlier, had fetched $200 million from its Saudi buyers in the depth of Texas's real estate crash, a windfall sale for Texas Commerce Bank at a time when it was difficult to give away commercial office space in Houston. The involvement of Mahfouz, and thus possibly BCCI, might be embarrassing to James Baker, whose father and grandfather founded Texas Commerce Bank. (The bank later merged with Chemical Bank, providing Baker with approximately $2 million in Chemical Bank stock.) Baker had served on the family bank's board of directors until he became Reagan's chief of staff. He remained a major shareholder and presumably benefited from the remarkably profitable sale, which came at an opportune moment for the fortunes of Texas Commerce. Another important Texas Commerce shareholder and board director at the time was then Secretary of Commerce Robert Mosbacher.

There is no evidence that the purchase of the bank property at such favorable terms influenced James Baker, but the nexus is disturbing. Khalid bin-Mahfouz represented both BCCI and Saudi Arabian interests. The other principal in the Texas Bank Tower purchase was Rafik

Hariri, a Lebanon-born, Saudi-based billionaire who has acted as a diplomat for Saudi Arabia and has demonstrated a knack for overpaying politicians. In 1989 he paid $2 million more than the assessed value for the McLean, Virginia, home of Congressman Bill Nelson, who used much of the windfall to underwrite his election campaign.

BCCI itself is still being officially "liquidated"—meaning that the accounting firm of Touche Ross & Co. has been hired to try to track down the bank's assets in order to pay off its liabilities. The latest estimate is that, of the $23 billion in assets, roughly $2 billion is recoverable and therefore available to pay off depositors. Though he has been arduously courted by the Bank of England, Zayed has not yet agreed to indemnify any depositors outside of Abu Dhabi. He has proposed that he inject roughly $2 billion in cash in exchange for immunity from lawsuits. BCCI has been either shut down, rescued and renamed, or merged into other institutions in the rest of the world. The vast majority of its depositors have seen at best a small fraction of the money they entrusted to the bank. Alleging negligence, breach of duty, and breach of contract, Touche Ross recently sued both Price Waterhouse and Ernst & Young for $8 billion—a sum that, if awarded by a jury, would bankrupt both firms.

Where is BCCI's money? Tied up in loans to the likes of the bankrupt Gokals or the bankrupt Ghaith Pharaon; funneled off into Abedi's foundations, from which it was invested elsewhere; or stolen outright by BCCI employees. For example, the estimated $1 billion that Ali Akbar and his associates accumulated in "commodities trading" losses in the mid-1980s may have been in part the result of extraordinary stupidity and mismanagement. Or, as several BCCI employees (including Masihur Rahman) have it, these "losses" were merely a convenient way of siphoning off money and concealing the paper trail. Commodities trading is, after all, the latest and most sophisticated form of money laundering.

Trying to trace the missing billions by pursuing BCCI's deceptive books and ledgers is largely a hopeless task. The hundreds of millions, or perhaps billions, of dollars involved in BCCI's weapons dealings don't show on BCCI's books at all. Nor do the profits from money laundering or narcotics trafficking.

Beyond the zero on the bank's balance sheets is the larger truth: The environment that permitted BCCI to perpetrate such a high-volume fraud still exists, scarcely changed at all. There have been repeated calls for reform of the various offshore and onshore tax havens created specifically to allow corporations and individuals to avoid taxes. The blind cutouts in the Cayman Islands, and in scores of sovereign imitators from Vanuatu to Montserrat—combined with the bank secrecy laws of countries such as Luxembourg—create a climate in which money laundering is both highly profitable and inevitable. Yet the outcry over the BCCI scandal during the summer of 1991 was muted, and business as usual has resumed in the financial centers that were designed expressly to conceal and disguise. Huge volumes of cash are remitted every day to and from the United States from places like Panama and the Cayman Islands without a question asked, though no one here really believes that all that cash represents dollars exchanged for local currency by tourists shopping for rugs or straw hats.

Aside from political rhetoric about curbing drug-money laundering, no one seems to be interested in taking steps that might curtail the exploding volumes of cash coming from overseas—the sort of activity that was BCCI's stock in trade. No administration with an eye to the United States balance-of-trade problems has ever wanted to cut off the flow of capital flight into America, and tough banking disclosure laws could dry up the multibillion-dollar river overnight. That unspoken imperative is so strong that some inside players, such as former National Security Council economist Roger Robinson, dismiss the idea that there needed to be a conspiracy to handicap an investigation or prosecution of BCCI. "Baker didn't pursue BCCI because he thought a prosecution of the bank would damage the United States' reputation as a safe haven for flight capital and overseas investments," Robinson said.

The cure is simple, but it is politically unpalatable even though it would cripple the drug trade. If banks such as BCCI are to be controlled, the United States must deal with the nations that guarantee the secrecy they rely on. The mechanism to accomplish this is financial: Two thirds of the world's trade is conducted in dollars. And more than 99 percent of all international dollar transactions—some $3.5 trillion a day—passes through the banking clearinghouses in New York. If the United States' banking regulations prohibited those dollar transactions with countries with such unsound banking practices, such impenetrable bank-secrecy laws, the development of the next BCCI would not be inevitable as it is today.

When BCCI used the Caymans and Luxembourg to avoid having to account to a national central bank of any kind and to take advantage of banking secrecy laws, the bank was only mimicking some of the world's largest and most prestigious banks, which were doing basically the same thing, often for the same reasons. BCCI collapsed solely because of the absurd scale of the fraud it had undertaken: A bank built on phony capital, with a succession of billion-dollar holes punched in its balance sheets, could not survive for long with even the cleverest bookkeepers. And yet, had Abedi and BCCI exercised just a bit of moderation, the bank—and the fraud—might still be going today, and Naqvi's secret accounts might still be sitting safely in his desk.

Since none of the rules has changed, there is nothing to prevent other BCCIs from springing up to operate in the artfully created regulatory gaps. And no one in authority wants the rules to change. Which means that however successful Robert Morgenthau is in achieving his goal of exposing the money men behind the drug business, there is absolutely nothing in place to prevent entry into this sort of business. BCCI played by existing rules, albeit with extraordinary criminal intent and a stunning global vision of empowerment. Like Dr. No, Abedi relied upon secrecy, privacy, and invisibility. All of these are just as easy to come by in 1993 as they were when a much younger Abedi set out in 1972 to create the world's first Third World multinational consortium bank.

EPILOGUE

It was a Friday afternoon in Washington, and Beaty and Blum were having a late lunch on the veranda of Duke Zeibert's restaurant, overlooking Connecticut Avenue. The technology-transfer lawyer, the one who helped them identify the Navstar photos liberated from the Kremlin safe, had joined them. The sound and fury of the BCCI scandal had passed, and Clark Clifford's trial lay in the future. They were talking about what it all had meant when Beaty looked up in surprise. Condor, whom he had not seen for weeks, nodded to the group, pulled up a chair, and sat down.

"Jonathan, I have an answer to the question you asked," he said. "The technology for the Colombine Heads got out of the country when it was leaked to the Israelis in 1983. The man who accomplished it was James Guerin, the original manufacturer of the mechanism: Guerin was a Hardy Boy, one of Casey's private agents."

All three listeners were nonplussed. Both Blum and the lawyer had helped Beaty in his search to discover what the Columbine Heads were, and they knew what Condor was talking about: critical components of the fuel-air bomb. And while Beaty had never heard of him, both lawyers knew who James Guerin was.

"But how could anyone get secret hardware like that out of the country?" Beaty asked.

"He didn't," Condor said very quietly. "He took the plans out of the country, and they built a new manufacturing plant in South America. Apparently Casey wanted to give the fuel-air bomb to the Israelis; they had beseiged the Carter administration for the technology but had been turned down flat. Things were different under Reagan, but Casey knew he would never get approval for the transfer from Congress. So he had Guerin give it to them."

There was a long silence.

"But if that was 1983 or 1984, how did BCCI acquire three heads in 1989 to sell to Saddam Hussein?" Beaty finally ventured.

"I don't know. I can only assume that BCCI had something to do with the original plans to build a plant out of the country. There is some indication Pakistan received the technology too."

Then Condor stood up. "That's all, Kid. You've pulled me into this too deeply and now I'm out of it. Don't come to me with any more questions; you're on your own."

He walked off without another word.

Beaty had a plane to catch, but he tarried long enough for Blum and the other lawyer to give him Guerin's background: A self-made millionaire and defense contractor, Guerin founded International Signal Controls in Lancaster, Pennsylvania, which manufactured exotic fusing devices and other highly secret technology. He had business associates such as onetime Secretary of State Alexander Haig, and when ISC merged with Ferranti, the British arms and electronics firm, Admiral Bobby Inman, the former deputy director of the CIA, joined the Ferranti-ISC board of directors. Presumably to keep an eye on American secrets.

Then Ferranti declared bankruptcy and sued Guerin for claiming to have hundreds of millions of dollars' worth of pending contracts that had never materialized. The nonperforming contracts turned out to be military deals with Pakistan and Abu Dhabi, and it was Guerin's contention that they had come unraveled after General Zia was killed in 1988.

"He was just recently tried for fraud in the United States," Blum explained. "Inman told the court Guerin had once been very helpful to the agency, but it did him no good. He was convicted of fraud, money laundering, and exporting arms to South Africa, and he's headed for prison. I think there were allegations that he also sold cluster bombs to Iraq. That may have had something to do with Banco Nazionale del Lavaro in Atlanta—that's the BNL branch that loaned Saddam $600 million. I told you you should be looking into that."

Beaty nodded. The emerging BNL scandal was part of an embarrassment being dubbed "Iraqgate," and the Bush administration was being accused of dragging its feet in the investigation of the bank. The Justice Department and the CIA accused each other of failing to act on intelligence information that the BNL was funneling money—including U.S. agriculture loans converted to militarily useful goods instead of grain—to build up Saddam Hussein's war machine. A lot of that money rolled through BCCI on its way to the Middle East.

He pushed back from the table. "This is all interesting, folks, but I've got to catch my plane. And Jack, please do me a favor. Don't tell me about any more banks."

Beaty called Gwynne a few days later. "Sam, we've got to get moving. I've got a jailhouse interview lined up with Christopher Dragoul, the former manager of BNL's branch in Atlanta. He claims the United States knew all about the loans to Iraq. And we need to go interview a guy named James Guerin who's also in a federal slammer," Beaty added quickly.

"I don't know if what Condor told me about him is true, but we've got to go ask Guerin himself. Wait until you hear what I've found out so far."

NOTES

A NOTE ON THE SOURCING OF THE MATERIAL IN CHAPTERS 1 THROUGH 5, 10, AND 11

Because of the narrative approach taken in large segments of this book, we have selectively omitted the usual chapter notes. Chapters 1 through 5, 10, and 11 contain a detailed and personal account of how the story began and how we developed and used the principal sources in our reporting for *Time*. It would thus be redundant here to explain the sourcing of our material, except to say that we developed many more sources than we cite in the text, most of whom contributed important but not necessarily noteworthy information about the case. Many of those sources were in the business, banking, and regulatory communities in the United States. The sources we have chosen to describe in these chapters were the most important for us in terms of defining how we looked at BCCI.

A NOTE ON ABBREVIATIONS

The Senate Subcommittee on Terrorism, Narcotics, and International Operations is cited after the first reference herein as "the Kerry subcommittee."

CHAPTER 6. END OF EMPIRE

1. Jim McGee, "Billions in Losses Led to Seizure of BCCI; Action Disrupts Sale of Stake in 1st American," *Washington Post*, 9 July 1991.
2. Nick Kochan and Bob Whittington, *Bankrupt: The BCCI Fraud* (London: Victor Gollancz, 1991), 145–146.
3. Editorial, *Daily News* (Karachi), 7 July 1991.
4. "West's Move Unfair, Biased," *Dawn*, 9 July 1991.
5. Senator Alan Cranston presiding at Kerry subcommittee hearing, referring to an article in *The New York Times*, 2 August 1991.

6. Jonathan Beaty and S. C. Gwynne, "Scandal? What Scandal?" *Time* (29 July 1991).

7. Najam Sethi, "I Am Not Responsible for Current Crisis: Abedi," *Dawn*, 15 July 1991.

8. *Ibid.*

9. Jason Nisse, "Column Eight," *The Independent*, 16 August 1991.

10. Virgil Mattingly, general counsel, Federal Reserve Bank, interview with authors, March 1992.

11. John Moscow, Virgil Mattingly, interviews with authors, March 1992.

12. Senate Subcommittee on Terrorism, Narcotics, and International Operations, *The BCCI Affair: A Report to the Senate Committee on Foreign Relations*, 30 September 1992.

13. Virgil Mattingly, interview with authors, March 1992.

14. Federal Reserve memo, McQueeney to O'Sullivan, 18 December 1990.

15. John Moscow, Virgil Mattingly, interviews with authors, March 1992.

16. Kerry subcommittee final report, 30 September 1992.

17. Jonathan Winer, counsel to Kerry subcommittee, interview with authors, July 1991. And audit of BCCI by Price Waterhouse, 1985.

18. Abdur Sakhia, testimony before the Kerry subcommittee, 22 October 1991. And BCCI documents in Kerry subcommittee records.

19. Audit of BCCI, by Price Waterhouse, 22 June 1991.

20. Abdur Sakhia, testimony before the Kerry subcommittee, 22 October 1991. And BCCI documents in Kerry subcommittee records.

21. Daniel Yergin, *The Prize* (New York: Simon & Schuster, 1991), 718–719.

22. *Ibid.*, 747.

23. Audit of BCCI by Price Waterhouse, 22 June 1991.

24. *Ibid.*

25. Susan Kennedy, "Idyll, Cache," *Palm Beach Life* (November 1991).

26. *Ibid.*

27. Audit of BCCI by Price Waterhouse, 22 June 1991.

28. Yakoob Wadalawallah, former BCCI Paris branch manager, interview with authors, September 1991.

CHAPTER 7. OUT OF THE BLUE

1. "Nervous," *Financial Times*, 10 July 1991.

2. Peter Mansfield, *The Arabs* (New York: Penguin Books, 1990), 340.

3. Wilfred Thesiger, *Arabian Sands* (New York: E. P. Dutton, 1989), 246.

4. Shahid Javed Burki, *Pakistan: The Continuing Search for Nationhood* (New York: Westview Press/Pak Book Corp., 1991), 11.

5. Steve Coll, "Abedi: A Courtier's Ruin," *Washington Post*, 1 September 1991.

6. *Ibid.*

7. *Ibid.*

8. Ahmed Rashid, "BCCI: The Inside Story," *The Independent*, 14 July 1991.

9. Thomas W. Lippman, *Understanding Islam: An Introduction to the Muslim World* (New York: Mentor Books, 1990), 139–141.

10. Najim Sethi, "BCCI Founder: These Things Happen," *Wall Street Journal*, 29 July 1991.

11. Burki, *Pakistan*, 41.

12. Various authors, "BCCI Behind Closed Doors," a collection of articles, *Financial Times*, 9–16 November 1991.

13. Sethi, "BCCI Founder: These Things Happen."

14. Jonathan Raban, *Arabia* (New York: Touchstone Books, 1979), 53.

15. Lawrence Ziring and S. M. Burke, *Pakistan's Foreign Policy* (Karachi: Oxford University Press, 1990), 422.

16. J. B. Kelly, *Arabia, the Gulf and the West* (New York: Basic Books, 1980), 208.

17. Ziring and Burke, *Pakistan's Foreign Policy*, 425.

18. Nigel Bance, "The Mysteries Behind Abedi's Bank," *Euromoney* (July 1978).

19. Rashid, "BCCI: The Inside Story."

20. Steve Coll, "Pakistan's Illicit Economies Affect BCCI," *Washington Post*, 1 September 1991.

21. A. J. McIlroy, "The Muslim Bank," *Daily Telegraph*, 12 August 1991.

22. Raban, *Arabia*, 129.

23. Siddiki quotes in *Forbes* (15 May 1978). Geoffrey Smith, "Banking: Who Gets the Petromoney."

24. *Ibid.*

25. Abdur Sakhia, testimony before the Kerry subcommittee, 22 October 1991.

26. "The Concept That Controls Governments," *New Statesman* (16 September 1981).

27. "Arab Banks Grow," *Business Week* (6 October 1980).

CHAPTER 8. GILT BY ASSOCIATION

1. Art Harris and Ward Sinclair, "White House's Friendly Arm Still Rests on Lance's Shoulder," *Washington Post*, 9 April 1978.

2. Bert Lance, interview with authors, March 1991. And Lance, testimony before the Kerry subcommittee, 23 October 1991.

3. *Ibid.*

4. *Ibid.*

5. Harris and Sinclair, "White House's Friendly Arm."

6. Telex, Abdus Sami to Agha Hasan Abedi, 30 January 1978.

7. "Democrats' Mr. Fixit," *Time* (26 September 1977).

8. Sidney Blumenthal, "The Essential Clark Clifford," *Washington Post Sunday Magazine* (5 February 1988).

9. Clark Clifford and Richard Holbrooke, *Counsel to the President, A Memoir* (New York: Random House, 1991), 263.

10. "Democrats' Mr. Fixit."

11. Clifford and Holbrooke, *Counsel*, 368–369.

12. Neil A. Lewis, "Washington at Work," *New York Times*, 5 April 1991.

13. Marjorie Williams, "The Man Who Banked on His Good Name," *Washington Post*, 9 May 1991.

14. Lewis, "Washington at Work."

15. Attorney's affidavit from 1978 lawsuit Financial General Bankshares, plaintiff, vs. Bert Lance, BCCI, Agha Hasan Abedi, et al., Civil Action #78-0276, County of New York, 28 August 1978.

16. *Ibid.*

17. *Ibid.*

18. Jerry Knight, "Some FG Shareholders Doubling Money on Takeover," *Washington Post*, 25 May 1980.

19. Clark Clifford, testimony before the Kerry subcommittee, 24 October 1991.

20. Federal Reserve document, from public hearing on Financial General acquisition, 23 April 1981.

21. Larry Gurwin, "Who Really Owns First American?" *Regardie's* (May 1990).

22. Gurwin says this comes from a 1981 Jack Anderson column saying that Shorafa was a weapons dealer.

23. Documents from House Banking Committee hearing, 11 and 13 September 1991.

24. Abdur Sakhia, testimony before Kerry subcommittee, 22 October 1991.

25. McGee, "Who Controls First American Bankshares?"

26. Indictment of Clark Clifford and Robert Altman by New York district attorney, 29 July 1992.

27. McGee, "Who Controls First American Bankshares?"

28. Robert Lacey, *The Kingdom* (New York: Avon, 1981), 338–339.

29. Knight, "Some FG Doubling Money on Takeover."

30. Gurwin, "Who Really Owns First American?"

31. Jerry Landauer, "Some Arab States Helped in Plane Sales," *Wall Street Journal*, 4 December 1975.

32. *Ibid.*

33. Gurwin, "Who Really Owns First American?" citing 1977 Amnesty International report, among others.

34. Lacey, *The Kingdom*, 393.

35. From House Banking Committee Minority Staff Report, *BCCI and Its Activities in the United States*, 10 September 1991.

36. Paul Eddy and Sara Walden, "No Questions Asked," *Daily Telegraph*, 11 September 1991.

37. Peter Applebome, "Southern Hospitality and BCCI," *New York Times*, 28 August 1991.

38. Dale Murray, former president and CEO, Chris-Craft Boat Company, interview with Kerry subcommittee staff, 18 September 1992.

39. *Ibid.*

40. *Ibid.*

41. Eddy and Walden, "No Questions Asked."

42. Youssef M. Ibrahim, "Ghaith Pharaon and Co.," *New York Times*, 25 November 1979.

43. *Ibid.*

44. G. Pierre Goad, "Influence of Ghaith Pharaon Spreads to Canada via Cement Company," *Wall Street Journal*, 6 August 1991.

45. Allan Sloan and Elizabeth Bailey, "Buying by the Seat of His Pants," *Forbes* (29 May 1979).

46. "Condor," anonymous source, interview with authors.

47. NBG internal loan document contained in the House Banking Committee Minority Staff Report *BCCI and Its Activities in the United States*, 10 September 1991.

48. Roy Carlson, interview with authors, March 1991.

49. Eric Pianin, "In Georgia, Where Money Talks, Probers Allege Voice Was BCCI," *Washington Post*, 4 September 1991.

50. Federal Reserve Civil Action vs. Clark Clifford and Robert Altman, 29 July 1992.

51. Robert Altman, deposition in Virginia Bankshares lawsuit, 43.

52. Pianin, "In Georgia, Where Money Talks."

53. Dale Murray, interview with Kerry subcommittee staff, 18 September 1992.

54. Clark Clifford, testimony before Kerry subcommittee, 24 October 1991.

CHAPTER 9. THE BLACK RAJ

1. Ingo Walter, *The Secret Money Market* (New York: Harper Business, 1990), 59–70.

2. Abdur Sakhia, testimony before Kerry subcommittee, 22 October 1991.

3. Craig Forman, "Cameroon Experience Shows Extent of Bank's Role in Building Local Business," *Wall Street Journal*, 6 August 1991.

4. Alan J. Kreczko, deputy legal adviser, Department of State, testimony before Kerry subcommittee, 1 August 1991.

5. Forman, "Cameroon Experience."

6. *Ibid*.

7. "BCCI Behind Closed Doors," *Financial Times*.

8. Carter staff, interview with authors, March 1991.

9. Jimmy Carter, interview with John Martin of ABC Television's *Nightline*, 7 August 1991.

10. Abdur Sakhia, testimony before Kerry subcommittee, 22 October 1991.

11. Mark Fineman, "BCCI Left Its Mark on Bangladesh," *Los Angeles Times*, 2 November 1991.

12. *Ibid*.

13. *Ibid*.

14. Much of the material here is drawn from a civil RICO suit filed in the United States District Court, Southern District of Florida, Republic of Panama, plaintiff, vs. BCCI and Amjad Awan, 16 January 1990, and subsequently amended.

15. Fernando Olivera, member Peruvian House of Deputies, testimony before Kerry subcommittee, 2 August 1991. And Morgenthau staff, interviews in New York district attorney's office with authors.

16. Report of internal investigation of Munther Bilbeisi, et al., Holland & Knight. Philip Manuel Resource Group, November 1990.

17. From documents of sale compiled by James F. Dougherty, Esq.

18. From cashier's checks and deposition of Marcelle Walters, records of James F. Dougherty, Esq.

19. In the words of a high-level executive, when asked about his bank's reputation for helping people avoid financial laws, "To be honest, all foreign banks try to work around the controls. BCCI did it more blatantly."

20. Indictment, United States of America vs. BCCI Holdings, S.A., Sheikh Mohammad Shafi, Syed Nadim Hasan, Tariq Nasim Jan; United States District Court, Southern District of Florida, August 1991.

21. *Ibid.*

22. *Ibid.*

23. Walter, *The Secret Money Market.*

24. *Ibid.*, 44.

25. *Ibid.*, 25.

26. *Ibid.*, 32.

27. *Ibid.*, 25.

CHAPTER 10. ROCK AND ROLL

1. John Connolly, "Dead Right," *Spy* (January 1993).

CHAPTER 12. THE HIDDEN ALLIANCE

1. S. J. Burki, *Historical Dictionary of Pakistan* (New York: The Scarecrow Press, 1991), 25.

2. *Ibid.*

3. One of those partners, Ali Reza Saheb, described the overpowering effect of Abedi's spending power and hospitality during those negotiations to Nick Kochan and Bob Whittington, authors of *Bankrupt: The BCCI Fraud.* "Ali Reza Saheb remembers one negotiation in Zurich when his wife and Abedi's newly married second wife, the air hostess Rabia, went on a spending spree on a Saturday. Money was no limit, but the two women ran out of cash, so Abedi told Naqvi to find the treasurer of the United Bank's branch in Zurich, who opened the safe and took out the cash."

4. A U.S. State Department official in close contact with Benazir Bhutto and her family, interview with Beaty, September 1992.

5. Thomas Petzinger, Jr., and Peter Truell, "Ex-BCCI Officials Undergo Questioning by Abu Dhabi aide," *Wall Street Journal,* 23 September 1991.

6. Mark Fineman, "BCCI Founder's Aides Tell Another Tale," *Los*

Angeles Times, 30 July 1991. Generally speaking, the U.S. press ignored the worldwide ramifications of the unfolding BCCI scandal, but the *Los Angeles Times* and *The Wall Street Journal*, along with *Time* magazine, stretched their coverage. Fineman's excellent work examining Abedi and his bank in Southeast Asia was perceptive and original.

7. Kerry subcommittee final report, 30 September 1992, part 4, 369.

8. Filed by the San Diego law firm of Milberg Weiss Bershad Specthrie & Lerach, the class-action complaint is a consolidation of three separate suits filed in August 1992 on behalf of several BCCI depositors. Bank of America has vigorously denied any illegality and described the lawsuit as a "flagrant attempt to assign guilt by association."

9. Bank of America spokesman, interview with Beaty, July 1991.

10. Mark Fineman, "BCCI Left its Mark on Bangladesh," *Los Angeles Times*, 2 November 1991.

11. Leonard A. Spector, *Nuclear Ambitions* (New York: Westview Press, 1990).

12. *Ibid.*

13. New York grand jury indictment of Agha Hasan Abedi, Swaleh Naqvi, et al., 1992.

14. *Ibid.*

15. Fineman, "BCCI Founder's Aides Tell Another Tale."

16. Letter, Charles Saphos to Gerald Lewis, 13 February 1990.

17. Lawrence Lifschultz, "Inside the Kingdom of Heroin: Bush, Drugs and Pakistan," *The Nation* (14 November 1988).

CHAPTER 13. MR. CASEY'S BANK

1. Count de Marenches and David A. Andelman, *The Fourth World War: Diplomacy and Espionage in the Age of Terrorism* (New York: William Morrow and Co., 1992), 83.

2. Bob Woodward, *Veil: The Secret Wars of the CIA* (New York: Simon & Schuster, 1987).

3. Lifschultz, "Inside the Kingdom of Heroin."

4. Kerry subcommittee final report, 30 September 1992.

5. De Marenches and Andelman, *The Fourth World War*.

6. Lifschultz, "Inside the Kingdom of Heroin."

7. Woodward, *Veil*.

CHAPTER 14. THE BIG SLEEP

1. House Judiciary Committee's Subcommittee on Crime and Criminal Justice, chaired by Rep. Charles Schumer (D-New York), *Subcommittee Staff Report Regarding Federal Law Enforcement's Handling of Allegations Involving the Bank of Credit and Commerce International*, 5 September 1991.

2. Abdur Sakhia, testimony before Kerry subcommittee, 22 September 1991.

3. *Ibid.*

4. CIA memo regarding 1985 report to the Department of the Treasury, declassified 9 April 1992.

5. *Ibid.*

6. Assistant to Donald Regan, interview with authors, April 1992.

7. Richard Kerr, acting director, Central Intelligence Agency, testimony before Kerry subcommittee, 25 October 1991.

8. Laurence Pope, associate coordinator for counterterrorism for the U.S. Department of State, testimony before Kerry subcommittee, 25 September 1991.

9. Abdur Sakhia, interview with authors, April 1992.

10. Jack Blum, interview with authors, February 1991.

11. Glenn R. Simpson, "The Words Sound Familiar," *Roll Call* (20 April 1991).

12. Dean Baquet and Jeff Gerth, "Lawmaker's Defense of BCCI Went Beyond Speech in Senate," *New York Times*, 26 August 1992.

13. Kerry subcommittee final report, 30 September 1992.

14. House Judiciary Committee's Subcommittee on Crime and Criminal Justice, chaired by Rep. Charles Schumer (D-New York), *Subcommittee Staff Report Regarding Federal Law Enforcement's Handling of Allegations Involving the Bank of Credit and Commerce International*, 5 September 1991.

15. Dean Baquet, "Drug Dealers' Fast Withdrawals Raise Suspicion in Bank Inquiry," *New York Times*, 27 October 1991.

16. Robert Merkle, interview with authors, April 1991.

17. Michael Rubinstein, assistant U.S. attorney, Tampa, Florida, interview with authors, March 1991.

18. Robert Genzman, deposition before Kerry subcommittee, 1 November 1991.

19. Dexter Lehtinen, district attorney, Miami, Florida, interview with authors, November 1991.

20. William von Raab, testimony before Kerry subcommittee, 1 August 1991.

21. Letter, Charles Saphos to Gerald Lewis, 13 February 1990.

22. Letter, Gerald Lewis to Charles Saphos, 14 February 1990.

23. Letter, Charles Saphos to Gerald Lewis, 16 February 1990.

24. Unsigned letter, anonymous U.S. Customs agent to John Kerry, October 1991.

25. Dexter Lehtinen, testimony before Kerry subcommittee, 14 May 1992.

26. House Judiciary Committee's Subcommittee on Crime and Criminal Justice, chaired by Rep. Charles Schumer (D-New York), *Subcommittee Staff Report Regarding Federal Law Enforcement's Handling of Allegations Involving the Bank of Credit and Commerce International*, 5 September 1991.

27. *Ibid.*

CHAPTER 15. BEYOND ZERO

1. House Judiciary Committee's Subcommittee on Crime and Criminal Justice, chaired by Rep. Charles Schumer (D-New York), *Subcommittee Staff Report Regarding Federal Law Enforcement's Handling of Allegations Involving the Bank of Credit and Commerce International*, 5 September 1991.

2. Kerry subcommittee, final report.

INDEX

ABOUT THE AUTHORS

JONATHAN BEATY is a senior correspondent for *Time* magazine. He lives in Hermosa Beach, California. S. C. GWYNNE is *Time*'s national economics correspondent in Washington, D.C. For their work on the BCCI scandal, the authors won the Gerald Loeb and John Hancock awards for excellence in business and financial reporting, and the Jack Anderson Award as the top investigative reporters of the year.

ABOUT THE TYPE

This book was set in Caledonia, a typeface designed in 1939 by William Addison Dwiggins for the Merganthaler Linotype Company. Its name is the ancient Roman term for Scotland, because the face was intended to have a Scotch-Roman flavor. Caledonia is considered to be a well-proportioned, businesslike face with little contrast between its thick and thin lines.